100 DAYS
IN
TEXAS

THE ALAMO LETTERS

100 DAYS
IN
TEXAS

THE ALAMO LETTERS

Wallace O. Chariton

Wordware Publishing, Inc.
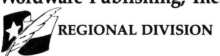
REGIONAL DIVISION

Library of Congress Cataloging-in-Publication Data

Chariton, Wallace O.
    100   Days in Texas / by Wallace O. Chariton.
        p.   cm.
    Includes index.
    ISBN   1-55622-131-2
    1. Alamo (San Antonio, Tex.) — Seige, 1836. — Sources. I. Title.
II. Title: One hundred days in Texas: The Alamo Letters.
F390.C47 1989
976.4'03 — dc20   89-5802
                                                               CIP

1506 Capital Avenue
Plano, Texas 75074

ISBN   1-55622-131-2
10 9 8 7 6 5 4 3 2 1
8908

All inquiries for volume purchases of this book should be addressed to
Wordware Publishing, Inc., at the above address. Telephone inquiries
may be made by calling:

(214) 423-0090

Contents

Chapter One — Introduction   *1*

A brief account of some of the more important events in Texas history that contributed to the conflict between Anglo Americans and Texans.

Chapter Two — The First Fall of the Alamo   *11*

December 9 through December 31, 1835. 13
The Texans, bolstered by their stunning victory over the Mexicans in the Alamo, prepare to invade Mexico. Sam Houston begins to try and assemble an Army.

Chapter Three — The Collapse of the Texas Government   *93*

January 1 through January 31, 1836 95
The ill-fated Matamoras expedition is underway, and Santa Anna is marching toward Texas. Before the months end the shaky government of Texas collapses leaving the men of the Alamo alone on the prairie to fend for themselves.

Chapter Four — The Enemy Advance   *195*

February 1 through February 22, 1836 197
Sam Houston leaves to treat with the Indians and William B.Travis and David Crockett arrive at the Alamo. Santa Anna and his army enter Texas and march steadily toward San Antonio.

Chapter Five — The Siege   *257*

*Santa Anna arrives totally unexpected and the siege begins.
For thirteen days, the outnumbered Texans in the Alamo
stall the inevitable. But on Sunday, March 6, 1836, the end
comes swiftly.*

Chapter Six — After the Fall   *341*

*Independence is declared and news of the fall of the Alamo
spreads quickly across the frontier. Scared Texans flee to the
East as Sam Houston struggles to bring together what is
left of the army to prepare to avenge the men of the Alamo.*

Preface

Although there are no statistics to support the position, it seems a good bet that the Alamo saga is one of the most written about events in the annals of American history. There have literally been hundreds — perhaps thousands — of books, magazine and newspaper articles, pamphlets, brochures, short stories, poems, and even movie scripts done on the subject. If we were to include the number of school term papers done on the Alamo, in Texas alone, the number would probably zoom into the hundreds of thousands, or maybe millions.

So why is the Alamo so popular a subject? Ironically, one of the earliest Alamo historians, Reuben Potter, may have given us the answer. He said in an 1860 article, "When horror is intensified by mystery, the sure product is romance." Everyone likes to write about romance.

The fact that over 180 Americans and perhaps three times that many Mexican soldiers died one Sunday morning in and around an old Spanish mission is not most people's idea of romance. But when you include concepts such as patriotism and the bravery of oppressed men battling against tyranny under the cry of victory or death, then you have the romance of men willing to give their all to be free, which is surely romance of the dearest kind.

I first became infatuated with the romance of the Alamo saga in the late 1950s. Even though I grew up in the shadow of the Alamo in San Antonio, Texas, it was not the close proximity to the old mission which spawned my interest. It was, of all people, a very popular early rock and roll disc jockey named Ricki "The Rockin' Ghost" Ware who first ignited a spark of Alamo interest somewhere deep in my soul.

The fact that Ware was a disc jockey actually had little to do with the story except that he was spinning those vintage platters for KTSA radio, located next door to Bethany Methodist Church, which the Ware family and my family attended. On Sunday mornings, when "The Ghost" was not on the air he was in church teaching my Sunday school class. It may have been the only time in history when parents did not have to prod their kids into attending Sunday school.

In those days, Ricki was one of the leading San Antonio disc jockeys; however he was always into other things to help maintain his popularity because no one knew how long rock and roll was going to last. As I recall, Ware spent some time racing cars on a dirt track, recording a few tunes, and dabbling in acting. When John "The Duke" Wayne came along with a fat wallet and a script for the movie *The Alamo* ol' Ricki landed himself a bit part. When the movie finally opened, my entire Sunday school class was in attendance, watching every frame looking for our teacher. He finally appeared, toward the end of the film, as a guard in the camp of General Sam Houston. In the scene, a rider was approaching and Ware got to say his only line, "Halt, who goes there."

Although none of the parents of the members of our Sunday school knew it, until now, we actually strayed from the scriptures on occasion and discussed the Alamo saga. I remember Ware talking about patriotism and fighting for what you believe in. Those brief discussions sparked an Alamo interest in my heart that survives, like vintage rock and roll, to this very day.

A year or so after Wayne's movie debuted, Harper and Row published Walter Lord's *A Time to Stand* which chronicled the fall of the Alamo. I bought an autographed copy of the book and read it with great interest. Unfortunately, I ended up somewhat confused when the written words did not square with the movie — not even close. It was my first clue that what you see on the silver screen is not necessarily accurate.

The discrepancies between *A Time to Stand* and *The Alamo* created a desire somewhere deep in my Texas heart to seek out the truth. I resolved, even at that early age, to study the Alamo, decide on what was fact and fiction, and one day write my own definitive story of one of America's most epic struggles. Toward achieving that end, I followed the lead of Walter Lord and went back to the original sources. I began accumulating copies of the original documents and surviving records that pertained directly to the Alamo and associated events.

The documents I went after included primary documents actually written by participants, records of the official government (something called the General Council), personal diaries written at the time of occurrence, receipts and memos, muster rolls, inventories, and even some vintage Republic of Texas newspaper articles. Purposely omitted were highly flavored personal narratives and remembrances written well after the fact.

After years of research, I completed my collection of primary Alamo documents, which are those actually written by Alamo defenders. Of course, in this instance "complete document collection" has to be defined as all those documents for which copies, in one form or another, are available. Sadly, some few documents have either disappeared from archives or are in private hands and unavailable for reproduction. The good news is that most of the pertinent documents pertaining to the Alamo and related events are available. After considerable searching, some old fashioned luck, and the kind cooperation of many archivists, my collection is now complete, as far as is known.

Once I had the primary material, I added other selected documents that helped tell the entire story. My intention was to put everything in chronological order, study every detail of the material, and then embark on writing *the* story of the Alamo. Somewhere in the middle of that undertaking, it occurred to me that the men who lived through and died in the adventure had already written the true story of the Alamo. In the words left behind by those participants it is possible to trace exactly what happened. It became clear that the original true story of the Alamo would be hard to improve on, so I decided the best course would be to reproduce the documents, as they occurred.

The premise of this book is simple. All the material is presented as it was written, in chronological order. If you begin at the beginning, you will see the entire story develop just as the people of Texas did in 1836. You will see the glorious early victory and the optimism that followed; you will see that optimism slowly turn to fear and despair. You will see the Texans comfortable in their beliefs that any reprisal would not happen until spring of 1836 but, unlike most of those early Texans, you will see the advancing Mexican army as Santa Anna closes in for the kill. You will see first hand the desperate pleas for help from the Alamo. If you read carefully, you will see the devout patriotism, the frustrations and triumphs, and you will even see some subtle humor as the entire Alamo saga unfolds before your very eyes.

After the decision was made to reproduce the documents, there was the problem of deciding where to start and where to end the story. The actual siege of the Alamo lasted just 13 days from February 23, 1836 to March 6, 1836, but that is certainly not the entire story. So much happened prior to and immediately following the actual siege that had to be included if the story was to be complete. Accordingly, this story begins on December 9, 1835, the day the Mexican army first flew a white flag over the Alamo in response to a Texas siege of the mission. The surrender of the Mexicans placed the Alamo in Texans' hands for the first time. They did not have it long.

The end of the story was not on March 6, 1836, the day the Alamo fell. Given the poor means of communication which existed during the period, it was several days before word of the fall began to spread through the province of Texas. This story actually ends with another beginning.

By March 17, 1836, Texas had declared herself free from Mexican rule, issued a brand new constitution, and the government adjourned to either take up arms or take to the hills and escape the advancing Mexicans in what would become the "Runaway Scrape." By that date, Sam Houston was sure the Alamo had fallen, he had ordered a full retreat of the meager army and burned Gonzales. It was also on that date when General Sam Houston first wrote that the Alamo must be avenged.

So this Alamo story begins on December 9, 1835 and runs through March 17, 1836, exactly 100 days — perhaps the most dramatic and eventful 100 days in the entire history of Texas. The next problem was deciding exactly which documents were to be included in the story.

There were many factors which contributed directly or indirectly to the fall of the Alamo. One factor certainly was an ill-fated expedition against Matamoros, Mexico that was supposed to take war out of Texas. It failed miserably in achieving that purpose, but did manage to contribute to the fall of the Alamo. Then there was the enemy from within — the political intrigue which ultimately left the men of the Alamo garrison alone on the harsh prairie. And, of course, there was Colonel James Walker Fannin, Jr., who, with his 400 plus men at Goliad, might have marched to the relief of the Alamo, but never did. In an effort to tell the entire story, documents pertaining to contributing factors were included.

There are also some totally unrelated items, namely interesting newspaper clippings from period publications, which are also included. These articles are intended to provide some sense of life in Texas during the period which is essential to the overall story.

The reproduction of the actual documents presented an entirely new set of problems. When dealing with old documents, the best approach is to obtain the clearest possible exact copy of the original and reconstruct exactly what was said. In making that attempt, however, you have to deal with poor and strange handwriting; you must also contend with weird grammar, strange spellings, words often omitted, damaged documents, and the use of words not common in modern vocabularies. All things considered, translating many of the old documents is akin to translating a Greek play into the Queen's English. For someone like myself, who cannot read his own handwriting when it gets cold, trying to decipher those fragile old documents can be a frustrating challenge.

Fortunately, for researchers of Texas history, some brave souls have preceded us and actually transcribed many of the original documents into published collections. The papers of Sam Houston, Stephen F. Austin, M. B. Lamar, Antonio Lopez de Santa Anna, and others have all been accumulated into collections. There is also *The Papers of the Republic of Texas, 1835-1836*, edited by John Jenkins, that is a ten-volume set containing virtually every document from those critical days of the Republic of Texas that could be found at the time the set was produced.

While these collections go a long way toward providing information, they also can present some problems of their own. It must be remembered that someone, somewhere, had to interpret the original document, which means that person faced the spelling and grammar problems. Unless the transcript is compared to the original document, there is no way to verify accuracy. Since making such comparisons is often very time consuming (and sometimes impossible since the original is missing) the decision must be made as to whether or not to trust the reproduction. For the purpose of the material in this book, that decision was made in the affirmative.

Once I decided to trust someone else's transcripts, I had to overcome the problem of methodology used in producing those transcripts. Since many of the old documents cried out for editing and correction, the person reading the document had to make a decision as to either presenting the material literally, as originally written, or to make subtle corrections to enhance readability. Since there is no universally accepted method on how old documents are to be presented, the decision was generally left to the preference of the editor. Thus, some collections are presented literally and some edited.

Since the purpose of this book was to tell the true story of the Alamo in as readable a format as possible, some slight and silent alterations were made. When obvious words were omitted, they were added without brackets. When unknown words were obviously omitted, the document was presented as originally written to allow the reader to make his own determination as to what was intended to be said. As to spelling, only the absolutely worst cases were corrected. When the original writer got close, the misspelling was left intact and the universal symbol [sic] used to indicate misspelling was omitted as being a useless distraction.

Concerning grammar, in most cases, the style (or lack of style) of the original writer was left undisturbed. Thus, you will see strange word uses, odd capitalization, and some very creative sentence and paragraph structure. Only in a few cases was the grammar silently corrected and then only so the reader could easily understand what was being said.

Many of the letters were very long and contained material that was not germane to the purpose of this book. In those cases, some of the documents were edited to omit portions of the material. Generally, the omitted items were of either a highly personal nature or on subjects deemed not essential to the story of the Alamo or of general interest. In cases where material was omitted, either by myself or some previous editor, a series of dots (. . .) was used to indicate the omission. In a few instances, the dots will indicate portions of letters that are missing. In no case was any letter written by an actual Alamo defender edited in any way.

One final consideration on content has to do with documents written in Spanish. I have lived in Texas all my life but I only know enough Spanish to help me find a bathroom, a telephone, or a cantina should the need arise. Therefore, when it came to Spanish documents, I either had to ignore them or trust the translations of others. I chose to trust the translations of others, when available, knowing full well that the translators faced language problems as well as the spelling and grammar problems.

It is sincerely hoped that none of the slight editorial treatments of the material will take away from the flavor of what has been presented. With few exceptions, what follows are the actual words of the men who lived and died in Texas for 100 days between December 9, 1835 and March 17, 1836. It is, after all is said and done, the true story of the Alamo.

Wallace O. Chariton

All goes well and glorious for Texas — the whole country is in arms and moved by one spirit, which is to take Bexar, and drive all the military out of Texas — This is as it should be — no halfway measures now — war in full. . . . I hope to see Texas forever free from Mexican domination of any kind — It is yet too soon to say this publicly — but that is the point we shall end at and it is the one I am aiming at. But we must arrive at it by steps and not all at one jump —

Stephen F. Austin
San Felipe de Austin, Texas
October 5, 1835

Dedication

To future writers of Alamo history. May this humble offering calm some of the stormy waters always encountered when historians go searching for the truth.

Acknowledgements

Like all other books ever published, this one is the result of the concerted efforts of many people, some of whom deserve much of the credit.

For Bernice Strong of the DRT Library at the Alamo, I would especially say thank you. She has her finger on the pulse of Alamo history and never ceased to amaze me when she could come up documents based on the barest of information. Thanks also to Mrs. Strong for pointing me in the direction of many documents that I not have otherwise uncovered. And I will always be grateful for the hours we spent talking about the Alamo.

Dianne Stultz deserves perhaps the biggest thank-you of all for this book because she had the dubious task of editing the manuscript. Since the material was reproduced exactly as written in 1835-1836, Mrs. Stultz had to decipher whether it was I or the original author who had committed the spelling and grammar errors. It was not an easy job but I appreciate her dedication and all the hours she spent laboring over the manuscript trying to decipher the material.

Michael Green and the staff of the Texas state archives in Austin provided invaluable assistance in tracking down primary documents and in suggesting other more obscure documents that ought to be included. The wonderful folks at the archives make researching Texas history a sheer pleasure.

The entire staff of Wordware Publishing, Inc. deserves much of the credit for this book ever becoming a reality. Thank you to Russ Stultz and Kenni "Jet" Driver for believing in the project. Thank you to Jana Gardner-Koch for keeping the project moving forward and for caring about quality as much or more than I do. If possible, I believe Jana was even more excited about this book than I.

And then there is Martha McCuller, the nice lady who was handed a tiny computer disk and asked to turn it into a book. I know dealing with the material almost drove Mrs. McCuller over the edge and I would thank her, not only for the quality of her work, but for only allowing her frustration to really boil over once, and then for such a brief moment. I really do appreciate everything you did, Martha. Thanks also to Alan McCuller for the fantastic cover design and for always seeming to have the answer when an art or graphic question arose.

And of course, a special thank-you is in order for Judy, Gage, and Jennifer. They know why it is the biggest thanks of all.

CHAPTER ONE

Introduction

Setting the Stage

Hostilities between the leaders of the Mexican Republic and the Anglo-American settlers in the province of Texas were probably inevitable from the very beginning. There were too many cultural differences in traditions, customs, language, and even religion. But although the seeds of discontent were planted early, it would take those seeds more than ten years to blossom into open and armed conflict.

After more than three hundred years of Spanish rule, Mexico finally won her independence in 1821. The fledgling young Mexican republic struggled for stability. There were ambitious leaders more interested in furthering their own position than that of the nation. There was damaging political and military intrigue from the very beginning. And there was the problem of what to do about the vast wasteland known as Texas.

The Spanish had tried for almost a century to colonize the huge expanse of land located to the north of the Rio Grande River. Their efforts had been less than successful and in 1821 the Spanish instigated a program to encourage colonization of the area by Anglo-Americans from the North. The new regime of the Mexican Republic decided to continue that policy in hopes of keeping the region from being totally overrun by savages.

News of the liberal Mexican colonization policy spread quickly through the southern part of the United States. Settlers, hungry for land and opportunity, discounted the dangers of life in a hostile frontier. Stephen F. Austin, carrying on in his father's footsteps, began shepherding the first settlers from his "Old Three Hundred" colony into Texas during November of 1821.

From that meager beginning the population of Texas would grow from an estimated 2,500 European colonists in 1821 to almost 40,000 Anglos, blacks, and Mexicans in 1836.

In the early stages of colonization, relations with Mexico were reasonably palatable. In 1823 Mexico passed the first in a series of Imperial Colonization Laws. The act allowed for farmers to receive a bounty of one labor (177 acres) of land; cattle raisers would receive one league (4,428 acres) of land; and those who both farmed and raised cattle, which was true of most settlers, would receive both a labor and a league of land. Another important provision of the law was the suspension of tariff laws for seven years. Two "catches" in the 1823 Law required that land owners had to be Roman Catholic and the trafficking in slaves was expressly prohibited.

In 1824, when a new Mexican constitution was written, the Anglo-Americans in Texas were not represented, although Stephen F. Austin did confer with Mexican leaders about the content of the document. The 1824 Mexican Constitution loosely resembled the United States Constitution but was patterned after the Spanish constitution of 1812. Highlights of the new Mexican Constitution included making Roman Catholic the official state religion to be supported by the public treasury; a president and vice-president to be elected, with limited powers, by representatives of legislative bodies from the individual states; and the establishment of a two-house Congress, Supreme courts, and district courts. Under the 1824 Constitution, individual states in the Mexican confederation were left to frame their own constitution to define their individual rights so long as the executive, legislative, and judicial powers were separated.

The Texas colonists would have been overjoyed to write their own state constitution and define their own rights had it not been for another provision of the 1824 Mexican document which required that the province of Texas be combined with the state of Coahuila to form a single new state. The capital of the new single state was moved from San Antonio 365 miles south to Saltillo, Mexico, and government representation of the people of Texas was limited to two as compared to eleven for the people of the former state Coahuila.

Effects of the disproportionate representation became obvious in March 1827, when the constitution for the combined Texas-Coahuila state was published. Although the document did guarantee liberty, security, property, and equality to the citizens of the state, slavery was forbidden and Roman Catholicism was established as the state religion. Provisions calling for trial by jury were never enacted and a promised school system did not materialize. All laws were published only in Spanish which was a foreign language to most of the Anglo-Americans in the region.

Naturally, the new Texans were sorely disappointed in their constitution. The general feeling was that rights available to them under the Mexican National constitution had been denied and the Texans greatly resented being combined with Coahuila. Relations with the Mexican government began to slip at an alarming rate. Those relations took a dramatic turn on April 6, 1830, when the Mexican government passed new laws forbidding further colonization from the United States, levying tariffs for the first time, ordering soldiers to enforce tax laws, and allowing convict-soldiers to live and work in the colonies. Although a liberal interpretation of the colonization law did allow some continued emigration into the Austin and DeWitt colonies of Texas, the tariff issue was destined to become a festering problem.

By 1832, politics in Mexico were in turmoil, thanks in large part to the actions of an upstart general named Antonio Lopez de Santa Anna who incited a revolution in his quest for power. In Texas, a series of attacks at Velasco, Nacogdoches, Tenoxtitlan, and Anahuac resulted in the removal of Mexican garrisons. At Anahuac, near the mouth of the Brazos River, long simmering political animosity erupted in violence. Following a series of disagreeable actions by the Mexicans that included the removal of a surveyor who was to issue land titles, unreasonable custom clearance regulations, and the arbitrary impression of Texas slave labor without compensation, the Anglos finally struck back. The action that precipitated the backlash was the unfair arrest of Patrick Jack and William B. Travis, both local activist lawyers. A force of citizens, aided by a company from Brazoria, was able to effect the release of the prisoners, get the director of the local custom house relieved of his duties, and force the suspension of tariff collections. Colonists who participated in the Texas insurrections claimed they were cooperating with Santa Anna in forcing the garrisons of Mexican President Bustamante to close.

Politically, the Texans were growing uneasy so they held a consultation to draft their grievances with the Mexican government. Essentially, the Texans wanted the tariff exemptions extended; they wanted to be separated from Coahuila and allowed to form their own government; and they wanted colonization restrictions removed. Unfortunately, their petition was never delivered to the Mexican government.

By 1833, the Mexican revolution was over and the liberal Santa Anna had been elected president. He won with a promise of a democratic form of government and that he would maintain the Mexican Constitution. Texans, still disgruntled at the mismanagement of politics in their region, called another convention (or consultation) to explore their options. In the second convention the issues were largely the same as in 1832, and the Texans decided to draft a proposed constitution for presentation to the

Mexican government. The plan was for Texas to be separated from Coahuila and the Anglo citizens to be allowed to govern themselves as provided for in the original 1824 Mexican Constitution. When the Texas document, which was patterned after the Massachusetts Constitution of 1870, was complete, Stephen F. Austin headed for Mexico City to plead the case of the Texans. The Mexican government agreed to repeal the colonization law and ordered the tariff issue held in abeyance, but no action was taken on the matter of individual statehood for Texas. For all his trouble, Austin was imprisoned on his way home and charged with inciting rebellion. It would be eighteen months before he would see Texas again.

Less than a year after his election, Santa Anna's true colors began to show through when he announced that the Mexican people were not sufficiently advanced to live under democratic rule and he installed himself as military dictator. The arbitrary acts of Santa Anna, the self-proclaimed "Napoleon of the West," riled many Mexicans as well as Anglo-Texans, but the dictator quickly showed he would tolerate no insurrections when he and his army crushed a rebellion in the Mexican state of Zacatecas.

Santa Anna also acted against Texas when he announced that the state government would be reorganized, and then he boldly sent troops to reopen the custom house at Anahuac in 1835. When Andrew Briscoe was arrested for tariff violations, William B. Travis led a detachment of twenty men and stormed the custom house, freed Briscoe, and demanded the troops withdraw. The actions of Travis and the rest infuriated Santa Anna who dispatched his brother-in-law, General Martin Perfecto de Cos, to expel all Americans who had come to Texas since 1830, to disarm all Texans, and to arrest anyone opposing the dictator's regime. Cos landed with 1,200 men and twenty-one pieces of artillery and marched to San Antonio.

Travis' actions also evoked the ire of many Anglo-Texans who professed loyalty to the new Santa Anna-led government. Mass meetings around the province condemned the actions of Travis on the grounds that he had incited war. The opinions of most of those angry Texans slowly changed, however, as it became evident that Santa Anna was determined to have Texas under military rule. It became increasingly clear to most Texans that they were in serious jeopardy of losing what few rights had been promised under the 1824 Mexican Constitution. Before the summer of 1835 was over, the tide of opinion in Texas had turned to rebellion.

Political opinion in Texas was generally divided. Some, the so called Peace Party, favored working for restoration of their democratic rights that had been provided for under the 1824 Mexican Constitution but dismantled by Santa Anna the dictator.

Others, the War Party, were in favor of establishing Texas as an independent republic free of any sort of Mexican rule. One point everyone seemed to agree on was that regardless of the cause, there would be fighting to be done, so the call for volunteers went out. Quickly, a meager army began to take shape.

On October 2, 1835, the first shot in what would soon be a full revolution was fired at Gonzales, Texas. A detachment of Mexican dragoons approached Gonzales to retrieve a small cannon which had been loaned to the townspeople for protection against Indians. The Texans challenged the Mexicans to "come and take it" and then fired on the dragoons. The Mexicans withdrew, leaving behind the cannon. The war was on.

On the political front, a consultation of the chosen delegates of all Texas was called to determine what course was to be followed. While the delegates met in San Felipe to haggle over political recourse, the fighting heated up. In Goliad, a small Texas force rousted the Mexicans out of LaBahia mission. Near San Antonio, Stephen F. Austin, who had finally been released from the Mexican prison, was preparing to attack the town and the Alamo fortress held by General Cos. On October 27, 1835, in a prelude to what was expected to be a major fight for San Antonio, a Texas patrol led by James Bowie was attacked by a company of Mexicans near Concepcion Mission, two miles south of San Antonio. After a brief thirty-minute skirmish, the Mexicans withdrew and the Texans had another victory.

Public sentiment among the Texans was running high for re-establishment of their rights. An article in the October 26, 1835 issue of the *Telegraph, and Texas Register* summed up the feelings of many:

> There can be as little doubt of the right of Texas to object to the system of centralism, or a combined government as to consent. She was an integral yet sovereign state of a federal republic, and cannot be induced into the action of any different form of government without the consent of her citizens, or by means of military coercion. Emigrants tool lands under a republican government; and to such only do they owe allegiance. That was supposed to be guaranteed to them, and they are not bound to be component parts of any dictatorial or monarchical government adverse to the protection and privileges by which they were induced to settle here. They are, therefore, fully justified in separating from the government, and in either declaring their state to be sovereign and independent, or seeking to be admitted as a member of the United states.

Since war was obviously being waged on the frontier, the delegates to the consultation meeting in San Felipe decided to publish a Declaration of Causes to explain to the world, and to the Mexican people, why Texans were taking up arms against Mexico. The Declaration, issued on November 7, 1836, was as follows:

> Whereas, General Antonio Lopez de Santa Anna and other Military Chieftains have, by force of arms, overthrown the Federal Institutions of Mexico, and dissolved the social Compact which existed between Texas and the other Members of the Mexican Confederacy — Now, the good People of Texas, availing themselves of their natural rights,

SOLEMNLY DECLARE

1st. That they have taken up arms in defence of their rights and Liberties, which were threatened by the encroachments of military despots, and in defence of the Republican Principles of the Federal constitution of Mexico of eighteen hundred and twenty-four.

2d. That Texas is no longer, morally or civilly, bound by the compact of Union; yet, stimulated by the generosity and sympathy common to a free people they offer their support and assistance to such Mexicans of the Mexican Confederacy as will take up arms against their military despotism.

3d. That they do not acknowledge, that the present authorities of the nominal Mexican Republic have the right to govern within the limits of Texas.

4th. That they will not cease to carry on war against the said authorities, whilst their troops are within the limits of Texas.

5th. That they hold it to be their right, during the disorganization of the Federal system and the reign of depotism, to withdraw from the Union, to establish an independent Government, or to adopt such measures as they may deem best calculated to protect their rights and liberties; but that they will continue faithful to the Mexican Government so long as that nation is governed by the Constitution and Laws that were formed for the government of the Political Association.

6th. That Texas is responsible for the expenses of her Armies now in the field.

7th. That the public faith is pledged for the payment of any debts contracted by her agents.

8th. That she will reward by donations in Land, all

who volunteer their services in her present struggle, and receive them as Citizens.

These Declarations we solemnly avow to the world, and call GOD to witness their truth and sincerity; and invoke defeat and disgrace upon our heads should we prove guilty of duplicity.

Any lingering thoughts that war might be avoided were gone. Out on the frontier, General Austin departed for the United States to try to borrow money for the Texas cause. He left General Edward Burleson in charge of a small army of about 400 men that was in a difficult situation. They were poorly equipped and badly outnumbered by the Mexicans hemmed up in San Antonio and the nearby Alamo mission. For over a month Burleson insisted the men wait for reinforcements while making certain the Mexicans did not receive fresh supplies. For volunteers itching to fight, the wait-and-see attitude was not popular. By the first part of December 1835, it appeared the army might disband and return home in frustration.

Possible disaster to the cause of Texas was averted when John W. Smith and Samuel Maverick escaped from San Antonio and brought word to the Texans that the morale of the Mexicans was waning and their supplies were running desperately short. Bolstered by such information, Colonel Ben Milam boldly asked, "Who will follow Old Ben Milam into San Antone?" Three hundred men answered the call.

On the morning of December 4, 1835, while Colonel James C. Neill diverted the attention of the Mexicans with artillery fire, the Texas army attacked. For three wet and cold days, the Texans advanced, literally from house to house, amid fierce fire from the enemy. By nightfall on December 8, the town of San Antonio de Bexar belonged to the Texans and the Mexicans had withdrawn to the relative safety of the huge Alamo mission.

By morning on December 9, 1836, General Cos had come to realize the seriousness of his situation. Although he commanded a far superior force, he was cut off from supplies and had no reason to expect reinforcements. It appeared to the general that surrender was the only way to save his force and he ordered a white flag hoisted. The Alamo saga was set to begin.

The period from December 9, 1835, the day the Mexicans surrendered the Alamo, to March 17, 1836, the day the self-proclaimed Republic of Texas finally got its own constitution, were destined to be the most dramatic and eventful one hundred days in Texas history.

CHAPTER TWO

The First Fall of the Alamo

December 9, through December 31, 1835

On December 10, 1835, the terms of the Mexican surrender of the Alamo were completed and Texans took control of the fortress. They would have it just eighty-seven eventful days.

The provincial government of Texas, at the time, consisted of an appointed governor, Henry Smith, and a General Council comprised of elected delegates from the principal municipalities. Members of the council generally leaned in favor of fighting for restoration of the Mexican constitution, as did the commander in chief of the army, General Sam Houston. Governor Smith, on the other hand, favored full independence from Mexican rule. The controversy over what course to follow would contribute directly to internal strife in the government at a time when harmony would be greatly needed.

The Texas victory at the Alamo set the wheels of war in motion both above and below the Rio Grande River. Sam Houston began working on organizing an army and the calls went out across the United States for volunteers. A wild, rather radical scheme was also beginning to gain favor. It was suggested, even encouraged, by some that the Texans ought to take the war to Mexican soil. The council received the plan with great favor while the governor and Sam Houston feared such a scheme might cost Texas the support of liberal Mexican citizens living in the province. Smith, however, relented and ordered Houston to set the expedition in motion. Houston responded by ordering James Bowie to organize a force and proceed against the port town of Matamoros, Mexico. Bowie did not receive the orders, however, until after the first of the year and thus took no immediate action.

The General Council, meanwhile, suggested to Frank W. Johnson, commander of the Texas volunteers in San Antonio, that an expedition like the one being considered against Matamoros might be an excellent idea. Johnson, with the assistance of Dr. John Grant, reacted immediately even though he had no specific orders. By the end of December, Johnson and Grant had looted the Alamo of vital supplies and organized two hundred troops to march on Matamoros. The Alamo garrison was left helpless on the Texas frontier and the government was on a collision course with self-destruction.

While the Texans were preparing to take the war to Mexico, Santa Anna was making plans to invade Texas, retake the Alamo, and then wage a war of extermination all the way to the Sabine River, which was the boundary between Mexico and the United States. The general set about making extensive preparations for outfitting an invading army of 6,000 men. On December 7, while his brother-in-law was battling the Texans from the Alamo, Santa Anna issued his instructions for the campaign against Texas and the Anglos. In one paragraph, he summed up his objectives:

> . . . The foreigners who wage war against the Mexican Nation have violated all laws and do not deserve any consideration, and for that reason, no quarter will be given them as the troops are to be notified at the proper time. They have audaciously declared a war of extermination to the Mexicans and should be treated in the same manner. . . .

While the Texans struggled with internal strife and a severe lack of supplies and the means with which to wage a war, the Mexicans were preparing to invade. Neither side had any thoughts of possible defeat.

Wednesday, December 9, 1835
88 DAYS TO THE FALL

F. W. Johnson[1] to General Edward Burleson[2]

SAN ANTONIO de BEXAR: Sir, I have the honor to acquaint you,
that on the morning of the 5th inst. the volunteers for storming the
city of Bejar,[3] possessed by the troops of General Cos, entered the
suburbs in two divisions, under command of colonel Benjamin R.
Milam: the first division, under his immediate command, aided by
Major R. C. Morris, and the second, under my command, aided by
Colonels Grant and Austin, and Adjutant Bristeral.

The first division, consisting of the companies of Captains
York, Patten, Lewellyn, Crane, English, and Landrum, with two
pieces, and fifteen artillerymen, commanded by Lieutenant-
colonel Franks, took possession of the house of Don Antonio de
la Garza. The second division, composed of the companies of
Captains Cook, Swisher, Edwards, Alley, Duncan, Peacock,
Breece, and Placido Benavides, took possession of the house of
Berrimendi. The last division was exposed, for a short time, to a
very heavy fire of grape and musketry from the whole of the
enemy's fortification, until the guns of the first division opened
their fire, when the enemy's attention was directed to both
divisions. At 7 o'clock, a heavy cannonading from the town was
seconded by a well-directed fire from the Alamo, which for a
time prevented the possibility of covering our lines, or effecting a
safe communication between the two divisions. In consequence
of the twelve-pounder having been dismounted, and the want
of proper cover for the other guns, little execution was done by
our artillery, during the day. We were, therefore reduced to a
close and well directed fire from our rifles, which, not withstanding the advantageous position of the enemy, obliged them
to slacken their fire, and several times to abandon their artillery,
within the range of our shot. Our loss during the day was one
private killed, one colonel, and one first lieutenant severely
wounded; one colonel slightly, three privates dangerously, six
severely, and three slightly. During the whole of the night, the
two divisions were occupied in strengthening their positions,
opening trenches, and effecting a safe communication, although
to a heavy cross-fire from the enemy, which slackened towards
morning. I may remark that the want of proper tools rendered
this undertaking doubly arduous. At daylight on the 6th, the
enemy were observed to have occupied the tops of houses in our
front, where, under cover of breastworks, they opened, through
loop-holes, a very brisk fire of small arms on our whole line,
followed by a steady cannonading from the town, in front, and
the Alamo on the left flank; with few interruptions during the
day. A detachment of Captain Crane's company, under

Lieutenant W. McDonald, followed by others, gallantly possessed themselves, under a severe fire, of the house to the right, and in advance of the first division, which considerably extended our line; while the rest of the army was occupied in returning the enemy's fire and strengthening our trenches, which enabled our artillery to do some execution, and complete a safe communication from right to left.

Our loss this day amounted to three privates severely, and two slightly. During the night the fire from the enemy was inconsiderable, and our people were occupied in making and filling sand bags, and otherwise strengthening our lines. At daylight on the 7th, it was discovered that the enemy had opened a trench on the Alamo side of the river, and on the left flank, as well as strengthening their battery on the cross street leading to the Alamo. From the first they opened a brisk fire of small arms, which was kept up until eleven o'clock, when they were silenced by our superior fire. About twelve o'clock, Henry Karnes, of Captain York's company, exposed to a heavy fire from the enemy, gallantly advanced to a house in front of the first division, and with a crow bar forced an entrance, into which the whole of the company immediately followed him, and made a secure lodgment. In the evening, the enemy renewed a heavy fire from all the positions which could bear upon us; and at half-past three o'clock, as our gallant commander, Colonel Milam, was passing into the yard of my position, he received a rifle shot in the head, which caused his instant death; an irreparable loss at so critical a moment. Our casualties, otherwise, during this day, were only two privates slightly wounded.

At a meeting of officers held at seven o'clock, I was invested with the chief command; and Major Morris, as my second, at ten o'clock, P.M. Captains Lewellyn, English, Crane, and Landrum, with their respective companies, forced their way into, and took possession of the house of Don J Antonio Navarro, an advanced and important position close to the square. The fire of the enemy interrupted and slack during the whole night, and the weather exceedingly cold and wet.

The morning of the 8th continued cold and wet, and but little firing on either side. At nine o'clock the same companies who took possession of Don J. Antonio Navarro's house, aided by a detachment of the Greys, advanced, and occupied the Zambrano Row, leading to the square, without any accident. The brave conduct, on this occasion, of William Graham, of Cook's company of Greys, merits mention. A heavy fire of artillery and small arms was opened on this position by the enemy, who disputed every inch of ground; and, after suffering a severe loss in officers and men, were obliged to retire from room to room, until at last they occupied the whole house. During this time our men were reinforced by a detachment from York's company, under command of Lieutenant Gill.

The cannonading from the camp was exceedingly heavy from all quarters during the day, but did no essential damage.

Our loss consisted of one captain seriously wounded, and two privates severely. At seven o'clock, P.M. the party in Zambrano Row were reinforced by Captains Swisher, Alley, Edwards, and Duncan, and their respective companies.

This evening we had undoubted information of the arrival of a strong reinforcement to the enemy, under Colonel Ugartachea. At half past ten o'clock, P.M., Captains Cook and Patten, with the company of New Orleans Greys, and a company of Brazoria volunteers, forced their way into the priest's house in the square, although exposed to the fire of a battery of three guns, and a large body of musketeers.

Before this, however, the division was reinforced from the reserve, by Captains Cheshire, Lewis, and Sutherland, with their companies.

Immediately after we got possession of the priest's house, the enemy opened a furious cannonade from all their batteries, accompanied by incessant volleys of small arms, against every house in our possession, and every part of our lines, which continued unceasingly until half-past six o'clock, A.M. of the 9th, when they sent a flag of truce, with an invitation that they desired to capitulate. . . .[4]

Sam Houston[5] to D. C. Barrett[6]

HEADQUARTERS SAN FELIPE: I beg to suggest in consequence of your kind offers — that some difference should be made between the Regular troops & the volunteers which may join the army — viz, that the Regular soldiers should receive 24 dollars bounty one half to be paid at the time of their muster at Head Quarters, the other half 6 months after muster and also an addition of 100 acres to their present bounty making in all 740 acres of prime land. —

Feeling the most perfect confidence in the clearness and perspicuity of your views on this subject — renders a further explanation on my part unnecessary —[7]

Sam Houston, commander in chief of the Texas Army.

Thursday, December 10, 1835
87 DAYS TO THE FALL

Moseley Baker[8] to The General Council of Texas[9]

SAN FELIPE: The very critical conditions in which the volunteer army now before San Antonio is placed induces me without offering any apology to intrude myself upon your attention.

From various sources concurring information has reached this place and also the camp at Bexar that Col Ugartechear was on the march with about 700 men to reinforce gen Cos and when I left the army Ugartechear was looked for every day. An express reached you night before last informing you that Col Milam with three hundred men had taken possession of one part of the town and by that same express you were called upon to reinforce your fellow citizens as soon as possible.

That neither you nor the country may be led into a dangerous mistake and induced to believe that San Antonio has fallen I will explain to you the true condition of things in order that you may be enabled to act accordingly.

The position now occupied by our troops is certainly a very important one and one from which the enemy may be very much annoyed but it by no means gives our party possession of the town — They occupy three stone houses — distant from water and wood — and until they gain possession of other parts of the town one half of the army must necessarily be retained at its old encampment — in order to relieve them, supply them with provisions and cover their retreat should one become necessary — Between them and the church there are three strong stone buildings occupied by Mexican troops who have to be dislodged before our party can advance further — even when these are taken other strong buildings independent of the church which is strongly fortified still remain in possession of the Mexicans — and when all these are taken they can still retreat to the Alamo. Thus you see that Bexar is not yet taken — but I have no doubt that if properly reinforced — that our Brave fellow citizens who have gained so important an advantage will press forward and successfully complete the work they have commenced and before the ushering in of the new year — that Texas and Liberty will be shouted from the walls of San Antonio.

But if this reinforcement is not sent and if the army is not immediately reinforced a different shout will be heard and a different work accomplished — situated as our army is at this time — the arrival of Ugartichear will be its ruin — the shout of victory will be on the Mexican side and the work accomplished will be the destruction of Texas — I am disposed gentlemen to speak to you in plain and direct language — I am just from the army — I have participated with it in its toils and privations and dangers — and I have seen men without a blanket to cover them — with only a thin pair of trousers and some without jackets clinging with desperate resolution to the army and swearing never to return until San Antonio fell — I have seen one universal feeling of patriotism pervading the army, such as never was and never will be surpassed — I have seen them all heroes and all willing to be martyrs — and yet they were fighting and contending only for what you were equally interested in.

Gentlemen I repeat to you this army is in danger — Texas is in danger — a heavy responsibility rests on you at this moment. I regret to see so little done to reinforce them — and so little prospect of their being reinforced — I suggest to your body the propriety of immediately appointing someone to enroll volunteers to go to their relief. The individual you may appoint should appoint persons of influence to go to the different settlements on the Brazos & Colorado and raise volunteers all to meet at Gonzales on the 20th of this month — In that way the army can be reinforced and I see no other practicable way of doing it at the moment — Gentlemen if you adopt this course in behalf of our suffering army and suffering Texas I intreat you to do so at once — some of our fellow citizens have already tasted the bitterness of Death others are severely wounded and all are tired and worn out with constant fatigue and fighting — For my own part I shall return to my fellow citizens in arms, I think it the duty of every man to go — but before going I will use my every exertion to rouse up my fellow citizens — and induce them to go where honor and duty calls them — where Danger and Destruction threatens their Relatives — their Friends and Fellow Citizens — and above all threatens the Brave — and Heroic volunteer army of Texas —

Respectfully
Moseley Baker[10]

J. W. Hicks[11] & others to the Honorable the President & Council of Texas

NACOGDOCHES, TEXAS: We the subscribers volunteers in the cause of Texas now on our way to San Antonio respectfully represent, — that we have been informed by Messrs Jesse & W. Badget,[12] known to judge Chambers as men of truth, and verily believe, that there are one hundred and twenty men, volunteers in the same just cause in which we have embarked, who left Natchitoches, Louisiana on or about the first day of December; — that under the impression that the provisional government of Texas has provided the means of forwarding volunteers they are unprovided for further than Nacogdoches and cannot come on further unless the honorable Council shall see proper to meet them there through an agent with the means of defraying their expenses to the army.

Joseph W. Hicks
[illegible]
M Hawkins[13]

General Council to the People of Texas

SAN FELIPE: We, the undersigned, having been appointed by the General Council of Texas, a committee for the purpose of drafting an address to you, and preparing resolutions on the subject of our gallant army now before Bexar, approach this subject with great diffidence, and under a full view of the deep responsibility which rests upon us, in the discharge of this important duty.

It is not necessary for us to go back and trace the causes which have led us in the defence of our constitutional rights, into the present war with the minions of a tyrant. It is sufficient that we are now in the war, and that a noble and heroic band, composed of our fellow citizens, and disinterested patriots from the United States are now in an exposed and critical situation, before the walls of a strong fortress of the enemy, and have made an appeal to you through this Council, for ammunition and reinforcements. They are contending without the necessary munitions of war, and without the usual comforts extended to armies, against a force more than equal their number, who are well supplied with ammunitions and strongly fortified. And from information of a positive character in our possession, the enemy will be, if they have not been already reinforced by large numbers.[14] If your army is not immediately reinforced, they will be forced to retreat or be slaughtered. Will you abandon this army, who have marched to the field of danger at the first tocsin of alarm? Will you give the enemies of the constitution, and the hireling slaves of a tyrant, the first victory? — Will you destroy the last hopes of the "Liberals" of the Mexican Republic? Will you disappoint the expectations of your friends? Will you compromise your own honor? Will you expose the defenceless women and children of the frontier to the ravages of an enemy, whose only check to their conduct, is the extent of their power? No, you will not! Rise up, then, with one accord, and shoulder your rifles, march to the field of battle, and teach the hirelings of a tyrant that they can not battle successfully with citizen freemen.

D. C. Barrett, Chairman; R. R. Royall, Henry Millard,
Committee[15]

Council Hall, San Felipe

By the laws of Creation and Nature, all men are free and equal, of these natural rights no man can be forcibly deprived of the principles of immutable justice: a desire for domination and power in man over his fellowman, subjects the weak and unambitious to the machinations of the more subtle and strong — to avoid such evils social compacts or Governments are formed for mutual protection: — to this end each member of a community surrenders certain of his natural rights for common security; — thus, of necessity, all the legitimate powers of any Government are immediately derived from the governed. The people are sovereign, and all the officers designated for the execution of their civil compact are agents and accountable for their fidelity: — when such agents assume the character of principals or dictators, and attempt of their own will to subvert the form and true principles of the Governmental Compac and substitute another without the consent of the people [resistance] is necessary and a virtue: in this situation are the citizens of Texas and a considerable portion of the Mexican Republic of which Texas is a part — resistances is, therefore, a duty. The protection of our liberties — one natural and reserved right to make it so . . . — arms are the resort, and in arms the people will find their only security from the oppression of ambitious tyrants, whose chains are forged to manacle our citizens and subdue them to their will: courage and bravery in resistance, and prudence in council will restore to us the natural sovereignty of all Governments: — one civil compact or constitution is destroyed and another must be formed to guarantee the purposes and ends of political associations: A Provisional or temporary Government, however wisely formed or prudently administered, is at best uncertain and insecure — permanency and strength should be the basis of all Governments — therefore,

Be it resolved, That in virtue of the powers vested in the "Provisional Government of Texas" by the Representatives of the people in convention assembled, and it is hereby resolved, by the General council of the Provisional Government aforesaid, that a Convention of Delegates of the people for each Municipality of the three departments of Texas shall be called, to assemble on the first day of March next, at the town of Washington.

Be it further resolved, That the Delegates elected by the people clothed with ample, unlimited, or plenary powers as to the form of government to be adopted: provided, that no constitution formed shall go into effect until submitted to the people and confirmed by a majority thereof.

Be it further resolved, That the acting Judge, or in the case there be no acting Judge, the Alcalde of each Municipality be required to issue writs of election to some competent and respectable citizen of each election district, to hold the election in the said district district on the first day of February, 1836 allowing all free white males and Mexicans opposed to a Central Government a vote: provided, that no proxy votes shall be received — excepting, nevertheless, all the Citizen Volunteers in the Army, each of whom shall have a right to his vote, which he shall write upon paper over his own signature, and send to the Judge or Alcalde . . . to be received on or before the day of the election aforesaid;

Be it further resolved, That with a view to as just an equalization of representatives as can be at present determined, that the Municipality of Austin shall elect three delegates, Brazoria four, Washington four, Mina three, Gonzales two, Viesca two, Harrisburg two, Jasper two, Matagorda two, Jackson two, Tenehaw two, Jefferson two, Refugio two, Goliad two Bexar four, Guadalupe Victoria two, and the citizens of Pecan Point two.

Be it further resolved, That the governor shall . . . issue his proclamation for carrying into effect the preceding Resolutions.[16]

Friday, December 11, 1835
86 DAYS TO THE FALL

Jose Juan Sanchez Navarro Diary Entry
"All has been lost save honor!" I do not remember, nor am I in the mood to remember, what French king said this, perhaps under better circumstances than those in which we are today, the eleventh of December, 1835. Bexar, and perhaps Texas has been lost, although the majority of the faithful subjects the Supreme Government had here for its defense cannot be blamed for such a loss. This is my humble opinion. . . .

We were surrounded by some gross, proud, and victorious men. Anyone who knows the character of the North Americans can judge what our situation must have been.[17]

CAPITULATION, entered into by General Martin Perfecto de Cos of the Permanent Troops and General Edward Burleson, of the Colonial Troops of Texas
Being desirous of preventing the further effusion of blood and the ravages of civil war, we have agreed on the following:

1st. That General Cos and his officer retire with their arms and private property, into the interior of the republic, under parole of honour; that they will not in any way oppose the re-establishment of the Federal Constitution of 1824.

2d. That the 100 infantry lately arrived with the convicts, the remnant of the battalion of Morelos, and the cavalry, retire with the General: taking their arms and ten rounds of cartridges for their muskets.

3d. That the General take the convicts brought in by Colonel Ugartechea, beyond the Rio Grande.

4th. That it is discretionary with the troops to follow their general, remain, or go to such point as they may deem proper: but in case they should all or any of them separate, they are to have their arm, &c.

5th. That all the public property, money, arms, and munitions of war be inventoried and delivered to General Burleson.

General Edward Burleson

6th. That all private property be restored to its proper owners.

7th. That three officers of each army be appointed to make out the inventory, and see that the terms of the capitulation be carried into effect.

8th. That three officers on the part of Cos remain for the purpose of delivering over the said property, stores, &c.

9th. That general Cos with his force, for the present, occupy the Alamo; and General Burleson, with his force, occupy the Town of Bexar; and that the soldiers of neither party pass to the other, armed.

General Martin Perfecto de Cos

10th. General Cos shall, within six days from the date hereof, remove his force from the garrison he now occupies

11th. In addition to the arms before mentioned, Cos shall be permitted to take with his force a four-pounder, and ten rounds of powder and ball.

12th. The officers appointed to make the inventory and delivery of the stores, &c., shall enter upon the duties to which they have been appointed, forthwith.

13th. The citizens shall be protected in their persons and property.

14th. Gen. Burleson will furnish Gen Cos with such provisions as can be obtained, necessary for his troops to the Rio Grande, at the ordinary price of the country.

15th. The sick and wounded of General Cos's army, together with a surgeon and attendants, are permitted to remain.

16th. No person, either citizen or soldier, to be molested on account of his political opinion hitherto expressed.

17th. That duplicates of this capitulation be made out in Castillian and English and signed by the commissioners appointed, and ratified by the commanders of both armies.

18th. The prisoners of both armies, up to this day, shall be put at liberty.

The Commissioners, Jose Juan Sanchez, adjutant inspector; Don Ramon Musquiz, and Lieutenant Francisco Rada, and interpreter, Don Miguel Arciniega; appointed by the commandant and inspector, General Martin Perfecto de Cos, in connection with Colonel F. W. Johnson, Major R. C. Morris, and Captain J. G. Swisher, and interpreter, John Cameron; appointed on the part of General Edward Burleson: after a long and serious discussion, adopted the eighteen preceding articles, reserving their ratification by the Generals of both armies.

In virtue of which, we have signed this instrument in the city of Bexar, on the 11th of December, 1835.

> Jose Juan Sanchez,
> Ramon Musquiz,
> J. Francisco de Rada,
> Miguel Arciniega, Interpreter,
> F. W. Johnson,
> Robert C. Morris,
> James C. Swisher,
> John Cameron, Interpreter.

I consent to, and will observe the above articles.

> Martin Perfecto de Cos.

Ratified and approved.

> Edward Burleson,
> Commander-in-Chief of the Volunteer Army.[18]

Moseley Baker to the General Council of Texas

SAN FELIPE, TEXAS: you will not I am certain consider any one intrusive who may presume to offer you his opinions on the importance and practicability of reinforcing the present volunteer army before Bexar.

I am not the particular authorized representative of our fellow citizens now comprising that army — but I consider myself authorized to represent them in any manner when I consider that I may be serviceable in forwarding to them assistance in their very critical condition —

The letter I had the honor to address to your body on yesterday morning — was called forth by the deep conviction that our friends were in danger and that relief ought to be extended to them — immediately — I think you ought if possible to forward that relief without one moment delay — for the loss of one week may result in the loss of our army —

The appointment of Capt Fanning[19] if he was present would undoubtedly be a good one — but inasmuch as he is not here and will not be for a week at least I cannot but consider it as unfortunate — unless others are associated. If gentlemen you would appoint agents who would go to work today volunteers might be on the way in three days and 8 days or 10 days gained to our suffering army before Bexar.[20]

My individual acquaintance in the Brazos Country enables me probably to be better acquainted with the individuals who can forward this desirable object than most of the members of your body — I would suggest that inasmuch as Capt. Fanning is not present that until his arrival that Horatio Chriesman — for Coles settlement — John Lott for Washington. Phillip Coe for Newyears Creek — Samuel Pettus for Mill Creek — John Bird for San Felipe — [blank] Lester and Jesse Burnham for Colorado — [blank] Thompson for Navidad [blank] for Menifees Neighborhood Randall Jones for Fort settlement James J Foster for Lake creek [blank] for Harrisburg — Warren D C Hall for Columbia J. S D Byrom for Brazoria — [blank] for Caney [blank] for Matagorda be appointed to enroll volunteers and forward them on as soon as possible —[21]

Nothing gentlemen but the conviction that our army is in danger could have induced me again to intrude myself on your notice and you will not regard it as springing from any other motive than an anxious desire to serve the army

Respectfully
Moseley Baker[22]

The General Council of Texas to the Mexican People

SAN FELIPE: The people of Texas have taken up arms in defense of their rights and liberties, menaced by the attacks of military despotism, and to sustain the republican principles of the constitution of 1824. The Mexican nation ought to be fully informed on this subject, in order to correct the falsehoods circulated by the Centralists, who have attempted to calumnate the Texians by giving to the revolution here, a character very different from the true one, and painting it in the blackest colors.

Texas has solemnly declared her principles in the declaration of the 7th November last . . . and has called God to witness the sincerity and purity of her intentions. The people of Texas could not have acted in any other manner, and every freeman would have done the same who appreciates his own dignity and was able to avert slavery.

Texas was left without any government, owing to the imprisonment and dispersion of the Executive and Legislature authorities of the state by the military Centralists, and everything was rapidly falling into anarchy and ruin. It is certainly not the fault of the Texians that this state of things existed. The truth is, that a storm which originated elsewhere, threatened to involve them in its desolating ravages. They wish to save themselves as they have a right to do, by the law of nature.

Faithful to their oaths, they wished to defend the constitution, and for this their enemies have declared a war of extermination against them, and are trying to deceive the liberal Mexicans with false reports that their objects are different from those expressed in the before mentioned declaration. God knows this to be a malicious calumny, circulated for the purpose of consolidating centralism, by trying to unite the Federalists in its ranks against their friends the Texians

Very dearly indeed have the Texians acquired their homes in this country, which but a short time since was a wilderness infested by hostile Indians. It is just and natural that they should wish to preserve them, in conformity with the guarantees of the Federal compact under which they were acquired. It is equally so, that they should obey the first law which God has stamped upon the heart of man civilized or savage, which is self-preservation.

The Texians have therefore taken up arms in defense of their constitutional rights, in fulfillment of their duties to the Mexican confederation and of the most sacred obligations to themselves.

They have organized a Provisional Government, to provide for their security as a part of the Mexican confederation should it again be re-established. Can it be possible that the whole nation will declare war against us because we wish to comply with our obligations in favor of the constitution, and because we wish to defend the rights which God has given to man, and which the Mexican nation has solemnly guaranteed to us? No, it cannot be believed. The free Mexicans are not unjust, and they will take part in our favor.

To arms then patriotic Mexicans. The Texians although a young people, invite and call you to the contest which is the duty of all to sustain against the purjured centralists, separate as we have done from the Central Government, and declare eternal war against it, let us sustain the federal compact, restore the federal system and firmly establish the liberties and happiness of our country. In this great work you will receive aid and assistance from the Texians, so far as their limited resources will permit, as they have offered in the second article of their declaration.

The foregoing address having been read, it was resolved that it be signed by the officers of the Council, and all members present, and that 500 copies be printed in Spanish and 200 copies in English.[23]

Council Hall, San Felipe
Mr. Hanks from the select committee appointed to procure and forward ammunition to Bexar, presented the following report:

Bought of Joseph Urband, 2 kegs Dupont's powder at fifteen dollars each,	$30.00
Bought of Jones & Townsend, 1 keg gunpowder,	14.00
Bought of Joshua Fletcher, 1 keg gunpowder,	14.00[24]

Saturday, December 12, 1835
85 DAYS TO THE FALL

Jose Juan Sanchez Navarro Diary Entry
Today is December 12. I am writing this when, by order of the Commandant General, I went to Bexar to compare the invoices for the ponchos, hats, and shoes that I brought from Leona Vicario.[25]

Sam Houston to People of Texas

PROCLAMATION TO THE CITIZENS OF TEXAS
Your situation is particularly calculated to call forth all your manly energies. Under the Republican constitution of Mexico, you were invited to Texas, then a wilderness. You have reclaimed and rendered it a cultivated country. You solemnly swore to support the constitution and its laws. Your oaths are yet inviolate. In accordance with them you have fought with the liberals against those who sought to overthrow the Constitution, in 1832, when the present usurper was the champion of liberal principles in Mexico. Your obedience has manifested your integrity. You have witnessed with pain the convulsions of the interior, and a succession of usurptions. You have experienced, in silent grief, the expulsion of your members from the State Congress. You have realized the horrors of anarchy and the dictation of military rule. The promises made to you have not been fulfilled. Your memorials for the redress of grievances have been disregarded; and the agents[26] you

have sent to Mexico have been imprisoned for years, without enjoying the rights of trial, agreeable to law. Your constitutional executive has been deposed by the bayonets of a mercenary soldiery while your state congress has been dissolved by violence, and its members, either fled, or were arrested by the military force of the enemy. The Federation has been dissolved, the constitution declared at an end, and centralism has been established. Amidst all these trying visissitudes you remained loyal to the duty of citizens, with a hope that liberty would not perish in the Republic of Mexico. But while you were fondly cherishing this hope, the Dictator required the surrender of the arms of the civil militia, that he might be enabled to establish upon the ruins of the constitution, a system of policy which would forever enslave the people of Mexico.27 Zacatecas, unwilling to yield her sovereign rights to the demand which struck at the root of all liberty, refused to disarm her citizens of her private arms. Ill fated state! her powers as well as her wealth aroused the ambition of Santa Anna, and excited his cupidity. Her citizens became the first victims of his cruelty, while her wealth was sacrificed in payment of the butchery of her citizens.28

The success of the usurper determined him in exacting from the people of Texas submission to the central form of government; and to force his plan of depotism, he dispatched a military force to invade the colonies and exact the arms of the inhabitants. The citizens refused the demand, and the invading force was increased. The question then was, shall we resist the oppression and live free, or violate our oaths, and bear a despot's stripes? The citizens of Texas rallied to the defense of their constitutional rights. They have met four to one, and, by their chivalry and courage, they have vanquished the enemy with a gallantry and spirit which is characteristic of the justice of our cause.

The army of the people is now before Bejar, besieging the central army within its walls. Though called together at a moment, the citizens of Texas, unprovided as they were in the necessary munitions of war and supplies for an army, have maintained a siege of months. Always patient and untiring in their patriotism and zeal, in the cause of liberty, they have born every vicissitude of season and every incident of the soldier, with a contempt of peril which reflects immortal honors on the members of the army of the people.

Since our army has been in the field, a consultation of the people, by their representatives, has met and established a provisional government. This course has grown out of the emergencies of the country; the army has claimed its peculiar care. We were without law and without a constitutional head. The Provisional Executive and the General council of Texas, are earnestly engaged in their respective duties, preparing for every exigency of the country; and I am satisfied from their zeal, ability, and patriotism, that Texas will have everything to hope from their exertions in behalf of the principals which we have avowed.

A regular army has been created, and liberal encouragement has been given by the government. To all who will enlist for two years, or during war, a bounty of twenty-four dollars and eight hundred acres of land will be given. Provision has also been made for raising an auxiliary volunteer corps, to constitute part of the army of Texas, which will be placed under the command, and subject to the orders of the commander in chief. The field for promotion will be open. The terms of service will be various: to those who choose to tender their service for or during the war, will be given a bounty of six hundred and forty acres of land; an equal bounty will be given to those who volunteer their services for two years; if for one year, a bounty of three hundred and twenty acres; and those who volunteers for a shorter period, no bounty of land will be given but the same liberal pay, rations, &c. will be allowed them as other members of the army. The rights of citizenship are extended to all who will unite with us in defending the republican principles of the constitution of 1824.

Citizens of Texas your rights must be defended. The oppressors must be driven from our soil. Submission to the laws, and union among ourselves will render us invincible; subordination and discipline in our army will guarantee to us victory and renown. Our invader has sworn to extinguish us, or sweep us from the soil. He is vigilant in his work of oppression, and has ordered to Texas ten thousand men to enforce the unhallowed purposes of his ambition. His letters to his subalterns in Texas have been intercepted, and his plans for our destruction have been disclosed. Departing from the chivalric principles of warfare, he has ordered arms to be distributed to a portion of our population, for the purpose of creating in the midst of us a servile war. The hopes of the usurper were inspired by a belief that the citizens of Texas were disunited and divided in opinion, and that alone has been the cause of the present invasion of our rights. He shall see the fallacy of his hopes, in the union of her citizens, and their *ETERNAL RESISTANCE* to his plans against constitutional liberty. We will enjoy our birth-right, or perish in its defense.

The services of five thousand volunteers will be expected. By the first of March next, we must meet the enemy with an army worthy of our cause, and which will reflect honor upon freemen. Our habitations must be defended; the sanctity of our hearths and firesides must be preserved from pollution. Liberal Mexicans will unite with us. Our countrymen in the field have presented an example worthy of imitation. Generous and brave hearts from a land of freeman have joined our standard before Bejar. They have, by their heroism and valour, called forth the admiration of their comrades in arms, and have reflected additional honor on the land of their birth. Let the brave rally to our standard.[29]

Sam Houston,
Commander in chief of the Army[30]

**Telegraph,
and Texas Register**[31]

NOTICE

On about the 20th of May last I forbid all persons harboring or trusting my wife, Matilda Tylee, on my account, she having left my bed and board without any just cause. I now repeat, for the information of the public, (that they may not be imposed upon by her false representations) that I will not pay any debts of her contracting on my account.
James Tylee[32]

BARKER & BORDENS

Respectfully inform the citizens of Texas that they have established a Printing Office in the town of

SAN FELIPE DE AUSTIN

where they are prepared to execute every description of BOOK and

JOB PRINTING,

at the shortest notice, and upon reasonable terms.

Their extensive stock of materials, being entirely new, and upon the most approved principles, will enable them to do all work entrusted to their charge in the best manner: they therefore confidently solicit a share of public patronage.

Sunday, December 13, 1835
84 DAYS TO THE FALL

Micajah Autry[33] to Wife

NATCHITOCHES, LOUISIANA:[34] About 20 minutes ago, I landed at this place after considerable peril. About 20 men from Tennessee formed our squad at Memphis, and all landed safely at the mouth of Red River. Major Eaton and Lady were on board the Pacific, to whom I suppose I was favourably introduced by Mr. Childress,[35] from that however or from some other reason Gov. Eaton paid me the most friendly and assiduous attention . . . I have not met with a more amiable and agreeable man than the Governor. By his persuasion a Major Arnold from Tennessee (a cousin of Gen'l Arnold) and myself left the rest of our Company at the mouth of Red River and went down to Orleans for the purpose of learning the true state of things in Texas as well as which would be the best possible route. The result was that the war is still going on favorably to the Texans, but it is thought that Santa Anna will make a descent with his whole force in the Spring, but there will be soldiers enough of the real grit in Texas by that time to overrun all of Mexico.

The only danger is in starvation, for the impulse to Texas both as to soldiers and moving families exceeds anything I have ever known. I have little doubt but that the army will receive ample supplies from Orleans both of provisions and munitions of war, as the people of Texas have formed themselves into something like a government, which will give them credit in Orleans. I have had many glowing descriptions of the country by those who have been there . . . We have between 400 and 500 miles to foot it to the seat of government, for we cannot get horses, but we have sworn allegience to each other and will get along somehow . . . The smallpox has recently broken out here very bad, but I fear the Tavern bill a great deal worse. Such charges never were heard of and we have to stay here probably several days before we can procure a conveyance for our baggage. I suppose we shall join and buy a wagon.

Write to me at this place all the letters you send by mail, perhaps the general intercourse from here to Texas, will enable me to get them conveniently. Write me in Texas by every private opportunity, and I will do the same . . . I send this by Mr. Sevier who promises to put it in the post office at Bolivar or Middleburg. . . .

P.S. The company of young men that left Jackson before I did passed through here about 20 days ago.[36]

Henry Smith to the Legislative Council
SAN FELIPE de AUSTIN: That the Mexican population within
our limits, particularly where they are unmixed with other
population, could not be tested at an election to know whether
they were in favor of centralism or not, that being the touchstone
for eligibility. Under existing circumstances, I consider one fact
plain and evident, that they who are not for us must be against
us. In my own opinion they should be so considered and
treated. Actions always speak louder than words, and a very
great proportion of the inhabitants of Bexar afford fair examples.
They have had, it is well known, every opportunity to evince
their friendship by joining our standard. With very few
exceptions they have not done it, which is evidence, strong and
conclusive, that they are our enemies. In many instances they
have been known to fight against us. I therefore consider that
they should be neither entitled to our respect nor favor, and as
such, not entitled to a seat in our Council.[37]

F. W. Johnson Report on Stores
INVENTORY
of military stores delivered in conformity with the capitulation
entered into on the 11th of December, 1835, between General
Martin Perfecto de Cos, of the Permanent Troops, and General
Edward Burleson of the Colonial Troops of Texas.
    IN BEXAR: 30 useless muskets; 5 boxes ammunition; 4 drums;
4 boxes with 66 hats and 49 blankets of the company of Lancers;
1 bale of 12 dozen blankets; 1 four pound cannon, mounted; 1
chinesco; 2 trumpets; 2 clarions; 1 lg clarion; 2 cymbals.
    IN THE ALAMO: 2 four pound cannon, mounted; 2 small
brass, ditto; 1 four pound field piece; 1 ditto, three pound,
complete; 1 rammer; 1 cannon, four pound, with carriage and
rammer; 1 iron culverine, of 9 inch calibur, mounted; 1 howitzer
of 5 inch calibur; 1 cannon of six pound; 1 field piece, four
pound; 1 cannon, 3 pound mounted; 1 ditto, six pound
mounted; 257 carabines and muskets.
    IN THE ARSENAL: 11,000 musket cartridges; 2 cartouch
boxes; 10 bags grape shot; 9 ditto with cartridges; 18 swivel
worms; 8 howitzer ditto; 100 small cannon cartridges; 18 pkgs
musket ditto; 10 port fires; 16 swivel worms; 40 swivel
cartridges; 1 bag containing 100 pounds of powder; 50 pkg's
cartridges; 1 box cartridges, damp; 1 box musket cartridges; 1
box powder; 1200 musket cartridges; 1 ammunition box with 20
cannon balls; 10 quick matches' 1 box howitzer worms; 3 boxes
musket cartridges; 2 ammunition boxes with 40 cannon balls; 1
match cord; 1 box howitzer worms; 1 box cartridges; 2 ditto
ditto; 7 empty ammunition chests; 17 muskets; 1 bugle; 2 boxes
ammunition; 1 rammer; 1 lanthron; 4 large cannon; 2 swivels; 1 4

pound canon, mounted; 1 box 26 stands of grape; 1 box musket cartridges; 1 bag powder; 1 bag gun flints; 1 drum; 15 carabines, out of order; 11 pieces small ordinance delivered by Manchaca; 76 muskets; 15 coats; 9 gun locks; 49 duck jackets; 1 bunch of wire; 3 bars of steel; 1 small ditto of iron; 1 bunch flax thread; 15 skiens sewing silk; 63 duck jackets; 2 barrels containing 166 bayonets; 9 aparejos; 58 lances; 1 pair scales with weights; 1 piece of linsey; 50 muskets with bayonets; 13 lances.

Delivered By: Juan Cortina, J. Francisco de Rada, Francisco Herrera

Received By: James Cheshire, William G. Cook, W.H. Patton[38]

Monday, December 14, 1835
83 DAYS TO THE FALL

Edward Burleson to the Provisional Governor

HEADQUARTERS, BEXAR: I have the satisfaction to enclose a copy of Colonel Johnson's account of the storming and surrendering of San Antonio de Bejar,[39] to which I have little to add that can in any way increase the lustre of this brilliant achievement, to the federal arms of the volunteer army under my command; which will, I trust, prove the downfall of the last position of military despotism in our soil of freedom.

At three o'clock in the morning of the 5th instant, Colonel Neill, with a piece of artillery, protected by Captain Roberts and his company, was sent across the river to attack, at five o'clock, the Alamo, on the north side, to draw attention of the enemy from the advance of the divisions which had to attack the suburbs of the town, under Colonels Milam and Johnson. This service was effected to my entire satisfaction; and the part returned to camp at nine o'clock, A.M.

On the advance of the attacking divisions, I formed all the reserve, with the exception of the guard necessary to protect the camp, at the old mill position; and held myself in readiness to advance, in case of necessity, to assist when required; and shortly afterwards passed into the suburbs to reconnoiter, where I found all going on prosperously, and retired with the reserve to camp. Several parties were sent out mounted, under Captains Cheshire, Coleman, and Roberts, to scour the country, and endeavor to intercept Ugartachea, who was expected, and ultimately forced an entry, with reinforcement for General Cos. Captains Cheshire, Sutherland, and Lewis, with their companies, were sent in as reinforcement to Colonel Johnson, during the period of attack; and Captains Splane, Ruth, and Lieutenant-Colonels Somerville and Sublett, were kept in readiness as further assistance if required. On the evening of the 8th, a party

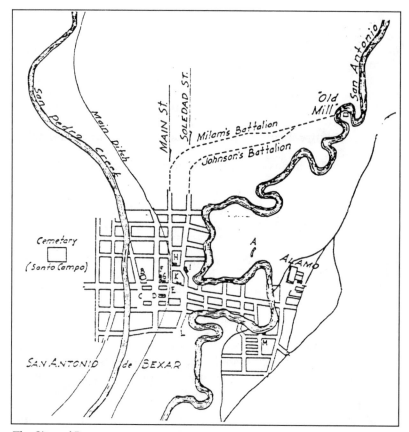

The Siege of Bexar

Line of attack by the Texans against the Mexican forces occupying
Bexar and supported by the Mexican garrison then in the Alamo, from
December 5 to 10, 1836.

A. Mexican Redoubt
B. Mexican Redoubt
C. Military Plaza
D. San Fernando Cathedral
E. Main Plaza
F. Zamorano Row
G. House of Antonio Navarro
H. House of de la Garza
I. House of Veramendi
K. House of the Priest
L. The Cottage (Quinta)
M. House where Gen. Cos signed terms of capitulation

from the Alamo, of about fifty men, passed up in front of our camp and opened a brisk fire, but without effect; they were soon obliged to retire precipitately, by opening a six-pounder on them, commanded by Captain Hunnings, by sending a party across the river, and by the advance of Captain Bradley's company, who were stationed above.

Colonel Ben Milam, one of the casualties of the siege.

On the morning of the 9th, in consequence of advice from Colonel Johnson, of a flag of truce having been sent in, to intimate a desire to capitulate, I proceeded to town, and by two o'clock, A.M. of the 10th, a treaty was finally concluded by the commissioners appointed, to which I acceded immediately, deeming the terms highly favourable, considering the strong position and large force of the enemy, which could not be less than thirteen hundred effective men; one thousand one hundred and five having left this morning with General Cos, besides three companies and several small parties which separated from him in consequence of the fourth article of the treaty.

In addition to a copy of the treaty, I enclose a list of all the valuable property ceded to us by virtue of the capitulation.

General Cos left this morning for the mission San Jose, and tomorrow commences his march to the Rio Grande, after complying with all that had been stipulated.

I cannot conclude this dispatch without expressing in the warmest terms, my entire approbation of every officer and soldier in the army, and particularly those who so gallantly volunteered to storm the town, which I have the honour to command, and to say that their bravery and zeal on the present occasion, merit the warmest eulogies which I can confer, and gratitude of their country. The gallant leader of the storming party, colonel Benjamin R. Milam, fell gloriously on the third day, and his memory will be dear to Texas as long as there exists a grateful heart to feel, or a friend of liberty to lament his worth. His place was most aptly filled by colonel F.W. Johnson, adjutant-general of the army, whose coolness and prudence, united to daring bravery, could alone have brought matters to so successful an end, with so very small a loss, against so superior a force, and such fortification. To his shinning merits on this occasion, I bore ocular testimony during the five days' action.

I have also to contribute my praise to Major Bennet, quarter-master-general, for the dillegence and success with which he supplied both armies during the siege and storm.

These despatches, with a list of killed and wounded, will be handed to your Excellency by my first aid-de-camp, Colonel William T. Austin, who was present as a volunteer during the five days' storm, and whose conduct on this and every other occasion, merits my warmest praise.

Tomorrow morning, I leave the garrison and town under the command of Colonel Johnson, with a sufficient number of men and officers to sustain the same in case of attack, until assisted from the colonies: so that your excellency may consider our conquest as sufficiently secured against every attempt of the enemy. The rest of the army will retire to their homes.[40]

James C. Neill Discharge

BEXAR: This is to certify that Col James C. Neill, Commander in chief of the Artillery department of the Federal Army of Texas entered the Army of the same 28th September and has discharged the dutys of that office with fidelity and as a patriot soldier and is this day honorable discharged from this army with my warmest respects.

Edward Burleson
Commander in chief
of the Voluntary Army[41]

Santa Anna to Don Vicente Filisola

HEADQUARTERS, SAN LUIS POTOSI, MEXICO: The captain of the Regiment of Veracruz who will place this in Your Excellency's hands is delivering the 30,000 pesos which are to be used with the greatest possible economy for the pay of the troops under Your Excellency's command. I have acquired this remittance with a thousand difficulties and there will probably not be another until I march with the remainder of the Army. God and Liberty.[42]

Tuesday, December 15, 1835
82 DAYS TO THE FALL

Council Hall, San Felipe de Austin; To Stephen F. Austin, et al
Citizen Commissioners: Bexar has fallen! Our brave citizen volunteers, with a persevering bravery and heroic valor, unparalleled in the annals of warfare, have triumphed over a force of twice their number and compelled the slaves of depotism to yield, vanquished by the ever resistless arms of freemen soldiers. We have not time to enter into full details of all that preceded the glorious Thursday of December the tenth, when the final capitulation of Cos and Ugartechea was signed.

The unconquerable Texians, with their equally brave auxiliaries from the United States of the North, could not be dislodged and the battle raged with murderous fury, with advantage to us, and to the discouragement of the enemy, who became dismayed and disheartened in a contest that but weakened them, and strengthened our valorous brethren in arms, raised the signal of submission.

Citizen Commissioners you will enter upon your duties with increased ardor and brightened hopes of full success. . . .[43]

Council Hall, San Felipe de Austin; To Edward Burleson, Colonel F. Johnson and all the brave officers and soldiers of the citizen volunteer army in Bexar
FELLOW CITIZENS: The Representatives of your General council, were this hour greeted with the welcome intelligence of your glorious victory and triumphant conquest, over the post of Bexar, with all your enemies prisoners, together with all the arms, munitions and provisions. We expected no less from our heroic citizens, and brave compatriots of our northern brethren. — We felt that you were invincible, and that our enemies, although greatly out-numbering you, must yield to the sons of freedom. Their cause is that of oppression and tyranny, ours, that of liberty and equal rights. They are but the hireling slaves of an usurper. You are the brave sons of Washington and freedom, and you have proved yourselves worthy of your glorious origin. You have fulfilled the expectations of your country, and the hopes of all the lovers of liberty on earth. Your representatives extend to you the cordial hand of congratulation and gratitude, as well as in behalf of our fellow-citizens and our families, as for themselves. You have nobly and vialiantly acquitted yourselves of the high trust which your country's danger caused you to assume, and your names will be enrolled in the first pages of your country's history of heroes, as well as imprinted on the hearts of your fellow-citizens. But in the midst of joy there is mourning, and whilst we shout your victory, the tears of holy sorrow bedew

our faces. The brave and heroic Milam has fallen in the arms of victory; and the cause of his injured country. In him we have lost a precious gem from the casket of brilliant heroes. God rest his soul! while his memory shall survive as long as freeman has a standing in Texas.

Other brave men have also mingled their blood with their country's sacrifices. Their honor is imperishable. That your first noble example may be followed, is the ardent wish of your Representatives, whose efforts in their sphere have been anxiously directed for your aid and comfort; and had your country's means at command been equal to her generous gratitude, your every want had been supplied.

Citizen Soldiers: — Many of you have long been in the field of honor and danger, separated from your families and your homes. A respite from your labors and your privations must be desirable; and it is reasonable, in anticipation of this glorious event to be achieved by your arms. Your government have been solicitously engaged in organizing a regular army, upon a proper footing, together with provisions for an auxiliary volunteer corps, that you might be released and get rest among your families and friends, until the future calls of your country again place you in defence of her, and your just rights. To such calls you have always proved your hearty response. We address you in much haste but with feeling not to be repressed. Your joy is our joy, your sorrows our sorrows; and with assurance of unabating sympathies with you, and all our fellow-citizens in the present glorious epoch in our country's annals.[44]

Executive Committee to Col T. J. Rusk

SAN FELIPE: The undersigned being appointed to write dispatches to our agents beg leave to communicate the very happy intelligence of the fall of Bexar. Majr Gay and other Gent. entitled to credit have just arrived and bring the pleasing and very happy Intelligence of the Capture of Bexar Ugartachea reached Bexar, a day or two before the capitulation and surrendered with the reinforcement he brought with him the number not known the terms of surrender are that officers and troops are to depart (without arms, or any other Public property) on parole of Honour, the troops behaved well the N. O. Greys are particularly spoken of but we are sorry to be under the necessity of communicating the sad intelligence of the loss of the Brave Milam he was killed by a Ball in the head on the second day of the action.

This account though not official the council has thought it unquestionable and request that you will continue your unremitted exertions to raise troops for the term of 3 months as volunteers or recruit for the regular army providing at the same time every means to afford them comfort on the road.

We have gained by this engagement a considerable amount of Public stores arms and Ammunition as well as a great many horses.

The troops spread over the place by working and fighting for five days and nights cutting through the stone walls from House to House and Cutting passes under the streets between corner building. . . .[45]

J. A. Mexia to Henry Smith

COLUMBIA, TEXAS: The day before yesterday I have dispatched from this place the American company, commanded by Capt. Allen to the camp before Bexar, and yesterday the Balance of my forces left here with direction to the Copano by way of Velasco, to take with them the Cannon, arms, and munitions of war which I have there, and to convey them to the camp. I also leave here to day, for Quintanna, to arrange matters there, and to proceed in person (to Bexar) if it should be necessary. All of which I will advise Y. E.[46] in due time.

I am Y. E. most obedt. Servt
Jose Antonio Mexia[47]

Sam Houston to Colonel D. C. Barrett

SAN FELIPE de AUSTIN: Having learned that you have been appointed by the General Council for the purpose of drafting an address to the army of the People, I take pleasure in suggesting to you my views in relation to the protection of our frontier.

I propose placing a field officer in command of San Antonio de Bexar with a sufficient number of Troops for the defense of the station, I also design, the employment of an Engineer and [to] have the fortifications and defenses of the place improved. La Bahia must be occupied by a force amounting [to] from 50 to 100 men, and commanded by a competent officer. The main force will be placed in a situation where it can command the port of Copano — Refugio Mission will probably be the best situation for a force to be stationed. San Patricio, will also be within the range of the cordon of posts to be established for the purpose of the reception of troops until the campaign of the spring will open. In the meantime I will forward, as promptly as possible the Volunteers which may tender their services; to the several points designated as they may arrive and are received into the service.

It is so manifest that the occupation of the points designated is necessary for the defence of the frontier, that I shall not detain you with my reasons.

Sam Houston

P.S. Engineers for the various stations will be indispensable for the construction of works, as well as for the selection of sites and the designs necessary.[48]

Wednesday, December 16, 1835
81 DAYS TO THE FALL

Eli Mercer to Henry Smith
EGYPT, TEXAS: The bearer of this letter Mr John Foster, reached
here last evening with public Drove of horses from San
Antonio[49] accompanied with a letter from General Austin directing me to take charge of the horses as public property and take
care of them until Spring, the letter requiring me to give an
account of their number and their condition. Mr. Foster says
when he took charge of them their number was more than 300
he reached here with 97 Generally very poor; but the winter
range in the bottom here is very good and I think they will do
very well. They will be delivered only to your order. I received
an appointment from under your hand authorising me to assist
in organising the Militia at the Jurisdiction of Austin; which I had
determined to attend and had appointed a meeting for the board
accordingly; But I feel it more particularly my duty to go to the
army, and Shall Set out on tuesday morning next and past for
San Antonia and as I expect to remain there some time, and as I
think it highly important for the Safety of the Country that an
organisation Should take place as son as possable, I hope you
will appoint Some other person to act in my place if you please I
would propose Mr. Menifee.[50]

Council Hall, San Felipe
Mr. Hanks,[51] from the committee on military affairs made the
following report:
   Your committee are of the opinion, that the regular army of
Texas, should be augmented. From the intercepted correspondence we are satisfied, that not less then eight or ten thousand
central troops under the command of Santa Anna's bravest and
most experienced officers will be sent to invade Texas, between
now and the ensuing spring, in addition to those already within
the borders of our State. From every indication, Texas will have
to battle single handed against the combined forces of the central
party, with Santa Anna for their leader, throughout Mexico. The
power and influence of the Priest, will also be extended against
us. Church and state are thus combined for the overthrow and
demolition of free institutions; and the friends and advocates of
Constitutional liberty, in the interior, are so few and weak, that
they dare not resist the encroachments and usurpations of
power, which have been made by this tremendous engine of
despotism — the union of church and State! — Texas alone has
dared to resist these usurptions; to vindicate her rights, and to
repulse the hireling soldiery of the ruffian tyrant . . .
   Under this view of our situation, your committee believe that

the establishment of a sufficient force to be the only means by which we can sustain ourselves in the present struggle, and no man will contend for a moment that the regular army will be able to resist and repel the combined forces of all of Mexico. What? Protect a sea coast of three hundred and fifty miles, an extended frontier, and a scattered population of seventy or eighty thousand inhabitants, with eleven or twelve hundred men, against the forces of a nation containing eight millions of inhabitants; and that nation denouncing us as rebels and traitors. Yes! Our frontier is already invaded by their troops, and all the orris of war brought within our country. An augmentation of the army, is therefore absolutely necessary for our safety and security; for the establishment and permanency of free institutions in Texas, rest entirely upon the success of our arms. Your committee are also of opinion, that one of the most important parts of the army has been overlooked, to wit, the establishment of a troop of cavalry. A troop of cavalry is indispensable for many reasons. No part of the army, infantry especially, can move with that celerity to any part of the country, which may be attacked by the enemy: Also to cut off the provisions and supplies, and intercept the communications of our enemies — to carry an express and do any act which requires celerity and promptness of movement. Your committee has consulted, gentlemen of experience and known abilities, relative to the creation of a troop of cavalry. It is the opinion of Col. Fannin that the regular army should be increased.

General Austin, General Houston and W. B. Travis, Esq. all concur with your committee in the immediate necessity of creating a troop of cavalry. It is true that it will cost several thousand dollars, to raise, organize, arm and equip an efficient troop of cavalry. Yet no one can be so blind as to renounce the lasting prosperity and greatness of Texas, rather than spend a few thousand dollars, or a million if it were necessary.[52]

Thursday, December 17, 1835
80 DAYS TO THE FALL

Sam Houston to His Ex. Henry Smith, Governor of Texas
HEADQUARTERS, SAN FELIPE de AUSTIN: On Yesterday I had the Honor to receive your order, directing the establishment of the headquarters of the army at Washington. It will give me pleasure to obey the order at the earliest moment.

In the meantime, I do earnestly solicit the attention of your excellency to the subject of an appropriation to cover the recruiting of the army. And I would beg leave to suggest the necessity of establishing a system of accountability in all its departments; requiring ample security of all the officers, who may be entrusted with funds, agreeably to the system established in the United States, if the provisions of the organic law are not sufficient.

More than a month has now elapsed since the adjournment of the consultation, and the army is not yet organized; and, though I have ordered some officers on the recruiting service, it has been on my own responsibility.

It is extremely painful to me to feel what I am compelled to experience, and believe to exist. I have never failed to render any information, when called on by the chairman of the military committee, and to furnish such books as he wished for his instruction. Yet, I am constrained to believe that he has interposed every possible obstacle to the organization of the army; and so far as I am identified with it, to delay the placing of Texas in a proper state of defence.

To arrive at the conclusion, it is only necessary to advert to a report which he made on the subject of the speedy organization of the army. In the report he took the liberty (though entirely unnecessary) of using remarks of a personal character toward myself. The honorable the general council deemed them so indecorous that they were stricken out of the report. To account for this course on the part of the chairman is not necessary.

I am careless of whatever individual feelings may be entertained toward me: but as a functionary of the government, placed in the most responsible situation, and so necessary to the salvation of the country, I am constrained to invoke and to hope for the necessary co-operation in discharge of the duties which I owe to the country and its laws. I am ready to make any and every sacrifice which my relations to the country may require of me.[53]

Governor Henry Smith to Sam Houston, Esq.
EXECUTIVE DEPARTMENT OF TEXAS GENERAL ORDER: Sir: You will adopt such measure as you may deem best, for the reduction of Matamoros — and the occupation of such posts as you may deem necessary for the protection of the frontier — keeping up a constant system of vigilance necessary for the protection of the country.

Henry Smith
Governor[54]

Governor Henry Smith to the Agents[55] of the People of Texas
SAN FELIPE, TEXAS: The honl. President and Members of the General council request me, by a resolution of their body, to instruct you as follows — viz

That you will not furnish any outfit to Mexicans who pretend to be our friends, such as Mexia and others; who profess to belong to the liberal party, but leave the matter for the Government here to judge, whose duty it is, and who will be governed by their acts and not by their promises. And I farther have to request of you that all your correspondence as Agents will be addresses as you have previously been instructed and not directed to the council. You will have agents in all the principal cities to correspond with us through you.

The Council requests you appoint agents in all the principal cities to correspond with the Govt. at least once in a month. This, however, I consider you will have managed through yourselves, or as you direct. Gentlemen, respectfully. Your Obst.

Henry Smith
Governor

Sam Houston to Colonel James Bowie

HEADQUARTERS, SAN FELIPE: Sir: In obedience to the order of his excellency Henry Smith, governor of Texas, of this date, I have the honor to direct that, in the event you can obtain sufficient number of men for the purpose, you will forthwith proceed on the route to Matamoros, and, if possible, reduce the place and retain possession until further orders. Should you not find it within your power to attain an object so desirable as the reduction of Matamoros, you will, by all possible means, comformably to the rules of civilized warfare, annoy the troops of the central army; and reduce and keep possession of the most eligible position on the frontier, using the precaution which characterizes your mode of warfare. You will conduct the campaign. Much is referred to your discretion. Should you commence the campaign, you will, from time to time, keep the government advised of your operations, through the commander-in-chief of the army. Under any circumstances, the port of Copano is important.

If any officers or men who have, at any time, been released on parole, should be taken in arms, they will be proper subjects for the consideration of court-martial. Great caution is necessary in the country of an enemy.

Sam Houston, Commander in Chief[56]

F. W. Johnson to Provisional Government

HEADQUARTERS BEJAR: List of officers of the Volunteer Army of Texas to be commissioned by the Provisional Government.

Commander in Chief - Col. Francis W. Johnson
Second in command - Col. James Grant
First Adjutant - Captain N.R. Brister
Second Do - Captain J. Vaughan
Surgeon In Chief - Dr. Albert M. Levy - N. Orlean's Greys
Assistant Surgeon - Wm M. W. Hart - Mobile Greys
Quarter Master - Captain V. Bennet

Paymaster Captain Francis Adams
Store Keeper - Mr. John Smith
First N.O. Greys, Captain Wm G. Cooke
Second N. O. Greys - Capt. Thos H. Breese
Third Company of Infy. Capt. T. Lewellyn
Artillery - Lieutenant J.C. Neill
            - Captain Almaron Dickenson
Artillery - First Lieutenant - W.R. Carey
Native Troops - Capt. John Cameron[57]

William B. Travis to James W. Robinson
MILL CREEK: I have understood, though not officially, that the General Council have done me the honor to appoint me first Major in the Artillery Regt. I feel highly sensible of this mark of distinction and I return my sincere thanks to the honorable body over which you preside for the honor they have intended me; yet believing that I could not be so useful in the artillery as elsewhere, I beg leave to decline the office or if I have been commissioned to resign same. You will do me the favor by communicating this to the council, although I am sensible that it is not regular, that I should make this communication until I should have been officially notified by appointment. I have taken the liberty of making this request of you, in order that the Genl Council may make another appointment immediately to prevent delay in the organization of the Regular Army which Texas has to look to for her ultimate defense, I would thank you to put Francis W. Johnson in nomination for the office of Major in the artillery to fill the vacancy. He is an old settler and has many claims to the favorable consideration of the council. I understand that he commanded in the storm of San Antonio after the death of the lamented Milam —

I hope the council will take measures to fit out an expedition immediately to take the port and city of Matamoros — I refer your excellency to a letter I have just written to Mr. Hanks of the military Com. for my views on this subject. and I hope you will agree with me —

I intend to join the expedition if one is gotten up, unless prohibited by superior orders, and I will execute to the best of my ability any command which the council may see fit to confer on me.

With consideration of high respect, I have the honor to be etc. etc. etc.

W. B. Travis

P.S. This letter is entirely private and not intended to be read to the Council, therefore I will thank you to make the requested verbally —

If it is necessary for my resignation to be in writing I can make it when I return to Town, which will be in a few days —

Travis[58]

This drawing of William B. Travis by Wiley Martin is thought to be the only likeness drawn from life.

Samuel Stivers and Amos Pollard to Governor and Council
HOSPITAL DEPARTMENT BEJAR: A correct detail of all the killed and wounded at the siege of Bejar commencing on the 5th Inst (morning) and ending on the morning of the 10th

Names	Killed	Wounded
Col B. R. Milam	Killed	
Francis Harvey	do	
E. F. Pulham		severely wounded
James McGehee*		do do
G. B. Logan		do do
Thos W Wardright		leg amputated
John Cook	mortal	
George Alexander	do	
Outlaw		slightly wounded
Saml G. Everitt		severely do
Lieut George W. Main*		do do
Dr. Mitchison*		do do
Capt. John W. Peacock		do do
Alexander Abrams		do do
Wm Thomas		do do
James Noland*		do do
James MCass		do do
Erastus Smith		slightly wounded
John Cornel		do do
John Hall		severely wounded
John Beldon		do do
Dr Grant**		slightly wounded

   * = later died in the Alamo
   ** = Commander of the Matamoros Expedition

We the undersigned having had special charge of the hospital at Bejar from the commencement of the siege at said Bejar up to the present date, do heare by certify the foregoing to be a true statement of the number killed and wounded at the above siege.[59]

General Sam Houston to President Andrew Jackson
SAN FELIPE de AUSTIN: Genl Houston has the honor of presenting to his best friend, President Jackson, the enclosed Proclamation,[60] with his sincere respects, and most cordial regards.

He begs leave also, to offer his joyous felicitations to the President, in the triumph of his principles, over an opposition, who sought to overwhelm him, and the country.

The most cordial wishes, for the Presidents long life, and future Glory; are tendered, with unceasing esteem and affection.

Genl Houston[61]

Friday, December 18, 1835
79 DAYS TO THE FALL

F. W. Johnson to His Excy. the Provisional Governor of Texas
HEADQUARTERS SN. ANTONIO de BEJAR: I have the honor to acquaint you that I have received advices this day from the interior, of the arrival of Genl. Ramerier Sesma at Laredo with 500 Cavalry & 1,000 Infantry for the purpose of reinforcing Genl. Cos to whom he had written recommending a vigorous defense until his arival, which he asserts will be in a few days. How far Capitulation may effect his movements it is impossible to say, but from further notices of the information of an Army at Sn. Luis Potosi, to be placed under the Command of President St. Ana, it is to be feared that they have immediate intentions of proceeding to offensive measures & every preparation should be made on our part with out delay, as I have too much reason to believe that the information received is as nearly as possible correct; and from the false representations of the Centralists, that we are fighting for independence instead of Liberty & the Constitution of 1824, we may dread the junction of both the great political parties against us unless prompt means are taken to undeceive the nations generally.

On the 16th Inst. I addressed your Excellency by Col. Bowie relative to the Arbitrary Conduct of Capt. Dimitt, and I now beg again to draw your attention to the importance of placing a man of prudence in Command of Goliad. Captn. Colingsworth who commanded at the taking of the place was named Generals Austin & Burlison to this charge, & I have no hesitation in recommending the propriety of his appointment. The threatened invasion renders it virtually important to place your frontier positions in a state of the best possible defense & this can only be done by having men of prudence & energy in charge. So soon as I am advised that the Command of Goliad is in such hands, I will order an officer of some experience on Fortifications to visit the garrison & give his advice as to the Works required for immediate defense.

It is of importance that some funds be remitted immediately for the purchase of Corn & Cattle and for the unavoidable current expenses, especially as I am now obliged to keep a party in advance on to Nueces to watch the movements of the enemy & and to act as a check in case of necessity — it will also be necessary to forward to this place all the Cannon balls & powder which can be procured now in the country.[62]

Saturday, December 19, 1835
78 DAYS TO THE FALL

Mathew Caldwell to His Excellency Govr Smith
GONZALES: I have the honor to give you a report of my
proceedings in the discharge of my public duty as Sub-Contractor
to the Volunteer Army of Texas which I hope will receive your
approbation. I am on the point of sending out a company in
pursuit of the Indians who committed last night depredations on
this neighborhood, and they have also been seen between this
and Cibolo.

Four wagons will leave this day for the army at Bexar with
supplies, consisting of Coffee, Sugar, Soap, Salt, Corn Meal and
blankets, forty beeves will also leave at the same time, with
about 5 cwt of iron and I intend contracting with Capt Bateman
for 10,000 lbs of Pork, all which I trust will be seasonable relief
Considering that two pieces of Artillery are requisite for the
protection of this frontier, I shall request the Commander at
Bexar to furnish me with them, say one 6 pounder and one 4
pounder. The funds placed at my disposal are nearly exhausted,
as per account annexed and I have respectfully to suggest a
further supply in order to meet immediate and pressing wants.
Five kegs powder & some lead remain on hand to be forwarded
when required.

Permit me to recommend to your Excellency my Assistant Mr
Edward Gritton, whose services have been useful, and who
lately performed an important one, in conveying supplies of
powder and lead to the army before Bexar.

Your Ob Svt.
Mathew Caldwell
Sub Contractor[63]

F. W. Johnson to the Provisional Governor
HEADQUARTERS ST. ANTO. de BEJAR: I have the honor to
acquaint your Excellency that in addition to the supplies already
mentioned, we require for the use of the Artillery & non-
commissioned officers Two hundred swords, & for the Infantry
three hundred cartouche Boxes with Belts.

I have the honor to be, Your Excellencies,

most obt. servt.
F. W. Johnson[64]

Albert Martin to D. C. Barrett
GONZALES: As there is a first Inspector to be appointed at the
Custom House at Lavaca, permit me to introduce to you for the
appointment Mr. Nicholas Peck who has been a sea Capt. and

upon whose integrity we can rely. Should the office be given to him I have no doubt that he will exert himself in the performance of the duties attached to his station.

Am in haste

Your Obt Servt
Albert Martin

I have been confined for some time to the house, owing to a serious cut in my foot from an axe, but am recovering fast. I have often thought of our frequent interviews. Our "cidevant" Commandant at Bexar (Urgatachea) In my opinion I think that Gen Cos is dead and was so before the fall of Bexar. I shall leave in few days for Bexar with an assortment of Spanish goods which I have fought for from time of their landing in this Country. My business has suffered much during the War. Remember me to Mr. Clements from this place.[65]

Sunday, December 20, 1835
77 DAYS TO THE FALL

**B. B. Goodrich to the Honl. President
and Members of the Legislative Council**
SAN FELIPE, TEXAS: I am requested by John Lott, contractor, to say to you, — that it is impossible for him to procure provisions for the Troops passing Washington without some immediate pecuniary assistance from your Honl body. — Corn is scarce and high, and can not be purchased without cash and such have been the heavy advances from his own purse to sustain the army on their march to San Antonio that his own funds are exhausted, and nothing in the way of provisions can be purchased on the faith of the Country.

Benjamin Briggs Goodrich

respectfully
B. B. Goodrich[66]

Council Hall, San Felipe de Austin

NINE O'CLOCK, A.M. On motion of Mr. Millard the rule of voting by ballot was suspended, and William Barret Travis unanimously elected lieutenant colonel of the legion of cavalry.

TWO O'CLOCK P.M. The House then proceeded to ballot for second lieutenants when Joseph E. Scott, James Butler Bonham, John M. Thurston, Manuel Carabajac James Drake J. Bevill, Jr. were duly elected second lieutenants of the legion of cavalry.

SEVEN O'CLOCK P.M. The house then proceeded to ballot for a first major of artillery, to supply the vacancy occasioned by the non-acceptance of William B. Travis; when Francis W. Johnson was duly elected.[67]

Santa Anna to Brigadier General Jose Urrea

HEADQUARTERS, SAN LUIS POTOSI: I hereby instruct Your Lordship to march to the Town of Guerrero, previously known as Presidio del Rio Grande, since it is no longer advisable for Your

General Antonio Lopez de Santa Anna, self-proclaimed "Napolean of the West."

Lordship to march to the Town of Laredo due to the fall of the City of Bexar into the hands of the insurgents. Your Lordship will join the First Brigade which is marching to Guerrero, and place yourself under the command of Most Excellent Major General Don Vicente Filisola, second in command to the commander-in-chief of the Army of Operations.[68]

Goliad Declaration of Independence
GOLIAD, TEXAS:

Declaration of Independence

Solemnly impressed with a sense of the danger of the crisis to which recent and remote events have conducted the public affairs of their country, the undersigned prefer this method of laying before their fellow-citizens, a brief retrospect of the light in which they regard both the present and the past, and of frankly declaring *for themselves*, the policy and the uncompromising course which they have resolved to pursue for the future.

They have seen the enthusiasm and the heroic toils of an army bartered for a capitulation, humiliating in itself, and repugnant in the extreme to the pride and honor of the most lenient, and no sooner framed than evaded or insultingly violated.

They have seen their camp thronged, but too frequently, with those who were more anxious to be served by, than to serve their country — with men more desirous of being honored with command than capable of commanding.

They have seen the energies, the prowess, and the achievements of a band worthy to have stood by Washington and receive command, and worthy to participate of the inheritance of the sons of such a Father, fritted, dissipated, and evaporated away for the want of that energy, union, and decision in council, which, though it must emanate from the many, can only be exercised efficiently when concentrated in a single form.

They have seen the busy aspirants for office running from the field to the council hall, and from this back to the camp, seeking emolument and not service, and swarming like hungry flies around the body politic.

They have seen the deliberations of the council and the volition of the camp distracted and paralyzed, by the interference of an influence anti-patriotic in itself, and too intimately interwoven with the paralyzing policy of the past, to admit the hope of relief from its incorporation with that which can alone avert the evils of the present crisis, and place the affairs of the country beyond the reach of an immediate reaction.

They have witnessed these evils with bitter regrets, with swollen hearts, and indignant bosoms.

A revulsion is at hand. An army, recently powerless and literally imprisoned, is now emancipated. From a comparatively

harmless, passive, and inactive attitude, they have been trans-
formed to one pre-eminently commanding, active, and imposing.
The North and East of Mexico will now become the stronghold of
centralism. Thence it can sally in whatever direction its arch
deviser may prefer to employ its weapons. The counter-revolu-
tion in the interior once smothered, the whole fury of the contest
will be poured on Texas. She is principally populated with
North-Americans. To expel these from its territory, and parcel it
out among the instruments of its wrath, will combine the motive
and the means for consummating the scheme of the President
Dictator. Already, we are denounced, proscribed, outlawed, and
exiled from the country. Our lands, peaceably and lawfully
acquired, are solemnly pronounced the proper subject of indiscriminate forfeiture, and our estates of confiscation. The laws and
guarantees under which we entered the country as colonists,
tempted the unbroken silence, sought the dangers of the wilderness, braved the prowling Indian, erected our numerous
improvements, and opened and subdued the earth to cultivation,
are either abrogated or repealed, and now trampled under the
hoofs of the usurper's cavalry.

Why, then, should we long contend for charters, which, we
are again and again told in the annals of the past, were never
intended for our benefit? Even a willingness on our part to
defend them, has provoked the calamities of exterminating warfare. Why contend for the shadow, when the substance courts
our acceptance? The price of each is the same. War — exterminating war — is waged; and we have either to fight or flee.

We have indulged sympathy, too, for the condition of many
whom, we vainly flattered ourselves, were opposed, in common
with their adopted brethren, to the extension of military
domination over the domain of Texas. But the siege of Bexar has
dissolved the illusion. Nearly all their physical force was in the
line of the enemy and armed with rifles. Seventy days' occupation of the fortress of Goliad, has also abundantly demonstrated
the general diffusion among the Creole population of a like
attachment to the institutions of their ancient tyrants. Intellec-
tually enthralled, and strangers to the blessings of regulated
liberty, the only philanthropic service which we can ever force on
their acceptance, is that of example. In doing this, we need not
expect or even hope for their co-operation. When made the
reluctant, but greatly benefited recipients of a new, invigorating,
and cherishing policy — a policy tending equal, impartial, and
indiscriminate protection to all; to the low and the high, the
humble and the well-born, the poor and the rich, the ignorant
and the educated, the simple and the shrewd — then, and not
before, will they become even useful auxiliaries in the work of
political or moral renovation.

It belongs to the North-Americans of Texas to set this bright, this cheering, this all-subduing example. Let them call together their wise men. Let them be jealous of the experienced, of the speculator, of every one anxious to serve as a delegate, of every one hungry for power, or soliciting office; and of all too who have thus far manifested a willingness to entertain or encourage those who have already tired the patience of the existing Council with their solicitations and attendance. Those who *seek* are seldom ever the best qualified to *fill* an office. Let them discard, too, the use of *names* calculated only to deceive and bewilder, and return like men to the use of words whose signification is settled and universally acknowledged. Let them call their assembly, thus made up, *a Convention;* and let this convention, instead of declaring for "the principles" of a constitution, for "the principles" of Independence, or for those of Freemen and Sovereignty, boldly, and with one voice, proclaim *the Independence of Texas*. Let the Convention frame a constitution for the future government of this favored land. Let them guard the instrument securely, by the introduction of a full, clear, and comprehensive bill of rights. Let all this be done as speedily as possible. Much useful labor has already been performed; but much is yet required to complete the work.

The foregoing, we are fully aware, is a blunt, and in some respects, a humiliating, but a faithful picture. However much we may wish, or however much we may be interested, or feel disposed to deceive our enemy, let us carefully guard against deceiving *ourselves*. We are in more danger from this — from his insinuating, sevret, silent, and unseen *influence* in our councils, both in the field and in the cabinet, and from the use of his silver and gold, than from his numbers, his organization, or the concentration of his power in a single arm. The *gold* of Phillip purchased what his *arms* could not subdue — *the liberties* of Greece. *Our* enemy, too, holds this weapon. Look well to this, people of Texas, in the exercise of suffrage. Look to it, Counselors, your appointments to office. Integrity is a precious jewel.

Men of Texas! nothing short of independence can place us on solid ground. This step will. This step, too, will entitle us to confidence, and will procure us credit abroad. Without it, every aid we receive must emanate from the enthusiasm of the moment, and with the moment, will be liable to pass away or die forever. Unless we take this step, no foreign power can either respect or even know us. None will hazard a rupture with Mexico, impotent as she is, or incur censure from other powers for interference with the internal affairs of a friendly State, to aid us in any way whatever. Our letters of marque and reprisal must float at the mercy of every nation on the ocean. And whatever courtesy of kindred feeling may do, or forbear to do, in aid of our struggle, prosecuted on the present basis, it would be idle and worse than child-like to flatter ourselves with the hope of any permanent benefit from this branch of service, without frankly declaring to the world, *as a people,* our *independence* of military Mexico. Let us then take the tyrant, and his hirelings at their word. *They* will not know *us* but as enemies. Let us, then, know them hereafter, as other independent States know each other — as "enimies in war, in peace, friends." Therefore,

1. **Be it resolved,** That the former province and department of Texas is, and of right ought to be, *a free, sovereign, and independent State.*

2. That as such, it has, and of right, ought to have, all the powers, faculties, attributes, and immunities of other independent nations.

3. That we, who hereto set our names, to sustain this declaration — relying with entire confidence upon the co-operation of our fellow-citizens, and the approving smiles of the God of the living, to aid and conduct us victoriously through the struggle, to the enjoyment of peace, union, and good government; and invoking His malediction if we should either equivocate, or, in any manner whatever, prove ourselves unworthly of the high destiny at which we aim.

Done in the town of Goliad, on Sunday, the 20th day of December, in the year of our Lord one thousand eight hundred and thirty five.[69]

Monday, December 21, 1835
76 DAYS TO THE FALL

Sam Houston to Lieut. Col James C. Neill
WASHINGTON: On receipt of this you will take command of the Post of Bexar and make such disposition of the troops there as you may deem proper for the security & protection of the place — causing reports to be made to me of the state of the place — the quantity of ammunition & the number of arms &c together with a list of property taken from the enemy as well as the statement of the force under your command — you will also cause a survey to be made by G.B. Jameson[70] of the different articles necessary for your Command & the number of Cannon & other munitions of war & also of provisions clothing &c — & you will immediately detail some capable officer to assist in fortifying the place in the best manner possible. A Tanner is ordered to report himself to you & detail him as you see fit.

Enclosed are Instructions for officers on the recruiting service which you will detail for that purpose from a list of officers herewith furnished you who are ordered to report to you also a blank form for volunteers which you will open for names at recollecting at same time that not less than a platoon of 28 men who are enlisted to one first Lieutenant. A company will consist of 1 Captain 1st and 1 2d Lieut 4 Sergeants 4 corporals and a battalion of 5 companies 1 lieut Col & 1 Major & a regiment of 2 Battalions & one Colonel. Herewith are also a list of the officers of the Regular Army to those who are in the army & who have not recd. a notification you will inform them of their appointment.

The Commander-in-Chief in depositing the high trust of the command of Bexar to Col J. C. Neill feels assured that the confidence is not misplaced & that he will always be able to respond to the country in defence of its rights.

By order of Sam Houston
Commander in chief
of the Army
Geo. W. Poe
acting Adjutant Genl[71]

Sam Houston to William Patton

HEAD QUARTERS WASHINGTON: Lieut Wm Paton, Sir You will proceed immediately on receipt of this to Velasco and there you are detailed for the duty of acting assistant Quarter master General you will in consequence remain there and inform all troops landing at the mouth of the Brasos, if they arrive in armed vessels to proceed on their voyage by sea to Copano & to occupy or position in the neighborhood of the port I would suggest Refugio Mission if in unarmed vessels to proceed to matagorda & from there to goliad. So far as practicable you will furnish them with supplies you can obtain.

You will report your arrival at the mouth of the brasos to Head Quarters at Washington & report from time to time anything interesting & if necessary by express & you will remain there until further ordered.

This order to be obeyed all orders to the contrary notwithstanding.

By Order of Sam Houston
Commander in chief
of the Army
Geo. W. Poe
acting Adutant Genl[72]

Council Hall, San Felipe de Austin

NINE O'CLOCK A.M. Be it resolved by the general council of the Provisional Government of Texas, that William Moore shall be, and is hereby appointed Sutler to the troops at Bexar; Provided, he shall be subject to the orders of the commandant of said post, accordingly to the rules and disciplines of war.[73]

Tuesday, December 22, 1835
75 DAYS TO THE FALL

Stephen F. Austin to F. W. Johnson, et al

QUINTANA: Dear Sirs, We expect to get off tomorrow in the Wm. Robbins; Archer, the two Whartons and myself and several other passengers.

There has been a great deal of low intrigue in the political maneuvering of a party who I am at last forced to believe have

Stephen F. Austin, the Father of Texas.

their own personal ambitions and aggrandizement in view, more than the good of the country. These men have operated on Archer until they have made him almost a political fanatic, preaching a crusade in favor of liberty against the city of Mexico, the only place short of which the army ought to stop, &c.

The Mexicans say that it is curious that the people of Texas should fight against military rulers, and at the same time try to build up an army that may, it its turn, rule Texas as it pleases. I think it probable there will be some thousands of volunteers from the United States in a few months. They nearly all wish to join the regular army on the basis of volunteers. What shall we do with so many? How to support them? I fear that the true secret of the efforts to declare independence is, that there must then be a considerable standing army, which in the hands of a few, would dispose of the old settlers and their interests as they thought proper.

The true policy for Texas is to call a convention, amend the declarations of the 7th of November last, by declaring Texas a State of the Mexican Confederacy under the basis laid down in the fifth and other articles of said declaration of the 7th of November, form a constitution and organize a permanent government. Every possible aid should be given to the Federal party in the interior; but it should be done as auxiliary aid, in conformity with the second article of the declaration. By doing this the war will be kept out of Texas. This country will remain at peace. It will fill up rapidly with families, and there will be no great need for a standing army. I believe that the combinations in the state of Tamaulipas are very extensive to form a new republic by a line from Tampico, west to the Pacific, and it is probable that the capitulation at Bexar was made to promote that object. In short, it is much easier to keep the war out of Texas, than to bring it back again to our doors. All that is necessary is for us not to do anything that will compel the Federal party to run against us, and if they call on us for aid let it be given as auxiliary aid, and on no other footing.

This takes away the character of a national war, which the government in Mexico is trying to give it, and it will also give to Texas just claims on the Federal part, for remuneration of the proceeds of the custom houses of Matamoros and Tampico, for our expenses in furnishing auxiliary aid. But if Texas sends an invading force of foreign troops against Matamoros, it will change the whole matter. Gen. Mexia ought to have commanded the expedition to Matamoros and only waited to be asked by the Provisional Government to do so.

I repeat: It is much easier to keep the war out of Texas and beyond the Rio Grande, than to bring it here to our own doors. The farmers and substantial men of Texas can yet save themselves, but to do so they must act in union and as one man.

This, I fear, is impossible. In the upper settlement Dr. Hoxey is loud for independence. Of Course he is in favor of a large standing army to sustain it, and will no doubt be ready to give up half, or all, of his property to support thousands of volunteers, &c. who will flood the country from abroad.

It is all very well and right to show to the world that Texas has just and equitable grounds to declare independence; but it is putting the old settlers in great danger to make any such declaration, for it will turn all the parties in Mexico against us. It will bring back the war to our doors, which is now far from us, and it will compel the men of property in Texas to give up half or all to support a standing army of sufficient magnitude to contend with all Mexico united.[74]

[Addressed to F. W. Johnson, Daniel Parker, D. C. Barrett, J. W. Robinson, Wyatt Hanks, P. Sublette, Asa Hoxey.]

Council Hall, San Felipe de Austin

BE IT RESOLVED: That Sam Houston, John Fortes, and John Cameron, be and they are hereby appointed commissioners to treat with the Cherokee Indians, and their twelve Associated Bands. Be it further resolved, &c. That said Commissioners be required to hold said treaty so soon as practicable.

Mr. Hanks, from the committee on military affairs made the following report: It is the opinion of you committee, that the appointment of a Paymaster for the troops at San Antonio de Bexar, is unnecessary at this time for several reasons.

In the first place, there is no money in the Treasury to pay the soldiers, or for any other purpose.

Secondly, a Paymaster has already been appointed, and will proceed to discharge the duties of his office as soon as the Government has funds. Beside the principal complaint against the General Council is, that too many offices have been created, and to create that number when there is nothing for them to do, the present impoverished state of our finances, would give just cause of complaint.

Your committee cannot under these circumstance recommend the appointment of any additional officer at this time; but as soon as money can be obtained to pay the troops at Bexar, it will be necessary to appoint a Paymaster.[75]

Wednesday, December 23, 1835
74 DAYS TO THE FALL

Henry Smith, Governor to the
President and members of the General Council
I herewith transmit to you various documents received from the commander at Bexar.

You will see various bills which they think necessary to be filled out, all of which you will compare and consider. The bills already forwarded to the United States to be filled by special agents, you will take into consideration, and see if anything additional should be ordered.

Of the article of bread stuff, they seem to be very scarce, and from verbal information, very little is on the way from Gonzales. What orders have been sent to commissaries for the forwarding of supplies from the West, by way of Labacca, I am not advised, but hope that the necessary means will be used to keep them supplied, with whatever the garrison may need.

You will also see an account in favor of Mr. Arnold, of which you will make the proper disposition.

The documents relating to the creation of officers in the camp, requiring commissions, &c. &c., I have passed over to General Houston, the commander-in-chief, with a request that he proceed to order the proper officers to that point to take command, and reduce the previous disorganization to system.

I also transmit to you, documents this moment received from Capt. Caldwell of Gonzales, who has been engaged in forwarding supplies to the army.

I have also received verbal information, that Capt. Caldwell has unfortunately received a wound which will probably retard the prosecution of his duties for the present. By verbal request of officers who have been in command of Bexar, I am informed a

Mr. Smith,[76] a deaf man, well known to the army for his vigilance and meritorious acts, has been severely wounded in storming Bexar, and that his family are daily expected in this place, with an expectation that the General council would exercise such guardianship over them as their situation may require. Their head remains in camp, as his services as a spy cannot well be dispensed with. All of which is transmitted to your honorable body for its imformation, and corresponding effects, by your

Obedient servant
Henry Smith, Governor[77]

Council Hall, San Felipe de Austin
SEVEN O'CLOCK, P.M. Mr. Barrett submitted a letter recommending G. B. Jameson, for an appointment in the engineer department, which was read and laid on the table.[78]

Sam Houston to Wm B. Travis,
Colonel 1st Regiment of Infantry
HEAD QUARTERS, WASHINGTON: On receipt of this you will proceed to St. Felipe and there establish your Head Quarters. Herewith you have a list of notifications to Officers directed to report themselves to you. From them you detail as many as you may think necessary to proceed to the United States or to any point you may think most likely to ensure success so that they will be able to return with their respective commands to your post by the first of March next. You will direct your officers to report to you weekly or semimonthly, & you will report semimonthly to head quarters, the Commander in chief expects that as order and discipline are the basis of an Army — that both your officers and men will be drilled.

By order of
Sam Houston
Commander in chief
of the Army
Geo. W. Poe
acting adjutant General[79]

Santa Anna to Colonel Ricardo Dromundo
HEADQUARTERS, SAN LUIS POTOSI: Since Your Lordship has been named Purveyor of the Army of Operations in Texas, and should march at once to the Town of Guerrero to gather food and stores for the above-mentioned army, I advise your Lordship to begin your march immediately, gathering in Saltillo, as well as in the above-mentioned villa of Guerrero, whatever you find available there, and consigning them to Bejar.

In the villa of Guerrero you will be supplied with the funds that you will need, for the purchase of said supplies, bearing in mind that your Lordship must have ready one thousand cargas of flour, one thousand of corn, brans, rice, lard and salt so that there shall be rations of two months supply for six thousand men. For God and Liberty.[80]

Edw Hall to the Govr & Council Texas

NEW ORLEANS: Gent: By the accompanying papers you will secure the Presidents message with all the other news, we have reports that Santa Anna is approaching Texas with an army of 6000 men, its also reported that the posts of Vera Cruz Tampico & Matamoros, have been shut to American Vessels, I have got some men at work making a Howitser & carriage & hope to have it done in 10 to 12 days. Men are coming in every day from various parts of the Country bound for Texas, many however are without any means. & I hope the Commissioners will soon arrive to provide some for all who are so anxious to join our cause.[81]

Capt R. B. Irvine to Genl Sam Houston

WASHINGTON: Two companies of about 80 volunteers from the United States under command of Col. Wyatt arrived in this place yesterday evening and await your orders. The Company being desirous of proceeding to their point of destination with as little delay as possible, you will confer a particular favor on the officers and privates of the company by sending them their orders as soon as you can, consistent with your convenience and inclination. It is undoubtedly the finest appearance, and best disciplined company that has yet entered Texas. The company has marched on foot from Natchitoches to this place, unless you can procure some horses, several of the men will be forced to remain in this place from fatigue and exhaustion.

Respectfully your obt. sert
R. B. Irvine
Capt. 1st Infty[82]

Thursday, December 24, 1835
73 DAYS TO THE FALL

F. W. Johnson to Wyatt Hanks & J. D. Clements, Members for the Committee of Military Affairs
HEADQUARTERS BEXAR: I have the honor to acknowledge the receipt of your communication of the 16th Inst. addressed to my predecessor Genl. Burleson, & it affords me the highest pleasure to observe that the conduct of the brave men under my command have merited your applause. —[83]

The hostility which several persons in power have evinced to the Volunteer Army, to which you allude, has been seen thro' for a length of time & nothing short of the absolute ruin of Texas which must have been the consequence of the dissolution of that body, could have kept the small band of patriots together so long, exposed to every privation — and above all to the frowns & culumny of those who should have been our staunchest supporters. — The painful consciousness of such decided opposition operated powerfully against a due organization & created a multitude of evils too numerous to mention — until a few resolute supporters of our sacred liberties, working upon the better feelings of a part of the mass, achieved what you so highly intole above its real merits, and out of disorder brought about regularity & a system of discipline which at this moment does high honor to the discernment of those who have submitted willingly to what our present position so imperiously demanded. —

The friendly intentions of the council towards the volunteer Army in framing the ordinance of which you enclose a copy, meets our gratitude; but as you will see by the enclosed documents[84] presented to me by the Captns. of the Companies who volunteered to stay for four months, in the principle of being commanded by the officers of their own choice, subject only to the Governor & Council in accordance with the decree of the Genl. Council for the formation of a regular Army, in which it is specifically stated that they are subject to their own Commander In Chief, unless they shall invite the Com. in chief of the regular Army to take the command — it is utterly impossible to induce the Army now here to become auxiliaries [to] the regular Army, or to subject them to the Comr [in] Chief. — At the same time they have willingly submitted to a system of due subordination & discipline as citizen soldiers — and they are ready & anxious to enter the field against the common enemy of our liberties — to sustain the principles of the declaration of the people of Texas, and otherwise to submit themselves in every respect to the disposition of the provisional Governor & Council with the reserve of the right granted to them by the Genl. Council as above alluded to. —

Their conduct hitherto in the field is but a slight specimen of what you may expect from them if the principles under which they were organized are respected and I feel persuaded that they will give new days of glory to Texas so soon as an opportunity is offered them of meeting the enemy. —

I will make immediate arrangement for an expedition against Matamoros as we are fortunate enough to receive your recommendation to take such a step. It will however be necessary to wait the arrival of reinforcements on the road, to enable me to leave a sufficient garrison at this important point. The difficulty which presents itself does not consist in a lack of volunteers for such an expedition, but on the contrary in persuading a sufficient number for garrison duty to remain behind — All wish to achieve new victories & to raise the glory of the Army of Texas, as well as to assist the friends of Liberty in the interior in throwing off the yoke of tyranny. —

To those worthy members of the council & Government who have befriended the only legitimate form of a free constitution — I tender my best thanks & the volunteer Army at large will ever cherish their merits & feel grateful for their support. —[85]

Charles Wilson to R. R. Royall
MATAGORDA: I have appointed Jas Collinsworth state Attorney. He will not I am afraid be here to investigate that Damnable league and combination that was at the pass — It would be well enough to appoint some other lawyer as I expect Collinsworth is on his way to the United States. If he writes me; Travis would be the man; I think our port and honors as good citizens ought to be protected by the strong arm of the Law. . . .[86]

Friday, December 25, 1835
72 DAYS TO THE FALL

Volunteers at Bexar to Genl. F. W. Johnson
ST. ANTONIO de BEXAR: We the undersign'd — Capt's of companies forming the body of forces who have the honor to serve under your command, having seen a decree of the general convention, by which the volunteer army is required to subject themselves to the Organic laws & comd'r. in chief of the Regular Army, beg respectively to represent, in our own in our companies names, that, this is in direct opposition to the tenor of a decree of the Gen'l Convention, by which the Regular army was ordered to be organis'd — That decree expressly allows the Individuals of the Voluntary army the privilege of electing their own officers, & not to

be subject to the Comdr. in chief of the Regular Army, unless he be invited by themselves to their command.

Under these stipulations we all Volunteer our services & our firm resolve, is to comply to the utmost of our ability, with the spirit of our compact, founded on the decree above alluded to, but in no case do we consider ourselves subject to variation or any infringement of our privileges during the term of our services, nor indeed, cou'd we induce our men under any circumstance to subject themselves to the Organic laws of the Regular Army, or to serve under any other terms than those under which they have at present volunteer'd.

Signed: Thos Lewellyn, B. L. Lawrence, Thos K. Pearson, Jon J. Baugh, David N. Burk, W. G. Cooke.[87]

Eli Mercer to Henry Smith

EGYPT, TEXAS: I take this method of communicating to you some of my views on public affairs. Our people met in a very disorganized manner, and, rather pr chance succeeded in taking San Antonia; and I think it reasonable to say it is time for Texas to be done with disorganized insubordinate undisciplined armies as that appears to have bean. It would appear necessary to organize a sufficient number of troops to garrison and fortify the post of San Antonio and to push forward supplies for their support. The contractor department I fear is very deficient; ample supplies for the support of the army should be laid in, in good time and forward to the proper places, and securely deposited to be in readiness for a spring campaign; as we may expect a strong force of the enemy to march against Texas at that time I deem it necessary for Texas to be ready to meat an army of eight or ten thousand strong in may next. Our army should be well organized and disciplined, to do which they should all be in the field by the middle of March; for it will require at least two months for men to be sufficient trained to insure success.

Subordination is also very necessary and cannot be dispensed in a regular army which also requires a length of time to put it into men.

Suffer me Sir, to close by saying my ernist desire is that every department may exert its self to have evry thing in readiness at any time and at all times to insure the Country the greatest Sucess.[88]

F. W. Johnson to J. W. Robinson

SAN ANTONIO de BEXAR: I have the satisfaction to acknowledge the receipt of your letter of the 15th to my predecessor Gen. Burleson, which I opened as it was not marked private on the cover.[89]

No apology is required by such a friend as you have proved to be to the Volunteer Army of Texas, for giving such hints as may appear to you conducive to the general good and to the success of the cause in which we are engaged. — On the contrary such hints would be gratefully received had they come from a person who had no influence on our movements and much more of course from one who has so immediate a share in their control

The expedition which you propose against Matamoros can be undertaken speedily with every rational prospect of success and every man in this garrison would willingly Volunteer to proceed to the interior, but as the position which we occupy is all important to maintain, it will be desirable to wait the arrival of considerable reinforcements now on the road to have a sufficient number to answer other purposes, and in the mean time every necessary preparation of suitable Artillery, Amn. and Stores can be made, all the animals required to convey the same procured. — An expedition of this nature you point out has occupied our attention for some time, and a small division of observation leaves this place to day for the Nueces to occupy the attention of the enemy at Rio Grande and Laredo, to open and keep up a communication with the liberals on the frontier and above all to procure positive information of the forces at each point, their condition and every other particular that can serve to guide us in our future operations. —

According to the last accounts from Matamoros the force of the enemy consisted of 200 men very little inclined to support the cause of Centralism, or desirous of opposing the favorers of the Federal Constitution. The frontier towns of Tamaulipas were arming to throw off the Yoke, and a movement was even attempted by the inhabitants of Matamoros against the Military, which from being immaturely made was suffocated. What bears particularly on the question of an attack on our part are the bodies of troops collecting at Loredo and Riogrande, which may be sufficient to oppose a considerable force — and frustrate an attempt of ours with less than 500 men, a number which I hope to unite in a few days; leaving 100 and 50 men here: — a sufficient number in my opinion, as we will naturally draw their attention in the other direction. — We can calculate with certainty on our liberals, now that the Council have made so explicit a declaration of our present intentions and victory must certainly be ours by following the ordinary maxims in such cases. We will then carry the war of Tejas and not only support ourselves out of the enemies resources, but likewise be able to ensure to Tejas a speedy reimbursement of her expenses in sustaining the present question with which our liberties and properties are so closely allied.

Matamoros is not a fortified town, but its possession by us will serve too important purposes — cripple the enemy in his resources, already worn thread bare, and support our armies and country amply, besides which it will scare the liberal party to action and give employment to Santa Anna and his minions in other parts of the Republic so as not to be able to make face against us . . . The moment is appropriate and should not be lost and you may rely on my embracing it with every soldier that can be spared now that I know your sentiments and those of several members of the council. — The discipline already established in the Volunteer Army will render us doubly formidable, and if we are not interfered with by the officers of the regular army, you may rely on all going well and to your wishes.—

Your frankness merits a due correspondence and for your private guidance I beg to acquaint you that the Volunteers arriving from the U.S. all declare that if we pretend to independence they will immediately quit us, as they consider the War in that case almost interminable. — It is likewise important that you should be aware that Genl. B lost entirely the confidence of this army in consequence of his having impedeuously given the attacking party Operating against this place an order to retire about half an hour before the enemy sent us their flag of truce, offering to capitulate on reasonable terms, of which order I send you a copy, he is so brave and honorable a soldier as any in the Army, but the extent of his capacity I leave you to learn from others. — I esteem him as a man but my duty to the service compels me to say so much. —

I wrote a long letter to the provisional Governor on the 17th Decr. requesting supplies which doubtless he has submitted to the council. — Among others I requested some funds for our absolute wants and for the proposed expedition 2000$ at least are of urgent necessity. —[90]

Committee on Military Affairs to Council and Governor

SAN FELIPE: The committee on military affairs, to whom was referred Maj. F. W. Johnson's letter, of December 18, 1835, from headquarters at San Antonio de Bexar, have had the same under consideration, and from the information contained therein, together with the movements of General Cos, after his departure from San Antonio de Bexar, learned from a private source, renders it necessary to concentrate on the frontier, at the most important points, all the troops that can be raised and that as speedily as possible.

We are also informed by the communication received from Bexar that advices have been received at that place that General Ramirez Sesma had arrived at Laredo with five hundred cavalry and one thousand infantry, for the purpose of reinforcing General Cos, and that an army was raising at San Luis Potosi, to be commanded by San Anna.

Your committee would therefore recommend that an express be sent to the commander-in-chief of the regular army of Texas, forwarding to him a copy of the letter received from Bexar of the 18th inst., and the private intelligence of the movements of General Cos and further, that Col. J.W. Fannin be ordered to proceed forthwith to the west and take command of the regular army and auxiliary troops, and that Colonel Travis be ordered to repair with all possible dispatch to the frontier, or seat of war, with all the troops he can bring into the field at this time under his command; and that the troops at Washington, and such as may be on the Guadaloupe, will be ordered to repair immediately to Goliad, Copano, or Bexar for the purpose of cooperating with and acting in concert in the general defensive or offensive operations which may be ordered or deemed necessary.

Your committee would further earnestly recommend, that the commander-in-chief be ordered to concentrate all the troops under his command, or that can be brought into the field, at Goliad or Copano, with all possible dispatch, taking care at the same time to procure, by his contractors, the necessary supplies of provisions for the sustenance of his troops, and that his orders be executed with all promptness and dispatch; and further, that the commander-in-chief be required to arrange and give orders to his recruiting officers and make such dispositions of his recruiting officers as may be deemed best by him.

Therefore your committee recommend the adoption of the following resolutions:

Inasmuch as the number of troops fit for duty now in the field is very much augmented, there being four hundred troops now at Bexar, seventy at Washington, eighty at Goliad, two hundred at Velasco, and several companies on their march to the different military posts and places of rendezvous, making in the aggregate seven hundred and fifty men now in service and ready for active operations, and at least one hundred more, not enumerated in the above aggregate, who will join the army in a few days, active operations should be immediately commenced; for the expenses of the above number of men, now in service, together with the officers and contingent expenses, are too great for Texas in the present state of her finances. Besides, to keep the troops idle who have entered the service will do us great injury at this time. It will induce those who are willing and able to aid us, to believe that we have no use for any more troops; it will give our enemies time to fortify Matamoros and Laredo, so they can demonstrate on us in the spring or whenever they think proper, knowing their fortifications would enable them to retreat safely, even if they were defeated, and should it become necessary to take either of the aforesaid places, for the security of the frontier, it would be far more difficult than it would be at this time, and no man can doubt the importance and necessity of striking a decisive blow at once. By taking Matamoros, we have the possession of the key; yes, the commercial depot of the whole country north and northwest for several hundred miles. We can then fortify the place; demonstrate, when the occasion presents itself, if necessary, at that point (Matamoros), at any time with perfect safety, and without incurring half the risk and expense we must at present. And we can also command the Gulf of Mexico from that point to the city of New Orleans, and land our troops and supplies wherever we please.

Therefore be it resolved, by the general council of the provisional government of Texas, That his Excellency, Henry Smith, governor, be and he is hereby earnestly requested to concentrate all his troops by his proper officers, at Copano and San Patricio, for the purpose of carrying into effect the objects expressed and contained in the foregoing report.

Be it further resolved, That no officer of the regular army of Texas shall receive pay until he is in actual service, under orders of the commander-in-chief.[91]

Daniel Cloud to Friend

NATCHITOCHES, LOUISIANA: We have found many situations suitable for the profitable employment of legal qualifications, but our hopes, our feelings, and sympathies urged us on, and now we stand on the shores of the United States, but next week, heaven willing, we shall breathe the air of Texas. Nor do we go to Texas as mere spectators of the momentous transactions now going on in that fertile region; no, we go with arms in our hands, determined to conquer or die; resolved to bury our all in the same ditch which ingulphs the liberties of Texas, or see it freed from this government. In 1823, thousands of Anglo-Americans settled in Texas, agreed to become, under a certain constitution, a state of the Mexican republic, bound by the same reciprocal ties as one of our states is to the present confederacy. Santa Anna, a military chieftain, overturns that solemn league, overruns Mexico and reduces all but Texas to his power. Finding resistance there, he actually offers to sell the whole province of Texas to the Rothchilds, of Europe, for ten millions of dollars. This offer, we learn on the best authority, was made eighteen months ago, without sanction of Texas. Failing in that offer of sale, he seeks to reduce the colony raises military law and pronounces them rebels. Inheriting the old Saxon spirit of 1640 in England, 1776 in America, the inhabitants of Texas throw off the chains of Santa Anna, assert their independence, assume a national sovereignty, and sends a corps of diplomatic agents to the parent state of Washington. Here these agents meet the commissioners of Mexico, charged, it is believed, with a project for the sale of Texas to the

United States — a sale of the sovereignty of that state, not a foot whose soil they possess beyond their very pickets.

Such is, we believe, the exact position of the two parties. In Texas the war continues — but what is it? Mexico can no more conquer Texas than she can Louisiana — She may occupy the extent of soil her soldiery encamp upon — but no more. Texas can battle it for years. Yet we do wish to see an end put to the further effusion of blood. The Government of the United States can do so if it chooses. Let but the independence of Texas be acknowledged at Washington, and there is an end to the difficulty. Recognize its government de facto if not de jute — invite its commissioners to open negotiations — assume the responsibility of aiding the holy energies of a people struggling for liberty, and General Jackson would entitle himself to even more regard than what he rightfully received in bringing the French question to a successful close. To such a course, Mexico could present no scriois [sic], no plausible objections. There is precedent on record of a recent date. When the republic of Columbia broke to pleas, — and Bolivar was overwhelmed, the United States immediately opened negotiations with the several new governments which sprung up from the ruins. Indeed it was the same principle and in pursuance of the same policy, that this country appointed diplomatic agents to many of the South American republics, long before their independence was acknowledged by Old Spain and while she in fact was sending out armies to reduce them.

It is only the same kind of conduct, on a smaller scale and nearer home, that is necessary for our government to pursue towards Texas — let her comissioners be received at Washington as the agents, of an independent state — and in return, let Gen. Jackson send a charge d'affairs or diplomatic agent to Texas. Then the Texas question is forever settled. But if our filled with virtuous indignation at this outrage upon good faith, upon humanity and human rights, they have hoisted the constitution of 1824 and are resolved to maintain the character and enjoy the immunities of freedom until the last beating pulse shall cease to tell. They appeal to all that is magnanimous in our natures, to all that is noble in our feelings, and implore that we will not permit the cause of liberty to be crushed in the bud. If we succeed, a fertile region and a grateful people will be for us our home and secure to us our reward. If we fail, death in defence of so just and so good a cause need not excite a shudder or tear.

Thousands of magnanimous youths from all quarters of this mighty nursery of freemen are pushing on to the seat of war, and many are destined to signalize themselves and win renown in the war of Texas.

When Texas becomes free I see in prospective a charming

picture; when the genial rays of freedom's sun whose fructifying beams have so long and so gloriously illuminated their portions of America, begins to shine with undiminished effulence upon Texas also, not one quarter of a century will stand between her and opulence, security, intelligence, religious and moral excellence, and social happiness and refinement. The tide of emigration will be onward and irresistible, and he whose life is spared fifty years will see the apostles of liberty and republicanism, the sons of our blessed country descending the western decliyities of the Rocky Mountains, bearing in one hand the olive branch of peace and the impliments of husbandry — in the other, the weapons of defence and security to shed on that benighted region the light of christanity and the blessings of civilization and free government, then the mighty waves of the monarch of oceans which wash the East Indies, the hoary empire of China and the Islands of Polynesia on the east, shall waft all their stores of plenty into the republican ports of our mammoth confederacy of the west. The prospect is grand, too much so for my feeble power of description to encompass.[92]

Saturday, December 26, 1835
71 DAYS TO THE FALL

Niles Weekly Register

MEMPHIS: The emigration to Arkansas is very great — "with large droves of negroes" — says a Little Rock paper; exclusive of those who are about to join the people of Texas. Col. Crocket has left Little Rock, with his followers, for Texas. Many others had the same destination.

Texan and Emigrants Guide[93]

NACOGDOCHES: It is said that the Texeans besieging San Antonio delight in being shot at, the balls of the enemy serve them in turn. All anxiously watch the flash of a Mexican cannon, and throw themselves flat on the ground, and in an instant rise and give chase to the ball bounding over the field, hallooing "stop that ball" and when unable to overtake it, "lost ball, Captain."

Emigration is very great into this country from the States. For several days past the roads have been full of wagons, carriage, &c on their way west. Many families have passed through this place during the present week and from their equipage and number of slaves, we suppose they are of the wealthiest and most respectable farmers of the southern States.

**Telegraph,
and Texas Register**

SAN FELIPE: We are informed that there are now in Brazos
8 vessels from different ports of the United States and more
are expected. It is also said that they have brought a large
number of volunteers in the cause of Texas. This information, if correct, is of the most flattering character.

We hear from an official communication from col F. W.
Johnson that there are fifteen hundred Mexican Troops (one
thousand infantry and five hundred cavalry) at Laredo, on
their way to Texas. The commander [of the Mexicans] not
knowing the fate of Bexar, wrote to general Cos urging him
to persevere in defense of the place and assuring him that
he would receive ample reinforcements.

Wyatt Hanks to Sam Houston

SAN FELIPE: The first drum that has beat for volunteers in Texas
for the Regular Army was on yesterday. It was done by Capt.
Allen & 12 or 13 enlisted. A report has been made & adopted
respecting the action of the Army a copy of which will be sent to
you. I hope it will meet with your approbation. We are told that
a great many volunteers from Georgia & Alabama has landed at
the mouth of the Brasos though no written or official recount.

I want to obtain your asistance in getting the appointment of
Sutler for the Army west of this.

Any recommendation from you as to that appointment would
have its influence with the Genl. council

If you see proper to do so, I shall consider myself under many
obligations, & will reciprocate the favour whenever an appointment presents itself.

Your friend & obt Sert
Wyatt Hanks[94]

Sam Houston to David J. Mitchell

HEAD QUARTERS WASHINGTON: Sir Should you find it
practicable to introduce Volunteers from the United States into
Texas by the first of March next they will be accepted by the
government. A Platoon will consist of 28 men rank & file 2
sergeants & 2 corporals — a Company of 2 platoons or 56 men
rank & file 1 Captain 1 first & one 2d Lieutenants 4 sergeants & 4
Corporals & 2 musicians — Five Companies will constitute one
Battalion & Two Battalions one Regiment commanded by 1
Colonel 1 Lieut Colonel & 1 Major. The monthly pay of the
privates will be 8$ per month Corporals 10$ Sergeants 11$. The
pay of the Officers & non Commissioned Staff will be the same

which is established in the Regular Army of the United States. The Volunteers will elect their own officers.

Bounty land given is 640 acres beside the right of citizenship to those who volunteer their services for 2 years or during the war & if for one year 320 acres of land. If for a shorter period than one year no Bounty of land will be given. To all accepted Volunteers will be given pay ration & clothing with the rights of Citisenship.

By Order of Sam Houston
Commander in chief of the Army
Geo. W. Poe
acting adjutant General[95]

Sam Houston to Henry Smith

HEADQUARTERS WASHINGTON: I have the honor of reporting my arrival here on yesterday, and my finding here Captain Wyatt,[96] with a company or detachment, consisting of less than fifty-six men from Huntsville, Alabama; also Captain King,[97] with about eighteen men from Paducah, Kentucky, with rifles — Captain Wyatt having fifty first rate United States muskets. Under the restrictions of the law, I find myself under the most painful difficulties in accepting the services of these volunteers. I will do the best I can for the country, while I render justice to them. I found in the ranks great discontent, and a disposition to abandon our cause. Today i have spent much time in explaining all matters to them. I hope they are satisfied —

Today there has been an arrival in six days from San Antonio, which reports all quiet, but no discipline. Ere this I hope my order has reached them, and will have a proper effect with the command. It is said that Bowie will be here tomorrow. Should he come to San Felipe I hope your excellency will be kind enough to order him to this point, as I can furnish him with a copy of the order[98] which I forwarded to him by your excellency's order.[99]

Daniel Cloud to I. B. Cloud

NATCHITOCHES, LOUISIANA: A long time has elapsed since we parted and long before this period, I expected to write to you, but continual traveling and employment have prevented it. After leaving Uncle Sloan's in Missouri which we did on the 29th of November, we journeyed South. I left the family well except Grandma, who was extremely ill. I have no idea that she lives yet. I left upwards of $30.00 with her besides the $10.00 sent her by Uncle William, which made between forty and fifty dollars, which I deem sufficient in the event of life or death. She had blankets and every kind of comfortable clothing and all that aunt could do to alleviate her suffering was done. We set off before

Aunt Rice and her family arrived, but were informed that they had good health and enough to eat and wear.

Now you wish me to say something of the country through which we have traveled, Viz, Illinois, Missouri, Arkansas and Louisiana.

The soil of Ill. North of 38 degrees is the best I ever saw and from all I can learn, the best body of land on earth of the same extent. The water is abundant and may be called good, many parts I regard as healthy, and the ridgeland between Ill. and the Mississippi River, I believe to be as healthful as the allegany mountains.

Yankees, Kentuckians and Ohion's etc., are filling up the state with a rapidity unparalled in the History of the West. I saw fine farms, good houses, barns, wagons, plows, horses, men, women, children, beds, tables, and furniture in Ill. as I ever saw in KY. I view this State at no distance day far in advance of any western State except Ohio.

The reasons which induced us to travel on were briefly these, First our curiosity was unsatisfied, second, Law Dockets were not large, fees low, and yankee lawyers numerous, Third the coldness of the climate. Missouris, like Ill. has too much praries and unlike her, has very poor praries, West of 15 degrees, west longitude from Washington city, the lands of both sides of the Mo. River about the depth of one County, including Boon, Howard, Carroll, Ray, Clay, and Clifton on the North, and Cooper, Saline, LaFayette, Jackson, Van Buren, etc on the south are very rich and well settled already.

Our reason for not stopping in Mo. were first we were disappointed in the face of the country and the coldness of the climate, but most of all the smallness of the docket. There is less litigation in this state than in any other state in the union, for its population as I was informed, by one of the Judges of the Supreme court, Judge Tomkins, and what is going on rebounds very little to the emolument of the practitioner. I was happy to find such a State of case existing, but while following the chase like other hunters, wish to go where game is plentiful, large and fat, we rode through Mo., from North to South, about six hundred miles the weather was growing cold we knew we could not settle, it was out of our way to go through Boonville and we had not an opportunity of presenting ourselves to Col. Boon and Mr. Grubbs, but we thank Brother Grubbs, for the letter of introduction which he gave us and which we yet keep.

We wish you to acquaint him with these facts, and to present our love and compliments to him and his family.

We found Ark. Territory, in some places rich, well watered, and healthy and society tolerably good, but the great body of the country is stony sand and mountains. In passing through we

traveled ten days constantly in crossing the Mountains. On Red
River the lands are immensely rich, and planters also many of
them worth two hundred and three hundred thousand dollars,
had we chosen to locate in Ark. we would have made money
rapidly, if blessed with health and life. Dockets and Fees being
large. The reason for our pushing still further on, must now be
told and as it is a Master one, it will suffice without the mention
of any other. Ever since Texas has unfurled the banner of
freedom, and commenced a warfare for liberty or death, our
hearts have been enlisted in her behalf. The progress of her
cause has increased the ardor of our feelings until we have
resolved to embark in the vessel which contains the flag of
Liberty and sink or swim in its defense.

Our Brethren of Texas were invited by the Mexican Government, while Republican in it's form to come and settle, they did
so, they have endured all the privations and sufferings incident
to the settlement of a frontier country, and have surrounded
themselves with all the comforts and conveniences of life. Now
the Mexicans, with unblushing effrontery call on them to submit
to a Monarchial Tyranical, Central despotism, at the bare mention
of which every true hearted son of Ky. feels an instinctive horror,
followed by a firm and steady glow of virtuous indignation.

The cause of Philanthropy, of Humanity, of Liberty & human
happiness throughout the world call loudly on every man to
come to aid Texas.

If you ask me how I reconcile the duty of a soldier with those
of a Christian, I refer you to the memorable conversation
between Col. Marion and DeKalb, on this point, and the sentiments of the latter I have adopted as my own.

If we succeed, the Country is ours. It is immense in extent,
and fertile in its soil and will amply reward all our toil. If we fail,
death in the cause of liberty and humanity is not cause for
shuddering. Our rifles are by our side, and choice guns they are,
we know what awaits us, and are prepared to meet it.

My Dear Brother, I am in the hands of the omnipotence and
rejoice in the hope of his favor and protection. Oh how I would
have rejoiced to receive a letter from some of you in Jefferson
City in compliance with the request I made in my letter from
Springfield, Ill.

I waited ten days and nothing came. I have not heard one
sylable from home since the day of our departure.

I now say again if you or any of our relatives will write to us
and direct your letters to Nachitoches, La., we may get them,
and would thank you most sincerely for them. If you have any
affection for us you will attend to this request, I now commission
you to bear me as a Son, as an affectionate Son, to my beloved
Mother and her husband, kiss sister and all the children for me,

Mr. Slack and Mr. Lewis must do the same with their children, to Uncle Samuel and William, and their families, remember me and inform them to Grandma's condition.

Dear Brother, we are of the same origin, the blood of the same Parents flows through our veins, and the same material tenderness watched over our infant slumbers, and the same councils instilled principles into our minds.

Many times have we slept the live long night locked in each others arms, May our united petitions to a throne of divine grace invoke the same bread of life and our souls united in love, finally nestle under the protecting shield of the same all-wise and all merciful redeemer.

Remember me to all the Brethern and acquaintances, who inquire and say to them that scarcity of paper prevents me from writing them personally.

We cannot go to Nachitoches for paper on account of the Small pox. In a few days we shall be in Texas and then having no means of writing you may not hear from us for many days, but when we can, we will write. The deed I made you on the 20th day of October for the 64 1/2 acres of land, is hereby confirmed.

Request Uncle Samuel, to inform D. Fishback by letter that he has his books, some of you must take the trouble of informing me at length of all that has occurred in Logan County. I am extremely anxious to hear.

Tell Brother Isham to write. I will sometime write to Brother Anderson, tell him I think well of the country about Quincy, Ill. I think he will be pleased if not too cold for him. My health has been tolerably good. I have suffered a great deal with my stomach, but am now considerable improved.

I hope I shall recover entirely the hardships I am destined to undergo. Mr. Bailey[100] has fine health, we have been traveling ten weeks, and have gone over about twenty five hundred miles.

If I were with you, I could talk enough to tire you. I hope we shall meet.

> Your Brother,
> D. W. Cloud[101]

Sunday, December 27, 1835
70 DAYS TO THE FALL

Sam Houston to U.S. Volunteers:

TO UNITED STATES VOLUNTEERS

Washington, Texas, Dec. 27, 1835

To all Volunteers and Troops for the Aid of Texas in her conflict:

I now recommend to come by sea, and to land at Copano, Coxes point, or Matagorda. The time employed will be less than one fourth that which would be needed to pass by land.

To those who would prefer to pass by land, I would recommend to bring Baggage Wagons; and to bring NO HORSES, unless for teams, or for packing.

By the first of March the campaign will open.

Sam Houston[102]

Martin Perfecto de Cos to Santa Anna
RANCH SALINAS: Army of Operations: E. S. (Supreme Excellency)

The 15th, from Ranch Salinas, fifteen leagues from the City of Bejar, General D. Martin Perfecto de Cos tells me as follows:

E. S.: after 56 days of siege, without the slightest hope of supplies of force, ammunition and food, I have withdrawn from Bejar by means of an honorable agreement which I was forced to sign in order to save the honor of the arms which have been trusted to me.

The arrival of Colonel Ugartecha with replacements, at the time my few soldiers[103] were fighting for the sixth day,[104] inch by inch over the Plaza, did not help, as we could not utilize them due to the fact they lacked training; were tired from a twenty three league march to the city; and they only aggravated matters by increasing the consumption of provisions of which there was an absolute lack.

In such critical circumstances, there was no other measures than to advance and occupy the Alamo which, due to its small size and military position, was easier to hold. In doing so, I took with me the artillery, packs and the rest of the utensils I was able to transport. In spite of the fact that two companies of the Presidales de Rio Grande with their officers, plus those at Agua Verde and some pikemen, with their captain, had deserted me. This occurence had demoralized the other soldiers so much that

almost all of them followed the example. Only 120 of the
Permanent Battalion, Morelos, and some Presidial Dragoons
remained faithful. The rest of those who had not deserted were
wounded or dead.

I was in a very difficult situation. My retreat was cut off, the
troops were dead tired and without a single horse to bring
provisions to maintain their position. Under those circumstances
I decided to take advantage of the evening's inaction at the
moment to draw up some terms, copies of which will be
forwarded to Your Excellency as soon as I arrive at Laredo where
I am now heading. I am taking with me more than 500 men,
including the replacements with their cartridge boxes full of
ammunition and a four-pounder; the rest of the armaments
remain in the power of the insurgents. I have stopped only for
today in order to acquire the necessary carriages to transport my
wounded and to furnish my subordinates with the indispensable
supplies to undertake a ten day's march, according to my
calculations.

And so I write this to you so that you may pass it on to his
Supreme Excellency, the Provisional President. I further state:
although losing the post of Bejar, I have the satisfaction of having
saved most of the garrison when it was thought that worse
would result.

God and Liberty![105]

Monday, December 28, 1835
69 DAYS TO THE FALL

Sam Houston to James Power
WASHINGTON, TEXAS: Colonel Wyatt, with two attachments
of auxiliary volunteers, is on his way to the vicinity of Copano,
for the purpose of protecting that point, so essential to the
nearest posture of our affairs. I hope that you will afford him all
the possible intelligence, and render to him all the necessary aid.

. . . Colonel Wyatt will relieve Captain Allen, who will repair
to New Orleans, and return by the first of March. Say to our
friends that, by the rise of the grass, we will be on the march.[106]

Santa Anna to Most Excellent Senor Vicente Filisola,
Second in Command
HEADQUARTERS, SAN LUIS POTOSI: I wish to advise you that
I have already ordered General Martin Perfecto de Cos to march
with all the men he can muster under his command, to the city
of Monclova, where he will replace the things which he needs,
to which end your Excellency will give him all things in your
power. I am ordering General Rameriz y Sesma to march

immediately with his division, as I arranged beforehand, to the villa Guerrero. Your Excellency must see that both movements are executed without fail or delay.

You need not have any worry about Port Matamoros, since General Francisco Vidal Fernandez has already marched there with a sizeable division.

All companies of the garrison of Laredo may remain there under the command of their officers to observe any movement of the enemy . . . God and Liberty.[107]

Henry Smith to Sam Houston, et al

SAN FELIPE: In the Name of the People of Texas sovereign and Free — To Whom these presents shall come, Be it Known.

That I, Henry smith, Governor of Texas; by virtue of the authority vested in me as Governor aforesaid, do hereby commission John Forbes, Sam Houston and John Cameron Esqrs as Commissioners on the part of the government of Texas, in conformity with the Declaration of the chosen delegates of all Texas in convention assembled in the month of November last, setting forth the external bounds within which certain Indians therein named are to be settled. And in conformity with an Ordinance and Decree passed by the Legislative Council of Texas under date of the 22 inst. authorizing the appointment of the said Houston, Forbes and Cameron for the purpose aforesaid to treat with the Indian Tribes in conformity with the superior declaration of the Convention, and pursuant to and in conformity with the said Ordinance and Decree as above designated, and to be governed by the accompanying instructions.

All acts performed by the said Commissioners on the part, and in the name of the People of Texas, within the purview and by virtue of this authority, shall be valid and ultimately ratified by this government, in good faith, when finally ratified or sanctioned by this Government.

In testimony of which I Henry Smith, Governor as aforesaid have hereunto set by hand and affixed my private seal, (No seal of office being yet provided)

Done and signed at my office in the Town of
San Felipe, this 28th day of December, Eighteen
Hundred and thirty five
Henry Smith
Governor[108]

Wednesday, December 30, 1835
67 DAYS TO THE FALL

Horatio A. Alsbury to General Sam Houston
BEXAR: I take the privilege of addressing you this note flattering myself that you will be pleased to know our operations at this place, but I am actuated more by the uneasiness I feel about our Country from the declaration of Dimitts part of La Bahia, & the disposition of the troops remaining at this place to second that declaration. You will excuse me therefore when I beg of you to inform me by letter the disposition of the Council & Texas in General relative to a premature declaration of Independence or an immediate declaration to that purport.

I will be truly grateful to you to give me candidly your own ideas on the subject of Independence. The army will leave here this evening to the number of 300 men for Matamoros where from authentic information they will meet the enemy fifteen hundred in number also many friends one body to the number of 200 that are waiting for them on the route. General Cos & his troops will not march for Matamoros.

Many persons here nominated to appointments in the Army under your command, will not accept, should you have any appointment to make of Command of Cavalry in this place and I may be thought worthy of such appointments, I will endeavor not to disappoint Expectations.

Any thing in which I can serve you in this place you may command me & it will afford me much pleasure to serve you. You will excuse this scrawl as I have danced all night & am indeed exceedingly dull this morning.[109]

S. H. Steedman to Henry Smith
CHILLISQUAQUE NEAR MILTON NORTHUMBERLAND, COUNTY, PENNA: Dear Sir I address You a Note as an individual Selected from among My Comrades for the perpose of Knowing Whether You have appointed an agent in any of our Commercial Towns for the perpose of freighing the expences of those who have a desire to render you relief If You furnish the means through Any agency You May have in Philadelphia or New York, to bear the expences & Equipage there can be a company of Young men from thirty to fifty and Probably amounting to one hundred raised — of the old Susquhanna River — Whose fathers faught & bled in ther Countries Cause. Your immediate answer will Much oblidge with

Respect Yours &c —
S. H. Steedman[110]

Sam Houston to Col. J. W. Fannin, Artillery
HEADQUARTERS, WASHINGTON: If possible I wish you to report in person at headquarters as soon as possible after receipt of this order.

You can detail such officer of your command as you may deem proper to succeed you during your absence from the district which has been assigned to you.

Lieut. Colo Neill has been ordered in command of the Post of Bexar.

The detail being special and at the same time indispensable he will remain until further orders.

Sam Houston, Commander in Chief of the Army[111]

Sam Houston to Don Carlos Barrett
WASHINGTON: On tomorrow by light I wish Capt Poe to set out for San Felipe, & Velasco. He will be with you on the first! You are advised!!! I wish you could send Wallace to me? What has become of the Indian Treaty business? Let that be done and Houston will be at Copano instaner!

I rely upon you to aid me in serving the country. God speed you! Salute my friends — you know them — The moment that I return from the Treaty, I will be on the march. Write to me, and often.[112]

Jose Maria Tornel to His Excellency, the President, General-in-Chief of the Army of Operations, Antonio Lopez de Santa Anna, Benefactor of His Country.
MEXICO: Under this date I have notified all commandants-general and the principal governors and political chiefs of departments and territories as follows:

CIRCULAR FROM THE MEXICAN GOVERNMENT

The Supreme government has positive information that in the United States of the North public meetings are being held with the avowed purpose of arming expeditions against the Mexican nation, of helping those who have rebelled against this government, of encouraging civil war, and of bringing upon our territory, all those evils attended upon civil war. Some expeditions have already been organized in that republic — our former friend — such as the one conducted by the traitor Jose Antonio Mejia to Santa Anna [the town] in Tamaulipas and others on their way to the coast of Texas. All kinds of war supplies have been sent to the said coast; and, due to this censurable procedure, the rebellious colonists have been able to carry on a war against the nation that has showered so many favors upon them. The supreme government has the most positive assurance that these acts, censured by the wise laws of the United States of the North, have merited the consequent disapproval of that government with which we maintain the best understanding and an unalterable harmony. The speculators and adventurers have succeeded in evading the punishment that awaited them in that republic, but we hope that it will still overtake them.

His Excellency, the President ad interim, who cannot see with indifference these aggressions that attack the sovereignty of the Mexican nation, has seen proper to command that the following articles be observed with regard to them. **1st.** All foreigners who may land in any port of the republic or who enter it armed and for the purpose of attacking our territory, shall be treated and punished as pirates, since they are not subjects of any nation at war with the republic nor do they militate under any recognized flag. **2nd.** Foreigners who introduce arms and munitions by land or by sea at any point of the territory now in rebellion against the government of the nation for the purpose of placing such supplies in the hands of its enemies shall be treated and punished likewise. I have the honor of transmitting these instructions to you for their publication and observance.[113]

Thursday, December 31, 1835
66 DAYS TO THE FALL

Council Hall, San Felipe

Mr. Hanks made the following report: Your committee, to whom was referred the communication of F. W. Johnson containing a list of such articles as it stated to be requisite for the safety, defense and actual wants of the troops at San Antonio de Bexar, have had the same under consideration. The only disposition, which we could recommend is to request the Governor order the captains of companies to report muster rolls setting forth the number of men, for what time they enlisted, when they enlisted, whether in the regular army or auxiliary corps, and everything relative to their condition and situation.

Your committee further recommends that the governor order his proper officers to report the true condition of the ordnance department at Bexar; how many pieces of artillery; the ammunition and supplies of said department; the tools and instruments for making and repairing fortifications; and, everything connected therewith.

Your committee recommends this course because it is impossible for the General council to order supplies, or make provisions for a garrison or any military post, without knowing its situation and condition in every respect.[114]

James Butler Bonham to Sam Houston

SAN ANTONIO: I take this opportunity of recommending Wm S Blount[115] from No Carolina to your consideration. I recommend him, from acknowledged conduct in the attack on Bexar or San Antonio, to [be] a Capt. in the Cavalry of the regular Service — If however There should not be such an appointment, which you can dispose of on him — let me, if I may have any weight with you — recommend him to the Lieutenancy of Cavalry, the same to which I am informed I myself have been appointed. I leave immediately for La Bahia. I remain with great regards yours

James Butler Bonham[116]

Endnotes

1. Francis White Johnson, of Virginia, participated in the storming of Bexar in early December of 1835 when the Texans gained control of the city and the Alamo. He later commanded the ill-fated Matamoros Expedition. He was one of five survivors of the massacre at San Patricio on February 17, 1836. He became active in the Texas Veterans Association and an avid collector of Texanna material. At the time of his death in 1884, Johnson was in Mexico collecting material for a book on Texas history. Eugene C. Barker later edited the material in Johnson's collection and it was published as F. W. Johnson's *History of Texas and Texans* in five volumes.

2. Edward Burleson, of North Carolina, succeeded Stephen F. Austin as commander in the siege of Bexar and later commanded the 1st Regiment of volunteers at San Jacinto. After the war, Burleson served in the House of Representatives and as Vice President of the Republic of Texas. He later represented the state of Texas in the U. S. Senate. He died in 1851 and Burleson county is named in his honor.

3. Bejar is the Spanish spelling for Bexar.

4. Henry S. Foote, *Texas and the Texans*, in two volumes (Philadelphia: Thomas, Cowperthwait & Co., 1841), 2:168-173. This document is actually undated but is assumed to have been written on December 13, 1835 since it is mentioned in an Edward Burleson communication of December 14, 1835. It is presented here since the material is a natural starting point.

5. Sam Houston, former governor of Tennessee, came to Texas to check on the Indian situation for his good friend President Andrew Jackson. Houston ultimately relocated to Texas, became commander in chief of the army of the Republic, and led his troops to victory in the battle of San Jacinto, often called the sixteenth most important battle in the history of the world because it eventually opened the entire western part of the present United States to exploration. Houston also served as president of the Republic of Texas, U. S. Senator from the state of Texas, and finally governor of Texas. His political career ended in 1861 when he refused to take the oath of allegiance to the Confederacy, fearing the South could never win the war. He died in 1863 after having achieved the reputation as one of the most colorful and controversial characters in the entire history of Texas.

6. Don Carlos Barrett served in the General Council of Texas and as judge advocate of the army for a short time until he resigned due to a disagreement with Governor Henry Smith. Barrett returned to his native Vermont for a short time but soon came back to Texas to practice law until his death, near Brazoria, May 19, 1838. Sam Houston apparently developed a strong dislike for Barrett in later years. Writing to John Swisher on November 29, 1853, the General said: "D. C. Barrett was, in my opinion, the worst man that was ever in Texas. He was so capable, and all his capability was turned to harm. I attribute to his management the fall of the Alamo, and the destruction of Fannin and Ward." Houston left no

full explanation as to why he blamed Barrett for the fall of the Alamo and in view of Barrett's service in the government, it seems a harsh condemnation. For more on D. C. Barrett, see "Don Carlos Barrett," by Eugene C. Barker in the *Southwestern Historical Quarterly*, (Austin: Texas Historical Society), 20:139-145. (*Southwestern Historical Society* hereafter cited as *SWHQ*.)

7. E. C. Barker and Amelia Williams [editors], *The Writings of Sam Houston*, in seven volumes. (Austin: University of Texas Press, 1938), 1:314.

8. Moseley Baker was active in the Texas Revolution and was wounded in the San Jacinto battle. He later led campaigns against the Indians, had a successful business career, and ultimately became a Methodist minister and religious publisher. He died when a yellow fever epidemic swept Houston in 1848. For more information on Baker, see *Heroes of San Jacinto* by Dixon and Kemp.

9. The General Council was the governing body in Texas from late 1835 until the constitutional convention opened March 1, 1836.

10. William C. Binkley [editor], *Official Correspondence of the Texas Revolution, 1835-1836*, in two volumes (New York: D. Appleton-Century Co., 1938), 2:180-182.

11. Hicks entered the Texas army after the siege of Bexar and later served with Fannin.

12. The Badget brothers were residents of San Antonio and Jesse later represented the Alamo Garrison at the constitutional convention and signed the Texas Declaration of Independence.

13. Binkley, 1:182-183.

14. At the time the Mexicans surrendered, General Rameriz y Sesma was on the march to reinforce the Alamo. His orders were changed when Santa Anna learned of the fall of the Alamo.

15. H. P. M. Gammel [complier and arranger], *The Laws of Texas, 1822-1897*, in ten volumes (Austin: Gammel Book Company, 1898), 1:651-652. Entries marked "General Council" or "Council Hall" are the proceedings or actions of the General Council of Texas, the governing body during the early days of the revolution.

16. Ernest Wallace [editor], *Documents of Texas History* (Austin: Steck Company, 1960), 94. These resolutions were actually vetoed by Governor Henry Smith but were passed by a constitutional majority on December 13, 1835. The document is presented here since this is the day it was written.

17. Helen Hunnicutt [editor], "A Mexican View of the Texas War: Memoirs of a Veteran of the Two Battles of the Alamo" *The Library Chronicle*, Volume 4 (Austin: University of Texas, summer, 1951), 60. Jose Juan Sanchez Navarro served as Adjutant Inspector of the Departments of Nuevo Leon and Tampaulipas in Santa Anna's army.

18. Foote, 2:173-175. General Martin Perfecto de Cos was Santa Anna's brother-in-law. He was in charge of the Alamo when it was surrendered in December of 1835 and although he agreed to never again take up arms against Texas, he subsequently participated in the siege and attack on the Alamo. Cos was wounded and captured at the battle of San Jacinto.

19. Fanning is James Walker Fannin, Jr. In many cases Fannin signed his name with such a flowing style and with a rubic ending that it appeared he was adding a "g" to the end.
20. Obviously Baker and the rest of the people in San Felipe had no way to know that the Mexicans had already surrendered to the Texans in San Antonio and the army was not, at the moment, in such a clear and present danger as Baker perceived.
21. Apparently Baker was not in a position to make nominations for each district since several were left blank as indicated. The records of the General Council show that one day before Baker wrote his letter, agents had been appointed for every district named by Baker. With the exception of San Felipe, where Baker himself was nominated, all the others were in agreement with Baker's proposal.
22. Binkley, 1:183-184.
23. Gammel, 1:651-652.
24. Ibid, 1:654.
25. Hunnicutt, 59. It appears Navarro is working on the inventory of captured goods. (See December 13, 1835.)
26. Stephen F. Austin was the agent sent to Mexico and imprisoned for more than a year.
27. The Mexican Congress, in April of 1835, passed a law that reduced state militia organizations to an amount equal to one armed man for every five hundred inhabitants.
28. When the citizens of the Mexican state rebelled against Santa Anna's rule, the General attacked the state and won a resounding victory that was associated with many cruelties and mass assassinations. Following the fighting, Santa Anna allowed his troops to pillage and plunder the area.
29. Houston obviously wrote this letter not knowing San Antonio had already been taken by the Texas forces.
30. Barker and Williams, 4:315-319.
31. The *Telegraph, and Texas Register,* edited by Gail Borden, Jr. and Joseph Baker, was one of the earliest newspapers in Texas. Printed weekly, originally in San Felipe de Austin, Texas, the paper provided a vital link between the struggling government and the people. Selected articles from the publication are presented throughout this collection of documents to illustrate the meager contribution of the press and to show the flavor of the news that was available to the Texans of 1835-1836. The material from the Telegraph was taken from actual copies of the publication in the Archives of the Texas State Library.
32. Apparently James Tylee did not have long to worry about the trouble with his estranged wife. Although not on every list of Alamo victims, a James Tylee of New York is on the Daughters of the Republic of Texas roll of Alamo victims. We have no record as to what might have happened to Matilda.
33. Micajah Autry was a Tennessee volunteer who died in the Alamo.
34. Natchitoches, Louisiana was a trading post on the Red River that served as a gateway to Texas for explorers, colonists, and volunteers in the army.

35. Autry met George C. Childress, the man who is credited with writing the Texas Declaration of Independence, while on his way to Texas. In a letter on December 7, 1835, Autry reported, "Childress thinks the fighting will be over before we get there, and speaks cheeringly of the prospects." Childress was wrong.
36. *SWHQ,* 14:318-319.
37. Gammel, 1:658-659. Henry Smith, of Kentucky, served as governor of the province of Texas until deposed in a squabble with the General Council. Following the war, Smith served in the House and Senate of the Republic before retiring to private life. He migrated to California in 1849 to search for gold and died in a mining camp in 1851.
38. *Telegraph, and Texas Register,* January 2, 1836.
39. See Johnson's statement of December 13.
40. Foote, 2:165-168.
41. From the actual document on file in the Daughters of the Republic of Texas Library at the Alamo. James C. Neill apparently did not stay discharged long. He served in the artillery at the siege of Bexar and was promoted to lieutenant colonel and given command of the Alamo garrison. He left that command on February 11, 1836 to attend to his family and try to secure funds for the post. He was attempting to lead volunteers back to Bexar at the time of the fall of the Alamo. Neill subsequently served with Sam Houston and was in charge of the Twin Sister Cannons at San Jacinto. He was wounded on April 20 and missed the battle of April 21. Neill later led campaigns against the Indians and negotiated treaties with his red brothers. He died in his home in 1845.
42. Richard G. Santos, *Santa Anna's Campaign Against Texas* (Waco: Texian Press, 1968), 13-14. Antonio Lopez de Santa Anna was president of Mexico and commander in chief of the army of invasion against Texas. He was captured after his forces were defeated at San Jacinto and was subsequently paroled to Mexico. He died in obscurity in Mexico City in 1876.

    Don Vincente Filisola, an Italian by birth, served as Santa Anna's second in command during the Texas campaign and was in charge of the evacuation of Mexican troops after San Jacinto. He was later tried for the loss of the war in Texas but exonerated himself. He died in a cholera epidemic in 1850.
43. Gammel, 1:666-667. Stephen F. Austin is often called the Father of Texas because he continued colonization plans started by his father. Austin was a general in the revolutionary army and subsequently negotiated loans from Americans sympathetic to the Texas cause. He died, while serving as Secretary of State for the Republic of Texas, on December 27, 1836.
44. Ibid, 1:664-665.
45. Binkley, 1:196-197. Thomas Jefferson Rusk was active in the revolution and served as Houston's secretary of war. He signed the Texas Declaration of Independence and served on the Republic of Texas Supreme Court. He and Sam Houston were the first U. S. Senators from the state of Texas. After a period of despondency over the loss of his wife, Rusk took his own life in 1857.
46. Your Excellency.

47. Binkley, 1:197. Jose Antonio Mexia was a Federalist Mexican opposed to Santa Anna's dictatorship. As a member of the Mexican Senate of 1834, he led an uprising against Santa Anna which failed and Mexia was exiled to New Orleans. He later led an unsuccessful expedition against Matamoros, Mexico and although he played a small role in the Texas war, he did not favor independence and thus was not trusted. He died in front of a Mexican firing squad in 1839.

48. Barker and Williams, 4:319-322.

49. This drove of horses may have been captured by William Barret Travis. See Binkley or Jenkins for a copy of Travis' report, of November 16, 1835, to Stephen F. Austin about capturing a cavalcade of Mexican horses.

50. Binkley, 1:202. Eli Mercer was an early colonist and supporter of Gail Borden and the *Telegraph, and Texas Register* newspaper. He helped evacuate the paper's presses when the Alamo fell and the "Runaway Scrape" began. He participated in the battle of San Jacinto and lived a long life in Texas, being active in the Baptist church and a charter trustee of Baylor University. He died in Egypt, Texas in 1872.

Mr. Menifee was a member of the Council and there is no record of any action on this proposal.

51. Wyatt Hanks, Chairman of Committee of Military Affairs of the Council.

52. Gammel, 1:670-671.

53. Barker and Williams, 4:321-322.

54. Sam Houston Papers, University of Texas Library, Austin.

55. The agents were Stephen F. Austin, Branch T. Archer, and William H. Wharton, each of whom is described later.

56. Barker and Williams, 3:322. James Bowie, the legendary knife fighter who was born in Tennessee and lived most of his life in Louisiana, came to Texas in 1828 and led a wheeler dealer's life. He was co-commander with William B. Travis in the Alamo Garrison until ill health forced him to relinquish any thoughts of command. He died, fighting to the end, on his cot in a small room in the Alamo.

James Bowie did not receive this order until the first part of January and by that time the General Council had already selected F. W. Johnson to lead the expedition.

57. Binkley, 213-214.

58. Charles A. Gulick Jr. [editor], *The Papers of Mirabeau Buonaparte Lamar*, 3 volumes (Austin: Texas State Library), 3:264. William B. Travis, of South Carolina, was an early activist in the cause of Texas independence. He inspired the ire of the Mexican government with a raid on the customs house in Anahuac, Texas in 1834. He was ordered to the Alamo with 30 men in early February 1836. He took over as acting commander when James C. Neill left the Alamo on February 11, 1836.

James W. Robinson was lieutenant governor until the General Council removed Henry Smith and Robinson became acting governor. After the fall of the Alamo, he enlisted in the Army and fought at San Jacinto. He continued active in various affairs of Texas until migrating to California in 1850.

59. Binkley, 2:212. Little is known of Samuel Stivers except that he served as a surgeon during, and for a short time after, the siege of Bexar. He apparently left the Alamo before the Mexicans arrived and was not heard of again.

Amos Pollard was chief surgeon for the Alamo Garrison and he died when the mission was overrun on March 6, 1836. Pollard submitted another list on December 27. The revised list included John West as severely wounded and James Bell as slightly wounded. John Cook and George Alexander originally listed as mortal are shown as having died on the revised list. John Peacock also died of his wounds. Stivers never again appears in the affairs of Texas but Amos Pollard returned to Bejar and served as surgeon in the Alamo.

60. See December 12, 1835.

61. Barker and Williams, 4:322. U. S. President Andrew Jackson and Sam Houston were friends. It was Jackson who first sent Houston to Texas to check on the territory and the Indian conditions.

62. Binkley, 1:220-221.

63. Ibid, 1:225-226. Mathew Caldwell, of Kentucky, was a signer of the Texas Declaration of Independence and served as a scout during the war. He was later active in the Indian affairs and was a part of the Santa Fe Expedition. He died in 1842.

64. Archives, Texas State Library.

65. D. C. Barrett Papers, University of Texas Library, Austin. Albert Martin, of Tennessee, was in the Alamo when the Mexicans arrived. He was sent out as a messenger, by William B. Travis, on February 24. He later returned with a small group of men from Gonzales, all of whom perished when the fortress was taken.

66. Binkley, 1:227. Benjamin Goodrich, of Tennessee, came to Texas in 1834. Benjamin was in Washington during the convention and anxiously awaited news of the fate of his brother, John, who was in the Alamo.

67. Gammel, 1:684.

68. Santos, 17-18. General Jose Urrea was the Mexican General who led his force against the Texans at San Patricio, Agua Dulce, and Goliad. He accepted the surrender of Col. Fannin and more than 400 on March 19. Urrea was on his way to join Santa Anna when the dictator was defeated at San Jacinto and Urrea retreated to Mexico.

69. D. W. C. Baker, *A Texas Scrap-Book* (New York: A. S. Barnes & Company, 1875).

This Declaration of Independence, the first in the Texas revolution, was signed by 91 men in Goliad. However, since the governing council of the province still favored restoration of the Mexican constitution of 1824 at the time this declaration was drafted, the document was suppressed. For a list of the names of the signers, see Baker, 64-65.

70. Green B. Jameson was the engineer for the Alamo garrison.

71. A. J. Houston Papers.

72. Ibid.

73. Gammel, 1:685.

74. Stephen F. Austin, *The Austin Papers,* complied and edited by Eugene C. Barker, volume 1 and 2 (Washington: Government Printing Office, 1924 and 1928), volume 3 (Austin: University of Texas Press, 1927), 3:289-290. Austin's efforts to convince the men against an expedition on Matamoros was too little too late. Johnson was already preparing for the march and a week after this letter was written, the Alamo had been stripped, and the expedition was underway. Also on this date, Austin wrote a similar letter to the Provisional Government. It was read in the Council Hall and ordered filed on January 2, three days after the Matamoros expedition departed San Antonio.

75. Gammel, 1:687 & 1001.

76. Erastus "Deaf" Smith, the famous Texas spy who was wounded during the siege of Bexar.

77. Gammel, 1:690-691.

78. Ibid, 1:692.

79. Stephen F. Austin Papers, University of Texas Library, Austin.

80. Filisola, *Correspondence of Santa Anna,* MA Thesis, University of Texas, 21-22. Ricardo Dromundo was Purveyor of the Mexican Army of Operations in Texas.

81. Archives, Texas State Library. Edward Hall was a partner of William Bryan in New Orleans and together they helped supply many needs of the Texas war effort.

82. A. J. Houston Papers. Robert Bruce Irvine was a captain in the infantry and one of the very few who voted against the Texans laying siege to Bexar. He was subsequently ordered by Houston to recruit volunteers for the army.

83. The actual letter from Hanks to Burleson, dated December 16, 1835, could not be located. However, it can be assumed that Hanks was reacting to the opinion of someone, probably Sam Houston, that the volunteers ought to be made part of the regular army, something the men were sorely opposed to. See Wyatt Hank's report to the council of December 16 and Sam Houston's letter of December 17.

84. See Volunteers at Bexar to Genl. F. W. Johnson dated December 25.

85. Binkley, 1:235-236. Wyatt Hanks, of Arkansas Territory, was an early Texas settler. During the war he was a quartermaster for a volunteer group that arrived after the battle of San Jacinto. Following the war, Hanks was involved in one of the earliest and bloodiest Texas feuds.

    J. D. Clements was a member of the General Council, representing Gonzales, and helped supply the army during the war.

86. Binkley, 1:234. Richardson Royster Royall was a member of the General Council and, after the war, organized a ranger company to round up stray beef for the army.

87. Ibid, 1:237.

88. Ibid, 1:239-240.

89. The letter from Robinson to Burleson suggesting the Matamoros expedition cannot be located, thus we have no clue as to what he apologized for.
90. Gulick, 272-273.
91. *SWHQ*, 5:313-315.
92. From a typescript of the original in the Daughters of the Republic of Texas Library at the Alamo. Daniel Cloud was a twenty-year-old volunteer from Kentucky who died in the Alamo.
93. An early Texas newspaper printed and distributed in Nacogdoches, Texas.
94. A. J. Houston Papers.
95. Ibid.
96. Captain Peyton S. Wyatt, of Huntsville, Alabama was sent to relieve Captain Phillip Dimmit, at Goliad, in mid-January. Wyatt and his men remained in Goliad under command of Fannin until that force was captured by the Mexicans. Wyatt, however, escaped the general massacre because he was away on leave at the time of the capture.
97. Amon B. King, not Aaron as is generally thought, was also with Fannin at Goliad and he died in the massacre. See *SWHQ*, 26:147-150 for information on King.
98. The order to lead an expedition against Matamoros, Mexico.
99. Barker and Williams, 3:325.
100. Peter James Bailey, of Kentucky, accompanied Daniel Cloud to Texas and the Alamo and became one of the victims of the fall.
101. From a typescript of the original letter in the Daughters of the Republic of Texas Library.
102. *Arkansas Gazette* (Little Rock), February 20, 1836.
103. As has been seen in the letters of Edward Burleson of December 14, Cos had perhaps 1,500 men against perhaps 300 or 400 Texans.
104. The storming of the Texans on San Antonio began on December 5, 1835. On December 9 the Mexicans offered to surrender and the offer was accepted the following day. Thus the battle did not last anywhere near six days.
105. Eugene C. Barker, Texas History Center, University of Texas, Austin.
106. Henderson Yoakum, *History of Texas From Its First Settlement in 1685 to Its Annexation to the United States in 1846*, 2 volumes (New York: Redfield, 1856), 2:455. James Power was a member of the Constitutional Convention and a signer of the Declaration of Independence. He was also instrumental in getting Sam Houston seated at the convention.
    There were several Captain Allens in the Texas army of the period. The one referred to here is thought to be John M. Allen of Kentucky. He was assigned several positions in the army including guarding the supplies at Copano, acting as agent for the Texas navy, and in recruiting volunteers after San Jacinto. After retiring from the army he served as mayor of Galveston and later as U. S. Marshall, a position he held until his death in 1847.

The "rise of grass" was expected to be the middle of March. By that time, the Alamo had fallen, Gonzales had been burned, the "Runaway Scrape" was underway, and Sam Houston was in retreat.

107. Filisola, 21-22.
108. Archives, Texas State Library, Austin.
109. A. J. Houston Papers. Horace (Horatio) Alsbury, of Kentucky, was one of Stephen Austin's original 300 colonists. He participated in the storming of Bexar and later fought at San Jacinto. He was killed during the Mexican War in 1847. His wife, Juana Navarro Alsbury, a native Mexican, is thought to have been in the Alamo during most of the siege but escaped a few days before the fall and reported conditions of the mission to Santa Anna.
110. Archives, Texas State Library, Austin.
111. Barker and Williams, 4:16. James Walker Fannin, thought to be the only officer and perhaps the only man in the Texas war with West Point experience. Fannin, a one time slave dealer, was active in the military affairs of Texas. Although he often doubted his own ability to command, Fannin was selected to lead the Matamoros expedition. When that operation failed, he retired to Goliad and was at that mission with more than 400 men when the Mexicans arrived in San Antonio, 95 miles away. He failed to go to the aid of the Alamo, subsequently surrendered to Mexican forces, and he, along with most of his force, was massacred on Palm Sunday, 1836.

The letter was endorsed: "Gen'l Houston to Fannin left in my hands by Fannin." Colonel A. J. Houston wrote below the endorsement, "The above is in the handwriting of Capt. Geo. W. Poe — A. General who delivered this order to Col. Fannin by whom it was ignored."
112. Ibid, 3:327.
113. Carlos E. Castaneda, *The Mexican Side of the Revolution* (Dallas: P. L. Turner, 1928), 55-56. Tornel was the Minister of War and Marine for Santa Anna.
114. Gammel 1:719-720.
115. Nothing is known of Wm S. Blount. He is not thought to have died in the Alamo with Bonham, he is not listed among the casualties in Fannin's command, and he did not serve with Houston in the San Jacinto Army. There is the bare possibility that the Wm S. Blount mentioned by Bonham was actually Stephen William Blount who was active in the Texas revolution and even signed the Declaration of Independence. However, S. W. Blount was from Georgia and settled in San Augustine when he came to Texas in 1835. It seems doubtful that Bonham would have gotten the name and place and origin wrong on a man he was recommending to Houston.
116. From a typescript in the Daughters of the Republic of Texas Library at the Alamo. James Bonham, a young lawyer from North Carolina, became one of the truly romantic heroes of the Alamo when he was sent out as a messenger twice and returned both times even though it meant certain death. On December 1, 1835, Bonham wrote Sam Houston volunteering his services to the army

without pay or other considerations. After writing this letter, James apparently did go to La Bahia (Goliad) because he was there when Houston arrived on January 16. Bonham was subsequently ordered to return to Bexar with James Bowie. The popular notion that Bonham and Travis were childhood friends in North Carolina is probably based on family legend since no appreciable evidence exists to suggest the two men knew each other before meeting in Texas.

CHAPTER THREE

The Collapse of the Texas Government

January 1 through January 31, 1836

By January 1836, the tide of opinion in Texas was beginning to turn in favor of independence. Stephen F. Austin, in the United States to borrow money for the cause, found Americans overwhelmingly in favor of Texas independence. Austin reversed himself and came out not only in favor of independence but suggesting the boundaries of Texas need not be limited. Sam Houston also got in line with Austin and Governor Smith favoring complete independence, but members of the council still clung to foolish notions of reestablishing the Mexican constitution.

Lt. Colonel James C. Neill, commander of the post at San Antonio, was in a tough spot at a tough time. Johnson and Grant had looted the Alamo garrison to outfit the ill-conceived Matamoros expedition, so Neill embarked on a letter-writing campaign to try and secure much needed men, money, and munitions. He did not have much success.

Sam Houston tried to help by dispatching James Bowie and a small detachment of men to Bexar and requesting others try to secure volunteers and march to the Alamo. The governor also tried to help by ordering William B. Travis and a small detachment of men to march toward the frontier at Bexar. Although disgruntled at the prospect of commanding such a small group, Travis nevertheless marched as ordered.

January wore on and Neill's position became precarious as more and more reports were received that Santa Anna was planning an invasion. It was widely believed that if the Mexican leader did launch an invasion, his first strike would be against

San Antonio and the Alamo. If that post were to fall, it was widely believed, all of Texas would be open to a quick defeat. Despite such sentiment Neill found it impossible to get any help.

One of Neill's urgent letters for assistance actually did more harm than good when it contributed directly to the end of the shaky government in Texas. When Governor Smith received the letter detailing the appalling conditions in the Alamo, he used it as a basis to belittle the General Council and demand the group immediately disband. The council responded by impeaching the governor but he refused to relinquish power. Many of the council delegates left in disgust and an advisory council was appointed to act for the council until a constitutional convention could convene on March 1, 1836. Lt. Governor James Robinson was tapped to try and continue the affairs of the executive branch but he met with little success. For all practical purposes, the government of Texas ceased to function by mid-January and the men of the Alamo were left in the breach of history, needing so much and with no one left to help them.

The air was ripe with rumors of political intrigue. The men in the Alamo supported the governor and offered to use armed force to sustain him in his struggle for power. The council became fearful that Houston was about to march against the council with troops so they relieved him of his position as commander in chief of the army. By the end of January, Houston had received a furlough and left to negotiate a treaty with the Indians.

While the Texans were squabbling over internal difficulties, Santa Anna was busy outfitting an army of 6,000 men. Before the month was over, he was on the march toward the Rio Grande and his sights were set on the Alamo. Many Texans picked up intelligence from spies that foretold of the rapid advance of the enemy but, for the most part, such information was ignored. Popular opinion, supported by such men as Sam Houston and William B. Travis, was that Santa Anna would not attempt any invasion until the grass was up in the spring. They were wrong.

Friday, January 1, 1836
65 DAYS TO THE FALL

Council Hall, San Felipe

Mr. Barret, from the committee on state and judiciary, made the following report accompanied with an ordinance:

Your committee to whom was referred the letter of the committee of safety at Beaumont, having duly considered its contents, and strongly impressed with the necessity of adopting some measures as recommended in said letter to prevent the importation or emigration of free negroes or mulattoes into Texas; being sensible from the experiences of other countries, that the residence of such free negroes and mulattoes among us, would prove an evil difficult to be remedied should it once be tolerated. To the slave-holder nothing could be of deeper interest than the timely adoption of some measure that will be effectually preventive of a course so much to be dreaded in a country, whose soil, from the nature of its productions must be cultivated by slave labor. The infusion of dissatisfaction, and disobedience into the brain of the honest and contented slave, by vagabond free negroes, who denied the society of whites, from necessity or choice, associate with persons of their own color cannot be too promptly and strongly guarded against.

Your committee would therefore recommend the adoption of the following ordinance and decree to be entitled.

An ordinance and decree to prevent the importation and emigration of free negroes and mulattoes into Texas.

Be it ordained and decreed, and is hereby ordained and decreed by the Provisional Government of Texas, that from and after passage of this ordinance and decree, it shall not be lawful for any free negro or mulatto to come within the limits of Texas, and if any free negro or mulatto, shall be found within the limits of Texas as aforesaid, and it shall appear, that he or she was within said limits prior to the passage of this ordinance and decree, it shall and may be lawful for any citizen of Texas, to apprehend said free negro or mulatto, and take him or her before the judge or alcalde of the municipality in which he or she may be so apprehended, and upon satisfactory evidence being adduced, that such free negro or mulatto emigrated into Texas, contrary to the provisions of this ordinance and decree, it shall be the duty of the judge or alcalde, before whom such free negro or mulatto may be brought, to expose him or her to sale at public auction, to the highest bidder, and the proceeds of such sale, after paying one third thereof to the apprehender and defraying the costs and charges, attending the conviction and sale of such free negro or mulatto shall be paid into the state treasury. And it is hereby declared, and made the duty of each judge and alcalde, and of each and every sheriff and other officer of the place, within each and every municipality throughout Texas, so to apprehend and cause to be apprehended all and every such free negro or free negroes, mulatto or mulattoes, offending against the provisions of this ordinance and decree, and that such officer or officers, who shall so apprehend such free negro or free negroes, mulatto or mulattoes, shall be entitled to the same compensation, that is by this ordinance and decree allowed to citizens, who may by such apprehension as aforesaid render the like service.

Be if further ordained and decreed, &c.: That it shall not be lawful for any master or owner of any ship or vessel, nor for any other person or persons whatever, from and after the passage of this ordinance to import, bring or induce, or aid in importing, bringing or inducing, any free negro or mulatto, within the limits of Texas, directly or indirectly, and if any master or owner of any ship or vessel, or any other person, or persons, whatever shall import, bring or otherwise induce, or aid or abet in importing, bringing or otherwise inducing, any free negro or mulatto into Texas as aforesaid, he or she so offending shall be deemed guilty of a misdemeanor at common law, and upon conviction thereof, in any court of record within Texas, shall be fined in the sum of five thousand dollars, and imprisoned, until the same together with the costs and charges of the prosecution shall be paid.[1]

Saturday, January 2, 1836
64 DAYS TO THE FALL

Telegraph, and Texas Register

LAW NOTICE

THE SUBSCRIBER will open a Law Office in Brazoria to receive such business as he may be favored with in his profession. He has with him licenses to practice law in South Carolina and Alabama of the United States of the North.   — James B. Bonham

DURING my absence, I have appointed Gail Borden, Jr. my special agent to collect any debts due me, and receipt for same.[2]   S. F. Austin

I HAVE appointed my brother-in-law, James F. Perry, my sole general agent to attend to all my business during my absence from Texas.   — S. F. Austin

Sam Houston to D. C. Barrett

WASHINGTON: To day I wrote to you by friend Major Hockley,[3] and recommended him to your kind notice — I have a moments leisure to write, and say that tho' one week has elapsed since my arrival here, I have not had one word of news from San Felipe. I hope Mr. Wallace[4] is on his way and will bring me news of importance — at least a letter from you on matters and things, in general. I am myself as usual pressed with business; and thank God my Christmas times are over, and I am most miserably cool & sober — so you can say to all my friends. In stead of Egg-nog; I eat roasted Eggs in my office. There was no fuss here, on yesterday, and I trust you had none in San Felipe, for if so our country, will be ruined — the world is now looking on us, and by our fruits, we shall be judged. Union & harmony will make us every thing that we could wish to be. Dissention will destroy Texas. I know well your feeling and your wishes — they are such as every Patriot will feel. God speed you!!

I learn from Judge Hanks[5] that you are about to make him a sutler! I have recommended him for one — there ought to be one to each Post where troops will be stationed.

Wou'd you have thought that the judge wou'd ask my recommendation? The age of wonders is not passed — I would like to know what is going on, but I know you will guard my rights.

So soon as I can proceed, and hold a Treaty with the Indians, I intend to detail a competent officer to command the Recruiting station, while I proceed to the frontier; and organize the army for a prompt movement in the spring.[6]

Samuel Williams to D. C. Barrett

LA VACA RIVER: . . . on my arrival here I learnt that the independent flag had been raised at Goliad & Bexar, under those circumstances the time that we are loosing is very precious as in my opinion 6 weeks will not elapse until Bexar & Goliad is besieged by the enemy — they will wait on the rio grande a short time to concentrate, and entrap any detachment, that may be sent to Matamoros and as soon as they learn that we are not coming to M, they march against Bexar & Goliad and perhaps at the same time send in troops by sea to excite the negroes & take possession of our parts — I learned that Bexar is in a bad situation to stand a siege or even to repel an enemy, as they are in want of provisions & more particularly ammunition — & Cannon balls, plenty of cannon has been taken but we want, grape, cannister, chain, double headed, & bar shot, and if I can sell what goods I have & get to Bexar in time there is materials there plenty to cast & make shot & shells sufficient for one ton of powder — I now have in my charge 13 kegs of rifle powder, some lead & that I am now trying to haul to Camp immediately

— The citizens of this part of the country have become individually responsible for two Barrels of Flour to be sent to B. and there is 70 more in the hands of Peter Carr — he wishes to dispose of it but will not take govt. security, but he at the same time introduced with a month 4 or 5000 worth of goods and has not paid any duty on them — Capt Hatch Mr. Clare — & Dr. Wells have given their individual notes payable in 30 days to Mr C, for the 10 Barrels of flour for the Army — and I now am trying to raise by subscription a sufficient amt. to buy the balance 70 Barrels — 700$ — if it is done, & any will follow me the flour shall be pressed for our starving Countrymen in Bexar

So soon as I can dispose of the goods I will remit to you a portion of the proceeds & the balance for Texas — please have me stationed at Bexar as that will be first attacked & the hardest fighting there — All the powder that was in Matagorda is now in my hands — & the merchants of this have already sent what they had to Camp by Mr. Moore, 200 lbs and San Antonio is in want of every thing that an army can want

I am Dr. Sr. your obd sevt and sincere Frend

Saml. Williams[7]

Sunday, January 3, 1836
63 DAYS TO THE FALL

F. W. Johnson to the General Council of Texas
SAN FELIPE de AUSTIN: I beg leave to represent to your honorable body that I have under authority of an official letter addressed to my predecessor Genl Burleson by the committee on Military Affairs, ordered an expedition against Matamoros of Five Hundred and thirty men Volunteers of Texas and from the United states — by whom I have been appointed to the command — The volunteers left Bexar on the 30th of December last for La Bahia and from thence to the destined point.

I have left in the garrison at Bexar 100 men under command of Lt. colonel Neill. This force I consider to be barely sufficient to hold the post and it will require at least fifty additional troops to place it in a strong defensive position. I have ordered all the guns from the town into the Alamo and the fortifications in the town to be destroyed.

I herewith present you the names of the officers to be commissioned for the exposition if it be consistent with the views of your honorable body viz —

Capt. B. L. Laurence — 1st Lieutenant David Thomas 2nd Lieutenant John Lowry[8]

Capt. Thos K. Pearson 1st Lieut Edwd. J. Johnson 2nd Lieutenant Henry Coney

Capt. D. N. Burke 1st Lieutenant J. B. McManing 2nd Lieutenant John Lowry[9]

Capt. Wm G. Cooke 1st Lieutenant C. B. Bannister 2nd Lieutenant John Hall

Capt. T. Lewellyn 1st & 2nd Lieutenants Bland Commissions

Capt. H. R. A. Wigginton, Blank Commissions for 1st & 2nd Lieutenants

The foregoing are the names who volunteered for Matamoros, in addition to which you will be pleased to forward the Commissions of those heretofore forwarded to the Governor.

In regard to the expedition I have no hesitation in saying that it is practical and that not one moment should be lost as the enemy are concentrating their force at many points in the interior with a view to suppress the liberals of the interior and also for the purpose of attacking Texas. Therefore I submit the foregoing to your consideration and ask your authority for making the expedition against Matamoros.

F. W. Johnson

N. B. Please issue Commissions to James Grant as colonel and N. R. Brister as adjutant —[10]

Council Hall, San Felipe

The President [of the Council] submitted a communication from F. W. Johnson for himself and other volunteers, for authority to proceed to Matamoros, which was read and referred to the committee on military affairs.

Mr. Hanks, from the committee on military affairs, reported the following: The communication of General F. W. Johnson respecting an expedition against Matamoros has had the same under consideration and beg to report that it is an expedition of the utmost importance at this time. It will give employment to the volunteers, until a regular army can be raised and organized.

And your committee take great pleasure in recommending Johnson to take the command of all the troops. Delay at this time on our part, would be dangerous. For if the volunteers on their march for Matamoros were defeated, the consequences resulting from it might prove fatal for Texas. But everyone must foresee the benefit that would result from occupying and keeping possession of that important and commercial depot. It would not only deprive our enemies of the immense revenue at that place, but aid us greatly in supporting our army.[11]

D. C. Barrett to Captain E. Hall[12]

SAN FELIPE: Yours of the ninth ult. has been received and read in Council. We rejoice that the proceedings of our Convention have been so well received by the friends of Texas in New Orleans. We hope the doings of the Council may prove equally satisfactory to those, whose good opinions and confidence, it is our wish and interest to secure. If patriotism and honest intentions can effect this object, we shall be gratified.

The fruits of our victory over the enemy and the capitulation of Bexar, have given us possession of more than thirty pieces of artillery of various calibre, and in a great measure superceded the necessity of the purchases to have been made by you in behalf of the government. But our work is by no means finished. The enemy is endeavoring to concentrate and bring upon us a large force which must be met and vanquished as soon as possible after he takes the field: munitions of war and supplies of provisions to be landed at or near the port of Copano as circumstances will admit, is all important to our present and contemplated future operations. Whatever can be done by you, in this way, and sending volunteers to the same destination, will aid your adopted country in the struggle for freedom and constitutional rights. A cordon of posts are being established from Bexar by Goliad to San Patricio on the Rio Nueces, and Government agents will be stationed at each post to receive and provide for volunteers, and take charge of all public stores. Indeed, we hope to extend the line to Matamoros at no very distant time.

The volunteers on board the Santiago have arrived, and will, we trust, be profitably and honorably, employed in the glorious cause. The gratitude of the country, and we hope more substantial testimonies will be secured to our brave and magnanimous brethren of the north. The struggle once over, and peace restored to the fair lands of Texas; what that the fondest wishes of the philanthropist could extend to man on earth, may not be expected here? The rich reward of our labors and our dangers is ever in view, and immediate possession but awaits the successful termination of the present struggle.

We hope you have met the government commissioners ere this and that success will attend all your efforts in favor of oppressed Texas. We shall expect to hear from you as often as your conveniences will permit, as matters of interest to our cause shall transpire.

Very respectfully, yours,

D. C. Barrett,
Chairman, of committee of State and Judiciary[13]

John T. Lamar to T. Ward
VELASCO: The Georgia Volunteers, composed of three Companies . . . are organized and commanded by Wm. Ward as Major — and the battalion is called the Georgia Battalion. The Governor

has ordered them to occupy Copano, a place on the Mexican frontier about 200 miles to the south of this place —

The fall of San Antonio has for the present put a stop to the war — many think it has terminated, that after the single defeat of Genl Cos that the Mexican Dictator will not again dare to invade the country. Others are of the opinion that Santa Anna will make another desperate effort in the spring to subjugate Texas to centralism, at the head of a powerful army; powerful at least in numbers — and I am inclined to the latter opinion but come as he may, he will meet a warm reception and the result will no doubt be favorable to the Texas Arms — 5,000 Americans are fully competent to fight and defeat 20,000 Mexicans — numerical force avails nothing against gallant freemen contending for their rights, their homes and their fire sides, aided by the volunteers from the United States. . . .

Let me advise you to come on with all the money you can command & invest in Texas lands — no such speculations were ever offered on this continent, and Capitalists who will purchase now will make overwhelming fortunes. The lands are the richest on the face of the globe and the title indisputable, no one can loose who will embark on speculation. Don't think I exaggerate when I tell you that Texas is capable with proper cultivation to produce as much cotton as is made in all the United States[14] — and that it is destined to do so at some period not very remote. The greatest speculations are generally made from small investments, if you wait until all difficulties are settled, until a free government is formed, & the people contented & prosperous, the value of lands will be enhanced ten times their present value — & perhaps cease to be a good speculation.[15]

Tuesday, January 5, 1836
61 DAYS TO THE FALL

Council Hall, San Felipe

On motion of Mr. Barrett, a select committee of two was appointed, to wait on Messrs. Fannin and Johnson, with the resolutions respecting an expedition to Matamoros, and learn their views respecting same. Messrs. Clements and Barrett were appointed on that committee.

The President submitted a letter from General Houston, recommending Wyatt Hanks for the appointment of sutler in the Texas army, which was read and referred to the committee on the state and judiciary.

Mr. Royall presented the following resolution, which was read and adopted.

Resolved, that the commandant of the post of Bexar be, and

he is hereby authorized to dispose of such public property as is
not needed for the support of the post on the best terms
possible, and apply the proceeds of the same for the benefit of
the post.

The ordinance and decree to prevent the importation and
emigration of free negroes and mulattoes, was taken up and read
a second time; the rule of the House was suspended and the
ordinance read a third time, when the question was taken on its
final passage, and decided in the affirmative.

Mr. Clements, from the select committee to wait on Messrs.
Fannin and Johnson, reported, that they had discharged that
duty, and that the gentlemen named fully concurred with the
resolutions.16

Wednesday, January 6, 1836
60 DAYS TO THE FALL

James C. Neill to the Governor and Council
at San Felipe de Austin

Sirs: Having informed officially the Commander in chief of the
Federal Army of Texas at Washington, the condition and situation
of my command, I deem it my infinite duty to make a corresponding representation to you, altho' so far as regards the social
intercourse desired between the Civil Authorities, the citizens,
and our Army, every thing has been harmonized Since the
Command has devolved upon me, to my Complete satisfaction,
and far beyond my most sanguine expectations.

You have doubtless heard from various Sources of the
arbitrary rule of the aids de Camp of Genl. E. Burleston, F. W.
Johnson, and James Grant the Town was surrendered on the 9th
Decr. and so long as they remained in command there was not a
move made by them to restore or organize harmony, or to
reestablish the civil functions of Govt. which continued up to the
30th ulto, and on that day and the next through the aid of major
G. B. Jameson, I had on the first day of this month all of the civil
functions of this department put in power — under the Constitution of 1824, and all things are now Conducted on a permanent
basis, the Army aids and sustains the civil authority, while the
Civil Authority aids us in getting horses, and such supplies as
the greatly impoverished vicinity affords.

It will be appalling to you to learn, and see herewith inclosed
our alarming weakness, but I have one pleasurable gratification
which will not be erased from the tablet of my memory during
natural life, that those whose names are herewith inclosed are to
a man those who acted so gallant in the 10 weeks open field
campaign, and then won an unparalleled victory in the five days

siege of this place — Such men in Such a condition and under all the gloomy embarrassments surrounding, calls aloud upon you and their country, for aid, praise, and sympathy.

We have 104 men and two distinct fortresses to garrison, and about twenty four pieces of artillery. You doubtless have learned that we have no provisions or clothing since Johnson and Grant left. If there has ever been a dollar here I have no knowledge of it. The clothing sent here by the aid and patriotic exertions of the honorable Council, was taken from us by arbitrary measures of Johnson and Grant, taken from men who endured all the hardships of winter and who were not even sufficiently clad for summer, many of them having but one blanket and one shirt, and what was intended for them given away to men, some of whom had not been in the army more than 4 days, and many not exceeding two weeks. If a divide had been made of them, the most needy of my men could have been made comfortable by the stock of clothing and provisions taken from here.

About 200 of the men who had volunteered to garrison this place for 4 months left my command contrary to my orders and thereby violated the policy of their enlistment and should not be entitled to neither compensation, nor an honorable discharge, leaving this garrison destitute of men, and at all times within 8 or 10 days reach of an overwhelming Enemy, and at all times great danger was apprehended from want of Civil order and Govt among the lower class of the mexican soldiers left behind, they have not even left here for our Government an english Copy of the Treaty, so derogatorily made.

I want here for this garrison at all times 200 men and I think 300 until the repairs and improvements of the fortifications is completed, a chart and index of which has been sent to Head-quarters at Washington, with the present Condition of the Fort, and such improvements suggested by Mr Jameson as has met my approbation, and I hope will be accorded by my Commander.

As I have stated to you before our exact situation here, I know you will make no delay to ameliorate our condition. The men have not even money to pay their washing, the hospital is also want of stores and even the necessary provisions for well men was not left the wounded by Grant, and Johnson, send us money in haste, the men have been here many of them more than three months and some of them have not had a dollar during the time.

I shall say to you as I have to my Commander in Chief, the services of Major Jameson to this army, and to his Country, can-not be too highly appreciated, the present army owes in a great part its existence to his exertions, and management, and so far as I am concerned in my Command, I assure you I cannot get along without him. I hope he will be continued in the army.

There are many subjects, that owing to the bearer of this letter being on the Eve of leaving, that has passed my attention of which you should be advised, and I will from time to time give you such information as may transpire here, and hope you will use all the exertions necessary in your power, to stimulate the men now under my Command to remain, and to award to each, and Every one of them, such praise as your patriotism may dictate, and I particularly recommend to your notice the officers now under my Command.

I further add that owing to our having no correspondence with the interior, that we Know not what day, or hour, an enemy of 1000 in number may be down upon us, and as we have no supplies of provisions within the fortress we could be starved out in 4 days by anything like a close siege.

I will say to you I know about the feelings of the Citizens of this place on the subject of Independence — they Know not whose hands they may fall into, but if we had a force here that they Knew could sustain them I believe they would be 3/4ths American and go for Independence and claim all to the Rio del Norte as they Know we want it and will have it —

The extent to which the impressment of Cattle and Horses, has been carried to by Johnson and Grant, has been the Cause of great Complaint and very much distress among the poorer class of the inhabitants, as several of them have been deprived of the means of cultivating their Crop for the ensuing Season, and which is their only means of support, owing to their Cattle being taken from them.

I beg leave to tender to his excellency the Governor and the Honorable Council the high regard I have for their patriotic exertions, in sustaining the present Federal Army of Texas, in my own name, and also in the name of all those I have the Honor to command at this post, and subscribe myself

Your obt Servt
J C Neill Lt Coln
Commanding

P.S. The troops who Engaged to Garrison this place for the term of 4 months, did so with an understanding that they were to be paid monthly and unless money comes in time there are several of them will return home —

I am just informed through a private source, that there are one Thousand Troops now on their march from Laredo towards this place, Should I receive any further information as to their proceedings or destination I will advise you without loss of time by express. . . .[17]

Sam Houston to Henry Smith
HEADQUARTERS, WASHINGTON: Sir I have the honor to enclose to your excellency the report of Lieutenant J. C. Neill,[18] of the artillery; and most respectfully request you will render to the cause of Texas and humanity the justice of bestowing upon it your serious attention, and referring it to the general council of the provisional government, in secret session. These, I may be permitted to hope, you will attend in person, that all the essential functionaries of the government may deliberate, and adopt some course that will redeem our country from a state of deplorable anarchy. Manly and bold decision alone can save us from ruin. I only require orders, and they shall be obeyed. If the government now yields to the unholy dictation of speculators and marauders upon human rights it were better that we yield to the despotism of a single man, whose ambition might have been satisfied by our unconditional submission to his authority, and a pronouncement, for which we were asked, in favor of his power.

In the present instances, the people of Texas have not even been consulted. The brave men who have been wounded in the battles of Texas, and the sick from exposure in her cause, without blankets or supplies, are left neglected in her hospitals; while the needful stores and supplies are diverted from them, without authority and by self-created officers, who do not acknowledge the only government known to Texas and the world.

Within thirty hours I shall set out for the army, and repair there with all possible dispatch. I pray that a confidential express may meet me at Goliad; and, if I shall have left, that it may pursue me wherever I may be.

No language can express my anguish of soul. Oh save our poor country! — send supplies to the wounded, the sick, the naked, and the hungry, for God's sake! What will the world think of the authorities of Texas. Prompt, decided, and honest independence, is all that can save them, and redeem our country. I do not fear — I will do my duty.[19]

Henry Smith to the President and Council
SAN FELIPE: I have ordered the Commander-In-Chief to establish his headquarters on the frontier, to concentrate all the troops in Texas, and occupy the most eligible points to afford protection, and keep the army in check and to have everything in a state of preparation for active operations, at the earliest possible day.[20]

Council Hall, San Felipe
On motion of Mr. Clements, the report of the committee on military affairs, and resolutions concerning the expedition to Matamoros, were called up and read, and Mr. Hanks presented a

letter from F. W. Johnson, declining any participation in the contemplated expedition, which was also read, and the House went into secret session, to consider and act upon the same.[21]

James Bowie to General Council

COUNCIL HALL, SAN FELIPE: James Bowie exhibited to the council orders from the commander-in-chief of the army, to proceed against Matamoros, and took leave of the council for his departure.[22]

Mr. Hanks, from the select committee appointed to wait on James Bowie, to obtain a copy of his orders, reported and presented a copy of same, which was ordered filed.[23]

Portrait of Colonel James Bowie, the legendary knife fighter.

Thursday, January 7, 1836
59 DAYS TO THE FALL

Wm. Pettus & Wm. B. Travis Certification

SAN FELIPE: I do hereby certify, that about the 28th of October last, — pressed a horse (a Bay Spanish horse) belonging to W. B. Travis, & delivered him to a man belonging to F. W. Johnson's Company & the horse has been lost in public service. He was taken from J. Urban's lot & he can tell his value.

Wm Pettus

This day came W. B. Travis and says the within account is Just and true & original and that the Horse was worth thirty-five dollars

Sworn to 7th January 1836 before me

J. W. Moody auditor[24]

Council Hall San Felipe de Austin

Your committee to whom was recommitted the report and resolution of the committee on military affairs, respecting an expedition against Matamoros, contemplating the appointment of J. W. Fannin and F. W. Johnson as agents: in consequence of Mr. Johnson's declining to act as agent, report the following resolutions:

1st. *Be it resolved*, by the General Council of the provisional government of Texas, That J. W. Fannin be and is hereby appointed and empowered as an agent, for in behalf of the provisional government of Texas, to raise, collect, and concentrate, at or near the port of Copano, as convenience and safety will admit, all volunteer troops willing to enter into an expedition against Matamoros, wherever they may be found, at the mouth of the Brazos, city of Bexar, or elsewhere, whether in Texas or arriving in Texas; and, when thus collected and concentrated, to report either to the commanding general, or to the governor or council, as he may prefer.

Sec. 2d. *Be it further Resolved*, That J. W. Fannin is hereby authorized to call upon the commissary Department for the proper and necessary munitions of war.

Sec. 3d. *Be it further Resolved*, That J. W. Fannin is hereby authorized to negotiate a loan of three thousand dollars.

Sec. 4th. *Be it further Resolved*, That on the concentration of the volunteers, an election be held for a commander and other officers.

Sec. 5th. *Be it further Resolved*, That J. W. Fannin shall make a descent upon Matamoros or such other point or place, as said agent may deem proper.[25]

F. W. Johnson to the General Council of Texas

SAN FELIPE: The rejection of my application for Commissions for the officers of the Volunteer Companies from the United States and for those raised in Texas, until now quartered in Bexar induces me again to address you.

Were I to consult my own feelings — I would probably indulge in a strain altogether different from what I shall but knowing as I do the irritable state of the public mind and however much predisposed it is — to contest the right you have to act, I refrain, — and I am content to bury in my own bosom all cause of complaint that I may have on my account — and although — I cannot but feel the unkindness and illiberality, not say injustice with which my application has been treated I yet shall not recur to it and instead of contemplated expedition I have only to say that I shall proceed in the contemplated expedition and do all I can for the safety and protection of Texas — And I ask no honor or compensation for myself — If by my exertions Texas is benefited I shall be well satisfied and it will never be cause of complaint to me that others may wear the laurels. —

On the 17th Decr. last I addressed a letter to his Excellency the Governor — relative to the condition of the Army at Bexar then under my command in which communication I enclosed a list of officers — requesting for them Commissions agreeably to your ordinances and in accordance with requests previously made to my two predecessors that such should be done — I could not suppose that the request was made in candor especially as Genl. Burleson and the Officers under him were commissioned upon application. — Those officers having certified the fact no commissions were given them. Why this has been the case I am unable to say. — I know of no offence committed by myself or the officers and men under my command, unless it was that in opposition to the wishes of many both out of the Army and in the field we dared to attempt the storm of Bexar and victoriously planted our standard on its walls. —

The Volunteers who had appointed me to the command were of Texas & men from the United States who had come here for no other purpose than to aid the cause of Texas. — They would not join the regular army and as there was no immediate call for their services, and they were anxious to be engaged in active operations and having received the official directions of the Military Committee of the date of the 16th. Utmo. requesting that a march on Matamoros might be made. I yielded to their desires and ordered a march on Matamoros. — In this as in all other acts of my public life I had solely the interests of the country at heart and was unwilling that Matamoros should be taken until I had commissions from your body for the officers — I considered that with commissions from your body — their acts would be those of Texas and the army subject to your orders — and as such when Matamoros was taken that the public property would be yours and the revenue sufficient in a short time to defray the heavy expense the war has created — Without Commissions my detachment would be necessarily compelled to act under color of some Mexican authority and consequently on the fall of Matamoros the public property and revenue and place itself would fall into the hands of the liberal Mexicans and not yours and by that means Texas would loose the benefit arising from the possession of the place and also an actual amount of money arising from the customs sufficient to pay our public debt a matter of great importance at this time. — Moved by these considerations I proceeded to this place . . . informing you of my intention and requested Commissions for the officers names I had previously reported to the Governor requesting Commissions — which were not extended. — It is to me a matter of great regret that your body has also declined granting the Commissions required. Not regret arising from any individual considerations — for I assure you that I have no feelings on my own account; but I regret it because I am aware your refusal is well calculated to alienate their feelings from the cause of Texas. — Because it drives them to the necessity of seeking authority from some liberal General in the interior and should Matamoros be taken deprives Texas of the benefits. — Five hundred and thirty men are surely an important consideration to Texas and ought not to be cut off. —

. . . In conclusion gentlemen I have to say that I shall still proceed on the expedition as I first contemplated and my every act shall have for its object Texas and the Constitution. —

Considering however the peculiar situation of the Volunteers under my command — recollecting their generous, disinterested and gallant services in the cause of Texas — I yet would suggest that some representation be made to them explaining why their commissions have not been extended and the reasons why an agent has been appointed in the manner contemplated in your decree — Such an explanation may have the effect of satisfying them and securing for Texas their services —[26]

Stephen F. Austin to General Sam Houston

NEW ORLEANS, LOUISIANA: In all our Texas affairs, as you are well apprised, I have felt it to be my duty to be very cautious in involving the pioneers and actual settlers of that country, by any act of mine, until I was fully and clearly convinced of its necessity, and of the capabilities of our resources to sustain it. Hence it is that I have been censured by some for being over cautious. Where the fate of a whole people is in question, it is difficult to be over cautious, or to be too prudent.

Besides these general considerations, there are others which ought to have weight with me individually. I have been, either directly or indirectly, the cause of drawing many families to Texas, also the situation and circumstances in which I have been placed have given considerable weight to my opinions. This has thrown a heavy responsibility upon me — so much so, that I have considered it to be my duty to be prudent, and even control my own impulses and feelings: these have long been impatient under that state of things which has existed in Texas, and in favour of a speedy and radical change. But I have never approved of the course of forestalling public opinion, by party or partial meetings or by management of any kind. The true course is to lay facts before the people, and let them judge for themselves. I have endeavoured to pursue this course.

A question of vital importance is yet to be decided by Texas, which is a declaration of independence.

When I left there I was of the opinion that it was premature to stir this question, and that we ought to be very cautious of taking any steps that would make the Texas war purely a national war, which would unite all parties against us, instead of it being a part war, which would secure to us the aid of the federal party. In this I acted contrary to my own impulses, for I wish to see Texas free from the trammels of religious intolerance and other anti-republican restrictions, and independent at once; and as an individual have always been ready to risk my all to obtain it; but I could not feel justifiable in precipitating and involving others until I was fully satisfied that they could be sustained.

Since my arrival here, I have received information which has satisfied me on this subject. I have no doubt we can obtain all and even much more aid then we need. I now think the time has come for Texas to assert her natural rights; and were I in the Convention I would urge an immediate declaration of Independence. I form this opinion from the information now before me. I have not heard of any movement in the interior, by the Federal party, in favour of Texas, or of the Constitution; on the contrary, the information from Mexico is that all parties are against us, owing to what has already been said and done in Texas, in favour of Independence; and that we have nothing to expect from that quarter but hostility. I am acting on this information, if it be true; and I have no reason to doubt it. Our present position in favour of the Republican principles of the Constitution of 1824, can do us no good; and it is doing us harm, by deterring those kinds of men from joining us, who are most useful. I know not what information you may have in Texas, as to movement of the Federal party in our favour, nor what influence they ought to have on the decision of this question, this being a matter which the Convention alone can determine. I can only say, that with the information now before me, I am in favour of an immediate Declaration of Independence.

Santa Anna was at San Luis Potosi, according to the last accounts, marching on rapidly, with a large force against Texas. We must be united and firm, and look well to the month of *March* and be ready. I shall try to be at home by that time.[27]

[Continued on January 8th]

Stephen F. Austin to Messrs. R. R. Royall and S. Rhoads Fisher
NEW ORLEANS, LOUISIANA: I am happy to inform you that the cause of Texas and of liberty stands high in this city and all over the United States. The spirit of the people is aroused by the evident justice of our cause, and they will sustain us. The universal wish and expectation in this quarter is that Texas ought to declare herself independent at once. . . .[28]

Washington, 7th Jan. 1838
My Dear Sir: - Events hurry themselves upon us. Every day, results in something important connected with the fate of Texas, and Liberty, a few individuals; at one time had denounced the Provisional authorities of the country, and were prepared to involve us in anarchy, but the firmness of the Governor and General Council sustained by the moral energies of the community soon put matters to rest. This matter will be known abroad, and it is fit that it should not be set down to the account of Texas; It must be imputed to those, who expect to realise advantages, from the continuance of our relations to the Mexican Government, by consummating vast land speculations. Many honest and clever men do not accord altogether, with what was done by the Consultation. It certainly was of advantage to Texas. It gave a government when we had none. The country was in war, the army had to be sustained, and without a Government nothing could be done. All was excitement and bustle - The remedy of all evils is at hand; and I do hope the Convention, to meet on the first of March next will apply the proper cure of all evils.

You are aware that I have been opposed to a Declaration of Independence up to this time. I was so, because I thought it premature and that some policy demanded of us a fair experiment - I now feel confident that no further experiment need be made, to convince us that there is but one course left for Texas to pursue, and that is,

an unequivocal *Declaration of Independence, and the formation of a constitution, to be submitted to the people for their rejection or ratification.*

It is the project of some interested in land matters, very largely, for Texas to unite with some three or four of the Eastern States of Mexico, and form a Republic - This I regard as worse, than our present, or even our former situation. Their wars would be our wars, and their evolutions our revolutions: While our Revenue, our lands, and our lives would be expended to maintain their cause, and we could expect nothing in return; but prejudice, and if we relied on them disappointment. Let Texas now Declare her Independence, and it will cost her less blood, and treasure to maintain it; than it would cost her to maintain her integral interest in such a confederacy; the preponderance, would be so decidedly against her, that she would have less influence is possible, than she has heretofore injoyed in the Congress of Coahuila and Texas.

The citizens of Texas can never be happy, until they are confident in the certainty of their rights - so long as they are subject to Mexican policy they never can be confident; Then if these are truths sanctioned by experience - *Texas must be free,* that her citizens may be happy.

I am your friend
SAM. HOUSTON,
To Colonel John Forbes-

Recreation of the original broadside printed January 7, 1836 in Washington-on-the-Brazos, Texas.

Friday, January 8, 1836
58 DAYS TO THE FALL

Stephen F. Austin to General Sam Houston

NEW ORLEANS: [Continuation of letter of the 7th]

This day we concluded a conditional loan for two hundred thousand dollars, which perhaps may be augmented fifty thousand more; we can only get ten per cent advanced now, which is all we can raise in this place. Huston and Wharton will commence their purchases tomorrow. Flour is eight dollars; but we will send about seven hundred barrels, two hundred of bread, and some beans.

Should a Declaration of Independence be made, there ought to be no limits prescribed on the south-west or north-west; the field should be felt open for extending beyond the Rio Grande, and to Chihuahua and New Mexico.

S. F. A.

J. C. Neill to Gov. & Council of Texas

HEADQUARTERS, BEXAR: We have this morning receiv'd an Embassador from the Comancha nation, who informs us that his nation is in an attitude of hostilities toward us.

They are, however, willing to treat with us, & propose to concede hostilities for Twenty days, for that purpose, & suggest that each party shall furnish Five Commissioners to form a Treaty of Amity, Commerce & Limits. I would suggest that Francisco Ruis & Don Gasper Flores of this place, be nam'd as two of the Commissioners, they are familiar with the Comancha character, and have acted in the capacity of negotiators to that nation. They propose to hold the Treaty at this place, at the time above nam'd, and it is hop'd that no time will be lost in the completion of an object involving such vital importance.[29]

James W. Fannin to Volunteers
ATTENTION, VOLUNTEERS !
To the West, Face: March !

An expedition to the west has been ordered by the General Council, and the Volunteers from Bexar, Goliad, Velasco, and elsewhere, are ordered to rendezvous at San Patricio, between the 24th and 27th instant, and report to the officer in command. The fleet convoy will sail from Velasco, under my charge, on or about the 18th, and all who feel disposed to join it, and aid in keeping the war out of Texas, and at the same time cripple the enemy in their resources at home, are invited to enter the ranks forthwith.

J. W. Fannin, Jr.[30]

Sam Houston to Henry Smith, *private*
WASHINGTON: I will set out in less than an hour for the Army. I will do all that I can. I am told that Frank Johnson and Fannin have obtained from the Military Committee orders to Proceed and reduce Matamoros. It may not be so. There was no Quorum, and the council could not give power. I will proceed with great haste to the army and there I can know all. I hope you will send me an Extract of Austin's letter about the New Confederacy,[31] and what he says about the "Capitulation" of Bexar. Please write to me of this.[32]

Santa Anna to Don Vicente Filisola
HEADQUARTERS, LEONA VICARIO, MEXICO: . . . I am informed that the two divisions commanded by Generals Don Joaquin Ramirez y Sesma and Martin Perfecto de Cos have recrossed the Rio grande; the former to establish itself at the Town of Guerrero, and the latter at the City of Monclova. I am also informed that Your Excellency is departing for the latter city as per my instructions, leaving the City of Laredo under the protection of its presidial company commanded by its captain acting under the instructions of which you sent me a copy and which leave nothing to be desired.

Considering the date upon which the officer carrying the 30,000 pesos left here, he should presently be in the immediate vicinity of Monclova . . . it is imperative for Your Excellency to conduct the necessary supplies and provisions to Monclova so that they may be paid for upon their arrival at that city.

Your Excellency will send the 20,000 pesos allocated for the division commanded by General Ramirez y Sesma, and the 10,000 pesos for the force headed by General Cos to cover the urgent expenditures, as soon as the said 30,000 pesos arrive.[33]

Santa Anna to Don Vicente Filisola
HEADQUARTERS, LEONA VICARIO, MEXICO: Your Excellency will order any troops from the towns of Revilla, Mier, Comargo, and Reynosa found in the Division commanded by General Cos to return to their respective towns to protect them from enemy raids. They are to recuperate at the respective towns and prevent the enemy from executing their malicious intentions. The troops are to act in accordance with the instructions given them by Your Excellency in case they are attacked.[34]

Santa Anna to Don Vicente Filisola
HEADQUARTERS, LEONA VICARIO, MEXICO: I herewith acknowledge receipt of Your Excellency's communique of the fourth of the current month informing me of the depredations

committed by the savages in the vicinity of Laredo and the measures which Your Excellency has seen fit to execute in order to contain them.[35]

Saturday, January 9, 1836
57 DAYS TO THE FALL

Telegraph,
and Texas Register

SAN FELIPE: The Organization of the militia in accordance with the ordnance upon this subject, passed by the General Council on the 25th and approved on the 27th November last, is a measure which the present circumstances of the country appear imperiously to demand. The defense of the country has hitherto depended upon the volunteer services of individuals, who merit the gratitude of every citizen, for their timely exertions in the cause of history. As the country is now threatened with invasion by a formidable force, nothing should be omitted which could contribute to the strength of the country, or place it in a better position to meet and repel its enemies.

Gail Borden, editor of the Telegraph, *and* Texas Register *went on to achieve world fame when he invented the process for condensing milk.*

James Gaines to J. W. Robinson
GAINES'S FERRY MUNICIPALITY OF SABINE: On my way
home I took some pains To inform myself as To the True state of
politics in Texas. From St Phillip to Nacogdoches one Entire Kind
of Independence pervades all Class of Men. At Nacogdoches
Much Canvas was flying with Liberty and Independence wrote
on It in large Letters: and Many of our dictators apeard Struting
under It a Belching Fury against the Acts of the General Council,
and but a very small share of attention apeard To be paying To
Volunteers, since which Time I am informed, that a Caucus has
been Calld by John Durst & Biesca which has caused the part To
hall down the great part of their flying Canvas and Repeat the
Shout For the Constitution of 24
   San Augustine has Generally followed suit to Nacogdoches
   Our people here Are Much pleasd with their Organization. We
Call our new Town Milam, We Shall Send our Two Members To
the Convention with Special Instructions To declare Texas Independent of the Central Government of Mexico, and To form a
Constitution, Keeping For Its Guide the Constitution of 87 and
not that of 24, as well as send a Representative To the Govern-
ment at Washington To Represent there such Matters and things
as the Convention May deem Necessary For Texas.
   I here insert a Toast drank Recently in nashville at a Great
party
   Texas the Eden of North American land Flowing with Milk and
honey, May the Star Spangled banner soon wave its proud
Stripes over the Valley of the Brassos, and its Stars like their
Glory dazzle the Eyes of the Mexican despot. You may Easily
learn my Opinion on Matters and things, as I am Too well
Acquainted with the Mexican Character To place any Confidence
in their Joining us in the support of the Constitution of 24 or any
thing Else Further than their private Interest may Dictate
   Although I in this as in Other Matters may be found in the
Minority Owing To a thorough acquaintance with the Many
parties Compossing the Leading Men of Texas, the Various
Clashing Interests Contending For by them all Should they unite
at all will be To Form a landed Aristocracy, the pledging of our
public Domain is intended by Some To Close The Scene, on that
subject, is Why I urge To drive the Matter through as Speedy as
possible For the General Good of the Bone and Sinew of our
Country the Actual Settlers;
   To Effect which Object I beg the Governor and Council and To
push their Joint Efforts, in Securing the Victory of Bexar by a
push To the Valley Of the River Grand of a force Sufficient To
Secure inviolate the possession of Texas So as the Right To the
public domain, of Texas may be considered ours or our Fathers
&c &c on which Liberty peace and prosperity may Rest in Safety

Be Assured that I Shall at all Times Be found doing my duty for the Good Of the Cause Of Texas and pray all To unite in the Same

My Compliments To the Council

I remain you Obt & Very Humbl Servt.

Jas. Gaines

P.S. Some rumors has been the Rounds that Cos has had his Runners acting Among the Cherekees and that they give him protection Such I think is the idle Chat of a few and Should it be a fact our Four or five Municipalities will award them in due Season For their Many Offenses, the prime of which is their Intruding themselves in the Burnett Colony and Claiming right by the Freedonian Treaty.

Your high Chief is said To be under March To Treat with his kindred nation peace of Course must follow[36]

Land Matters some important discoveries has Recently been made by some purchasors From the United States, that there is no Record in Texas of Said Titles the papers in the United is Said Will Shortly Set Forth the Matter in Its proper Colours

David Crockett delivered one of his Corner Speeches yesterday at San Augustine and is to Represent them in the Convention on the first of March[37] So much For the Times

10th the mail has arivd and brings us nothing neither From the Post Master General, by way of appointment instructions or otherwise, please name It to him that Something apears to me Intirely Necessary,

J. G.[38]

Council Hall, San Felipe

James B. Jamieson's letter of recommendation for the office of Engineer for the army of Texas was taken up, and at the suggestion of the President, ordered to be filed.

The resolution requiring Colonel Travis, under the order of the commandant to proceed to Matamoros, were taken up, and leave given Mr. Royall to withdraw them.[39]

Davy Crockett to Family

SAN AUGUSTINE, TEXAS: My dear Sone and daughter This is the first opportunity to write you with convenience. I am now blessed with excellent health and am in high spirits, although I have had many difficulties to encounter. I have got through safe and have been received by everybody with open cerimony of friendship. I am hailed with hearty welcome to this country. A dinner and a party of ladys have honored me with an invitation to partisapate both at Nacing docher [Nacogdoches] and at this place. The cannon was fired here on my arrival and I must say as to what I have seen of Texas, it is the garden spot of the world. The best land and best prospects for health I ever saw, and I do believe it is a fortune to any man to come here. There is a world of country to settle.

It's not required here to pay down for your League of land. Every man is entitled to his head right of 400 — 428 [4,428] acres. They may make the money to pay for it on the land. I expect in all probability to settle on the Border or Chactaw Bro or Red River that I have no doubt is the richest country in the world. Good land and plenty of timber and the best springs and will [wild] mill streams, good range, clear water & every appearance of

David Crockett, the Tennessee frontiersman who came to Texas searching for a new life and a "splendid fortune."

health — game a plenty. It is the pass where the buffalo passes from north to south and back twice a year, and bees and honey plenty. I have a great hope of getting the agency to settle that company and I would be glad to see every friend I have settled here. It would be a fortune to them all. I have taken the oath of the government and have enrolled my name as a volunteer for six months, and will set out for the Rio Grande in a few days with the volunteers of the United States. But all the volunteers is entitled to vote for a member of the convention or to be voted for, and I have but little doubt of being elected a member to form a Constitution for this province. I am rejoiced at my fate. I had rather be in my present situation than to be elected to a seat in Congress for life. I am in great hope of making a fortune for myself and my family, bad as my prospect has been.

I have not written to William but have requested John to direct him what to do. I hope you will show him this letter and also Brother John as it is not convenient at this time for me to write to them. I hope you will all do the best you can and I will do the same. Do not be uneasy about me. I am among friends. I will close with great respects. Your affectionate father. Farewell.[40]

Mathew Caldwell to Provisional Government
GONZALES: I now must inform you something of the present situation of this country. I have endeavored to Give assistance to the army every way in my power that is now in Bexar, Yesterday I have in Order to comply with the comdt of that place sent fifty bushels of corn meal, some beef cattle and are now collecting for that place, therefore I must now inform you, that articles necessary to furnish that army are Scarce here as the Volunteers ever since the war has been Furnished with very much from this place and there is now no more than is immediately needed for the families in this Munity and there is no funds here in my hands which has not been applied to public use, therefore I must say it is Out of my power to comply in contracting for the army any longer without funds being placed in my hands, to disburs as the people here cannot longer render their services individually nor their property or teams without pay, as they are for the preservation of their families bound to use their Money to their own individual purpose.

I have seen the Resolves regulating and providing for Rangers on the frontier, I only say to You, that in regard to the appointing the officers to command the rangers in this division the people will not organize under that regulation but if your honorable body will see fit to permit us to elect our own officers to command the company, up to a Captain in that Event I think a company may be made, which we must need, I am at this time much recovering from my wounds & afflictions, that i informed you of in my last communication, having nothing more of importance to inform you of at present. . . .[41]

General Jose Urrea Diary Entry
I arrived at Saltillo with my regiment and part of a squadron of Durango. This force was incorporated with the greater part of the army already gathered in the city by his Excellency, General Don Antonio Lopez de Santa Anna.[42]

Sunday, January 10, 1836
56 DAYS TO THE FALL

Phillip Dimitt to Henry Smith
FORT GOLIAD; I have the honor to inform your Excellency, that our Cavallado was seized yesterday, by order of Col. Grant, who had arrived a few days before from Bexar.

The Volunteers who were the first to open the war, who have taken this post and maintained it, and who were on the eve of being relieved from garrison duty, are by this act left without the means of transportation to their homes.[43]

Council Hall, San Felipe
Special Call of the House:
The Council met and the President read the following communication from the Governor:

I have recently received by express dispatches from Bexar containing information of a character which should be immediately laid before the Council.

And being informed that you do not meet today, I must beg the favor of you to call a secret session of your body. I wish all the members of your body to be present, as immediate action will be necessary.

The House met and went into secret session:

Gentlemen:

I herewith transmit to your body, the returns and correspondence of Colonel Neill, Lieutenant Colonel Commandant of the Post of Bexar.

You will in that correspondence find the situation of that Garrison. You will find there a detail of facts, calculated to call forth the indignant feelings of every honest man. Can your body say that they have not been cognizant of and connived at this predatory expedition?[44] Are you not daily holding conference and planning co-operation both by sea and land? Acts speak louder than words, they are now before me, authorizing a Generalissimo with plenary powers to plan expeditions on the faith, the credit, and I may justly say, to the ruin of the country. You urge me by resolutions to make appointments, fit out vessels, as government vessels, registering them as such, appointing landsmen to command a naval expedition by making representations urgent in their nature, and for what? I see no reason but to carry into effect by the hurried and improvident acts of my department, the views of your favorite object by getting my sanction to an act discouraging in its nature, and ruinous in effect. Instead of acting as becomes the counsellors and guardians of a free people; you resolve yourselves into low, intriguing, caucussing parties, pass resolutions without a quorum, predicated on false premises, and endeavor to run the country, by countenancing, aiding and abetting marauding parties, and if you could only deceive me enough, you would join with it a practical co-operation. You have acted in bad faith, and seem determined by your acts to destroy the very institutions which you are pledged and sworn to support. I have been placed on the political watch tower, I feel the weight of responsibility devolving upon me, and confidently hope I will be able to prove a faithful sentinel. You have also been posted as sentinels, but you have permitted the enemy to pass your lines, and Mexican like, you are ready to sacrifice your country at the shrine of plunder. I speak collectively as you all form one whole, though at the same time I do not mean all. I know you have honest men there, and of sterling worth and integrity; but you have Judas in the camp — corruption, base corruption has crept into your councils, men who, if possible would deceive their God.

Notwithstanding their deep laid plans and intrigues, I have not been asleep; they have long been anticipated, forestalled and counteracted. They will find themselves circumvented on every tack. I am now tired of watching scoundrels abroad and scoundrels at home, and as such I am prepared to drop the curtain. The appointment and instructions founded on the resolutions predicated on false premises, shall now be tested. I will immediately countermand the order made out in such haste, as you say, and as her register says, the armed vessel Invincible is a Government vessel, I will immediately order a suitable officer of the Government to go and take charge of her in the name of the Government, and hold her subject to my order. And if that be refused, I will immediately recall her register by proclamation to the world. I would further suggest to you that our foreign agents have been commissioned and specifically instructed to fill out our navy, and procure the proper officers and crews; and unless they can be certainly informed of the absolute purchase in time, to prevent their purchase of a similar one, the purchase, so made by you, shall never be ratified or become binding on this government; because you would do the government serious injury by meddling with matters which you have put out of your power by special appointment. You shall not be permitted by collusion or management, to act in bad faith to the injury of the Government. If the appointment of general agents, with latitudinarian powers, with the power of substitution, and many other things equally inconsistent, and ridiculous; which have been engendered in, and emated from your caucussing, intriguing body, recently, does not show a want of respect to my department, and a total neglect of the sacred oaths and pledges solemnly made by you, I must admit I am no judge. I wish you to understand, that the ground on which you stand is holy, and shall be guarded and protected with every assiduty on my part. Permit me again to repeat it, Mr. President, that it is not intended to touch either yourself or the honest and well intending part of your Council.

Look around upon your flock, your discernment will easily detect the scoundrels. The complaint; contraction of the eyes; the gape of the mouth; the vacant stare; the hung head; the restless fidgety disposition; the sneaking sycophantic look; a natural meanness of countenance; an unguarded shrug of the shoulders; a sympathetic tickling and contraction of the muscles of the neck anticipating the rope; a restless uneasiness to adjourn, dreading to face the storm themselves have raised.

Let the honest and indignant part of your Council drive the wolves out of the fold; for by low intrigue and management they have been imposed upon, and duped into gross error and palpable absurdities. Some of them have been thrown out of folds equally sacred, and should be denied the society of civilized men.

They are paricides piercing their devoted country, already bleeding at every pore. But thanks be to my God, there is balm in Texas and a physician near. Our agents have gone abroad; our army has been organized. Our general is in the field. A convention has been called which will afford a sovereign remedy to the vile machinations of a caucussing, intriguing and corrupt Council. I now tell you that the course here pointed out, shall be rigidly and strictly pursued, and that unless your body will make the necessary acknowledgements to the world, of your error, and forthwith proceed, and with the same facility and publicity, (by issuing a circular,) and furnish expresses to give circulation and publicity, in a manner calculated to counteract its baleful effects, that after twelve o'clock to-morrow all communications between the two departments shall cease; and your body will stand adjourned until the first of March next, unless from the emergencies of the country, you should be convened by proclamation at an earlier period.

I consider as the devisers of ways and means, you have done all contemplated by the organic law. That your services are now no longer needed, until the convention meets; I shall continue to discharge my duties as Commander-In-Chief of the army and navy, and see that the laws are executed.

The foregoing you will receive as a notice from my department, which will be rigidly carried into effect. You are further notified that audience will not be given to any member or special committee other than in writing. I will immediately proceed to publish all the correspondence had between the two departments by proclamation, and the causes which have impelled me to do it.

I am gentlemen your ob't servant

HENRY SMITH, Governor[45]

F. W. Johnson to Volunteers

PROCLAMATION OF THE FEDERAL VOLUNTEER
ARMY OF TEXAS

The Federal Volunteer army of Texas, the victors of San Antonio, then and now under the command of Francis W. Johnson, through him address themselves to the friends of Texas and of Liberty.

Under sanction of the general council of Texas, they have taken up the line of march for the country west of the Rio Grande. They march under the flag 1.8.2.4., as proclaimed by the government of Texas, and have for their object the restoration of the principles of the constitution, and the extermination of the last vestige of depotism from the Mexican soil. Texas herself, free from military rule, yet hears on her borders the insolent tone of the tyrant's myr- midons, yet hears the groans of her oppressed Mexican friends, and their call for assistance. Her volunteer army will answer that call; and with a determination to aid and assist them in reestablishing their constitution and their liberty, they march to victory or the grave. They invite into their ranks all friends to freedom, of whatever name or nation.

To arms! then, Americans, to aid in sustaining the principles of 1776, in this western hemisphere. To arms! native Mexicans, in driving tyranny from your homes, intolerance from your altars, and the tyrant from your country. Our first attack will be upon the enemy at Matamoros; our next, if Heaven decrees, wherever tyran- ny shall raise its malignant form. Between the 25th and 30th inst., it is expected the whole of the volunteer army of Texas will take up the line of march from San Patricio.[46]

Austin,[47] Archer,[48] and Wharton[49] to his excey Henry Smith

NEW ORLEANS: We have succeeded in affecting a loan in this city of two hundred and fifty thousand dollars for Texas. . . .

Some of the best informed persons of this place confidently assert that this loan insures the triumph of our cause and the independence of Texas. That in New Orleans, so near us, and so well acquainted with our situation, confidence enough should exist in us to induce a loan, speaks volumes in our favor and will give confidence every where else. The stock in this loan will soon be in the the hands of hundreds of capitalists who will feel as much interest in Texas and exert themselves as much for it, as those of us, who have long lived there. To prove this the lenders have offered to land in Texas within six weeks five hundred men officered, armed, and equipped to serve during the war on the terms of the military laws of the provisional government and convention, and after the war to receive pay for the costs of their arms and outfit with interest in the mean time at 8 pr. cent on the amount (with the option of being paid on the basis of this loan as an addition to it) from their arrival in Texas. This is the true way to obtain troops. To undertake to receive them here, and pay their way to Texas is now impossible — We have not the means, and it is an open violation of the laws of this country, than which nothing could more effectually injure our cause. Let volunteers not be recognized until they have presented them- selves to the governor or commander in chief. A sufficient num- ber will do this at their own expense. A man must have lived to little advantage, and will not be of much force when he joins us, if he be not able to spend thirty or forty dollars to get to Texas, especially when he will be paid for gun, horse etc. on his arrival.

All grants of land or certificates of citizenship or reception hereafter to those who are not now in Texas or who have not already acquired rights should be made with a special reservation of the priority of location stipulated for the four hundred thousand acres contracted away by this loan, and it should be so published and mentioned in the certificate that no body be deceived. Disposing of our land at fifty cents pr. acre for the purpose of getting money so particularly indispensable at this moment, appears to us very fortunate. In fact rather than have missed the loan, we had better borrowed the money for five years and given them the lands in the bargain.

We are of the opinion that in the next convention a stop should be put to granting league and quarter league tracts to all who come after that date, for otherwise the country will be taken up entirely before we have volunteers enough, and besides the pay and rations of the United States with a premium of six hundred and forty acres, will induce just as many to come . . .

The information from Mexico recd. here is, that the leading men of the federal party have united with Santana to invade Texas; consequently the position taken by the declaration of 7 November in favor of the republican principles of the constitution of 1824 can no longer do any good, the object of that declaration having been to extend light and liberty over Mexico, and thus secure the cooperation of the liberal party. On the other hand, mentioning the federal constitution in that declaration has done us an injury in this country and would ruin us if it were not confidently expected and believed that a new convention would soon meet and make an absolute declaration.

We hope to be home in March, and can then give more specific information. . . .

Augustus & William C. White[50] to Henry Smith

BANGER, MAINE: Sir to you Honor; we the subscribers wold render our services to your state and country we solemnly vow that we will act the Brav part of a soldier which you wold require of us; we will Try to get mor volunteers if necessary of corse it will be if you except of us we hope you will except of us to doing a good caus for you countrey we solomnly vow that we will fite or Dye for you an countrey & except of us as friends to a good caus.

we ask no more then your fraying our expences on there and supliing us with; War utencils and provisions we take youre 8the act that who, ever volunteered there cervices in her presant struggle, and reciev them as citisens and reward them by donations in land . . . pleas to Answer this with despatch[51]

Monday, January 11, 1836
55 DAYS TO THE FALL

Sam Houston to J. W. Robinson

BEASON'S: I thank you a thousand times for yr. kind letters, and ten thousand times for my dear Cousins regards and kind prognostics in my favor.

The bearer starts in a moment and the instant that I can reach the frontier I will write to you all about the subject of Sutler — This much — You may rely upon it that if you have a good station it is very valuable, and ought to be worth from $10 to $20,000$ per annum.

So soon as I can get to some place where I can write, I will write to you and the council on the subject of Hanks — But I now hereby do most solemnly revoke, the letter which I addressed to you in his behalf, as I do most seriously regard him, as the basest of all mankind.

I pray you attend in the most especial manner to the appointment of my friend Major Geo W. Hockley as a Captain — also Blonnell make Wm Blount[52] Lieut of Cavalry — Colonel Bonham, ought to be made a Major by all means. His influence in the army is great — more so than some who *"would be generals"* You may rely upon my doing every thing for your information on the Subject of Sutler. And if I can serve you; I will only say command me !

If Hanks hands you that letter retain it — I only; since I left San Felipe; have concluded the extent of his Villany ! ! ![53]

I pray to salute my dear cousin, with my love. Present me to my friends. Write by every express. send at least one every week.[54]

Council Hall, San Felipe

On motion of Mr. Hanks, all acts of the House done in secret session in regard to the governors late message, are released from the obligation of secrecy.

On motion of Mr. Barrett, the President is requested to wait upon the Governor this evening and confer with him and endeavor to avert from the country, if possible, the disorder and confusion likely to result from the course he is pursuing.

Your special committee to whom was referred the communication of governor Smith, Report: That they are unable to express any other views to this House, than indignation at language so repulsive to every moral feeling of an honorable man, and astonishment that this community could have been so miserably deceived in selecting for the high office of Governor, a man whose language and conduct prove his early habits to have been vulgar and depraved, and his present disposition, that of a tyrant.

That they repel the infamous charges preferred against this Council and its members, as false and unfounded in every part; and condemn the style and language as low, blackguardly and vindictive, and every way unworthy of, and disgraceful to the office whence it emanated, and as an outrageous libel on the body to whom it is addressed, and therefore advise the return of the paper accompanied by the following resolutions:

1st. *Resolved,* That the members of the General council are the immediate representatives of the Sovereign People and are charged with the safety of the country and amenable only to the people for the faithful discharge of their duties.

2d. *Resolved,* That each member individually, and as a body collectively, will sustain at all hazards the dignity of this government, and the rights of the good citizens of Texas, whom they have the honor to represent.

3d. *Resolved,* That Henry Smith, Governor of Texas, be ordered herewith to cease the function of his office, and be held to answer to the Council upon certain charges and specifications preferred against him, agreeably to the provisions of the fourth section of the Federal Constitution of Mexico of 1824; and the eleventh section of the organic law of the Provisional Government of Texas, as adopted in convention on the thirteenth day of November, A.D. 1835, and that a copy of said charges and specifications, be furnished to the Governor, Henry Smith, within twenty-four hours from this time.

4th. *Resolved,* That the Secretary to the Executive be forwith notified of these instructions, and that he be held responsible for every and all records, documents and archives of his office.

5th. *Resolved,* That the Treasurer, Commanding-General, foreign agents, and all others of this government be notified of the suspension of Henry Smith. . . .

6th. A committee be appointed to draft an address to the people of Texas, setting forth the circumstance and reasons which compel their representatives to adopt these measures.

On motion of Mr. Hanks, Messrs. Jones and Tucker were appointed a committee to return to the Governor his message of yesterday, together with the report and resolution thereon.

Your committee who was this day appointed by the General Council of the Provisional Government of Texas, to present to Henry Smith, Governor of said Government, a report and resolutions upon his message of the ninth instant; report as follows:

That the Governor, Henry Smith, stated, after reading said report and resolutions; "Well, you have adopted your course and I will pursue mine!" after which your committee left.

THREE O'CLOCK, P. M.

On motion of Mr. Barrett, the Lieutenant Governor, James W. Robinson, was sworn as acting Governor of Texas.

On motion of Mr. Jones, Messrs. Jones, Royall, Burnham, Tucker and Collard, were appointed a committee to draft an address to the people of Texas, setting forth the causes, &c. according to the report and resolutions upon the Governor's message and to act upon the articles of impeachment.[55]

Tuesday, January 12, 1836
54 DAYS TO THE FALL

Council Hall, San Felipe

The committee to whom was referred the governor's message of the ninth instant, made report thereon, together with resolutions and articles of impeachment against the governor, and an address to the people of Texas, all of which were adopted unanimously and ordered printed.

TO THE PEOPLE OF TEXAS

When, in the execution of delegated powers, the representatives of a sovereign People urged to the necessity of adopting harsh means, to protect the interests of their country, and save her from anarchy, it becomes their duty to their constituents to explain to them the circumstances under which they have acted, and the inefficiency of a milder course. Under these considerations, and a full sense of the high responsibility resting upon them, the representatives of the people of Texas, in General Council assembled, chosen and delegated to guard her rights and interests, in her present embarrassed and critical situation, are painfully compelled to disclose to their constituents and to the world, occurrences as unlooked for, as they are to be deplored and regretted. In a government like ours, formed for the present emergencies, hastily organized, and at a time when confusion and disorder prevailed throughout our oppressed land, it could not be expected that perfect harmony and concord would characterize all the facts of all its departments, or entire satisfaction could be given by all its legislations; but it was at least to have been hoped, and the hope was fondly cherished by the members of this Council, as well as by all patriots, that, by mutual compromises and a general spirit of concession, the present necessities of our beloved country could be answered. All immediate self-interest we endeavored to discard; all private ambition and individual jealousies to sacrifice on the altar of our country, and to unite in fraternal Council to promote and advance the general weal. That this department of the government has so far succeeded in their adherence to these principles, we appeal to our public acts and to all who have witnessed our deliberations. When complaints have been made to us, of our acts, we have endeavored calmly and considerably to revise our conduct, and correct, so far as we are able, all errors and inconsistencies. With the other department of the Provisional Government, we have endeavored to co-operate in the same spirit of consession, and allowance for all errors and misconceptions, and to avert the present lamentable state of affairs, has been our constant and unremitting care: but, unfortunately for the country, it was not to be prevented. From the very organization of the government we have witnessed with the deepest regret, and most painful apprehensions, the disposition of that department to abridge the powers of the General Council, which were designated as a check upon executive usurpation, and to assume to itself the provinces of both departments. The executive has from time to time, communicated his advice to the Council, which it has always received with that deference due to the office from which it came, and has maturely weighed and deliberated upon the same, but when the Council has adopted the measures recommended by him in his messages, he has withheld or delayed his signature to their ordinances, or neglected to comply with their requisitions; and at other times he has transcended all authority, violating the organic law, framed and enacted by the people's own immediate representatives, in General council assembled, and the republican principles of the constitution of Mexico of 1824, which he is solemnly sworn to support; and has imputed to the Council the evils resulting from his own acts. He has assumed the right of appointing and commissioning, and has so appointed and commissioned, private individuals to take command of armies, without the consent or advice of the Council, and in direct violation and contradiction of the organic law of the convention, to which he owes his official existence.

After the reduction of Bexar, the volunteer troops being idle within our boundary, numbers daily coming in to our assistance from the United Sates of the North, and the country not affording the means to support them, it was thought advisable by the Council and the Governor so advised them, to keep the war without our territories, and to have the volunteers actively and profitably employed. For that purpose the Council authorized Colonel J. W. Fannin to enlist volunteers, hold an election of officers; and the army when raised and organized, to make a descent upon Matamoros, specifying the manner, and prescribing the limits of Colonel Fannin's actions as the agent of the Government for that special purpose; for which they received from the Governor the vilest and most uncouth anathema, couched in the most vulgarly abusive language, charging them with appointing a generalissimo with plenary powers, to conduct a plundering and marauding expedition, and wishing to join with it a piratical co-operation; while he himself without the advice, consent, or knowledge of the council, and plainly and palpably in violation of the organic law, which he is unequivocally sworn to obey, had just given James Bowie, not known to the government as an officer of any rank whatever, orders, through the Commander-in-Chief, to raise an army and proceed against Matamoros; thus endeavoring by misrepresentations and false charges against the Council, to excite public indignation against them, and divert if possible, their attention from his own lawless and headlong course, trampling law under his feet disregarding his official oath, and breaking up the foundations of Government.

His dignity was insulted at the idea of the existence of the co-ordinate branch of the Government, to curb his acts and check his usurpation. He became more and more restless; his fury in a blaze, consumes his prudence, he orders the Council to disperse, shuts the doors of communications between the two departments and proclaims himself the Government!

Such is the purport of his last message, dated the ninth of January instant, accompanied with documents from Bexar, containing an account of the deplorable situation in which the troops of that garrison were left by Dr. Grant. The message he would make it appear, was induced by arrival of these dispatches, as he directed them to be read first, as an introduction to his message, in which he falsely charges the Council with having connived at, and sanctions the expedition under Dr. Grant, which he alleges is the cause of the distressed situation of the troops in Bexar. The council repels the charges, as false and unfounded, and denies having ever recognized in Dr. Grant any authority whatever.

The council met the occasion with all the calmness and

deliberation they could muster. Personal feelings and considerations were abandoned. What could the council do? He had shut the door of his office; it was, in effect, vacant. He had denied the authority that had created it; and as the guardians of the people's interests, they were compelled to proceed with the transaction of business, recognizing the lieutenant-Governor, as the acting Governor and they have preferred charges of impeachment against Governor Smith. Yes the Council met the occasion firmly.

Base perjury would have stamped her seal upon their acts if they had flinched. And while the armies are abroad in the defense of our beloved land, from the invasion of a foreign foe, they will ever guard and protect her from the insidious machinations of her internal foes, and will deserve the just condemnation and lasting reproach of their countrymen, if ever in danger, they desert their post.[56]

Henry Smith to F. C. Gray
SAN FELIPE: The legislative council of Texas have passed a bill that J. W. Fannin, as agent of the Government; given him lutiterdinarien powers, with the power . . . to raise men. fit out expeditions . . . at the expense, hazard, and on the credit of their Government. This authority has not been sanctioned by my Department.[57]

Henry Smith to members of the Council
SAN FELIPE: The communication sent to your body on the tenth inst., in which I used much asperity of language, which I considered at the time was called for from me; owing to what I deemed improvident acts of your body, in which I considered much intrigue and duplicity had been used, which was in their nature and tendency calculated to breed confusion and greatly injure the public good. Among other things the appointment of Colonel Fannin, was one which I deemed unwarranted by law and of injurious tendency. If the act of your body was ratified by me, it is plain and evident, that neither the Commander-In-Chief, the council, nor the Executive, could have any control over him. I therefore deemed it a gross insult offered by the Council to my Department and one which I was not willing to overlook. I admit I repelled it with a keenness and asperity of language beyond the rules of decorum; because I believed it was certainly intended as an insult direct. If therefore your body should think proper to acknowledge their error by an immediate correction of it, which I consider would only be their reasonable duty, all differences between the two departments should cease;

and so far as I am concerned be forever buried in oblivion. And that friendly and harmonious intercourse resumed which should ever exist between the different branches of the Government. I suggest and solicit this from the purest motives, believing the public good would thereby be advanced. Believing that the rules of Christian charity require of us to bear and forbear, and as far as possible to overlook the errors and foibles of each other. In this case I may not have exercised towards your body that degree of forbearance which was probably your due. If so, I have been laboring under error, and as such hope, you will have the magnanimity to extend it to me. And the two branches again harmonize to the promotion of the true interests of the county.[58]

Council Hall, San Felipe
Resolved, That this council has received the communication [above letter] in the spirit of compromise, at too late a period to be met by that spirit of accommodation offered and urged a short time since.

Resolved, That as the slanderous communication of Henry Smith, late Governor of Texas, has been acted upon and is now before the public, this council cannot, in justice to their constituetns and themselves, do otherwise than lay before the people all the facts connected with that unfortunate transaction, and the motive by which this council was actuated, and the circumstances which compel them to adopt this course.

Resolved, That the communication alluded to be returned together with a copy of the charges and specifications preferred against the said Henry Smith, late governor aforesaid, for malfeasance and misconduct in office, and that he be notified to reply within three days, or that trial will proceed thereon, before the General Council ex parte.

On motion of R. R. Royal, it is ordered that the resolutions of the House, appointing Col. J. W. Fannin the agent of Government, for raising and concentrating volunteers, and holding an election for officers to make a descent upon Matamoros, be forwarded to the printer for publication, with the address to the people yesterday.[59]

General Council to Henry Smith, Esq.
SAN FELIPE: Sir: The following are the charges and specifications preferred against you in substance and in form as contemplated by the fourth section of the organic law of the provisional government of Texas.

Charge first. For violating the republican principles of the Federal constitution of 1824, which as provisional governor, he has sworn to support.

Second. For neglecting to support the declaration of the Consultation of the chosen delegates of all Texas, in general convention assembled; and for endeavoring to prevent the general council from carrying into effect especially the second article as adopted by the said convention.

Third. For official perjury, in infringing and violating the organic law of the provisional government of Texas.

Fourth. For slanders and libels upon the general council as a body, and upon the members thereof individually, and contempt of its powers and authority, and attempting to dissolve the government, and assume dictatorial power over the good citizens of Texas, and by inconsistency, misrepresentation, and other official misconduct, has produced confusion and aimed at general disorganization.[60]

James W. Robinson to General Council

SAN FELIPE: I beg leave respectfully to ask your attention to the importance and necessity of having a secretary to the executive.

Letters and communications daily arrive in this place, through the post office, by express, and by private conveyance, directed to Henry smith, Governor of Texas.

I would ask you honorable body to direct me, as my legal advisors, whether being so officially directed I ought to open them as the only legal Executive. I am without the means of knowing what instructions have been given to our foreign agents or Indian Commissioners, or orders to the commanding general, or any officer either civil or military, neither do I know what laws are and what are not published, and as the order of your honorable body makes it my imperitive duty to cause them to be published . . . it will be difficult for me to perform my duty . . . unless I am put in possession of the public archives now in possession of my predecessor and by him pertinaciously withheld. . . .[61]

James W. Robinson was named acting governor when Henry Smith was impeached.

Wm R. Carey to Dear Brother & Sister

ST. ANTONIO DE BEXAR: To give you any satisfaction about my situation at present I should have to give you a history of Texas and the Mexican Government, but let me commence by saying that I am in the volunteer army of Texas. I arrived at Washington on the 28th of July. This is a small town situated on the Brazos river & there I intended to take up my final residence, but the unsettled state of affairs between Texas & the Mexican Government, I was called to the field. Movements on the part of the Mexicans aroused our suspicions. They want to establish Centralism or rather military depotism, a government that is repugnant to the principals of free born Americans, we remonstrated and sent commissioners, but we could not positively ascertain on account of their treachery and deceit. They denied it and still they were making preparations for it, but we were on the alert. I shall have to state the situation of this place and also the town of Gonzales as to give a little information on the affair. This place is an ancient Mexican fort & Town divided by a small river which eminates from Springs. The town has two squares in and around the church in the centre, one a military and the other a government square. The Alamo, or the Fort as we call it, is a very old building built for the purpose of protecting the citizens from hostile Indians. The Mexican army or rather part of them came to this place commanded by Martin de Perfecto de Cos, a bold aspiring young General. The town of Gonzales is about 78 miles below this place on the Warloupe[62] river. The enemy (as I shall now call them) sent about 200 of their troops to Gonzales after a cannon that they sent there for the use of the citizens to fight the Indians. We then were aroused and watched closely their movement. Volunteers was called for to fight for their country I was one of the first that started, about 150 of us ready in a moments warning, and we marched to Gonzales and put the enemy to flight, they retreated to this place. We then considered it essentially necessary for the security of our peace to drive them from this place, but we concluded to wait for reinforcements as we were so few in number, and they in a fortified place but unfortunately for us they commenced fortifying the town and strengthening the alamo until it became almost impossible to overcome them, our number increased gradually to the amount of 800 but on account of so many office seekers there was nothing but confusion, contention and discord throughout the encampment, which was within half a mile of the place, for we came up to endeavor to starve them out, and on the 4th day of December a retreat was ordered to the satisfaction of many, but to the grief of a few brave souls who was among the first that volunteered and who preferred Death in the cause rather than such a disgraceful retreat. We rallied around a brave soul (Colo Milam) and requested him to be our leader, he consented and 150 of us declared to take the place or die in the attempt, while a large number of them endeavored to discourage us and said we would all be butchered, but a few more seen we were resolute and joined until our number was 220, and on the next morning about day break we marched in the town under heavy fires of their cannon & musketry, but we succeeded in getting possession of some stone houses (which is outside of the square) that sheltered us a little from their fires until we could make Breastworks for ourselves we labored hard day and night for 5 days still gaining possession when on the morning of the 5th day they sent in a flag of truce to the extreme joy of us all, Thus a handful of militia of 220 in number stormed a strongly fortified place which was supported with two thousand citizens & soldiers (of the enemy) here I must remark, on the third day of the siege our leader fell in the battle, another userped the command who never was in favor of storming and had ordered the retreat but he was in time to make a disgraceful treaty, some strongly suspect bribery was the cause but whether or ignorance I cannot decide. The enemy on the third day of the siege raised a black flag (which says no quarters) and when we had whipped them by washing the flag with the blood of about 300 of them we should have made a Treaty and not a childs bargain however its done now and its too late to alter until we have another fight which we expect shortly.

Now a little about myself. I volunteered as a private and as a private in camp was always ready and willing to discharge the duty of a soldier when called on. I was out on a number of scouts and would frequently creep up to the Mexican sentinals at a late hour when they thought alls well and shout one or two of them of a night — and Oh! my dear sister and brothers how often have I thought of you when I have been walking the lonely wood or barren field as a sentinel exposed to all the inclemencies of the weather and suffering many privations which you can not have the least idea of, but all was sweet when I reflected on our forefathers in the struggle of liberty. about the 28th of October I was appointed 2d Lieut. of artillery and during the siege I was promoted to first on account of the first being Lieut, being cashiered for cowardice he always use the word go and I the word come on my brave boys. I thought & still think that nothing but fate save me we only had four killed and thirteen wounded three of the wounded & two of the killed received shots along side me when discharging their duty at a cannon that was ordered by a fool in the open street immediately before the enemies breastworks within 120 yards of their heavy fires, but he was my Superior and I did obey and when the men was killed & wounded I loaded and fired the gun assisted by two more instead of ten and escaped only slightly wounded, a ball passed through my hat and cut the flesh to the skull bone and my clothes received many shots until by a lucky shot made by me into the port-hole of the Enemy I dismounted their cannon which caused them to cease firing until we got away — but this is useless to state such trivial sercumstances, the wound prevented me from working the guns after we took the place and the child's bargain made, it was thought requisite for some to remain to protect it, volunteers was called for to inlist for four months and did those that came at the eleventh hour and remained in the camps expecting us all to be killed and they men of property in this country and have their all in Texas did they come forward to protect the place. No. They pilfered us of our blankets and clothes and horses and went home telling how they whipt the Spaniards reaping the laurels of a few.

Those that fired the first guns at Gonzales and who declared on victory or death. Those who came in when death stared them in the face, and labored hard day and night half starved and almost famished for water, it was them that volunteered to maintain the post until Texas government could make some provision to keep the Standing army here, and these men have now become almost naked, destitute of funds having expended all for food and munitions of war and not much to eat only some corn that we grind ourselves & poor beef this constitutes our dayly food, but we hourly expect supplies news has arrived that there is plenty of provisions & money and clothes on the way. I hope its true. I have strayed a little from the subject. when volunteers were called for they were to form into companies and elect their officers — fifty six brave souls joined into a company of artillery and chose me for their Captain. I accepted the command and my dear sister is it possible that the once ignorant weak and fickle minded W. R. Carey should now be at the head of so many brave men as their leader — It is a fact and with his parental name. have I deserved this post of honor, its not for me to say, but the brave proclaimed it. The forces here is commanded by Lieut. Colo J. C. Neill who has his quarters in the Town which is called the left wing of the forces and your brother William has the command of the Alamo which is called the right wing. I am subject to the orders of Colo Neill but he thinks a great deal of my judgement and consults me about a number of the proceedings before he issues an order. Brother & sister do not think that I am vain my friends here says I dont possess enough of vanity for my own good, except when we go to fight the Enemy and then I think a small number of us can whip an army of Mexicans — I know one thing, I am deceived in myself.

When I was in Natchitoches I wrote to you and stated I believe that soon I should look out for a companion. It would have happened this winter if the war had not commenced but fortunately it did. My selection was nothing to boast of she is tolerably ugly and tolerably poor and tolerably illiterate. but she is virtuous and a good housekepper, but there is no prospect now, as I was conversing with a Mexican lady the other day she remarked that in time of peace the ladies would gladly embrace the offer or accept the hand of an officer, but in these war times they would too soon become a widow. She may be right but I don't think it, however I have too much else to think about now, as I have not been a graduate at West point, I must study military affairs now for I am rejoiced at the opportunity to do something for myself. The men in this place have sometimes been discouraged on account of the distressed situation we are in, for want of clothes and food. The Colo and myself has twice called a general parade and addressed them in such a manner that they would get satisfied for awhile, but we are now discouraged ourselves, and unless the provisional government of Texas do speedily send us assistance we will abandon the place, we have sent and made known our situation to them and as the safety of Texas depends mostly upon the keeping of this place they certainly will as soon as possible do something for us especially when we expect to declare independence as soon as the convention meets.

Those of us here has already declared it with a recommendation to the convention of Declaring it but this place is so far in the interior that it takes some time for news to go and supplies to come. The Savage Comancha Indians is near at hand we expect soon to have a fight with them. Since I commenced writing this letter I have received an order to prepare and I have run over it quicker than I would have done as a friend of mine Wm. Guile is going to the States and I thought it a good opportunity as he will put it in the Philadelphia post office and you I think will get it.

I cannot close without saying something about my invincibles, as I call them, about twenty of my company (although the whole has been tried and I know them all) that will (to use their words) wade through h-ll, when I am at their head if I should give the order — O sister could you but see me at the head of those brave men marching forward (undismayed) to perform their duty. To relate circumstances of their bravery it would fill a large book. When the enemy ten to one has marched up as if they in one minute would send us all to eternity to see the invincibles rush foreword charge upon them and put them to flight except those we would either kill or take prisoners. We have had many such skirmishes since we left home. a circumstance occurred the other day which I must relate, a man for disobedience of orders and bad conduct was ordered to arrested (he was not under my command) The officer who received this order took a file of men and attempted to arrest him — he resisted and swore with pistols in his hands that he would shoot down the first man that attempted his arrest, the officer retreated without him the Colo immediately sent an order to me informing me of the circumstance and requesting me to take a file of my invinciples and bring the culprit to trial. I ordered three of the brave to prepare immediately I buckled on my sword and went to him he was then with two more who also swore he should not be taken, I approached him with my men he told me if I came one step further he would certainly shoot me down the other two swore the same and with great confidence too as he had put the other off but he soon found himself mistaken my men wanted to rush immediately upon them I ordered them to halt and I walked up to him and with a mild tone told him to disarm himself or I would cut him assunder he sheepishly laid down his pistols and gave himself up. the other two swore still that we should not take him. I insignificantly look up and told them if they attempted to move or put their finger on the trigger of their arms that they should fall on the spot they stood. I then walked up to them and took their arms likewise, my men stopt where I ordered them, watching minutely their movements ready at the twinkling of an eye to do what I should say, I told them to take those gentlemen to the guardhouse, which was done & there they remained until trial, the court marshall passed a sentence or would have passed a sentence of death upon the first. I found it out and went into my room and wrote two notes one to the court and the other to the Colo. and the sentence was remitted and he was drummed out of the army they all said that nothing but the invincibles with Capt Carey could have taken them as he expected to die any way if he was tried. When any thing of a dangerous character is to be done its by order Capt Carey will take a file from comp. of his men and go immediately and _____ . its always done. This should not come from me but as I am writing to Brothers and sister I think you ought to know something about these matters — I must close by saying that if I live, as soon as the war is over I will endeavor to see you all. Write to brother John or send this letter to him the reason why Brother I dont write to you is I dont know whether you are in Baltimore or not and brother William & sister I am nearly certain is in the same place yet — Write to me if you please and give as much satisfaction as you can — You will direct to Wm. R. Carey, Washington. Austin's Colony, Texas and I think I will get it, you will have to pay the postage as they will not be taken out of the office in New Orleans unless they are postpaid.

Your affectionate Brother

Wm. R. Carey[63]

SAN FELIPE, 12 JAN. 1836.

TO F. C. GRAY, Esq.

DEAR SIR.

The legislative council of Texas have passed a bill that J. W. Fannin, as the agent of the government; giving him lutitredinarion powers, with the power of substitution, to raise men, fit out expeditions, make decents at pleasure, &c. at the expense, hazard, and on the credit of the Government. This authority has not been sanctioned by my Department, nor can it ever be. We have already seen, and felt, the great evil growing out of a multiplicity of Commanders in Chief. The people in their sovereign capacity have elected one, and while he remains in office we should look up to, and respect him as such. Col. Fannin, has accepted a commission in the regular army, and as such he should obey his superior officer. If he would take the trouble to examine the ordinance, he would find he could not hold two appointments, and that the authority derived from the council by intregue, was of little validity, and a streach of power which will never be sanctioned. And out of fifty, or sixty, who aspire to the chief command, I think it more than probable, that the choice of the sovereign people in selecting Gen. Houston, should supercede all others. For in their selection of him, they have joined talent, integrity and ability - and a gentleman in every way calculated to do honor and credit to his high and important station.

This is therefore to notify all officers of the Government, and the citizens generally, that the proper officers of this Government will order and fit out expeditions whenever they deem it advisable to do so. And in the mean time all officers are required to submit themselves to their superiors and comply with the requisitions of the law. And that this Government will favor no predatory expeditions calculated to embarrass its circumstances or confront its honor.

HENRY SMITH, Governor.

N.B. You will also give notice through the medium of your paper, that the council as the divisers of ways and means, having performed all the duties contemplated by the organic law - they they were adjourned on the 10th inst. until the first of March next, unless from the emergencies of the county they should be convened by proclamation at an earlier period.   **H.S.**

Recreation of original broadside issued by Governor Henry Smith in San Felipe. The original printing was done by F. C. Gray in Brazoria, Texas.

Unknown gentleman residing in Matagorda, Texas

The report that St. Antonio with General Cos and his army, consisting of 1300 men, has surrendered to the Texans is correct; and after a solemn oath from both officers and soldiers, that they would not again take up arms against Texas, they were allowed to go home with a few arms, ammunition, and some stores sufficient to last ten days.

This shows the magnanimity and generosity of the Americans. Our army consisted only of between 3 and 4 hundred men, and by this conquest gained a strong fortress, and the only one of note on our borders. — A large quantity of stores, arms, ammunitions, horses, and heavy artillery were taken.

Gen. Cos was severely wounded and very many of his men killed, on our side Col. Milam was killed; and 6 others only, having from their favorable situation a good cover from the enemy.

When Cos sent into our Camp his white flag, our little army had but one keg of powder, besides a few rounds in their pouches. There was a singular Providence in this, and it seems a proof that the arm of the Almighty had been stretched forth to give us the victory.

We have now volunteers pouring in from all quarters, expecting another attack in the spring from Santa Anna, although many think he will not attempt it; but if he should, he will find no boy's play, as we can compete with any force he will dare send from home; a counter revolution in Mexico, and a constant desertion of soldiers from his army, will prevent his sending a large force.

If Santa Anna knows what is for his good, he had better let us enjoy the Constitution of 1824, unmolested. . . .[64]

John Forbes to James W. Robinson

NACOGDOCHES: . . . the internal Enemies of the Country have been uncommonly active for some time past, and are now regularly organized here, the late Mexican authorities emboldened by the support they receive from you know whom have had the hardihood to refuse giving up the Archives &c, &c and say that they know no provisional Government and will not obey its ordinances and decrees. . . .

. . . the Committee as it is now constituted have taken matters into their own hands, seized on the Public funds, and direct things at their pleasure and in opposition to the Council . . . I believe it is their intention if they can to have the Land offices Opened for the purpose of getting the money they may pay in, to be used by themselves in Disbursements as they will say for the use of the Volunteers —

. . . I was truly gratified to learn of Genl. Houstons departure for the army. it will have an excellent effect. . . .

I regret that a person in General Houstons Staff I mean J. K. Allen should have been the most bitter opposer of the Government. of another Individual of that staff, I could say much — I have been very busily engaged in attending to numerous Volunteers from the States fifty two of whom will leave here tomorrow for the frontier almost all are Gentlemen of the best respectability and mostly hailing from Tennessee They have come to fight the battles of Texas and maintain its rights, and while here have pledged themselves to sustain the Council against the speculators who have been tampering with them. I have had the honor of administrating the oath of allegiance to them the Celebrated David Crocket is of the number. . . .[65]

Vallejo to Jose Maria Ortiz Monasterio
DEPARTMENT OF FINANCE, MEXICO: Sir: His excellency the President ad interim has been pleased to declare the ports of Galveston and Matagorda, in the Gulf of Mexico, closed to foreign commerce, as well as to vessels wishing to take in provisions or to pursue the coasting trade.[66]

James W. Fannin, Jr. and Joseph Mimms partnership

Contract
Know all men by these present that Mr. Joseph Mimms & J. W. Fanning[67] Jr. have this day entered into the following partnership that is the said Mimms agrees to furnish eight head negro men & boys together with the following property & stock & to wit sixty head of stock cattle, two yoke of oxen & cart & yokes. four work mules, two horses, five ploughs & gears, three hundred bushels of corn, eighty head of hogs & three thousand & thirty acres of land, part of league No. fifty seven on the west bank of the San Bornordo [sic] adjoining Williams to the north & John Cummings to the south including all the improvements of said Mimms, it being the tract of land on which he now lives. Which property is valued at twenty five thousand dollars. And the said Fanning agrees to furnish twenty three African negros to wit twelve men, seven women and four boys, such negros are valued at seventeen thousand two hundred & fifty dollars, and it is agreed between the parties that the said Fanning shall pay the said difference of seven thousand seven hundred & fifty dollars in five equal annual installment with interest from this date at the rate of eight per centage per annum or should the tranquility of the country authorise it said Fanning is at liberty to pay the whole amount of said last mentioned amount of seven thousand seven hundred & fifty dollars in negros at fair valuation and have his bonds cancelled at once paying no further interest than may have accrued up to the time of said payment at the rate aforesaid.

The above named negros & stock are to be worked & used on said plantation above described for the term of five years under the exclusive & entire control of said Mimms and the profits arrising from the produce of said negros, stock & plantation during the aforesaid time fo five years after deducting all necessary expenditures for carrying on said plantation is to be equally divided between said contracting parties. The dividends to be disbursed annually.

And to the expiration of the aforesaid time of five years said land negros, stock & their produce & _____ shall be valued (should the parties themselves not agree) by a disinterested person chosen by each party & should they not agree they shall choose a third whose decision shall be final And said land, negros, stock, farming untensils &c After being valued shall be equally divided between said parties, but each of them shall be at liberty to retain the negros originally put in by him.

And it is further understood & agreed on by the above named parties that neither is at liberty to use the name or credit of the other on account of said partnership each being liable for his own contracts.

In confirmation whereof we have _____ to set our hands & affixed any seals this 12th day of January A. D. 1836. In presence of A. J. Pollock, Robert J. Patton, _____ Samuel C. Douglass

J. W. Fannin Jr.
Joseph Mimms[68]

Wednesday, January 13, 1836
53 DAYS TO THE FALL

Micajah Autry to Wife

NACOGDOCHES, TEXAS: I have reached this point after many hardships and privations but thank God in most excellent health. The very great fatigue I have suffered has in a degree stifled reflection and has been an advantage to me. I walked from nachitoches whence I wrote you last to this place 115 miles through torrents of rain, mud and water. I remained a few days in St. Augustine when Capt. Kimble from Clarksvelle, Ten, a lawyer of whom you may recollect to have heard me speak arrived with a small company of select men, 4 of them lawyers. I joined them and find them perfect gentlemen. We are waiting for a company daily expected from Columbia, Ten. under Col. Hill with whom we expect to march to head quarters (Washington) 125 miles from here, where we shall join Houston the commander in chief and receive our destination. I may or may not receive promotion as there are many very meritorious men seeking the same. I have become one of the most thorough going men you ever heard of. I go whole hog in the cause of Texas. I expect to help them gain their independence and also to form their civil government, for it is worth risking many lives for. From what I have seen and learned from others there is not so fair a portion of the earth's surface warmed by the sun.

Be of good cheer Martha I will provide you a sweet home. I shall be entitled to 640 acres of land for my services in the army and 4444 acres upon condition of settling my family here. Whether I shall be able to move you here next fall or not will depend upon the termination of the present contest. Some say Santa Anna is in the field with an immense army and near the confines of Texas, others say since the conquest of St. Antonio by the Texans and the imprisonment of Genl, Cos and 1100 men of which you have no doubt heard, that Santa Ana has become intimidated for fear that the Texans will drive the war into his dominions and is now holding himself in readiness to fly to Europe which latter report I am inclined to discredit, what is the truth of the matter no one knows or pretends to know.

Tell Mr. Smith not to think of remaining where he is but to be ready to come to this county at the very moment the government shall be settled, as for a trifle he may procure a possession of land that will make a fortune for himself, his children and his children's children of its own increase in value and such a cotton country is not under the sun. I have just been introduced to Mr. McNeil a nephew of Mr. S. who is now in this place and appears to be much of a gentlemen. Give my most kind affection to Amelia and Mr Smith and to my own Dear Mary and James give a thousand tender embraces and for you my Dearest Martha may the smile of heaven keep you as happy as possible till we meet.

M. Autry

Tell Brothers J. & S. I have not time to write to them at present as Mr. Madding and Sevier by whom I send this can not wait. Tell brother Jack to think of nothing but coming here with us; tell him to study law as this will be the greatest country for that profession, as soon as we have a government, that was ever known.

M. A.

P.S. We stand guard of nights and night before last was mine to stand two hours during which the moon rose in all her mildness but splendor and majesty. With what pleasure did I contemplate that lovely orb chiefly because I recollected how often I had taken pleasure in standing in the door and contemplating her together. Indeed I imagined that you might be looking at her at the same time. Farewell Dear Martha.

P.S. Col. Crockett has joined our company[69]

Henry Smith to Members of the Council
SAN FELIPE: On the ninth instant I notified your body that as the devisors of ways and means, I considered you had performed all the duties incumbent on you, contemplated by the organic law, and as such I consider the country would be relieved from a heavy tax by your adjournment until the first of March.

On the tenth I received notice that I was removed from office.

Not by death, inability or other casualty, but for exercising too
much capacity; and that by virtue of authority vested in your
body; that you had instaled a new governor and had created a
new organization.

I acknowledge receipt of the charges and specifications
preferred against me by your body, and feel able and willing in
convention to plead to them.

I would give your body this friendly advice, that the people
have given you the limit over which they will not permit you to
pass and any thing done by your body calculated to bring about
disorganization will be viewed as an outrage for which you will
be held amenable.[70]

Santa Anna to Filisola
GENERAL HEADQUARTERS, LEONA VICARIO: Your Excellency will aid the garrison companies located in Monclova, even
though they might not be of those that were in Bexar, from the
10,000 pesos that must be left over from the General Cos'
Division, as this Commissary can not, at the present time, aid in
any way.[71]

Thursday, January 14, 1836
52 DAYS TO THE FALL

James C. Neill to Major-General Samuel Houston
COMMANDANCY OF BEXAR: This is the third official since my
command at this place and they are all of the same nature,
complaining of the scarcity of Provisions, men and money, and I
think we have plenty ordinance, small arms, cannon and musket
cartridges, but no rifle powder.

The men in my command have been in the field for four
months, they are almost naked, and this day they were to
receive pay for the first month of their enlistment, and almost
every one of them speaks of going home, and not less than
twenty will leave tomorrow, and leave here only about 80
efficient men under my command, and there are at Laredo Three
Thousand men under the command of General Rameriz, and
two other generals and it appears by a letter received here last
night, one thousand of them are destined for this place and two
thousand for Matamoros, we are in a torpid defenseless situation, we have not and cannot get from all the citizens here
Horses enough since Johnson and Grant left, to send out a patrol
or spy company. Capt Salvador Flores a Mexican, has volunteer'd
to go with two others as spies, all the way to Laredo, to learn the
situation of the Enemy, or meet them on the road, and report to
us here the movements and destination of the Enemy.

I can say to you with Confidence, that we can rely on great aid from the Citizens of this town in case of an attack, they have no money here, but Don Gasper Flores, and Louisiana Navaro, have offered us all their goods Groceries, and Beeves, for the use and support of the army, but men will not be satisfied without some money to pay their incidental expenses which we must have.

I have sent to the command of Major Dimmit, three pieces of artillery and must have in return three loads of supplies, as per contract with the owners of said wagons.

I hope we shall be reinforced in 8 days or we shall be overrun by the enemy, but if I have only one Hundred men, I will fight one thousand as long as I can; and then not surrender — I have sent this day a similar letter to the Governor and Council at San Felipe, learning from Doctor Pollard that you would be in Goliad before this letter would come, I hope you will send me one Hundred men from Goliad, unless they have been already sent from some other quarter, as it is absolutely necessary for the support of this place.

Fourteen days has expired since I commenced informing my superior officers of my situation and not even an item of news have I received from any quarter. I hope tomorrow or the next day will bring something good.

There has been a Comancha Indian in here, wishing to treat with us as a nation, and has set the 20th of April[72] for the purpose of meeting our commissioners at this place to enter a treaty of amity, commerce and limits with us.

Private
You will learn what sneaking and Gambling has been done, to operate against you by J & G.[73] You will hear all about the Houston flag, and the Houston House in Bexar, for fear you would be elected Commander of the Volunteer army, they never would let it come near an election, but shuffled it off, and threw all the army into confusion several times, and the responsibility on the heads of several Captains. I am at all times ready to obey the several orders of my commander in chief in a respectful manner and remain with high regard, your obt. Servt J. C. Neill. Lieut. Coln. Comdg.[74]

James C. Neill to the Governor and Council,
San Felipe de Austin
COMMANDANCY OF BEJAR: I beg to refer you to my official communication, under date of yesterday,[75] since when, I am sorry to inform you, that our situation becomes such as to be compelled to acquaint you of it by express. There can exist but little doubt that the enemy is advancing on this post, from the

number of families leaving town today, and those preparing to follow; among which is that of John W. Smith, who has this evening engaged wagons to remove his family into the colonies. We are informed that the advance of the enemy is on the Rio Frio, and so situated are we for want of horses, that we cannot through our own exertions gain any information, not being able to send out a small spy company. The volunteers that entered for two or four months under Burleson or Johnson, did so with an understanding that they were, for that period, to be paid monthly; which not having been complied with, has weakened me very much, as several left yesterday and today and I have not more than seventy-five men fit for duty, and afraid that number will be considerably reduced in a few days. Unless we are reinforced and victualled, we must become easy prey to the enemy, in case of attack.

My frequent repetitions on the subject of our distress and the apprehensions of an enemy, arise from the interest I feel for my country, and a wish to preserve those lands she has acquired in the infant stage of her campaign; and being well convinced as above stated, that the enemy may be nearer than rumored, without a power of ascertaining it through our own men on whom we depend and would, if necessary, ascertain the movements of the enemy, however distant, had we but a few horses.

In this extremity I will assure you, that as far as our strength goes, we will, till reinforced, use it both in spy service and if drawn within the walls, will defend the garrison to the last.

P.S. The bearer of this takes a requisition to the chairman and members of the committee of safety, at Gonzales, to assist me with as many men and horses as possible, until I can receive reinforcements through orders of the government, from some other quarter.

I shall not again make application for aid, as considering it superfluous, but wait the result of either receiving aid or an attack before it should arrive; in which case I will do the best I can with the small force I have. I have been induced to make my situation known to you supposing in the chance through which I, as well as the country, may receive most immediate assistance.[76]

Council Hall, San Felipe

Your committee to whom was referred the letter of F. W. Johnson, of the seventh, report: That the statement of Col. Johnson, connected with the recent disclosure to this House, of executive acts heretofore kept secret from their knowledge, places the expedition got up for a descent upon Matamoros by the volunteers at Bexar, in a point of view, widely different from

that which was first presented to them. The strong objections of
the Governor to the movements of volunteers, induced the
apprehension that all was not right. But upon a further
knowledge of facts, it appears that the measure as adopted by
Col. Johnson, arose from an apparent legal authority from the
Provisional Government, and which this Council, will not, at this
time disclaim.

Your committee therefore advise that Colonel Johnson have
the approbation of this Government to conduct the volunteers
who have entered upon the expedition to Matamoros and that he
proceed to unite with J. W. Fannin.[77]

John Forbes, Ist Judge of the Municipality of Nacogdoches Muster Roll

NACOGDOCHES: Know all men by these present; That I have
this day voluntarily enlisted myself in the Volunteer Auxiliary
Corps, for and during the term of six months.

And I do solemnly swear that I will bear true allegiance to the
provisional Government of Texas, or any future Government that
may be hereafter declared, and that I will serve her honestly and
faithfully against all her enemies whatsoever and observe and
obey the orders of the Governor of Texas, the orders of the
present and future authorities and the orders of the officers
appointed over me according to the rules and regulations for the
government of the Armies of Texas. "So help me God"

H. S. Kimble	31	Tennessee
M. Authey [Autry]*	43	Tennessee
J. P. Bailey*	24	Kentucky
Daniel Cloud*	21	Kentucky
W. J. Lewis*	28	Pennsylvania
Wm. H. Furtleory*	22	Kentucky
B. M. Thomas*	18	Tennessee
R. L. Stockton*	18	Virginia
Robert Bowen	24	Tennessee
J. E. Massie	24	Tennessee
Wm. McDowelly*	40	Tennessee
John P. Raynolds*	29	Tennessee
Joseph Bayliss*	28	Tennessee

The above sworn to and subscribed before me, this 14th day
January, 1836.[78] [* indicates died in the Alamo]

Santa Anna to Don Vicente Filisola

HEADQUARTERS, LEONA VICARIO, MEXICO: I recommend
Your Excellency forward the 20,000 pesos to General Rameriz y

Sesma immediately because the distance makes it difficult to
send another.

Since it is no longer necessary to draft more men for the
Army, Your Excellency should ignore the instructions which I
issued from San Luis Potosi concerning this matter.

Your Excellency shall instruct the Purveyor General, colonel
Don Ricardo Dromundo, that besides the supplies and provisions
which he has been ordered to gather, he is to see to the making
of three to four thousand quintals of maiz biscuits [hardtack]
which are most essential.

I especially commission Your Excellency to see to the gathering
from the immediate haciendas of that area some 500 well fed,
broken horses which are to be kept on good pastures to augment
the Army's cavalry which is in a very poor condition. The horses
will be paid for upon my arrival at that place. God and Liberty.[79]

Friday, January 15, 1836
51 DAYS TO THE FALL

Council Hall, San Felipe
The President presented a communication from J. C. Neill, Lieut.
Colonel commandant at Bexar, enclosing a list of the men in that
Garrison which was read and on motion of Mr. Royall, was
referred to the committee on military affairs.[80]

James C. Neill Muster Roll of Alamo Defenders[81]
FIELD AND STAFF OFFICERS
J. C. Neill — Lieut. Colonel Commanding
G. B. Jamison — Major
E. Melton — Quarter Master
J. Baugh — Adjutant
A. Anderson — Quarter Master Sergeant
H. J. Williamson — Sergeant Major
J. Fetch (Fitch) — Insr. of Art
W. H. W. Mart — Assistant Surgeon
Amos Pollard — Assistant Surgeon

Ordinance Department

George (Robert) Evans	Master Ordinance
S. C. Blair	Assist.
Charles Lance	Assist.

Artillery Corps

W. R. Carey — Captain	*T. Holland
F. W. Jackson — 1st. Lieut.	*C. Haskill
B. F. Fry — 2nd. Lieut.	A. B. Mitchell

Wm. Herser — Sergt. (Wounded)
J. McGregor — 2 Sergt.
J. W. Heallie — 3 Sergt
J. Robertson — 4 Sergt.
C. J. (P.W.) Jennings — 1 Corpl.
Wm. Lightfoot — 3 Corpl.
M. B. Atkinson
S. (L.) Boatwright
J. Byrnes
J. Balentine
R. Cockran
P. Conrad
R. W. Cunningham
Wm. Lurdoff
S. Damon
S. (L.) Dust
J. S. (L.) Ewing — Sec. to Comd.
G. Narraw (Naran) Sec. Engr. Dept.
Wm. Edwards
*C. Grymes
*John Cain
*S. Johnson
*J. Kinney
*P. Lindley
*J. Lewis

Infantry
Wm Blazeby — Captain
John Jones —1st Lieut.
B. F. Musselman (Mussellman) — Sergt.
James Dockon — Sergt.
R. B. Moore
Robt Crassen (Crasseer) — wounded
Wm. Spratt
John Moran
Samuel Holloway
Wm. Bell
J. W. Garrand
Stephen Denison
Wm. Lynn — taken prisoner
Wm. Howell
H. J. Nelson (wounded)
Richard Starr
James McGee — wounded
Miles D. Andross — sick
Wm. Thomas — wounded
Wm. Marshall
W. Haze (Hage)

W. T. Malerie (Maleree)
J. Northcross
P. Preehouse
J. Preehouse
R. Perry
J. Rutherford
T. Ryan
R. W. Russel
William Smith
C. S. Smith
R. Tommel (Tommell)
F. Taylor
G. Tomlinson
Thomas Walters
G. Wyatt
A. Wolf
J. Bartlett
S. C. Connell
I. (J.) Ingram
H. Johnston
J. Walker
J. Shudd
J. Warnull
W. Howard
D. Bowe

S. W. Edwards
G. A. Fassitt — Capt.
Robt. White — Lieut.
Wm. A. Erwin — Sergt.
Jona T. Hobbs
Wm. Parks
Isaac Ryan
John Pickering
A. Devault
A. S. Summerlin
Thos. Hendrick
T. Harris
Chester Gorbit
H. K. (R.) Day
G. Washington
          Mitchell
S. Sewell
David Davis
S. W. Main—In Hospital
W. Walker — In hospital
T. C. Goodrich

[* later died in the fall of the Alamo]

General Jose Urrea Diary Entry

His Excellency received information regarding a party of colonists that was making its way to Matamoros for the purpose of taking possession of that port. In view of this, he immediately ordered me to set out for the said port with my cavalry and two additional pickets of mounted troops from the regiment of Tampico and the auxiliary troops from Guanajuato. Three hundred infantry from Yucatan were to join me at Matamoros. With this force I was ordered to begin the operations of our campaign along the coast as far as Lipantitlan, a fort situated on the right bank of the Nueces.[82]

Saturday, January 16, 1836
50 DAYS TO THE FALL

Telegraph,
and Texas Register

SAN FELIPE: The manager of the Natchez (Mississippi) theater announces that all the receipts of the 16th (December) shall be applied to the use of the patriots of Texas — New Orleans Bee of Dec 19th.

Useful volunteers — among the number of those who sailed from New York for Texas were six West Point cadets.

More Texian volunteers — A company of Germans has been embodied at Pittsburg, to proceed immediately to Texas.

Amos Pollard to Henry Smith

BEJAR: I have but a moment to write you as I am so busy in regulating the hospital. Things have been in the worst possible state here as you are aware — I hope and have reason to believe that they will soon become much better — I ought to have written by the express but knew not when it started — I have only to say that we are much in want of money and that some could be collected on goods being brought into this place and the commandant will do it yet he is ignorant of the rate of duties established by the government — Were he in possession of that knowledge he would avail himself of it now as there are goods here and he talks of charging but four percent — I am interested in this as you will see for the Hospital is in great want of a little money.

We will endeavor to elect as many of our countrymen as possible from this jurisdiction — What the prospect is I have not been able to learn — I think we have now an excellent opportunity to completely conquer our most formidable foe — our internal enemy — The Mexican Troy party of the country — I hope every friend of his country will be diligent at his post and from the righteousness of our cause we cannot but succeed.[83]

Council Hall, San Felipe de Austin: Resolutions providing for the Troops at Bexar

Sec. 1, *Whereas*, the troops garrisoned at Bexar being without the necessary provisions and clothing for their support and comfort, and the probability of its being some time yet before the necessary supplies from our agents in the United States for their support, sustenance and use of the army will be received, and it being absolutely necessary to make immediate provisions for the sustenance and support of those troops at Bexar, and it being impossible to drive beeves and procure provisions for their use without horses, — therefore,

Be it Resolved by the General Council of the Provisional Government of Texas, That Lieut. colonel James C. Neill, commandant at Bexar, be, and is hereby authorized and empowered to employ as many Mexicans, or other citizens, for the purpose of driving up beeves and procuring provisions for the troops under his command, as may be required for their support, and that this government shall respect the drafts of said commander for the pay of the said men in his employ.

Sec. 2. *Be it further resolved, & etc.* That the sum of twenty dollars per month, to the Mexicans employed by the commandant, for the purpose of getting beeves and other provisions for the use and support of the troops . . . is hereby acknowledged by this Government.

Sec. 3. *Be it further resolved*, That John W. Smith be, and is hereby authorized and empowered to collect the sum of one thousand dollars of the public dues, or any money to that amount belonging to this government in the department of Bexar, and give same to the commandant at that place; the same to be used for support of the troops.

Sec. 4. *Be it further resolved*, That an express be immediately procured to take these resolutions to the commandant at Bexar.

Passed January 16th, 1836.[84]

Sunday, January 17, 1836
49 DAYS TO THE FALL

William B. Travis to Sam Houston
SAN FELIPE: Militia and volunteers are but ill suited to garrison a town . . . Enthusiasm may keep up an army for a few days, but money, and money alone will support an army for regular warfare.[85]

General Sam Houston to Governor Henry Smith
HEADQUARTERS, GOLIAD: I have the honor to enclose for your information a communication from Lt. Col J. C. Neill, under date of the 14th inst. Colonel Bowie will leave here in a few hours for Bexar, with a detachment of from thirty to fifty men. Capt. Patton's company, it is believed, are there now. I have ordered the fortifications in the town of Bexar to be demolished, and if you should think well of it, I will remove all the cannon and other munitions of war to Gonzales and Copano, blow up the Alamo, and abandon the place, as it will be impossible to keep up the Station with volunteers. The sooner I can be authorized the better it will be for the country. In an hour I will take up the line of march for Refugio Mission with about 209 efficient men, where I will await orders from your Excellency, believing that the army should not advance with a small force upon Matamoros with the hope or belief that the Mexicans will cooperate with us. I have no confidence in them and the disaster at Tampico should teach us a lesson to be noted in our future operations.

I have learned that Colonel Gonzales is somewhere on the Nueces with one hundred and seventy men, but accounts vary as to the actual number. They are to cooperate in the eastern Confederacy, I am told.

I will leave Captain Wyatt in command at this post until I can relieve him with thirty-five regulars now at Refugio. I pray that your Excellency will cause all the regulars now enlisted to be formed into companies, and march to head quarters. It will be impossible to keep up a garrison with volunteers. Do forward the regulars. Capt. Smith had been relieved, and I met him on his way home today. Captain Patton will return to Lavaca country and bring on a company as soon as possible.

I have sent to Capt. Dimmit to raise one hundred more men and march to Bexar forthwith, if it should be invaded, and if not to repair to headquarters with his company. Capt. Patton will do likewise. I would have marched to Bexar with a force, but the Matamoros fever rages so high I must see Col. Ward's men. You have no idea of the difficulties I have encountered. Patton has told you of the men that make the trouble. Better materials never were in ranks. The government and all its officers have been misrepresented to the army.

I pray you send me copies of Austin's letters, or rather extracts. If the council is in session I do wish they would say something about the Confederacy.

Please send me frequent expresses and advise me of your pleasure.[86]

J. W. Robinson to Edward Burleson, J. C. Neill & et al

SAN FELIPE: You will forthwith on sight or knowledge of this or so soon thereafter as practicable, repair to the city of Bexar & meet and treat with such deputation of the Comanche Indians, as may be then and there assembled, and adjourn your meeting so such times and places as you may deem best calculated to effect the objects of your mission[87]

Council Hall, San Felipe

Be it Resolved by the General Council of Texas, That a committee of five shall be appointed to act, in the event of there not being a quorum of the members of the Council present. . . .

Be it Resolved by the General Council of Texas, That in the event of there not being a quorum of the council present, the acting Governor of Texas is hereby clothed with the full and ample power to enforce all ordinances, laws and resolutions enacted by the Council, and all other laws of Texas[88]

Stephen F. Austin to D. C. Barrett

NEW ORLEANS: Texas stands high all over the country. We have effected a loan for *two hundred thousand dollars,* and expect to procure another 40 or 50,000. The enclosed contract contains the terms of the first loan; it will no doubt be ratified by the Convention as stipulated. The credit and prospects of the country will be totally ruined if it is not. The last news from Vera Cruz and Tampico is, that the Federal Party had united with Santa Anna against Texas. This leaves us but one course, which is an absolute Declaration of Independence. Such a measure is expected and called for by the people of the United States, from one end of this union to the other. We could not have obtained the loan here except on the firm belief by the lenders that a Declaration of Independence would be made in March next by the Convention.

The negotiation that is now pending for another loan has been embarrassed by a rumor that there has been a mob at San Felipe to destroy the government, and restore the old state of things under Coahuila and Texas. I do not believe there has been any such thing. Texas must be united and act together and in harmony, and never recede one inch. It may, perhaps, be necessary to stop and rest awhile on the way, but never to retrace our political march. It must be forward. The country has rested a short time under the Declaration of 7th November, in order to look around and gain a little more strength and a little more information as to the road yet to be traveled over — and we are now ready for another move and a final one. What ever difference of opinion there may have been as to the time for this move, I hope there will be none now. The whole nation [Mexico] of all parties are against us; they have left us but one remedy — **Independence**. It is now necessary as a measure of self-defense. The United States, as a people, are ready to sustain it — we shall sink in their estimation if we do not adopt it. . . .

I shall try to be home by the first week in March and preach Independence.[89]

Monday, January 18, 1836
48 DAYS TO THE FALL

James Bowie Receipt

Provisional Government of Texas
To J. W. Nash for carrying express
By orders of Col Neill To San Felipe de Austin 11 days $10.00
Horse furnished self $10.00
Expenses furnished $13.00

Sworn to and subscribed before me in the absence of Col Neill.

James Bowie
Commandant at
the post of Bejar[90]

Green B. Jameson to Sam Houston
BEXAR: Believing that a letter will meet you at Goliad, and having had more time to make a better plot of the "Fortress Alamo" at this place I have embraced this opportunity to acquaint you more satisfactorily of the condition and progress of the department which you have so kindly assigned me.

I send you herewith inclosed a neat plot of the fortress exhibiting its true condition at this time, as also an Index being duplicates of my former addressed to you at Washington, added to which is a recapitulation more explanatory, and showing the improvements already made by me.

I am now fortifying and mounting cannon. The 18 pounder now on the N.W.[91] corner of the fortress so as to command the Town and the country around.

The officers of every department do more work than the men

and also stand guard, and act as patrol every night. I have no doubt but the enemy have spies in town every twenty-four hours, and we are using our utmost endeavors to catch them every night, nor have I any doubt there are 1500 of the enemy at the town of Rio Grande, and as many more at Laredo, and I believe they know our situation as well as we do ourselves.

We have received 100 bushels of meal and 42 beeves which will last us for two months yet to come, but no other supplies have come to our relief.

You have heard so much about our situation from our Commander that I shall say nothing further on the subject.

You can rely on aid from the citizens of this town in face of siege, Saguine [Seguin] is doing all for the cause he can, as well as many of the most wealthy and influential citizens.

You can plainly see by the plat that the Alamo was not built by a military people for a fortress, tho' it is strong, there is not a redoubt that will command the whole line of the fort, all is in the plain wall and intended to take advantage with a few pieces of artillery, it is a strong place and better that it should remain as it is after completing the half moon batteries than to rebuild it. The men here will not labour and I cannot ask it of them until they are better clad and fed. We now have 114 men counting officers the sick and wounded, which leaves us about 80 efficient men 40 in the Alamo and 40 in Town, leaving all of the patrol duty to be done by the officers and which for want of horses has to be performed on foot.

We have had loose discipline until lately. Since we heard of 1000 to 1500 men of the enemy being on their march to this place duty is being done well and punctually in case of an attack we will move all into the Alamo and whip 10 to 1 with our artillery.

If the men here can get a reasonable supply of clothing, provisions and money they will remain the balance of the 4 months, and do duty and fight better than fresh men, they have all been tried and have confidence in themselves.

I can give you full assurance that so far as I am concerned there shall be nothing wanting on my part, neither as an officer or a soldier to promote and sustain the great cause at which we are all aiming, and am at all times respectfully subject to your orders for the verification of which I refer you to my commander at this place, as well all as the officers and men. I have been much flattered for my exertions at this place. I have more than one time received the vote of thanks of the whole Garrison.

I have one other subject which interests me some; to ask you, if it is not too late, that is to recommend to your notice Capt. G. Navan, who is clerk in my department for the appointment of Sutler at this Post as he is in every way qualified to fill the office. I know of no man who merits it more than he does, as an

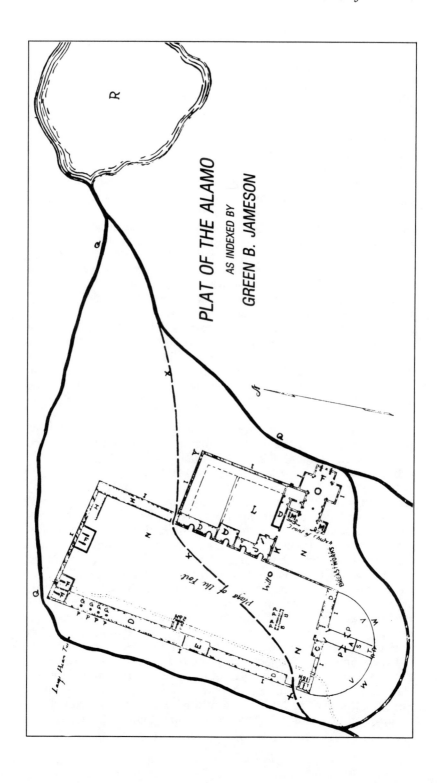

Index

A. Represents the entrance into the Alamo with two cannon.

B. Temporary redoubts of stakes on end and rocks and dirt between, ...

C. The Guard House.

D. Soldiers quarters built up of stone houses.

E. Headquarters of Alamo now occupied by 2 wounded officers.

F. Batteries and platforms where cannon are now mounted.

G. Cannon mounted on the ground with ports in the main wall.

H. Soldiers quarters built up doby houses and picketed all round as letter B.

I. Strong stone walls without pickets all around.

J. The hospital up stairs in a two story building of stone, the lower story being represented by the letter K. and now occupied as an Armory for our small arms.

L. A large stone quartel for horses adjoining the Church San Antonio, Hospitals and Armory.

M. The Magazine in the Church San Antonio two very efficient and appropriate rooms 10 feet square each, walls all around and above 4 feet thick.

N. All large vacancies inside the walls of the fortress, the Church San Antonio is in the Alamo and forms a part of the fortress and is marked by the letter O.

P. The cannon mounted in the Alamo. Their number corresponding with that of the letter.

Q. The aqueduct as around the fortress by which we are supplied with water, marked with red ink.

R. A lake of water where we contemplate supplying the fortress by ditching from one of the acqueducts laid down.

S. A pass from the present fortress to a contemplated drawbridge across a contemplated ditch inside a contemplated half moon battery as laid down on the plan.

T. A part of said ditch, as well as a trap door across said ditch, which is contemplated to be raised by a tackle from inside the half moon battery.

U. The hinges on which said bridge is to be raised.

V. The half moon baattery at each end of the fortress as contemplated.

W. A 12 feet ditch around the half moon battery as contemplated.

X. The contemplated ditch where we wish the permanent water to pass thro' the fortress and thence to pass out erecting an arch over each place and also a redoubt for a permanent cannon in case of seige.

Y. A ditch passing under the stone wall to the lake marked R.

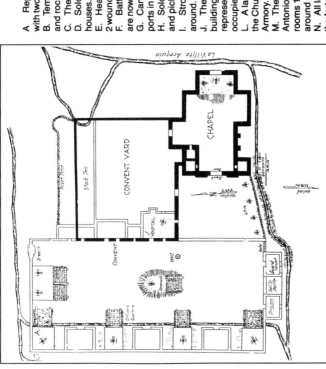

The Alamo ground plan compiled from drawings by Capt. B. Green Jameson, Texan Army, January 1836; Col. Ignacio de Labastida, Mexican Army, March 1836; and Capt. Reuben M. Potter, United States Army, 1841.

evidence of his patriotism he has absented himself from his family when he was also receiving a salary of $1800 per annum to aid us in our difficulties.

I am with esteem, Very Respectfully, Your obt. Servt.

ATTACHMENT: I will in my next give you a plan of the town as fortified when we took it. We have too few to garrison both places, and will bring all our forces to the Alamo tomorrow as well as the cannons. In excavating our ditches we can with perfect safety rely on a fall from the two ditches or aqueducts of at least 20 feet, consequently we can make our ditches deep enough with perfect safety, and the earth here is of such a nature that it will not wash, and we can ditch very near the half moon batteries with perfect safety. I will say all that is necessary in my answer to your official letter on this subject. In regard to the ditch we can have a flood gate at the mouth of it, which will answer for keeping in a supply of water in case of a siege, as also by raising, for cleaning the fortress. I am too much occupied to copy these papers but I shall be able to show you by demonstration when I have nothing else to attend to that I will not be wanting in my abilities as a topographical Engineer.[92]

Henry Smith to L. W. Groce

SAN FELIPE: Much difficulty & confusion has to be encountered. Necessity has compelled to adjourn the council. They have joined with the mob to ruin the country. You know they used to threaten to break us up — they now use stronger means, their money — My council became basely corrupt. A veto is useless, and in place of a veto, I sent them to the Devil, in the shape of an address. It was a fancy article intended alone to tickle their own delicate ears. It was not intended for the public eye, but addressed to them in secret session. They felt it severely and it was just what I intended. They however by way of creating sympathy in their favor, have made it public with a bloated tissue of falsehood attached to it, all of which I have their own acts to refute, but they have been so bent on mischief they can not recollect their own acts. I have since tried to purge the hive, but in vain — the worms had so artfully _____ [93] themselves in that nothing short of fire and brimstone would drive them. I threw it in abundantly and such a buz you can not imagine. I was alone entirely and expected the whole to be upon me. But honest necessity compelled me to bluff the whole. They notified me I was removed from office &c and a new Governor was made &c. I knew however they could not break me to make a new one — and I could adjourn them by force, that is by cutting off all communications with them. The council has been the means of fitting out marauding parties from Bexar & now doing everything in their power to join a piratical co-operation at the risk, cost & credit of the Govt. This they do to favor a corrupt part. Bexar has now but Seventy men to defend it, striped of ammunition, clothing, provisions, Horses, oxen, wagons and the whole country round stripped by impressments and the party has now arrived at Goliad for the same purpose but there I hope they will be headed by Genl Houston & a stop put to their plans and it is more than probable, some of their necks broken. An express has just arrived from Bexar that the Mexicans hearing of their weak situation, was on the march with a large army to make an attack and retake it, and was within 60 to 80 miles, and the inhabitants were all leaving as fast as possible. This state of things has been brought about by the management of base men, who have not the good of the country at heart. It is annoying to me — and some of my council even deserves death, for aiding and abetting. They have preferred charges against me to be tried before the convention. I am able & willing to plead to my charges — but I am not amenable to the council and will be tried only by my peers.

My health is bad & I have trouble enough to keep it so, for I have but little rest. I still remain however in good heart and can bear all they can heap upon me. But when my own council turn traitors and attempt to deceive me, it is too bad. They have not however been spared nor have they anything better to expect at my hands. I have numbers, money, and talent to contend with, and I am now entirely alone. The worst of it is, they dont even offer me a divide — and I really considered it was time to dissolve the partnership. You need not be discouraged about this difficulty. I can fight them all; and honesty is the best policy and will ultimately succeed. An unequivocal Declaration of Independence will save the country & that is all that can. You will certainly be alive to this, come down and see me, don't stay at home — up with the Hypo. I am not thus troubled, and I know no reason why you should. If you had the half of my troubles you might complain, so come down, and see me and hear what is going on. I can not write half — two hours with me would cure you — Please remember me to your brother and ladies. It is late and I have much writing to do yet.[94]

Council Hall, San Felipe

The Council met pursuant to adjournment.

There not being a quorum present, adjourned till nine o'clock tomorrow morning.[95]

Stephen F. Austin to Gail Borden Jr.

NEW ORLEANS: Texas continues to rise all over this country, our rise in public opinion and confidence is however based entirely on the prospect of a speedy declaration of independence. I have assured everyone that this measure is certain and will be unanimous, as all the reason in favor of the declaration of 7 Novr. have entirely ceased owing to the federal party having united with Santanna against us —

My health is greatly improved — had it been as good before I left home, I should have come on from San Felipe by land and avoided the excitement which I found blazing at Quintana and other places in the low country. I shall preach independence all over the U.S. wherever I go — What do you think of the inclosed idea for a flag?[96]

James W. Robinson to Gen. Sam Houston
SAN FELIPE de AUSTIN: Inclosed in the printed document, you will find the late Gov. Smith's Bullying message, and some of the proceedings of the General Council; by them you will perceive the most flagrant usurptions of power attempted to be exercised by the late Gov. & the utter impossibility of his maintaining his foolish notions & policy.

It is rumored here that the plan now issuing by him was suggested by you that [you] will be here with troops to support him against the council; now so foolish & utopian an idea, I know could not originate with you and I hope you will speedily satisfy the Council of your innocence for the impression is gaining ground and may ruin you. . . .[97]

Wednesday, January 20, 1836
46 DAYS TO THE FALL

D. P. Cummings to Father
GONZALES: The scarcity of paper together with other difficulties I have had to labor under has prevented me from writing before this and indeed it is a matter of Claim whether this letter will ever reach the United States.

I arrived at the mouth of the Brazos about a month ago in a vessel from New Orleans and have traveled on foot by San Felipe to this place leaving my trunk with books, and two rifles with Mr. White at Columbia 10 miles above Brasoria having sold my best rifle for $30 at San Felipe. I saw Genl. Houston and Presented him your letter. He advised me to get a horse & proceed to Goliad where he would see me in a short time again — I have accordingly come on thus far with the intention as to connect myself with a Company of Rangers on the Frontiers to keep off the Indians, But it is most probable I will go to San Antonio de Bexar and there remain until I can suitably connect myself with the Army or until an occasion may require my services. Every man in this country at this time has to go upon his own footing as the Government at present is unable to make any provisions for the Army. However a change for the better is expected soon and affairs is expected to be in a better condition.

Provisions are very scarce here and traveling or living is attended with considerable expense — Allowing to the great number of Volunteers from the U. States besides the Emigration of Families into the upper Colonies is unprecedented for the past five months.

Tho under rather indifferent circumstance myself at this time, I have no reason to complain of my coming to this country as I find nothing but what might have been expected. On the contrary I have satisfaction of beholding one of the finest countries in the world and have fully determined to locate myself in Texas. I have to be better situated to write you more about this country, and as I have not much time Can say very little at present, More than inform you what I am about &c &c.

A Gentleman is going East today by whom I intend Sending my letter.

Letters have been intercepted to the Mexican citizens of Bexar informing them of the arrival of 2,000 troops on the Rio Grande, and now coming on to retake that place in consequence of which, Many of the Mexicans have secretly left the place, and preparations are now making to fortify the town. All of our troops have been ordered to Copano to proceed against Matamoros.[98]

J. W. Robinson to Advisory Committee

1st The ports of Mexico are blocked against American vessels and the ports of Tampico & Matamoros even against Mexican vessels, which argues that Mexico is making great preparations against Texas and resorts to the blocking of her ports in order to cut off communications with Texas — and keep from us the knowledge of her preparations —

2nd It is said a line of sentinels is stationed along the Rio Grande to prevent all communications with Texas — which if true would be conclusive to my mind that great preparations are making against Texas — and if so the want of organization in the Militia department leaves Texas in a very exposed situation —

3rd The bill proposing to organize the Militia has not answered the purpose — In Austin the Militia has not been organized and it is the same in many of the other Jurisdictions

4th It is said the enemy are now advancing & the Militia are not in a situation to be called out and we have to depend on the uncertain assistance of volunteers — to remedy which I would propose that

5th That the council authorize you to appoint one aid de

camp for each Municipality whose duty it shall be to superintend the organizing of the Militia — and Report to you forth with the number of men in their respective Jurisdictions enrolled in the militia the amount of ammunition number of Rifles, muskets, Shot guns — the — probable quantity of Provisions — The most suitable places for Depots of Provisions & ammunition & arms — which will enable you to make such arrangement and understandably give such orders in case of an invasion as may be necessary —

6th Let the council pass another Bill — ordering the alcaldes to organize the militia and under heavy penalties & report to you through the aid de camp

7th Let the Militia be then divided into four parts — and drafted to serve 3 months — Let the draft be made of all — so that one fourth can be called out at a moments warning — & if necessary the 2nd fourth and so on to the whole if circumstances should require it — & By this means the whole force of Texas will be in a situation to be called out at short notice

The present System of 3 Commissioners will not answer — one says to the other "do it" — & he refers it back again & by that means nothing is done — Compel the Adcaldes under heavy penalties to do it and something may be done otherwise Texas is left a prey to the Enemy

I very Respectfully recommend the foregoing plan of organizing the militia for the defense of Texas, to the consideration of the advisory committee, for their opinion and advice; and as one great arm of defence the organization of the Militia deserves to be attended to without delay.[99]

Advisory Committee to J. W. Robinson

To the Acting Govr — The advisory committee are of opinion that three hundred dollars should be placed in the hands of Andrew Ponton, of Gonzales, subject to the orders of the Govt contractor at that place, for purchase of supplies for the garrison at Bexar.

To the Committee of finance — You will please draw for the within amount from the contingent fund.

In accordance with the Resolution passed by the General council and approved by the acting Governor on the 17th of January A D 1836 together with the foregoing instructions of the Advisory Committee and the acting governor — The committee on Finance do hereby authorize and instruct J W Moody Auditor to draw on the Treasury for Three hundred Dollars in favor of the Chairman of committee of finance to be placed by him in the hands of Andrew Ponton of Gonzales for the purpose stated to be drawn out of the Contingent fund.

To the acting Govr.

The advisory committee of the executive are of the opinion that the sum of three hundred dollars, drawn by the committee on finance, for aiding the contractor at Gonzales, in supplying the garrison at bexar, should be sent to Andrew Ponton, Esqr. of the former place, for the above purpose; and that General Burleson is a suitable man by whom to send it, provided he will have it forwarded with dispatch —

In according with the foregoing advice, I recommend & direct the committee on Finance to pay the above sum of three hundred dollars to General Burleson, and take triplicate receipts for the same.[100]

M. Hawkins to Governor Henry Smith

BEJAR: While I am waiting to carry an express to General Houston, I take the opportunity of giving my sentiments by our express to San Felipe.

By the documents you will receive you will perceive our indignation at this post at the disorderly and anarchical conduct of the council. Were it not for a proclamation issued from headquarters which arrived here last night, you would have MEN, not sentiment at San Felipe to sustain you in the discharge of your duty as first Magistrate of the nation. Be consoled! Fight the good fight and we are with you to a man. Let the low, intriguing land and Mexican speculators know, that the sons of Washington and St. Patrick will not submit to delusion, rascality and usurption. We are bound to you in the proper discharge of your duties and will not submit to anarchy and misrule. May God bless you and prosper you is the sincere wish of an honest son of Erin and a friend to Texian Independence.

P.S. We will sustain you by arms.[101]

Edward Burleson [receipt]

COUNCIL HALL, SAN FELIPE: Received this day of Wyatt Hanks, Chairman of the Finance Committee, Three hundred dollars ($300.—) to be taken to Andrew Ponton Esqr. at Gonzales, for the purpose of purchasing supplies for the troops garrisoned at Bexar — The same being an appropriation made in accordance with the special advice and instruction of the Advisory Committee & acting Governor for said troops.[102]

Santa Anna to Don Vicente Filisola

HEADQUARTERS, LEONA VICARIO, MEXICO: I herewith acknowledge being informed . . . of the present state of the City of Bejar and of the expedition heading towards Lipantitlan.

According to the latest intelligence, The Mexicans accompanying

Gonzales, with whom he arrived at Lipantitlan and which number only forty, abandoned that place before the 15th of the current month.

I have ordered Sesma, and also instruct Your Excellency, to cease all communications with Bejar, and not to permit the passage of any goods, and to allow only trustworthy spies to pass who may be able to report with certainty the actual state of the City and intentions of the rebels.[103]

Thursday, January 21, 1836
45 DAYS TO THE FALL

William B. Travis to W. G. Hill

SAN FELIPE: I have this day sent you orders about contracting with McKinney for our uniforms and equipment. I wish you to attend to it immediately. I spoke to him about my uniform,

which I have written to him to purchase. I am ordered off to the defense of San Antonio, which is threatened with an attack from the enemy. I shall leave in two days. Do all you can to make recruits and get the remain.[104]

This widely publicized portrait of William B. Travis, painted years after his death, is responsible for the notion that Travis wore a fine uniform. In truth, there is no record the uniform he ordered arrived before the fall of the Alamo.

William B. Travis Notebook Entry[105]

Paid	for	flour	$5.00
do	do	Tin ware	2.50
do	do	Twine	1.00
		3.00 2.00	
do	do	Leggins & Spurs	5.00
		5.00 1.00	
do	do	Flag & powder flask	6.00
		4.00 15	
do	do	Bridle 3 blankets	19.00
		12.00 1.25	
do	do	Tent frying pan	13.25
		6 ft	
do	do	Rope	.75

Austin and Archer to A. J. Yates[106]
NEW ORLEANS: You are hereby authorized to draw on William Bryan the General agent of the Government of Texas, in the city of New Orleans, for the sum of Twenty Thousand dollars, payable at the bank of New Orleans, at the time that the installment hereafter to become due on the Loan negotiated by the Commissioners on the 11th instant, shall become due, and you are to account to the Government of Texas for the proceeds of said draft, in conformity with the letter of Instructions. . . .

Friday, January 22, 1836
44 DAYS TO THE FALL

William B. Travis Receipt[107]
Rec'd from Governor Smith by the hands of C B Stewart one hundred Dollars for the use of the Army.

W. Barret Travis
Lt. Col. of Cavalry

William B. Travis Notebook Entry

Paid	for	Corn to Made	1.00
do	do	to Burnam for corn	1.00

Santa Anna to D. Vicente Filisola
HEADQUARTERS OF LEONE VICARIO: Several complaints having been called to my attention about the divisions of Generals Sesma and Cos, and of some bold pickets who have been demanding, on credit, supplies of all kinds from the towns and farms in their transit . . . Your Excellency will see to it that the above mentioned generals pay the amounts which they may owe . . . warning them that nothing shall be taken without paying for it at its fair price, because a favorable opinion of the army demands it. . . .

[another letter, same date, same addressee]
I am advised of the wise dispositions which General Sesma has ordered taken to facilitate the crossing of the Rio Grande, which measures meet with my approval.[108]

Austin and Archer to Governor Henry Smith
NEW ORLEANS: We have deposited ten thousand dollars in the Bank of Orleans subject to the orders of the Govt. which must be drawn for in the manner stated in our instructions.

El Mosquito Mexicano

Decree from Jose Maria Tornel

Attention! Civil wars are always bloody. Our soldiers ever aspire to shed the blood of foreigners who seek to take away from us our rights and menace our independence. This war is righteous, and should be without remorse; and this nation will adorn with flowers the tomb of its defenders. Remember, soldiers, in civil war triumphant victories must always be accompanied by the mourning and by the tears of widows and orphans. It is in the face of such reflections that our brave troops start out on a campaign so full of privation to retrieve the disasters at Bexar. So many misfortunes have already been suffered and so many more may come that the Supreme Government is supremely indignant and ardently desires vengeance. It therefore esteems it very fitting that it should pass the following law:

Art. I. The war against Texas is national;

Art II. To reward services that the army will make in this campaign and in wars of like nature, there is established a military order to be called the LEGION OF HONOR;

Art. III. In order to be admitted to this order it is necessary to have made the Texas campaign or to serve in Tampico or other points of foreign aggression. The General-in-Chief of the army himself will record the merits of each one.

[Eight articles follow containing details on service necessary for decoration of this order]

Art. XI. The candidate for the honor must kneel and swear: "I swear to be faithful to the country, the Government, and to honor and do all that constitutes the duty of a reliant loyal gentleman of the Legion of Honor!" The soldiers and sergeants swear together to fight with extra ordinary valor on the day of battle.

The insignia of the Legion shall be a cross or star with five double radiants. The centre shall be surrounded by a crown of laurel; at one side shall be the national arms, on the other the motto HONOR, VALOR and COUNTRY. On the other side of the medal in the centre shall be the campaign or action for which the decoration is awarded, on the other Republica Mexicana. This cross shall be of silver for the cavalryman and of gold for all officers. The Grand Crosses will wear a band with a red border on each edge across the right and left shoulder. This is a purely military order and shall be considered the highest honor a Mexican soldier can merit. None besides soldiers ought to obtain it.[109]

Saturday, January 23, 1836
43 DAYS TO THE FALL

David Crockett Receipt
WASHINGTON: This is to certify that John Lott furnished my self and four other volunteers on our way to the army with accommodations for our selves & horses. The government will pay him $7.50 cts —

David Crockett[110]

This is to certify that John Lott furnished myself & Mr. Kerr & two horses on our way to the army for Four Dollars which Government will pay

Wm. B. Harrison Cap

William B. Travis Notebook Entry
Paid   for   to Burnam for corn   1.00

Telegraph,
and Texas Register
SAN FELIPE: SATURDAY: We learn that an armed schooner, named Bounty, mounting six guns, has just arrived on our coast from Boston and is intended for the service of Texas. It is said that she is a very fine, fast sailing vessel, and is well calculated for service. It is gratifying to see that our Yankee brethren have not forgotten us in the time of trouble, but have already given us proof of their liberality, and of the interest they feel in the welfare of their suffering brethren of Texas.

TO THE CANDIDATES FOR THE CONVENTION
GENTLEMEN, — Inasmuch as the destinies of Texas will be placed in the hands of those of you who may be elected; it is proper that you should distinctly explain to the people your political sentiments, and the course you will pursue. You are all requested to declare "are you for adhering to the Constitution of 1824, or for a declaration of Independence?"

A voter

LAW NOTICE
THE PARTNERSHIP heretofore existing between Travis & Nibbs, has been dissolved by limitation. The unfinished business entrusted to them will be attended to by Travis & Starr.

W. B. Travis and Franklin J. Starr have associated themselves in the practice of law, and will attend to business in the courts of San Felipe, Washington, and the adjoining municipalities. One or both of them will be constantly found in San Felipe.[111]

From the New York Herald

TEXAS

IMPORTANT DIPLOMATIC MOVEMENTS — We are informed, on high authority, that a few days ago, Joaquin Maria de Castillo, charge de Affairs of Mexico, sent a strong and stormy note to the Secretary of State, remonstrating on the popular movements in certain parts of this country, particularly in New Orleans, relative to the affairs of Texas. The people of Texas, he represented as rebels from the central government of Mexico, and the minister claimed the interference of the United States, on the principle of the laws of nations, to put down at once all armaments or movements that might be attempted in this country, to aid the inhabitants of that colony.

We are also informed, that when the note of the Mexican minister was read or heard by General Jackson, his natural spirit in favor of liberty and right could not brook the insolent taunts, the concealed sneers, the empty pretensions, of De Castillo. The good old general started on his legs, strode across the room, and swore that the cause of liberty, in Texas or elsewhere, should never be impeded or put down by any act of his government.

James C. Neill to the Governor & General Council

COMMANDANCY OF BEXAR: I hasten to inform you that a courier has arrived here last night in twenty days from St Louis Potosi dispatched by Eugene Navarro to his brother bringing intelligence that Santa Anna has arrived at Saltillo with three thousand troops, also that there are at the Town of Rio Grande sixteen hundred more and that he makes Saltillo his headquarters for the present, and further that he is instructed by the Government to raise forthwith Ten Thousand in such manner as he may think proper and proceed against Texas, which he says he will reduce to the state it originally was in 1820. I was also or at least Col. Buoy [Bowie] was informed yesterday confidentially by the priest of this place who is a staunch Republican that it was the intention of Santa Anna to attack Copano and Labahia first and send but a few hundred cavalry against this place at the same time.

If teams could be obtained here by any means to remove the Cannon and Public Property I would immediately destroy the fortifications and abandon the place, taking the men I have under my command here, to join the commander in chief at Copano, of which I informed him last night immediately on the above information being Communicated to me.

The foregoing information is received thr'u such a channel that the most implicit reliance may be given to its correctness and veracity, as the parties are personally Known to colo Buoy and he says deserving the utmost confidence.[112]

James C. Neill to Henry Smith

I ask the privilege of you to send me here at this place a writ of Election for the Volunteer Army now under my command to authorize them to elect two delegates to the Convention to be held at Washington. The reason that I request this is that not a man here under my command will or can have a voice in an election only by and through that method. They are all Volunteers are all in favor of independence.

Such men should have representation in the Council of their country and that too by men chosen from among themselves. The citizens have all declared for us and will on the first next month take the oath to support the provisional Govt. You have the highest regards of the whole Army, and you shall be sustained for your firmness and Philanthropy.[113]

John W. Smith to D. C. Barrett

GONZALES: You will no doubt be surprised to find my letter dated in Gonzales. I am here and have my family also here. I did not wish to pass again into the hands of Centralists now [nor] was I willing to leave my family in their power for which reason I have brought them here and tomorrow I go with Mrs. Gritton to San Antonio there to remain until times is a little settled.[114]

James Robinson to Stephen F. Austin, Wm Wharton and B. T. Archer

SAN FELIPE: In the discharge of my official duty, it becomes incumbent on me, to communicate to you the painful and humiliating fact that Henry Smith Esq. has been and is now suspended from acting as Governor, and the council has preferred serious and weighty charges and specifications against him, and cited him to trial.

The state of things has grown out of the expedition to Matamoros, the Govn. being opposed to it, and the council in its favor and I confess I was warmly in favor of the measure and I hope in God it will prosper as it is now under way, and the late Govn. cannot stop it I Hope!

I am now performing the duties of Governor by virtue of a resolution of the council and I do most seriously say upon my honor much against my will, and my interest, and every effort but the total abandonment of my post has been made by me, to avoid doing so I have pleaded with the late Governor to desist but in vain the printed enclosed paper will show you our proceedings in this matter.

The Expedition against Matamoros will go on. The enemy of that measure cannot defeat it.

We have information that Genl. Santa Anna was a short time since at San Luis Potosi with 5 to 6000 troops and advancing upon us. Let him come, he shall be welcome. I hope we will give a Good account of him in our report to the world and I hope that the common enemy making his appearance upon our frontier will dispel all little diversions among us.

Sunday, January 24, 1836
42 DAYS TO THE FALL

M. Hawkins to J. W. Robinson

BEXAR: You will perceive by the express which leaves here today, that we may in short time expect stormy gales from Mexico; That Santa Anna has proscribed every individual, without distinction of age or sex, from the Grande to the Sabine. He will be warmly received and nobly encountered, and find to conquer Mexicans is one thing, but Americans another, if the latter only do their duty by preparing with energy. Let the tocsin of war be only sounded in all the colonies between these two rivers, the meneces of the despot be proclaimed, and every man capable of bearing arms invited into the field, let a copy of the express of to day be published, and circulated as far as practicable throughout the United States, and Sta. Anna will boast no more, Americans will be triumphant and Texas FREE. Energy and action be the signal note of preparation. So far for our military politics. I understand with insufferable pain that our patriotic first magistrate is threatened with assassination. Accused and withered be the unhallowed hand that at such a crisis dare be raised agt him, or at any time. Should this be the case Texas is lost forever, and the blood of heroes has been shed in vain. I have been informed that the speculative, disorganizing, troy part are as vigilant as Argus and as active as Cataline, to make their preparations for swaying the councils of the nation in the next Convention. Men and horses are going night and day to seduce the people to their views. Can no measure be adopted to counteract these nefarious designs? If not, Texas is lost. She has more danger to apprehend from internal than external enemies, more from disunion than a hostile foe. Pardon the Liberty I have taken in making any suggestions to such an able and efficient officer of state. Write me of your views if you can spare a moment from the arduous duties of your place; communicate this, and present my devoted services to his excellency H Smith. . . .

PS I would have written more but the Carrier waits. The whole army is delighted with Houston who met the shock of disorganizers at La Bahia, with firmness and success Every man here is for independence.[115]

[Appended slip]
We are very badly off for want of money; this morning after applying to head quarters I could not raise a bit[116] to pay for washing a shirt and must go with a dirty one. Nibbs informs us that 5000$ public money is in the hands of Nixon at Nacogdoches. Could we not have a part of it or for what is it deposited there?[117]

B. M. Thomas Receipt
WASHINGTON: This is to certify that John Lott furnished myself and horse one night for which the government will settle

B M Thomas
one of

$1.25   D Crocketts Com[118]

William B. Travis Notebook Entry

Paid	to	Mouly for corn	2.00

Monday, January 25, 1836
41 DAYS TO THE FALL

William B. Travis Notebook Entry

Paid	for	Burnam for blankets	
		for 2 soldiers	10.00
		4.00 3.00	
do	do	coffee sugar	7.00

Tuesday, January 26, 1836
40 DAYS TO THE FALL

William B. Travis Notebook Entry

Paid	for	Jackson for blanket	
		for soldier	5.00
do	do	Winburn for do	
		2 blankets	8.00
do	do	McDaniel	2.50
do	do	to soldiers for	
		bounty	17.00
		Amount Carried over	$107.00

Citizens & Soldiers of San Antonio de Bexar to Council, San Felipe

At a large and respectable meeting of the citizens and soldiers of this place, held this 26th day of January 1836, to take into consideration the recent movements at San Felipe, James C. Neill was called to the chair, and H. J. Williamson appointed secretary. The object of the meeting having been stated by the chair, on motion of Col. J. B. Bonham, a committee of seven was appointed to draft a preamble and resolutions for the consideration of the meeting; whereupon the following were appointed by the chair. Chairman of Committee J. B. Bonham. Jas Bowie, G. B. Jameson, Doctor Pollard, Jesse Badgett, J. W. Seguin, Don Gasper Flores.

Preamble:

Whereas we have been informed from an undoubted messenger that the Executive Council and its President, a subordinate and auxiliary department of the government, have usurped the right of impeaching the governor who, (if we would imitate the wise institutions of the land of Washington) can only be impeached by a body set forth in the constitution which constitution must have been established by the people through their representatives assembled in general convention. Moreover, the said council and its president, whose powers are defined to aid the governor fulfilling the measures and objects adopted by the general consultation, have taken it upon themselves to annul the measures of the said general consultation. They are about to open the land offices, which were temporarily closed until a general convention of the people should take place, thereby opening a door to private speculation, at the expense of the men who are serving their country in the field. Moreover the said council have improperly used, and appropriated to their own purposes a *FIVE HUNDRED DOLLAR LOAN,* from a generous and patriotic citizen of the United States intended to pay the soldiers in the garrison of Bexar. Moreover, that private and designing men are, and have been embarrassing the governor, the legitimate officer of the government, by usurping, contrary to all notions of order and good government, the right of publicly and formally instructing and advising the governor and the people on political, civil and institutional matters subject. Moreover that a particular individual has gone so far as to issue a proclamation on the state of public affairs, and to invite volunteers to join him as the commander of the Matamoros expedition, when that particular individual must have known that General Houston the commander in chief of all the land forces in the service of Texas has been ordered by the government to take command of that expedition. This particular individual is also fully aware, that all officers under the commander in chief are elected by the volunteers themselves, and that therefore there was neither room nor necessity for another appointment by the council. Still in the possession of these facts, he has issued his proclamation, and continues to aid all those who are embarrassing the executive.

Therefore, be it resolved 1st That we will support his excellency Governor Smith in his unyielding and patriotic efforts to fulfil the duties, and to preserve the dignity of his office, while promoting the best interests of the country and people, against all usurptions and the designs of selfish and interested individuals.

Resolved 2nd That all attempts of the president and members of the executive council, to annul the acts of, or to embarrass the officers appointed by the general convention are deemed by this meeting as anarchical assumptions of power to which we will not submit.

Resolved 3rd That we invite a similar expression of sentiment from the army under Genl Houston, and throughout the country generally.

Resolved 4th That the conduct of the president and members of the Executive Council in relation to the *FIVE HUNDRED DOLLAR LOAN*, for the liquidation of the claims of the soldiers of Bexar, is in the highest degree criminal and unjust. Yet under treatment however illiberal and ungrateful, we cannot be driven from the Post of Honor and the sacred cause of freedom.

Resolved 5th That we do not recognize the illegal appointments of agents and officers, made by the president and members of the Executive council in relation to the Matamoros Expedition; since their power does not extend further than to take measures and to make appointments for the public service with the sanction of the governor.

Resolved 6th That the Governor Henry Smith will please to accept the gratitude of the army at this Station, for his firmness in the execution of his trust, as well as for his patriotic exertions in our behalf.

Resolved 7th That the Editors of the Brazoria Gazette, the Nacogdoches Telegraph and the San Felipe Telegraph be requested, and they are hereby requested to publish the proceedings of this meeting.[119]

Wednesday, January 27, 1836
39 DAYS TO THE FALL

James C. Neill to Henry Smith
BEJAR: I have received a copy of the resolutions enacted by the council and approved by James W. Robinson Acting Governor as signed empowering me (as said therein without giving me the

means) to do sundry acts to my own relief as commander of this place. In my communications to the Executive I did not ask for pledges and resolves but for money, provisions and clothing. There has been money given or loaned by private individuals expressly for the use of this army and none has been forwarded. Mr. Clay from Ala. gave or loaned $500 (in the presence of our express and on the pledge that the sum will keep the army here for the present) to the council for the use of this garrison expressly. My express after having been detained two days to receive that $500 was told by the committee that they had appropriated it otherwise. But it appears that a legitimate Executive has not had my returns by express before him. I wish to be advised. I wish to keep up a correspondence with you public or private. Enclosed are our resolves, they speak their import. Certain intelligence in confirmation of fact 1400 troops of the Central Army are on the Rio Grande making every preparation to attack us was received this morning.[120]

James C. Neill to Prest. & Members of the Executive Committee of Texas

BEJAR: Gents, I have received your dispatches per express and am truly astonished to find your body in such a disorganized situation. Such interruptions in the General Council of Texas have tendencies — they create distrust and alarm and at this critical period of our History are much to be lamented. I do hope, however, to hear of a reconciliation of matters. Our Govt. appears to be without a legitimate head and unanimity of action is certainly necessary to answer the ends and to effect the objects contemplated by the Consultation.

I enclose you a copy of the Proceedings of a meeting held in this place 26th Ult. which will convey to you some idea of the feelings of the Army on the subject.

I enclose to you the address of the Commandant of the Post of Saltillo to his subalterns. Every courier from the west seems to corroborate the previous statements in relation to the preparations of the Mexicans for war.[121]

Amos Pollard to Henry Smith

BEJAR: I perceive that the troy party have brought up your council and instead of being an assistant to you as intended they have usurped the government to themselves — but the people will not stand this — you will see by our resolution here that we are determined to support you at all hazards — I did hope the provisional government would continue till we could establish another and a more firm one — this we will endeavor to do in March and God grant that we may create an independent government — should we be previously invaded I hope that the council will come back from its corrupt course and meet the exigencies of the country — Reports say that troops are now on their way Rely my dear sir on every support that my feeble efforts can give you in endeavoring to ensure the liberties and establish the Independence of our adopted country. . . .[122]

Thursday, January 28, 1836
38 DAYS TO THE FALL

William B. Travis Notebook Entry
Paid   for   To Chadorn for corn   3.00

James C. Neill to The Provisional Government of Texas
SAN ANTONIO de BEXAR: A friend to the cause of Texas who arrove yesterday from the Presidio de Rio Grande, which place he left 9 days back has communicated to me the following intelligence of the enemies movements which I deem sufficient important to transmit by Express to the Provisional Government as derived from a source entitled to credit.

The commander in chief, General Rameriz y Sesma of the army of the centralists destined to operate against Texas, had assembled at Rio Grande, 1600 infantry and 400 cavalry of the Presidial companies, 80 wagons and 400 mules with supplies and baggage, including 3000 mules loads of flour, 300 fanegas of biscuit &c &c two mortars and 6 pieces of artillery supposed to be twelves and had sent to Dr Beales colony of dolores for two boats wherein to pass the infantry &c for the purpose of taking up their march into the colonies, which in Ramirez y Sesma language are to be Exterminated if they offer any resistance. A forced loan of one per cent had been imposed upon all property and hires made of horses, mules, oxen wagons corn &c in order to fit out the expedition, even women had been compelled to grind corn and prepare the bread for the invading army, and the country presented a scene of extortion and oppression, which when inflicted upon friends and countrymen, we may expect to behold inflicted with double rigor upon ourselves. Extraordinary measures of severity were adopted towards those guilty of distortion of which some symptoms had been manifested, and on the day of my informants departure these were to be shot for that offence. The roads between this and the Rio Grande, which is fordable, are now good as the season there has been a dry one.

As I expect the Enemy to be on the point of commencing their march, I intend sending out tomorrow a spy to reconnoiter and on the arrival of Col. Travis and his men I shall also dispatch them to cut off their supplies, a policy I conceive to be at his juncture most expedient as by depriving the enemy's troops of their provisions & of the means of progressing they will become discouraged and be induced to return. The first misinformation that may happen to them far from this place will be productive of the best effects. I shall instruct Col. Travis to cut down the bridges over the Leona and Nueces to embarrass the enemy in crossing those streams, with the men, say 25, under that officer's command the force of this garrison will consist of 130 Americans and with 600 to 1000 men, I can oppose an effectual resistance.

On my Couriers arrival from San Felipe minds became excited and the Resolutions sent out were the result. But fellow citizens, the time has arrived and a second epoch is to be from this day dated in the affairs of our adopted country in which domestic dissentions should be hushed and rancour should be the watchword. United the attempts of the enemy can be baffled even if Santa Anna with his 3000 men do come on. Texas ought and must again arouse to action, another victory will secure us forever from the attack of Tyranny and our Existence will no longer be doubtful but prosperous and glorious to attain so desirable an end. I am ready to sacrifice my all . . . from the time of my taking the field in the defense of Texas liberties up to the present moment, my labours and watchfulness have been unremitting and they shall continue to be so until I see the land of my adoption free.

I have respectfully to advise that the efforts of the government be all concentrated and directed to the support and preservation of this town, that supplies of Beef, pork, hogs, salt, &c be forthwith forwarded, and if wagons cannot be procured let as much as possible come by hand, men, money, rifles and cannon powder are also necessary. I shall consult with some of the influential Mexicans known to be attached to our cause, about obtaining the effectual assistance of these citizens of whom I judge that 4/5 would join us if they entertained reasonable expectations of reinforcements —[123]

William B. Travis to his Excellency Henry Smith
Governor of Texas

BURNAM'S, COLORADO: Sir: In obedience to my orders I have done everything in my power to get ready to march to the relief of Bexar, but owing to the difficulty of getting horses and provisions, and owing to desertions, etc. I shall march today with only about thirty men, all regulars except four. I shall however go on and do my duty, if I am sacrificed, unless I receive new orders to counter march. Our affairs are gloomy indeed The people are indifferent. They are worn down and exhausted with war, and in consequence of dissentions between contending and rival chieftans, they have lost all confidence in their government and officers. You have no idea of the exhausted state of the country. Volunteers can no longer be had or relied upon. A speedy organization, classification and draft of the Militia is all that can save us now. A regular army is necessary — but money and money only can raise & equip a regular army — Money must be raised or Texas is gone to ruin. Without it war cannot be again carried on in Texas. The patriotism of a few has done much; but that is becoming worn down. I have strained every nerve. I have used my personal credit and have slept neither day not night, since I recd orders to march — and with all this exertion, I have barely been able to get horses & equipment for the few men I have — Enclosed I send you a list of men who deserted on the roads from Washington & San Felipe to this place. I understand from rumor that His Excellency the Commandant General, Saml Houston is gone to San Felipe — Will you be good enough to show this communication to him & request him to write me — as I wish to be in communication with him —

I have the honor to be your Excellency's obt Ser
W. Barret Travis
Lt Col Comdt.

List of Deserters on the road from San Felipe —
A. White
John Cole

From Washington
—— Baker — with a roan horse, saddle & bridle —
Andrew Smith — with a sorrel horse saddle & bridle —
blanket — gun & shot pouch
—— Ginnings with a dun horse — saddle & bridle —
valued at $150 —
Mr. Smith
Solomon Bardwell
Alfonso Stele[124]
—— Wiley
Reported by Sergeant J. G. Smith —
W. B. Travis
Lt. Col. Comdt.[125]

J. W. Fannin to His Excellency James W. Robinson
Gen. Council of Texas
ARANSAS BAY: I have the honor to inform you that, agreeable to the last Communications from Velasco — I sailed & arrived here safe some days or so after — but the wind being ahead cannot go up until a change —

I have about 200 men — & 80 more waiting at Matagorda —

and am informed that since I left Brazos, the liberty & four sails under convoy, with men & munitions & provisions &c had arrived there — and will be here tomorrow —

Rest assured that I will do all in my power to promote the public service, regardless of the consequences — or my own personal safety. . . . Gen Mexia writes me, the report & his information stated that Santa Anna was in Matamoros —

I will not give an opinion — but simply suggest that if it be correct we may expect a *vigorous onset* — *& speedily* —

Will it not be prudent — nay is [it] not necessary to order out *all the disposable force of Texas* — from East North & South — to concentrate at Bejar, Goliad and Nueces &c and that *forthwith*. If this is not done — you may not be surprised to hear your officers are being compelled to make retrograde movements if they do not suffer the most disastrous defeats. Aid them and the brave men who are in the field. Do your duty as you have done, and you need not fear the consequences. "Westward, Ho," should be the order of the day, and watch word by night.

I recd. a few minutes before I sailed a letter from "Henry Smith" a copy of which I ordered made out — & forwd. to you — It was nearly equal to the one I referred to in my last — & from which I quoted — You will see from the back, that he reports an Express from Bejar, saying 2500 Mexicans were advancing to retake the Post. I suspect the cause of this rumor — and will be governed by such orders, emanating, from such persons, as may be above suspicion, as may be recd, at the Copano — or Refugio —.

I will make farther report from that point — and trusting that you will take my suggestions into consideration & act on them promptly — I am as ever, With high consideration, yr obt servt.[126]

Governor Henry Smith to Sam Houston
Commander-in-Chief, Army of Texas

SAN FELIPE, TEXAS: Sir: You are hereby furloughed until the 1st day of March next, for the purpose of adjusting your private business, preparatory to your necessary absence from home, in the country's service.

Your absence is permitted in part by the illegal acts of the council in suspending you, by the unauthorized appointment of agents to organize and control the army, contrary to the organic law, and the ordinances of their own body.

In the meantime, you will conform to your instructions, and treat with the Indians.[127]

Mexican Secretary of War[128]
CIRCULAR
The supreme Government has received official notice that the rebels of Texas have adopted a strange banner. It is known also that vessels, armed and fitted out by those traitors, carry this device, and that recently one of those vessels from the coast of Texas sailed into New Orleans with this flag at her masthead.

This flag is unknown to the Mexican nation and is not recognized, and His Excellency the President orders that all vessels sailing under this new flag be considered and treated as pirates.[129]

Friday, January 29, 1836
37 DAYS TO THE FALL

William B. Travis to his Excellency Henry Smith
Governor of Texas
BURNAM'S, COLORADO: This will be handed to you by Capt. Jackson who will explain to you the situation of things here. I leave here with the troops under Capt. Forsythe, but shall await your orders at Gonzales or some point on the road. I shall however keep the 30 men of Forsythe's company in motion toward Bexar, so that they may arrive there as soon as possible.

Not having been able to raise 100 volunteers agreeable to your orders, and there being so few regular troops altogether, I beg that your Excellency will recall the order for me to go on to Bexar in command of so few men. I am willing, nay anxious, to go to the defense of Bexar, and I have done everything in my power to equip the enlisted men and get them off. But sir, I am unwilling to risk my reputation (which is ever dear to a soldier) by going off into the enemies country with such little means and so few men, & them so badly equipped — the fact is there is no necessity for my services to command so few men. The company officers will be amply sufficient. They should at all events be sent to Bexar or to the frontier of Nueces. They may now go on to San Antonio under command of Capt. Forsythe, where they can be employed if necessary, and if they are not needed there may be sent to San Patricio or some other point. I am now thoroughly convinced that none but defensive measures can be pursued at this inclement season. If the Executive or the Major-General desire or order it, I will visit the post of San Antonio or any other for the purpose of consulting or communicating with officers in command there — or to execute any commission I may be entrusted with, but I do not feel disposed to go to command a squad of men, and without the means of carrying on a campaign. Therefore I hope your Excellency will take my situation into consideration and relieve me from the orders which I have hitherto received, so far as they compel me to command in person the men who are now on the way to Bexar. Otherwise I shall feel it due to myself to resign my commission. I would remark that I can be more useful at present, in superintending the recruiting service.[130]

Advisory Commission to J. W. Robinson
COUNCIL HALL SAN FELIPE: The advisory Committee to the Executive appointed to act in that capacity during the absence of a quorum of the Council, regret to be informed of the dissatisfied and disorganized state of the volunteers who left Bejar for the expedition against Matamoros. It is evident however that these evils and misunderstandings have arisen either from the want of correct information or from the intrigues and misrepresentation of designing men, all of which may be corrected by communicating truly and frankly, the acts and the objects of the government in regard to volunteers generally, together with all special acts with the Matamoros Expedition.[131]

Saturday, January 30, 1836
36 DAYS TO THE FALL

William B. Travis Notebook Entry

Paid	for	Dement[132]	
		for shoeing horses	6.00
do	do	Kimballs bill for corn	2.00

Sam Houston to Governor Henry Smith
WASHINGTON; I have the honor to report to you that, in obedience to your order under date of the 6th inst., I left Washington on the 8th and reached Goliad on the night of the 14th. On the morning of that day I met Captain Dimit, on his return home with his command, who repeated to me the fact that his caballade of horses (the most of them private property) had been pressed by Dr. Grant, who styled himself acting commander-in-chief of the federal army, and that he had under his command about two hundred men. Captain Dimit had been relieved by Captain P. S. Wyatt, of the volunteers, from Huntsville, Alabama. I was so informed by Major R. C. Morris that breadstuff was wanted in camp; and he suggested his wish to remove the volunteers farther west. By express, I had advised the stay of the troops at Goliad until I could reach that point.

On my arrival at that post I found them destitute of many supplies necessary to their comfort on a campaign. An express reached me from Lt. Colonel Neill, of Bexar, of an expected attack from the enemy there. I immediately requested Colonel James Bowie to march with a detachment of volunteers to his relief. He met the request with his usual promptness and manliness. This intelligence I forwarded to your excellency, for the action of the government. With a hope that supplies had or would immediately reach the port of Copano, I ordered the troops, through Major R. C. Morris, to proceed to Refugio mission, where it was reported there would be an abundance of beef — leaving Captain Wyatt and his command, for the present, in possession of Goliad, or until he could be relieved by a detachment of regulars under the command of Lieutenant Thornton, and some recruits that had been enlisted by Captain Ira Westover. On the arrival of the troops at Refugio, I ascertained that no breadstuffs could be obtained, nor was there any intelligence of supplies reaching Copano, agreeably to my expectations, and in accordance with my orders of the 30th of December and 6th of January inst. directing the landing and concentrating all the volunteers at Copano. I had also advised Colonel A. Huston, the quartermaster-general, to forward the supplies he might obtain at New Orleans to the same point. Not meeting the command of Major Ward, as I had hoped from the early advice I had sent him to Major George W. Poe. I determined to await his arrival and the command of Captain Wyatt. With a view to be in a state of readiness to march to the scene of active operations at the first moment that my force, and the supplies necessary, could reach me, I ordered Lt. Thornton with his command (total twenty-nine) to Goliad, to relieve Captain Wyatt; at the same time ordering the latter to join the volunteers at Refugio. I found difficulty in prevailing on the regulars to march until they had received either money or clothing; their situation was truly destitute. Had I not succeeded, the station at Goliad must have been left without any defence, and abandoned to the enemy, whatever importance its occupation may be to the security of the frontier. Should Bexar remain a military post, Goliad must be maintained, or the frontier will be cut off from all supplies arriving by sea at the port of Copano.

On the evening of the 20th, F. W. Johnson Esq., arrived at Refugio, and it was understood that he was empowered, by the general council of Texas, to interfere in my command. On the 21st, and previous to receiving notice of his arrival, I issued an order to organize the troops so soon as they might arrive at that place, agreeably to the "ordinance for raising an auxiliary corps" to the army. A copy of the letter I have the honor to enclose herewith. Mr Johnson called on me, previous to the circulation of the order, and showed me the resolutions of the general council, dated 14th of January, a copy of which I forward for the persual of your excellency.

So soon as I was made acquainted with the nature of his mission, and the powers granted to J. W. Fannin Jr. I could not remain mistaken as to the object of the council, or the wishes of individuals. I had but one course left for me to pursue (the report of your being deposed had also reached me), which was, to return, and report myself to you in person — inasmuch as the objects, intended by your order were, by the extraordinary conduct of the council, rendered useless to the country; and by remaining with the army, the council would have had the pleasure of ascribing to me the evils which their own conduct and acts will, in all probability, produce. I do consider the acts of the council calculated to protract the war for years to come; and the field which they have opened to insubordination, and to agencies without limit (unknown to military usage), will cost the country more useless expenditures than the necessary expenses of the whole war would have been had they not transcended their proper duties. Without integrity of purpose and well-devised measures, our whole frontier must be exposed to the enemy. All the available resources of Texas are directed, through special as well as general agencies, against Matamoros; and must, in all probability, prove as unavailing to the interest as they will to the honor of Texas. The regulars at Goliad can not long be detained at that station, unless they should get supplies; and now all the resources of Texas are placed in the hands of agents unknown to the government in its formation, and existing by the mere will of the council; and will leave all other objects, necessary for the defense of the country, neglected, for the want of means, until the meeting of the convention in March next.

It was my wish, it if had been possible, to avoid for the present the expression of any opinion which might be suppressed in the present crisis. But since I reported to your excellency, having had leisure to peruse all the documents of a controversial nature growing out of the relative duties of yourself and the general council, requiring of me an act of insubordination and disobedience to your orders, demands of me that I should inquire into the nature of that authority which would stimulate me to an act of treason, or an attempt to subvert the government which I have sworn to support. The only constitution which Texas has is the "organic law." Then any violation of that law, which would destroy the basis of government, must be treason. Has treason been committed If so, by whom, and for what purpose? The history of the last few weeks will be the best answer that can be rendered. . . .[133]

I do not consider the council as a constitutional body, nor their acts lawful. They have no quorum agreeably to the organic law, and therefore I am compelled to regard all their acts as void. The body has been composed of seventeen members, and I perceive that the act of "suspension," passed against your excellency, was by only ten members present; the president pro tem. having no vote. Only ten members remain, when less than twelve members could not form a quorum agreeably to the organic law, which required two thirds of the whole body. I am not prepared to violate either my duty or my oath, by yielding obedience to an act manifestly unlawful, as it is, in my opinion, prejudicial to the welfare of Texas.

The lieutenant-governor, and several members of the council, I believe to be patriotic and just men; but there have been, and when I left San Felipe there were, others in that body on whose honesty and integrity the foregoing facts will be the best commentary. They must also abide the judgement of the people.[134]

J. W. Robinson to James Tarleton, B. C. Wallace[135] and T. H. McIntire

EXECUTIVE DEPARTMENT, SAN FELIPE de AUSTIN: *private*

1st. You will immediately repare to the Camp of the Volunteer army of Texas, and on your way to that place, if you meet or overtake any troops or citizens, you will fully explain our situation at the seat of Gov. & of the disposition of the authorities here to meet their wishes — of the arrival of the Wm Robbins at Velasco, with A. J. Wharton on board, who informs us that our agents in N. Orleans has effected a loan of 250,000$, to be pd on our draft, & also bringing ample supplies of provisions, & arms & ammunition, that will be sent to the army —

2d. On your arrival in Camp, you will request the commander, if they have elected one, or the captains of companies, in the event of their not having elected a Commander, to assemble the men in hollow squares or otherwise & have read, the information that you have from this place, and distribute the same among the troops, so that the same may be generally and fully known, throughout this camp.

3d. And you will also by your conversation, in camp, and at all times promote harmony among the troops and citizens generally, & assure the troops that they are fully authorized and empowered to elect company officers, and also a commander of the expedition against Matamoros, & urge the importance & necessity of an immediate attack of that place, and that they will be fully sustained by all means in the power of the Government of Texas in that moment.

4d. Assure them no doubt is entertained, on the part of the

Government, of the ability of the country to fully compensate them for their toil & Labour in money & Land.

5th. Give your aid in any way, you may think best calculated to promote the great object of the campaign, in organizing the volunteers, permanently under the auxiliary Law, or temporarily, if that does not meet the views of the troops, and any other mode you may think proper, not inconsistent with existing Laws —

6th. You will use these instructions as you may think proper — you may shew them or not as may seem best, & the interest of the service may, in your opinion require —

James Robinson
Acting governor[136]

F. W. Johnson to the Honble the Genl. Council of Texas

SAN PATRICIO: I have the honor to acquaint that I joined the Bexar division of the Volunteer Army at Refugio on the 20th Inst, but at same time regret to have to say, that much mischief has been done during my absence by disorganizers both at Goliad and Refugio, founded on claims of the Comdr, in Chief of the Regular Army [Sam Houston] to direct the movements of the Volunteers, & every obstacle was thrown in the way of an advance, into the neighboring state — a measure tho' approv'd of by your honbl. body, which was represented as unauthoris'd & contrary to the interest of Texas. One company was dissolved in Goliad & only a small fraction came on to the mission, three other companies (Cook's Burks & Lawrenc's) with the fraction alluded to, remain at the Mission, under the impression that they were not authoris'd to move with me without express orders to that effect from Genl Houston. —

Two companies and a few who segregated from the other companies accompanied me to this place —

Such is a true but most mortifying picture of the present state of the Volunteer Army of the Frontiers, & unless an explicit declaration is made to the seceding Captns by the Executive of their being authoris'd to join the expedition to the interior, without reference to the orders of the Comdr. in Chief of the Regular Army, many valuable men will be lost to the service of Texas — & what is worse all those who return to their country will give us so unfavorable an account, of the unhappy dissentions arrising from party spirit, as will deter many from joining in the support of our rights and liberties —

I am still without any intimation of the movement of Col. Fannin, and quite at a loss to account for the want of due information on this head — The mischiefs that may arise from delay, at the present moment are to obvious to require my adverting them —

By advices recd from Monterey, up to the 18th Inst—& from Matamoros up to the 20th same, the following may be said to be the present state of the political & military operations. — Santa Anna is in Saltillo, with a force of 2300 men, and a considerable train of heavy and field Artillery. — so far on his way to invade Texas, but in consequence of the rising of the liberals, both in Zacatecas & Guadalaxara, his supplies have been cut off, his progress arrested & he seems to be at a loss whether to advance or retreat, his forces are deserting daily — & he does not detach assistance to Matamoros, fearing that the Troops on leaving the Camp wou'd declare against him — The army which was collecting at Laredo, barely 1,000 men, including the remains of Coss' Troops under Felisola, have left that place for Monclova some time back, in consequence of the revolution in the interior. — Matamoros may be said to be entirely defenceless, & the genl in command ready to join the liberals on their appearance, of 160 militia, which were sent as a reinforcement late in Decr to Matamoros I am assur'd that only 10 existed, all the rest having deserted — The whole force at that place does not exceed 200 men.

In the present state of St. Anna's army, one blow at this moment wou'd free us, from the efforts of the Centralists & leave both Texas & the northern part of the Republic, in full enjoyment of peace — Such a blow given by the troops of Texas, wou'd raise her at once to a position, in which she might dictate to her sister States —

Col. Gonzales, is with a detachment on the Bank of the Rio Grande opposite to Mier, & from the reinforcements on the way to join him it may be safely calculated that he has ab't 300 men to date — The moment we move Gonzales will start to join us near Matamoros. —

Much alarm has been created even among the liberals of the adjoining states, by rumours of a desire to declare Texas independent of the Republic of Mexico.

Every step has been taken to do away with this impression, both by our friends here & in the Interior, as a junction of all parties wou'd inevitably result from such measure & the consequences wou'd too, probably be ruinous to Texas at this moment. — I deem it my duty to keep your honbl. Body inform'd of all these matters, for the guidance of the people of Texas, & I hope soon to be able to lay before you a correct copy of St' Annas plan of his intended campaigns for your Gov't — In the mean time I hope that the Gov't & Council, will be pleas'd to use every endeavor to augment the forces intended for the Interior, & that the present inviting opportunities of carrying the war under which such favorable auspices out of Texas may not be lost. —

Every true friend to his country, every lover of liberty and order will see the propriety of laying aside every minor feeling, arising from party or any other spirit — & embracing with warmth the present opportunity of ensuring us peace and quiet — by one effectual effort at a moments so truly auspicious —[137]

Sunday, January 31, 1836
35 DAYS TO THE FALL

General Jose Urrea Diary Entry
Our division arrived in Matamoros, having spent the time intervening in marching through the towns of the north.[138]

Endnotes

1. Gammel, 1:720-721.
2. Stephen F. Austin left Texas to try to borrow money for the war effort.
3. George Washington Hockley, of Philadelphia, came to Texas in 1835. On March 4, 1836, when Sam Houston became commander in chief of the army, Hockley became his chief of staff. On April 20 when Lt. Col. James C. Neill was wounded, Hockley assumed command of the artillery and held that position during the battle of San Jacinto on the 21st. Several weeks after the battle, Hockley was one of the commissioners assigned to escort Santa Anna to Washington City. He later served as Secretary of War during Houston's two terms as president of the Republic.
4. Benjamin C. Wallace served with James Walker Fannin and along with the colonel and J. M. Chadwick, signed the surrender following the aborted battle of Coleto. Wallace was one of the men who died when Fannin's men were massacred.
5. Wyatt Hanks was on the Executive Council of the Provisional Government and served a short time as Chairman of the Military Committee.
6. Barker and Williams, 1:330-331.
7. Binkley, 1:266-267. Samuel Williams, of North Carolina, was an early land speculator in Texas and he helped finance the war effort. Samuel Williams was not assigned to Bexar and was not among the Alamo casualties.
8. This Lowry served as a private in Capt. English's company from San Augustine and later in Captain Bradley's company. There is no record that he ever received a commission.
9. This Lowry served in the Mobile company and although Capt. Burke certified that this Lowry served as an officer, he was only allowed the pay of a private.
10. Binkley, 2:267-268.
11. Gammel, 1:727-729.
12. Captain E. Hall was a resident of New Orleans who worked to support the volunteer effort in Texas.
13. Gammel, 1:734.
14. Modern Texas does, in fact, produce more cotton than all the other states combined.
15. Gulick, 3:292-293. John T. Lamar was apparently a volunteer with Georgia Battalion. Thomas Ward was wounded at the siege of Bexar and lost a leg, which, legend has it, was buried with Ben Milam who was killed in the action. Though crippled, Ward served with Rusk at San Jacinto and later became the second Land Commissioner of the Republic of Texas.
16. Gammel, 1:738-739.
17. Binkley, 1:272-275.

18. The Neill letter Houston references is not the one written by the Alamo commander on this date, as surmised by many historians. For a full discussion of the letter that brought down the Texas government, see *Exploring the Alamo Legends*, by Wallace O. Chariton, (Plano, Texas: Wordware Publishing, Inc., 1990), 107-116.

19. Barker and Williams, 1:332-333.

20. Gammel, 1:740-741.

21. Ibid, 1:744.

22. James Bowie returned to Goliad but never participated in the Matamoros expedition. Instead, he was assigned by Houston to go to the Alamo.

23. Yoakum, 2:508-509.

24. This certification and endorsement are from a typescript in the Ruby Mixon papers in the Barker Texas History Center at the University of Texas in Austin. According to other information in the papers, John McMullen, Counter Pro Tem, approved the claim and a draft in the amount of $35.00 was issued January 8, 1835.

25. Gammel, 1:746-747.

26. Binkley, 1:275-278.

27. Foote, 2:194-196.

28. Austin, 3:299. S. Rhodes Fisher was a member of the Constitutional Convention and signed the Declaration of Independence. He later served as Secretary for the Republic of Texas Navy.

29. Binkley, 1:278.

30. Foote, 2:186.

31. See Stephen F. Austin to F. W. Johnson, December 22, 1835.

32. Barker and Williams, 3:334.

33. Santos, 23-24.

34. Ibid, 24.

35. Ibid, 25.

36. Gaines apparently referred to Sam Houston who had been named to treat with the Indians but had not, by this date, left on that mission.

37. Even though the actual election had not been held, Crockett expected to be elected. See his following letter.

38. Binkley, 1:282-284. James Gaines came to Texas from Virginia in the early 1800s and contributed to the war effort by operating a ferry on the Sabine River. He also served in the Congress of the Republic before heading for the California gold fields where he died in 1856.

39. Gammel, 1:757. Jamieson's name was actually Jameson. Also, no record has been found of an order requiring Travis to march to Matamoros. Perhaps Travis was inadvertently substituted for Bowie, who was ordered to go to Matamoros.

40. James A. Shackford and Stanley Folmsbee, *A Narrative on the Life of David Crockett* (Knoxville: University of Tennessee Press, 1973), 214-216. David Crockett, the famous naturalist from Tennessee, volunteered to fight for Texas with the rank of high private. He died in the Alamo. Despite being known as somewhat of a prolific writer, this is the only letter he is known to have written home while in Texas.

41. Binkley, 1:281-282. The General Council of Texas received this request for funds and, on January 14, 1836, declared that Caldwell was not known as a contractor so if he had been appointed a sub-contractor, he should settle with the person who appointed him. See Gammel's Laws of Texas, 1:780.
42. Carlos E. Castaneda, *The Mexican Side of the Revolution* (Dallas: P. L. Turner, 1928), 211.
43. Binkley, 1:284-285. Phillip Dimitt was active in many areas of the Texas revolution. He supported the Matamoros expedition, participated in the taking of Goliad, and helped author the Goliad Declaration of Independence. He apparently had some trouble with command and was relieved by Stephen F. Austin. He participated in the siege of Bexar and established a trading post along the gulf coast. He was captured by Mexican forces in 1841 and it is believed he took his own life to deny the Mexicans the pleasure of executing him. For a discussion on the possibility that Dimitt was an Alamo coward, see *Exploring the Alamo Legends* by Wallace O. Chariton.
44. The expedition against Matamoros, Mexico.
45. Gammel, 1:758-761.
46. *SWHQ,* 5:320-321.
47. Stephen F. Austin.
48. Branch T. Archer was active in the military and political affairs of early Texas. He was at the battle of Gonzales where the first shots of the Texas Revolution were fired and later served as a Texas Commissioner to the United States where he helped raise funds for the war effort.
49. William H. Wharton, of Virginia, was a Texas Commissioner to the United States and later became minister to the U.S. After helping secure recognition for the Republic of Texas in 1837, Wharton was captured and taken to Mexico. He managed to escape in time to return to Texas and get elected to the Senate. He died in 1839 when he accidently shot himself while dismounting a horse.
50. Although it is not known for sure, William White may have been the same one that was with Fannin for a short time before becoming sick.
51. This letter, reproduced as written, was in response to the Texas declaration of causes for taking up arms against Mexico, dated November 7, 1835. Section 8 of that declaration offered land and citizenship to all who would volunteer in the cause. See the introduction to this book for the complete declaration.
52. Many historians have concluded the Wm. Blount mentioned here was Stephen William Blount, a Georgia native who came to Texas and ultimately signed the Declaration of Independence. However, those historians probably did not have access to the letter written by James Butler Bonham of 12-31-1835 (the original has been missing for many years but a typescript was recently found in the Alamo Library) so they had no way to know Houston was responding to Bonham's request on behalf of Wm. S. Blount of North Carolina, of whom little is known.

53. Houston's protest against Hanks came too late. He was confirmed by the Council as sutler for the army on January 9, 1836. See Gammel, 1:757.

54. Barker and Williams, 3:335.

55. Gammel, 1:759-764.

56. Ibid, 1:764.

57. Thomas W. Streeter, *A Bibliography of Texas* (Portland, Maine: Anthoesen Press, 1955), document 144.

58. Gammel, 1:772.

59. Ibid, 1:773-774.

60. *SWHQ,* 5:326-327.

61. Gammel, 1:769. Incredibly, while the men of the Alamo desperately needed help, the acting governor of Texas was uncertain if he should even open the mail. The council issued resolutions calling for Henry Smith to relinquish the archives, which he ignored.

62. Guadalupe River.

63. *SWHQ,* 62:513-18. Letter was postmarked NATCHITOCHES, LOUISIANA, FEBRUARY 7, 1836.

64. Portsmouth, N. H. *Journal,* February 20, 1836.

65. Gulick, 1:295-296. John Forbes was active in Indian affairs and, along with Sam Houston, signed a treaty with the Cherokees in February 1836. Forbes then served in Houston's army as aide-de-camp. Forbes was in charge of the spoils of war following San Jacinto and he kept Santa Anna's sword for himself. He was later a mayor of Nacogdoches and was buried there after his death in 1880.

66. Jenkins, document number 1767.

67. Fannin's signature often appeared to have a "g" on the end.

68. DRT Library, the Alamo. This contract between Fannin and Mimms is often cited by historians as having occurred in 1834 or 1835. However, a review of a clear copy of the actual document reveals clearly it is dated in 1836. The document is presented both as evidence of slave trading in Texas and as perhaps an indication that Fannin's attention was not totally focused on the war in Texas.

69. *SWHQ,* 14:319-320

70. *Proceedings of the General Council,* 227-28.

71. Filisola, 40.

72. On April 20, 1836, James C. Neill was actually in command of the artillery at San Jacinto and preparing for the battle of the 21st. On the 20th, however, Neill was wounded in an artillery skirmish with the Mexicans and subsequently missed the battle.

73. F. W. Johnson and Dr. John Grant.

74. Binkley, 294-295.

75. No letter can be found from Neill dated on the 13th. Since he says it was an official, a designation he apparently used for letters to Sam Houston, his commander, it is possible he meant the other letter he wrote on the 14th.

76. *Telegraph, and Texas Register,* January 23, 1836.

77. Gammel, 1:777-779.

78. *SWHQ,* 14:320-321.
79. Santos, 26-27.
80. Gammel, 1:788.
81. *Muster Rolls of the Texas Revolution* (Austin: Daughters of the Republic of Texas, Inc., 1986), 40-42. This muster roll is often thought to have been dated February 11 or 12 and that it was perhaps submitted by Neill when he left the Alamo. However, since this is the only list known to have been submitted by Neill, it may be assumed to be the one mentioned in the council records. Also, since the list does not contain the names of James Bowie, David Crockett, James Butler Bonham, and William Barret Travis, all of whom were in the Alamo by early February, it is doubtful this muster roll was done at that time.
82. Castaneda, 211-212.
83. *SWHQ,* 37:269-270.
84. Gammel, 1:1037-1039.
85. Yoakum, 2:59. This letter was referenced and briefly excerpted in Yoakum's History of Texas but a complete copy of the document cannot be located. It was assumed Travis was writing from San Felipe.
86. Barker and Williams, 3:339-340.
87. Binkley, 3:302-303.
88. Gammel, 1:1050-1051.
89. Foote, 2:196-197.
90. Document in private hands. Most historians believe Bowie did not arrive at the Alamo until January 19, 1836. Bowie did sign this receipt dated the 18th but it could have been written prior to his arrival. This receipt is the only known evidence that Neill was not in Bejar on the 18th and it is also evidence that Bowie assumed command.
91. On the plat the eighteen pounder is clearly marked at the S. W. corner.
92. Adina De Zavala, *History and Legends of the Alamo and Other Missions In and Around San Antonio* (San Antonio: By the Author, 1917), 23-25. Green B. Jameson was about twenty-seven years old, from Kentucky, and he served as the post engineer for the Alamo.
93. This space was left blank in the original document.
94. Binkley, 1:304-305. Leonard Waller Groce was an early settler from Georgia who was active in supplying beef to the war effort. He also operated Groce's Landing, started by his father, and helped fit out the "Twin Sister" cannons when they arrived from Cincinnati.
95. Gammel, 1:802. The council never again achieved a quorum. An advisory committee acted in place of the council but was largely ineffective. For all practical purposes, there was no official governmental body until the constitutional convention convened on March 1, 1836.

96. Barker and Williams, 3:306. Borden was active in Texas during the revolution and contributed much through his *Telegraph, and Texas Register* newspaper. In later life, he achieved much fame as an inventor. His most recognized invention was the process for condensing milk.

97. A. J. Houston Papers.

98. Court of Claims Vouchers, 4271, File A-C, General Land Office, Austin, TX.

99. Archives, Texas State Library. Cummings was a twenty-seven-year-old volunteer from Pennsylvania who died in the Alamo.

99. Binkley, 316-317.

101. Archives, Texas State Library. The only Hawkins known to have been in the Alamo was Joseph M. of Ireland. Since this Hawkins was an express rider, he possibly was not in the Alamo when it fell and simply faded into oblivion. Hawkins was obviously aware of the problems between the governor and the council and was offering to use arms to help the governor retain his office.

102. Ibid.

103. Santos, 29-30.

104. Ruby Mixon Papers, Barker Texas History Center, UT Austin. William G. Hill was a private in the Texas army and participated in the battle of Concepcion, the grass fight and the siege of Bexar. Despite the popular notion of Travis wearing a splendid uniform, it appears he went to the Alamo without one. The Mexican who retrieved Travis' jacket after the battle said it was made of homespun Texas jean material.

105. Ibid. William B. Travis kept a small notebook where he recorded his expenses on behalf of Texas. That notebook was used to verify claims on the part of Travis when his estate was settled. The executor of Travis' estate, John R. Jones, included the following note when the expenses were submitted: "The foregoing is taken from the original entries in Col. Travis' handwriting made in a small morocco bound book with his name on it," The information presented is from a typescript done by Ruby Mixon when she was working on her Masters thesis for the University of Texas. Other notebook entries are found at January 22, 23, 24, 25, 26, 28, 30, February 3, 7, 8, 12, and 16. They are all from the Ruby Mixon Papers in the Barker Center.

106. Andrew Janeway Yates, of Connecticut, enlisted in the Texas army but was selected as loan commissioner under Stephen F. Austin.

107. Ruby Mixon Papers, Barker Texas History Center, UT Austin. On January 21, 1836, Travis announced that he had been ordered to Bexar. The $100 was apparently all the government could spare at the time for the relief of the Alamo although it was hardly enough. On February 22, C. B. Stewart submitted the receipt to the government as proof he had given the cash to Travis.

108. Filisola, 51-54.

109. *SWHQ*, 36:108. *El Mosquito Mexicano* was a Mexican newspaper of the period.

110. Ruby Mixon Papers, Barker Texas History Center, UT Austin. Very little is known of Crockett's movements from the time he enlisted in the army in Nacogdoches on January 9, 1836 until he arrived at the Alamo in February. Judging from this receipt, it would appear Crockett and some of the Tennessean volunteers were in Washington on the 23rd. These two receipts were written on the same page but the Harrison portion was torn off so it could be separate. It has been speculated that Crockett was traveling with a group of from thirteen to seventeen men total. Judging from this receipt, the one by B. M. Thomas on the 24th, and the one by Daniel Cloud on February 11, it appears the Tennesseans were not moving across Texas as a group.

111. By the time this notice appeared in the paper, Travis had already been ordered to the Alamo. He never again was in San Felipe to practice law.

112. Binkley, 1:328

113. Ibid, 1:329

114. D. C. Barrett Papers, University of Texas Library, Austin. John Smith, of Virginia, was twice selected as an Alamo messenger by Travis. He left on February 23 with Travis' first message and he left on March 3 with Travis' last official message. Although many believe Smith was the last messenger sent out, evidence suggests at least one other messenger left after Smith.

115. The men in the Alamo were, indeed, overwhelmingly for independence rather than restoration of the 1824 Mexican constitution.

116. A bit equals twelve and one half cents.

117. Gulick, 3:307-308.

118. Ruby Mixon Papers, Barker Texas History Center, UT Austin. This receipt is perhaps further proof that Crockett and his men were not traveling as a group. However, Thomas did note that Crockett was considered in command.

119. *SWHQ*, 14:55-58.

120. Ibid, 37:271.

121. Ibid.

122. Binkley, 2:345-346.

123. Ibid, 2:349-351.

124. Alfonso (Alphonso) Steele is listed here as a deserter but he may have left the army because independence had not been declared. He rejoined the army in March of 1836 and fought in the battle of San Jacinto where he was one of the few Texans wounded. At the time of his death on July 7, 1911, Steele was the last survivor of the San Jacinto army.

125. Ruby Mixon Papers, Barker Texas History Center, UT Austin.

126. Gulick, 3:309.

127. Yoakum, 2:509-510.

128. Jose Maria Tornel was Mexican Secretary of War.

129. DRT Library at the Alamo.

130. Binkley, 1:362-363.

131. Ibid, 1:363-364.

132. It is possible Travis meant Phillip Dimitt, former commander at Goliad. On January 17, Dimitt was ordered by Sam Houston to round up volunteers and march to Bexar. Since Dimitt is known to have been at the Alamo on February 23, it seems possible that he might have marched with Travis after shoeing the horse.

133. At this point in this very long and detailed letter, Houston provided his version of the history of Texas for the previous few weeks. He traced the development of the Matamoros expedition and sighted many documents presented elsewhere in this work. The point of Houston's history led to the conclusions presented. Following the writing of this letter, the General departed for treaty talks with the Indians and he did not return until February 29, six days after the Alamo had been attacked.

134. Yoakum, 2:460-470.

135. Benjamin C. Wallace was assigned to secure volunteers to prepare for the Matamoros expedition and when that effort stalled, he went to Goliad. He was captured with Fannin and signed the terms of surrender. He was one of the Goliad men killed on Palm Sunday, 1836.

136. Binkley, 365-366.

137. Ibid.

138. Castaneda, 213.

The Enemy Advance

February 1 through February 22, 1836

By February 1836, there was no longer any doubt that independence was the cause for which the revolution would be fought. There was also no longer any doubt that Santa Anna was coming with a large, well-trained, well-fed, angry army to put down the rebellion and exterminate the rebels. By the middle of the month, the Mexican army had crossed the Rio Grande and was closing on San Antonio. Rumors flew among the Texans. It was impossible to determine exactly what was happening with the enemy. Some felt the attack was eminent and others still hung on to the belief it would be mid-March before the Mexicans would attempt an invasion. Incredibly, some Texans still believed Santa Anna would not be foolish enough to chance any invasion into Texas.

In the Alamo, William B. Travis and 30 men arrived on February 3. The legendary Davy Crockett arrived on the 8th or 9th with a handful of mounted volunteers, and a few more Tennesseans arrived several days later. On the 11th, Lieutenant Colonel James Neill suddenly left his post under an excuse that he had to attend to sick family members. He named Travis to act as commander in his absence which produced some political intrigue within the garrison. The volunteers demanded they be able to choose their own commander and Travis let them decide the issue in a vote. Bowie was their unanimous choice which created the untenable situation of co-commanders: Travis for the enlisted men and Bowie for the volunteers. The situation was ultimately resolved by an agreement between the two men that they would issue orders and sign correspondence jointly.

Together, Bowie and Travis had little success in getting any assistance from the government and they were left wanting men, money, and provisions. Urgent pleas for help to James Walker Fannin in Goliad went unanswered, although Fannin did make one aborted attempt to march to Bexar. He was forced to turn back when his wagons broke down. About the only bright note in the Alamo was an election to select their representatives to the upcoming constitutional convention.

The government continued to flounder while making little, if any, progress. Everyone seemed content to wait for the convention where all the problems of the government could be resolved. The acting governor and commander in chief of the army, James Robinson, still held on to faint hopes that the Matamoros expedition might be the salvation of the Texas cause; but thanks to dissension among those troops and the conflicts in the government, the expedition was basically in shambles before the end of the month.

Santa Anna, on the other hand, was closing quickly. So quickly in fact that he out-marched some vital elements of his army, namely the artillery and hospital supplies. His desire was to take the Alamo quickly and march on to the interior and smash the rebellion before it could really take form.

By February 22, Santa Anna and his advance force was camped on an open plain just eight miles below Bexar. Incredibly, the Texans were totally unaware of the presence. So secure were the Texans in their position, that a fandango was held in honor of George Washington's birthday. Thanks to a well-established spy network and sympathetic local citizens, Santa Anna learned of the planned party and decided on a bold stroke. He immediately dispatched his cavalry with orders to take the Texans while they danced and drank and enjoyed what few pleasures they could on the desolate prairie. If a sudden rain storm had not caused a river to swell rapidly preventing the cavalry from crossing, the entire battle for San Antonio and the Alamo might have been over before it got started. But the river did rise.

So the Mexicans camped and rested while the Texans partied. Young Bill Travis still believed the Mexicans would not arrive before March 15. He was wrong. In fact, by March 15, Travis would be nine days dead.

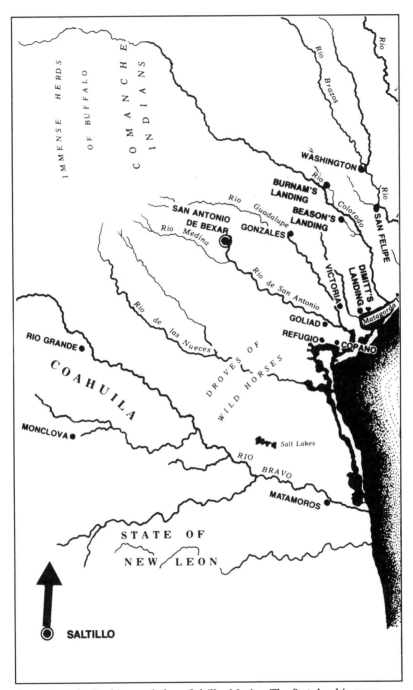

Santa Anna begins his march from Saltillo, Mexico. The first day his army marched 16 leagues to Hacendia Mesillas.

Monday, February 1, 1836
34 DAYS TO THE FALL

Almonte Diary Entry

At 8 A.M. — The President set out from Saltillo for Monclova, passing by the way of the Hacendia of Santa Maria, 6 leagues distant; thence to Carretas, 5 leagues; thence to the Hacendia de Mesillas, 5 leagues; making in all 16 leagues of good wagon road. In Carretas there is running water, no pasture, the road passes through high ridges and hills, and with little stone. There is a shorter road to Saltillo from Los Arcos, or a bridge near to the Hacendia of Santa Maria. Mesillas has no running water, but a reservoir; the running water being 1 1/2 leagues distance; there is a large house, corn and corn stalks.[1]

Jose Juan Sanchez Navarro Diary Entry

The Most Excellent President, to whom I introduced myself and who recognized me — we were classmates in officer's training . . . has granted the request I made him [to permit me] to return to the Texas campaign . . . There is much activity by way of preparation for this purpose. There are many troops and there is much noise; but I see no indications of good political, military, and administrative systems.

His Excellency himself attends to all matters whether important or most trivial. I am astonished to see that he has personally assumed the authority of major general . . . of quartermaster, of commissary, of brigadier generals, of colonels, of captains, and even of corporals, purveyors, arrieros, and carreteros.

Would it not be better for His Excellency to rid himself of such troublesome work which will occupy his time, which is more needed for the execution of the high duties of his office, by keeping each individual member of the army in complete exercise of his authority according to provisions of the general ordinances. . . ?

What will become of the army and of the nation if the Most Excellent President should die? Confusion and more confusion because only His Excellency knows the springs by means of which these masses of men called the army are moved. The members of the army in general have no idea of the significance of the Texas war, and all of them believe that they are merely on a military excursion. If, when questioned, one tells the truth about what one has seen there, one is considered a poor soul. As if the enemy could be conquered merely by despising him. . . .

Today the Most Excellent President left with his General Staff. He was accompanied by General Cos as far as Santa Maria. It is said that His Excellency is very economical, even miserly. Those close to him assert that whoever wants to, can make him uncomfortable by asking him for a peso; and they add that he would rather give a colonel's commission than ten pesos. Can all this be true? Even if it is, would it not be better not to mention it? I believe so. But the facts speak for themselves. When we took leave of each other, His Excellency shook my hand and expressed surprise that I was not wearing the insignia of lieutenant colonel, and he told me so.[2]

Wm. Fairfax Gray Diary Entry
NACOGDOCHES: This is the day designated by the Provisional Council for a general election of members of the new Convention. This place is much divided on the question of adhering to the Mexican Constitution of 1824, or declaring for absolute and immediate independence. Much excitement prevailed. . . .[3]

Soldiers at Bexar to the Constitutional Convention
SAN ANTONIO de BEXAR: A memorial of the Undersigned Officers in and over the Army Stationed at Bexar, to the President and members of the Convention of Texas to be held at Washington on the 1st day of March next, respectfully showed that:

Whereas, it is evident as well from the Resolution of the Consultation which provides for the calling of a Convention of all Texas, as from the clear equity of the case, that an equal representation of all persons & interests was aimed at and intended;

And whereas the volunteer and regular soldiers in the actual service of the country, are by the same Consultation, declared to be citizens and raised to the right of suffrage;

And whereas it is but right on the grounds of population, and appears, from the early date of the aforesaid Resolution, to be intended, that the resident Mexican citizens of Bexar should have four representatives in the Convention;

And whereas our officers perceived that impediments were put in the way or our men voting, such as requiring an oath of actual citizenship in this municipality before the vote would be taken; and furthermore they wished to prevent any, the least, breach in the good understanding which has so happily existed between the citizens and our garrison;

And whereas no facilities and insufficient time was afforded to such individuals in the army as live in a certain Municipality, to send their votes, and at the same time a large portion of the army, whilst they possess the declared right of voting for members of this Convention, do not yet possess any local habitation whatsoever;

And whereas it is of great importance that this army should have representatives in the Convention who understand their wants and their wishes, and are participants of their feelings; and of importance also to all Texas, since she would proceed with less hesitation on any great measures whilst having the voice of all;

And whereas if the army here would so far neglect their interests and their duty, as not to send members of their own choice, it is evident the wants of the Army and the necessity of maintaining & supplying this important garrison in a manner required by the public safety, might be forcibly seasonably urged on the attention of the government — inasmuch as the members sent from their municipality, though they have the best intentions, are yet unable, from the difference of language & habits, to represent the Anglo American and Army interests;

And whereas the reasonableness as well as the particular advantage of such a representation has gained the hearty good wishes of the Mexican as well as the Americans at this place;

And whereas by general wish, under the influence of these powerful reasons, an order was issued to three respectable gentlemen, who are captains, in this service, to hold an election for two members to the Convention, the Certificate of whom, with the return of the votes taken, is transmitted with this memorial;

And whereas on the election being held at the time and in the manner prescribed by law, and in strict conformity with common usage, it appeared on summing up the votes, as the result of the election that, by a vote which was almost unanimous, Samuel A. Maverick and Jesse B. Badgett, Esquires, were elected as members of the Convention,

Therefore, for these and other good reason it is the united petition of ourselves and of the army under our command that the said Samuel A. Maverick and Jesse B. Badgett shall receive seats as members of your honorable body and be admitted to full participation in all the rights, powers, privileges and immunities enjoyed by the other members; all of which, your memorialists very respectfully submit to the President and members of your honorable body, & will ever pray.

Samuel A. Maverick

Signed: J. C. Neill, Lt. Coln. Comd. Bexar; R. White, Capt of the Bexar Guards; Wm A Irwin, 1st Lieut; Wm R. Carey, Capt of Artillery; W. C. M. Baker, Capt; Saml C. Blair, Capt; Geo. Evans, Mast Ord; Wm Blazeby, Captain of the Orleans Greys; W. Barret Travis, Lt. Col of Cavalry; James Bowie; G. B. Jameson; E. Melton 2 Q. M; Almaron Dickenson, Lt; W. H. Patton, Capt.4

Tuesday, February 2, 1836
33 DAYS TO THE FALL

Election Certificate, Alamo Garrison

Certificate

We certify that in pursuance of an order from the senior officer in command here & influenced by an urgent general request, we proceeded by order of Lt. Col J. C. Neill, to an election of two persons as members of the convention to represent the citizens of Texas now here on duty, in the convention ordered by the late General Consultation and to sit at Washington. The election was held in the Alamo Fort on the first day of February, in strict conformity with the law and with general usage. The within we certify to be a correct return of the polls as kept _____ by our own clerk, whose name is hereunto appended. The return exhibits one hundred and four votes; one hundred and three votes were given to Samuel A. Maverick, one hundred to Jesse B. Badget and one vote given to each of two other persons. We therefore return Maverick and Badget as elected. Given under our hands at Bejar this 2nd day of Feby 1836.

E. Melton, Clerk of the election. Judges, W. C. M. Baker, Samuel Blair, Capt., Wm. Blazeby[5]

James Bowie to Henry Smith

BEXAR: Sir: In pursuance of your orders, I proceeded from San Felipe to La Bahia and whilst there employed my whole time in trying to effect the objects of my mission. You are aware that Genl Houston came to La Bahia soon after I did, this is the reason why I did not not make a report to you from that post. The Comdr. in Chf. has before this communicated to you all matters in relation to our military affairs at La Bahia, this makes it wholly unnecessary for me to say any thing on the subject. Whilst at La Bahia General Houston received dispatches from col Comdt. Neill that good reasons were entertained that an attack would soon be made by a numerous Mexican army on our important post at Bexar. It was forthwith determined that I should go instantly to Bexar; accordingly I left Genl Houston and with a few very efficient volunteers came on to this place about 2 weeks since. I was received by Col Neill with great cordiality, and the men under my command entered at once into active service. All I can say of the soldiers stationed here is complimentary to both their courage and their patience. But it is the truth and your Excellency must know it, that great and just disatisfaction is felt for the want of a little money to pay the small but necessary expenses of our men. I cannot eulogize the conduct & character of Col Neill too highly: no other man in the army could have kept men at this post, under the neglect they have experienced. Both he & myself have done all that we could; we have industriously tryed all expedients to raise funds; but hitherto it has been to no purpose. We are still laboring night and day laying up provisions for a siege, encouraging our men, and calling on the government for relief.

Relief at this post in men, money, and provisions is of vital importance and is wanted instantly. So this is the real reason of my letter. The salvation of Texas depends in great measure in keeping Bejar out of the hands of the enemy. It serves as the frontier picquet guard and if it were in the possession of Santa Anna there is no strong hold from which to repell him in his march towards the Sabine. There is no doubt but very large forces are being gathered in several of the towns beyond the Rio Grande, and late information through Senr. Cassiana & others, worthy of credit, is positive in the fact that 16 hundred or two thousand troops with good officers, well armed, and a plenty of provisions, were on the point of marching, (the provisions being cooked &c) A detachment of active young men from the volunteers under my command have been sent to the Rio Frio; they returned yesterday without information and we remain yet in doubt whether they intend to attack on this place or go to reenforce Matamoros. It does, however, seem certain that an attack is shortly to be made on this place, and I think it is the general opinion that the enemy will come by land. The citizens of Bexar have behaved well. Colonel Neill and myself have come to the solemn resolution that we will rather die in these ditches than give up this post to the enemy. These citizens deserve our protection and the public safety demands our lives rather than to evacuate this post to the enemy. — again we call aloud for relief; the weakness of our post will at any rate bring the enemy on, some volunteers are expected: Capt Patton with 5 or 6 has come in. But a large reinforcement with provisions is what we need.

James Bowie

P.S. I have information just now from a friend whom I believe that the force at the Rio Grande (Presidia) is two thousand complete; he states further that five thousand are a little back and marching on, perhaps the 2 thousand will wait for a junction with the 5 thousand. This information is corroborated with all that we have heard. The informant says that they intend to make a decent on this place in particular, and there is no doubt of it.

Our force is very small, the returns this day to the Comdt. is only one hundred and twenty officers & men. It would be a waste of men to put our brave little band against thousands.

We have no interesting news to communicate. The army have elected two gentlemen to represent the Army & trust they will be received.

James Bowie[6]

R. R. Royall to Govnr. & Genl Council

MATAGORDA: I herewith send you a copy of a bill of Lading, of supplies for the Texas army, which arrived in our port on the day before yesterday. I have no orders from the Government, and no discretionary powers, but will take the liberty to order the supplies, to Dimmit's Landing on the La Baca (well knowing that our troops at Goliad and Bexar are much in want of Provisions) and shall instruct Capt. Dimmit to furnish the proper officers of the Government, such Provisions as they may require, until he may receive orders from the Government, and in order that all may be timely understood I wish the order issued as early as possible.

The supplies being Delivered in this Port will necessarily cost from $425 to $700 to convey them to Dimitts. I shall Draw on our Agent Mr Bryan for the Freight &c. I send you also a copy of a Letter Recd. from Mr Bryan on the subject.

Your Obt servant
R. R. Royall

N B I shall Instruct Mr Bryan to ship in future to Dimitts unless ordered otherwise by the Govt.

R R R

Without Pretending to determine who is the acting Govern. I have forwarded two exact copies one to James W. Robinson and this to your Excellency.

R R R[7]

George Poe to Henry Smith

COLUMBIA: I have seen & heard a great deal relative to Council matters since I have been here — & I beg leave now to state to you my firm adherence to the Governor of Texas — if you would say what we shall do — for we have heard Houston is no longer General — but that Fanning is appointed, for any information if you give me some orders & inform me what will become of the army &c. — I would esteem it an honor —

Yesterday our election was held here the results is Byrom 45 Waller 42 Collinsworth 37 Brigham 35 the opposition ticket at highest did not get more than 19 the result from Brazoria I have not learned —

I shall be in a few days at San Antonio. If I can be of any service to you there command me in all things

Very truly Yr friend
Geo W Poe[8]

Almonte Diary Entry
Started for Ancho at 7 1/2 A.M. — To the reservoir of San Felipe, &
leagues; road almost level; little stone; the water in the reservoir
somewhat scarce; there is some pasture; no house; we camped in a
small valley; there we met the second division under command of
Tolsa; we arrived at 5 P.M. having a short halt.[9]

Col F. W. Johnson to J. W. Fannin
SAN PATRICIO: . . . By advice from Monterey of the 18th ult —
and from Matamoros of the 20th. ult, — I learn that Santa Anna
was in Saltillo with 2300 men, and a good train of artly — That
on his imprudently advancing so far, the states of Zacatecas and
Guadalaxara en mass, had taken to arms in his rear . . . The
troops which occupied Laredo have retired to Saltillo &
Monclova — those at Rio Grande (town) it is supposed will
likewise make a retrograde movement . . . defection has crept
into the arch tyrants ranks . . . 20 & 30 men desert daily & tho
Matamoros is almost entirely without a garrison, he is afraid to
send off assistance least they should revolt on leaving camp. . . .
    Everything looks most prosperous, and unless our head strong
countrymen, by a premature Declaration of Independence, rouse
the jealousy of the Federal party victory is secured and by one
blow, we may calculate over throwing the Tyrant Santa Anna and
his Minions. . . .
    Matamoros is poorly supplied with troops — our friends are in
power — I have to believe, that if a quick movement is made,
not a shot will be fired —[10]

Wednesday, February 3, 1836
32 DAYS TO THE FALL

Almonte Diary Entry
A 8 1/2 A.M. — Started to the Hoya, 8 leagues; no people; well
dry; two small poor houses — to Bejar, 6 leagues; very good road;
some dry pasture; no water in the road. The Infantry arrived at 7 1/2
P.M. and rested the day following; many soldiers sickened with
diarrhoea, and some with blistered feet; plenty of water, but no
fodder; corn; corn a 2 rials [reals] the almad [almud][11]

William B. Travis Notebook Entry
3.00   1.50
Paid for corn & wood (at San Antonio)[12] 4.50

F. W. Johnson to the General Council of Texas
SAN FELIPE DE AUSTIN: I beg leave to represent to your
honorable body that I have, under authority of an official letter

addressed to my predecessor, General Burleson, by the committee on military affairs, ordered an expedition against Matamoros of five hundred and thirty men, volunteers of Texas and from the United States — by whom I have been appointed to the command. The volunteers left Bexar on the 30th December last for La Bahia and from thence to the destined point.

I have left in the garrison at Bexar one hundred men under command of Lieutenant-Colonel Neill. This force I consider to be barely sufficient to hold the post and it will require at least fifty additional troops to place it in a strong defensive position. I have ordered all the guns for the town into the Alamo and the fortifications in the town to be destroyed.

In regard to the expedition I have no hesitation in saying that it is practicable and that not one moment should be lost, as the enemy are concentrating their forces at many points of the interior and also for the purpose of attacking us in Texas. Therefore I submit the foregoing to your consideration and ask your authority for making the expedition against Matamoros.

P.S. — Please issue commissions to James Grant as colonel, and N. R. Brister as adjutant.[13]

John Smith report on Bejar Public Stores Inventory
Report of the Public Stores and the manner in which the articles contained in my report of 31st December 1835 were disposed of.

	12-31	M.O.	Neill	Q.M.	Blaz	Fay	Dick	Delv'd
Muskets Carabines etc	357	368						368
Barrels of Carabines etc	5	8						8
Blunderbuses	1	1						1
Bayonets	420	451						451
Cartridges	19300	19300						19300
Aparajos	12	12						12
Lances	7	7						7
Boxes Musket balls	1	1						1
Camp hones	1	1						1
Doubletrees	1	1						1
Troughs or canales	18	18						18
Leather stocks	11	11						11
Round brushes	12	12						12
Cases instruments	3	3						3
Boxes Buckles, etc	1	1						1
Lots of cartridge boxes	1	1						1
Drum hoops	11	12						12
Case bottles	46	46						46
_____ bottles	3	3						3
Frails	6	6						6
Flag staffs	1	1						1
Bullet molds	3	3						3
Balls for cannons	22	45						45

	12-31	M.O.	Neill	Q.M.	Blaz	Fay	Dick	Delv'd
Small shells	4	4						4
Sm Bags of Powder	7	7						7
_____ hoes	3		1					1
Frames for lamps	1	1						1
Boxes Gun locks	1	1						1
Swords	1	1						1
Pieces Iron & Steel	4	4						4
Iron in sq bars	4			4				4
Iron in round bars	5		2	3				5
Bundles Rd Bars Iron	1			1				1
Wool hats	5		3	2				5
Socks	44		47					47
Kegs Powder	1/2	1						1
Shoes	102		90	3	3		1	97
Shirts	11		13					13
Pieces domestic	96		81			34		119
Frying Pans	4		4					4
Pounds of thread	5	3	1			1		5
Spades	33	4		31				35
Axes	12	5						12
Bags Coffee	2		1	1				2
Lances	57	57						57
Pigs of lead	1	1						1
Bars of lead		36						36
Bags of flints	2	2						2
Rifles			1					1

Note the deficiency in the shoes of five pairs will be accounted for when Wm. Fitch returns from San Felipe where he is now gone.[14]

Bejar 3rd February 1836   John W. Smith P. S. K.

Further note the difference in the account of muskets, bayonets & cannon balls carries from my having gathered up scatiering [sic] ones after Johnson left this [place] for Matamoros.

[Attached certificate, dated same day]
I certify that after a careful examination of the within report, it appears to me to be correct and corresponds with the vouchers posted.
Garrison of Bejar Feb 3 1836   J.C. Neill, Lt. Coln Comd Bejar[15]

[Editor's note: This is the exact inventory of material in the Alamo as of Feb 3. The categories are 12-31, the inventory as of that date; M.O. stands for delivered to Master of Ordinance; Neill stands for ones delivered per Neill's orders; Q.M. stands for the material delivered according to Quarter Master orders; Blaz means those materials used by Captain Blazeby; Fay means those materials delivered to Captain Fayete; Dick stands for those materials delivered to Captain Dickenson; Delv'd is the final inventory of those materials delivered to the garrison.]

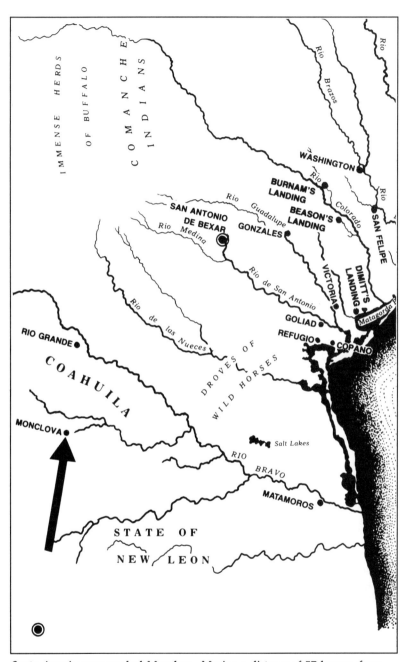

Santa Anna's army reached Monclova, Mexico, a distance of 57 leagues from Saltillo.

Thursday, February 4, 1836
31 DAYS TO THE FALL

Almonte Diary Entry

Started at 8 A.M. to the Hacendia de Castanos, 10 leagues; running water, good and abundant; to Monclova, 3 leagues; good road; corn and stalks, but few provisions. From Saltillo to Monclova, according to our count, there are 57 leagues; according to the Itinerary, 52 leagues[16]

J. W. Fannin Jr. to His Excellency James Robinson
Govr. of Texas

COPANO, TEXAS: I have the honor to inform you that I have succeeded in disembarking my men and have marched them up to the Mission of Refugio, a distance of fifteen miles — I have not yet succeeded in getting Carts and Teams, to transport our baggage &c — tho, I hope to have them tomorrow — or the next day —

I have been daily expecting the arival of the Liberty and convoy, with stores, men &c — having been informed by Capt Brown of the Invincible that they were to follow him in one or two days —

I recd. an express from Col. Johnson this day under date 2d Feby He is at San Patricio, a distance of 50 miles, with only about 100 men — They are waiting my arrival. when we will take up the line of march for Rio Grande — I learn from Col. Johnson, that Col Gonzales has 420 men — and Capt Placadon 47 — and some other Mexican officer, some considerable force — and all are in wait for my advance, and stationed near Peubla — also about 400 more ready to join us, on this side of the Rio Grande —

I herewith give you an extract of Col Johnson's communication . . . in relation to the movements of the enemy

[see letter of Feb 2nd, Johnson to Fannin]

I dispatched a courier, on my first landing, and finding that Genl. Houston had suddenly left for San Felipe, to Bejar & Goliad — and recommended to Lt. Col Neill to remove all the Cannon from the Post, to Victoria & Gonzales, except barely enough to protect the Alamo — but to maintain his position until further orders or an enemy of a superior force rendered it a matter of necessity to make a retreat — If it be true that Santa Anna is in the predicament just represented [in the Johnson letter], there is no necessary at present for either — but it is safe to do the first, even now —

I shall proceed west — and must beg of you to order the naval force, to co-operate with me before Matamoros. . . .

It is useless for me to urge the necessity — It is too apparent to require a second word — I have the private & counter signals of all except the Brutus — and Can Communicate with them. . . .[17]

Friday, February 5, 1836
30 DAYS TO THE FALL

Almonte Diary Entry
The Thermometer at Monclova in the house at 59 degrees; in the afternoon arrived Messrs. Ampudia, Caro, Wall and Argo; I wrote New York; it rained in the night; stood guard; Mr. Moral arrived.[18]

Santa Anna to General Ramirez y Sesma
HEADQUARTERS, MONCLOVA, MEXICO: Since Your Lordship should be ready to march, I hereby instruct you to leave for San Antonio de Bejar with the entire division under your command on the twelfth of the current month, making proportionate daily marches so that the troops will be in good condition in case they should have to fight.

Your Lordship will add to that division one hundred men from the presidial companies gathered at that town selecting from among those better armed and mounted.

Your Lordship will attempt to take at least one month's provisions for the entire Division and a surplus of maiz and flour which you will have conducted in carts or whichever way possible for there are no provisions at Bejar.

Your Lordship will leave 25 well mounted lancers from the Regiment of Dolores under the command of a trustworthy officer to become my escort. I will leave this place on the eighth of the current month and will try to be there by the eleventh or twelfth, which information shall serve Your Lordship as guidance.

Since I will overtake Your Lordship enroute you will verbally receive from me your instructions for your operations in Bejar.[19]

Sam Houston to Colonel Bowl, Cherokee Nation
NACOGDOCHES: My friend, To-day I heard that you were in trouble, and that you have called upon the Red brothers of all the Tribes to come; and hold a Talk with you! When you were last in this place, we talked about your troubles, and you told me, that you would soon be in town again, I have looked for you, but you did not come!

If you had come, I would have gone with you to Mr. Rueg, the Political Chief, and you could have talked to him — He would have told you that he had heard from the government about the Cherokees, and other Tribes, and the Talk was good.

Mr. Rueg is a good man, and will not let anyone take your

An early woodcut of Sam Houston.

lands, or settle on them or survey them nor disturb your
cattle or any thing belonging to
the Indians! If it is tried by any
one after this, he will have
them punished, that trouble
you! It is only a few white men
who have tried to take your
lands, from you and the most
of the white people do not
know of it; or they would con-
dem those who have done it!
All the good men wish you to
have no trouble, but they wish
you to be happy and live upon
you own lands, in peace, and
buy from you what you bring
to sell!!

I never told you a lie, nor
any other friends, and I now counsel you to come down and see
Mr. Rueg, the political chief, and you troubles will leave you,
and not come back upon you, nor your people. Your sun will
shine bright upon you, and your sleep will not be troubled any
more! I would advise you to bring some chiefs with you, of the
other Tribes; that they too may be satisfied. The Political Chief
will tell you his orders from the government, and he is a good
man, and will not lie to you. I hope you will be happy! Your
Friend

Sam Houston[20]

Saturday, February 6, 1836
29 DAYS TO THE FALL

Almonte Diary Entry
*In Monclova, thermometer at 59 degrees, cloudy. The second division
arrived; Flores was ordered to deliver the command of the Division of
Gaudalaxara to his next in command; wrote under dictation of his
excellency the President; D. Ramon Musquiz left for Sta. Rosa;
Arago continues unwell; Moral on guard.*[21]

Santa Anna to General Don Vicente Filisola
HEADQUARTERS, MONCLOVA, MEXICO: Since I have to
march to the vanguard on Monday the eighth of the current
month, it becomes indispensable for Your Excellency to remain at
this place to expedite the departure of the brigades and supplies

which should follow the Army. I therefore advise Your Excellency that the First Infantry Brigade will leave here on the same, aforementioned eighth, the Second on the tenth, and the Third, the Cavalry, on the twelfth.

The Permanent Battalion of Morelos will join the Second Brigade and Your Excellency will order this to be made known in the General Order to be used by the Major General of the Army.

The four-pound cannon which exist in this city will be given to the Commanding General of the same armed force with whatever artillery crew, munitions and mules it might have.

Each infantry brigade will take one month's rations and the Purveyor General will complete whatever is lacking which might have been used or lost enroute. They will take the necessary carts and mules for transportation as well as three empty carts to carry the sick which the troops might have in transit and to replace any carts which become unserviceable. An appropriate number of oxen will also be taken to replace the tired ones.

The necessary foreman will be named to care for the oxen and carts and shall be paid four reales per day for their maintenance. Each cart will earn two pesos per daily march which will be accredited by the General Treasury of the Army.

The Cavalry brigade will take only pack mules.

The remainder of the mules will be placed at the disposition of the Purveyor General so that the remaining provisions which are to serve as reserves behind the Army may be transported after the departure of the Calvary Brigade, asking from the Civil Authorities for the necessary number of mules and carts to be found.

Each infantry brigade will take one sergeant and ten soldiers from the existing presidial companies at this city so that they may pasture the mules and oxen of each brigade.

The Treasury of the Army will take care to cover the salaries of the said forces for the entire present month.

Your Excellency will give each brigade commander his respective itinery to Bejar, instructing them not to delay at the Town of Guerrero any longer than necessary to cross the Rio Grande

The sick army personnel who may be at this city and cannot follow will remain here under the charge of a practioner for whom a house shall be made available to establish a hospital as well as the necessary funds for medicines and utensils. Meanwhile, a trustworthy officer will be placed in charge of the arms, equipment and attire of each soldier as well as their pay to the end of the month and which he shall collect from the respective troop commanders.

The aforementioned officer shall be instructed to return to the Army with the sick as soon as they have regained their health, and continue the march to Bejar after acquiring the necessary provisions.

From the cavalcade which His Excellency the governor of the Department [of Coahuila] was ordered to gather. Your Excellency will replace the horses of the cavalry units in poor condition which might be unable to continue the march, leaving the tired horses with the military commandant of this place so that he may send them to a good pasture to recuperate them, giving a receipt for them to the commanders who deliver them, as well as to the Most Excellent Governor for those he receives.

Your excellency may rejoin the General Staff after having set the reserve provisions on march. God and Liberty[22]

William Bryan to His Ex the Governor & Hon Council of Texas
AGENCY OFFICE, NEW ORLEANS: By the arrival of the John M. Brandel from Matamoros, I have the honor to communicate the following Important information, Gen Santa Anna is at Saltillo with 7,000 men, waiting provisions, which are very scarce in his army, he was supposed to have arrived there on the 12th of January, he had given permission to a House to import provisions free of duties, & a vessel was seen by the J M Brandal off the coast having the private signal of that House. His troops are represented as badly armed & provided & without discipline & that they cannot move without provisions. Santa Anna has issued a proclamation (which I have not seen) threatening extermination to all Texians who oppose him & protection to those who submitted, & that he should treat as pirates all American vessels taken conveying Arms or provisions to Texas. I am enabled to send this by the unexpected detention of the Durango. I have the honour to remain

Yours Respectfully &c
Wm Bryan
General Agent

The House who supplies provisions has a private signal White with a black cross[23]

R. C. Morris to James Fannin
SAN PATRICIO: Don Placido Benavides has just returned & brings disagreeable intelligence. Gonzales command is entirely dispersed, and twenty two men taken prisoners. Three hundred Cavalry and three hundred Infantry have arrived at Matamoros, which in addition to the garrison makes the effective force now there 1000 men, and more are expected shortly, Cos and all his officers from Bejar are raising troops to march on Texas. One thousand men are already on the Rio Frio. One thousand more on the march near the Rio Grande destined for some point in Texas; and forces are gathering rapidly in all directions for the

same object. It is believed an attack is intended on Goliad and Bejar simultaneously.

Roderigus has broken his parole since 5 o'clock this evening and as I have but 18 effective here and no horses, I could not pursue him.

The inhabitants of Tamaulipas are generally in favor of (1824) but are so much oppressed by the military, that many of the principal men having been arrested they are completely fettered. Santa Anna caused a report to be set afloat that he was with the troops at Matamoros, but it is ascertained beyond all doubt that he is on the way to the Rio Grande for the purpose of pushing on those forces.

Don Placido deems it of the utmost importance that troops be sent to Bejar as well as others retained in this direction and also assures me that Santa Anna wishes to draw the troops of Texas out to Matamoros in hopes to throw a strong force in their rear while he makes his attack on the upper part of the colonies. This information he received from the first alcalde of Matamoros. He has been within 20 leagues of the town and correspond with him.

The people of Tamaulipas as well as those of the Rio Grande complain much of Dimitt's Proclamation, and would have acted with more decision were it not for that act, but they fear it is now almost impossible; but are still anxious for the cause. The Cavalry are the choice troops from the interior, they are armed, every one, with lance musket, pistols and sword and Santa Anna has sworn to Take Texas or lose Mexico.

Doct. Grant has been out two days with thirty men. I feel very anxious about him. I intended to have sent you two more wagons tomorrow morning early, and in fact had the oxen yoked to start before day-light but shall now await your further orders.

Cos is actually with Seizma and also Ugartechea. They have 1000 spare horses and a large number of pack mules.

It is with regret, but I am absolutely obligated to give Doct. Hoit your horse to carry him with this.

P.S. To raise funds and provisions, Cos causes each man to give an inventory of all he posses with the valuation of each article on which he demands one percent, every twenty days, he then sends two men to make the appraisement over, and if he finds that they make a return higher than the owners, he demands three per cent in lieu of one; and each family has to furnish a fanega of corn also, every twenty days and even causes the women to grind it, without respect to station. His soldiers have assassinated many of the most influential citizens, and the wives and daughters are prostituted — the whole country is given up to the troops to induce them forward.

R. M.[24]

Sunday, February 7, 1836
28 DAYS TO THE FALL

Almonte Diary Entry

In Monclova, thermometer sixty two degrees, day clear. Orders issued at 6 A.M. the next day; Sr. Mora, assistant guard . . . the mail from Mexico arrives at Monclova, Tuesday, in the morning, and leaves Wednesday at night.[25]

Santa Anna to General Don Vicente Filisola

HEADQUARTERS, MONCLOVA, MEXICO: I have instructed the military commandant of this city, Captain Don Vicente Arriola, that as of eight in the morning beginning tomorrow, he is to establish ten men at Castanos from the presidial companies with an officer of his trust to patrol continuously all the trails and roads for apprehension of deserters, and are to remain there until after the departure of the Army. As soon as it has been completed, they are to pass on to the hacienda de Hermana where they are to establish themselves to accomplish same.

[Another letter, same date, same addressee]
I acknowledge being informed . . . that there remains only two of the eight mules which were conducting a howitzer for the place of Bejar. According to the poor condition which Your Excellency tells me of the said mules which are not able to continue. Your Excellency may order their sale and impress their price into the General Treasury of the Army[26]

James Fannin to His Excellency J. W. Robinson, and General Council

MISSION OF REFUGIO: I have to communicate to you, and through you to the people of Texas, the enclosed express just received from the advance Division of the volunteer army.
You will readily discover the great difference between this information and that contained in my report of the 3d instant. The first was then supposed to be entitled to credit, and accordingly made the subject of a communication; — I cannot now question the correctness of the last. Not the least doubt should any longer be entertained, by any friend of Texas, of the design of Santa Anna to overrun the country, and expel or exterminate every white man within its borders. May I be permitted to ask of them in sober earnestness, "Why halt ye between two opinions?" Your soil is again to be polluted by the footsteps of the hirelings of an unprincipled Despot. Will the freemen of Texas calmly fold their arms, and wait until the approach of their deadly enemy compels them to protect their own firesides? Can it be possible that they — that any American — can so far forget

the honour of their mothers, wives, and daughters, as not to fly to their rifles, and march to meet the Tyrant, and avenge the insults and wrongs inflicted on his own country-women on the Rio Grande? What can be expected for the fair daughters of chaste white women, when their own country-women are prostituted by a licensed soldiery, as an inducement to push forward into the Colonies, where they may find fairer game?

The question would seem to be useless; but when I tell you, that out of more than four hundred men at and near this post, I doubt if twenty-five citizens of Texas can be mustered in the ranks — nay, I am informed, whilst writing the above, that there is not half that number; — does not this fact bespeak an indifference, and criminal apathy, truly alarming? We calculate upon the service of our volunteer friends, to aid in the defence and protection of our soil. Do the citizens of Texas reflect for a moment, that these men, many of whom have served since November last, have not received the first cent's wages, and are now nearly naked, and many of them barefooted, or what is tantamount to it? Could they hear the just complaints and taunting remarks in regard to the absence of the odd settlers and owners of the soil, and total neglect in the officers of the Government, not providing them with even the necessities of life, this our main stay would not be so confidently relied on! Will you allow me to recommend the issuing of general orders, to be sent by express to every part of Texas, commanding the civic militia, under their present organization, to turn out, and march forthwith to the seat of war! At the same time call upon all volunteers to do the same, taking care to apprise our friends in the United States of our true situation, that a sufficient inducement may be held out to draw them to our standard, in this hour of trial. It is generally believed in the United States that the war is over, and indeed our own citizens seem to have indulged the same hope. We are now undeceived, and unless a turn out in mass be made, and that speedily, the force now in the field cannot keep the invaders in check long enough to prevent the fury of the war's being felt in the heart of the country — if ever Santa Anna crosses the Guadaloupe with 5,000 men, we have to fight east of the Brazos, if not the Trinity! I feel certain that, even in that event, his army would inevitably perish or surrender. But, should we not prevent such a dreadful catastrophe, and rally, to the rescue, every freeman of Texas? Evince your determination to live free or perish in the ditch.

In order to provide for the wants of the men, appoint contractors, and have established on the difficult routes west, depots, for beef, cattle, salt, &c., and such provisions as may be obtained, that the men may be pushed forward without delay, to such points as may be deemed most exposed. In the mean time,

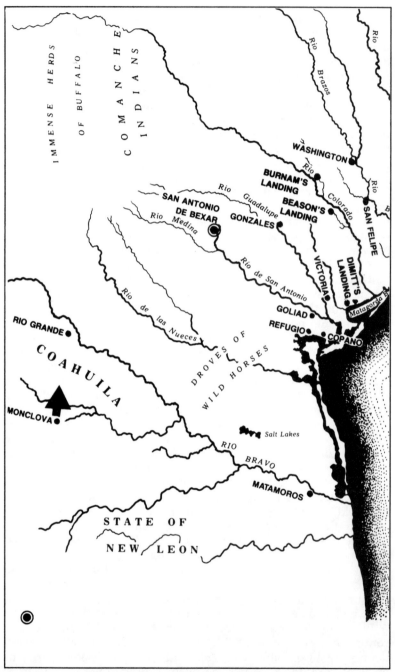

After four days rest Santa Anna's army departed Monclova to continue the march.

I would respectively recommend such measures be taken, as to form a corps of reserve on Colorado, at or between Bastrop and Gonzales, and also the Navidad and La Baca, in order to protect the settlers, and cover the advance, in case an enemy with a superior force should leave them in the rear, and march forward, calculating much upon our weakness and unprepared state of defence, and expecting much from our inexperiences and division of forces, which might be dispersed in detail, and leave the country as easy prey to the arch-Tyrant.

It is useless to controvert the fact that our true strength and geographical situation are well known to Santa Anna.

This expedition against Texas has long since been determined by Santa Anna; and Colonel Almonte was sent to Texas for the express purpose of ascertaining these facts, which you will see from his report he faithfully executed. In order to meet all the exigencies, allow me to urge you not to permit too many cavalry. But few horsemen will be resquite on the west side of Guadalupe; and experience has convinced me that the service will not be promoted by having any number of them: and extensive frauds, practised upon the government, in remunerating the owners for property never lost or destroyed in the service, and not unfrequently sold several times, on private account . . . .[27]

[to be continued, see February 8]

William B. Travis Notebook Entry

For corn for Forsyths company	6.00
do cash to soldiers Bounty	4.00

Monday, February 8, 1836
27 DAYS TO THE FALL

Almonte Diary Entry

Left Monclova at 7 1/2 A.M. arrived at the hacienda de Dos Hermanas and slept there.[28]

William B. Travis Notebook Entry

For corn for horses	2.00

**James Fannin to His Excellency J. W. Robinson,
and General Council**

[continued from February 7]

May I also urge the immediate necessity of causing suitable floating bridges, or boats, at private pass-ways, across all streams to the East of Guadalupe, should it be our unfortunate lot to be compelled to make one. This would at the same time secure the easy passage of our reinforcements, provisions, arms, &c. &c. It cannot be attended to, too soon, and I doubt not but the patriotic citizens, who have remained at home, will turn out readily and perform the work.

I must also urge upon you the absolute necessity of providing course clothing, shoes, &c., for the troops first in the field, and the following forthwith, powder, lead, &c We have enough for the present force, for a short time, and the rise of 500 new muskets brought down by me from Brazos, which will be distributed to those capable of bearing arms and entering our ranks.

I have not yet heard from the Bar, of the arrival of col. Wharton, but trust I may to-day or to-morrow, and have pilots below in order to bring them up, I have sent forward a reinforcement to San Patricio, to bring off the artillery and order a concentration of the troops at Goliad, and shall make such disposition of my forces as to sustain Bexar and that post, and keep up a communication with the colonies. In the mean time, I would recommend that some government officer be sent to La Bahia, to receive and forward stores, &c. and that point be selected for the present as our principal depot. I would also urge the immediate removal of all artillery from Bexar not requisite to the defence of that post.

Such orders have already been issued to Colonel Neill, or rather such recommendations, provided he could procure the necessary teams. I now feel authorized to give orders to that effect, and shall forward an express to him this today.

In conclusion, let me implore you to lose no time and spare no expense in spreading these tidings throughout Texas, and ordering the militia out "in mass" Spare us, in God's name, from elections in camp; organize at home, and march forward in order, and good may result from it.

I have barely time to say that an election was held on yesterday for Colonel and Lieutenant, and that myself and major Ward received nearly a unanimous vote. The returns have not yet been handed in, or I should make a report of it.

Look well to our coast; now is the time to use our small navy, and that to advantage; and unless soon afloat, we may fear the worst. . . .[29]

Tuesday, February 9, 1836
26 DAYS TO THE FALL

Almonte Diary Entry
To Lamparos, 5 leagues, (well water); to Laura, 5 leagues, (well water); good roads, all level, and good pasture.[30]

Jose Juan Sanchez Navarro Diary Entry
It is pitiful and despairing to go looking for provisions and beasts of burden, money in hand when there is plenty of everything in the commissaries, the almacenes, and depots, and to have everyone from the quartermaster general, who is General Woll, and the jefe politico to the humblest clerk reply — as if I were a Turk and the supplies I order and for which I offer to pay cash were for the russians — "We cannot sell that, we cannot let you have it because it is for the army." consequently, we are perishing from hunger and misery in the midst of plenty.

When we arrived in this city [Monclova], His Excellency the President had left for Rio Grande the day before. He is going to Bexar with inconceivable, rather astonishing haste. why is His Excellency going in such haste? Why is he leaving the entire army behind? Does he think that his name alone is sufficient to overthrow the colonists?[31]

F. W. Johnson to James Fannin
It is of importance that you should be aware of the actual state of Matamoros more clearly than I can state in a public letter — to avoid mens names being bandied about while they are still in the power of the enemy. If a force from 3 to 400 men is sent against Matamoros, Vital Fernandez, who commands with 800 Taumalips troops, will imeediately join you — And the whole of the frontier towns will immediately follow.

. . . [illegible] for the purpose of acquiring essential information and not inciting suspicion has gone for a few days to Saltillo to visit Santa Ana. He will be back to Montery ere this — Time is precious, and not a moment should be lost. Fear nothing for Bexar or Goliad or any point of Texas if an attack is made on Matamoros. The enemy will be compelled to change his plan of attack and we will maintain the war in his own territory with his own means with every advantage on our side. The true policy is to unite all your forces here, leaving a small force in Bexar and Goliad and proceed without delay into the interior. — with 150 or 200 men I will engage to keep Santa Anna's partizans in play from the town of Rio Grande to Requeta, cut off any reinforcements he may send to the coast and leave you this possession of Matamoros and even Tampico if necessary without his being able to send aid to those points. I can raise the whole country agst him and then the interior must move so as to compel him to a retrograde movement. Your Congres must be kept active to prevent any reinforcements by sea and then you play a perfectly sure game. Haste in your present movements will prove the salvation of Texas. Delays at all times are dangerous but more particularly so in this movement. All depends on you and I feel that you will warmly enter on your preparations and advance.

By a letter recd in Mier . . . from a person of credit in Saltillo it appears that movements in the state of Guadalajara and Zacetecas agst Santa Ana were likely to induce him to return incognito to the interior, leaving the command of the army to Gen'l Filisola. . . . Filisola is an old woman — Santa Anna will not retire unless everything is in an uproar.[32]

Wednesday, February 10, 1836
25 DAYS TO THE FALL

Almonte Diary Entry
To the river Sabinas at La Hacendia, 1 league; to San Jose, 9 leagues; good roads and pasture.[33]

Thursday, February 11, 1836
24 DAYS TO THE FALL

Micajah Autry, Daniel Cloud testimony
This is to testify that we in behalf of a squad of volunteers traveling to St. Antonio being out of provisions called upon John Y. Criswell who fed us in his own house with his own provisions for the night & next mornings breakfast, eight of us two meals @ 25. cts say five dollars for which the government will no doubt remunerate him we being authorized to draw on said gov. for provision.

M. Autry
D. W. Cloud
[?] Squad[34]

Green B. Jameson to His Excellency Henry Smith
BEXAR: I have been in the field on actual duty more than four Months and have not lost one hour from duty on account of sickness nor pleasure. But have served my country in every capacity I possibly could. when I left home it was with a determination to see Texas free & independent, sink or swim die or perish. And I have sanguine hopes of seeing my determination consummated. There is still a powerful force at Rio Grande say

2000 certain the last accounts we have is that they were preparing Ferry Boats to cross the River to march against us we know not when they may come. We are badly prepared to meet them. Though we will do the best we can.

A great number of the volunteers here will leave tomorrow as the end of their second month is up and no pay no clothes nor no provisions — poor encouragement for patriotic men who have stood by their country in the hour of trial. $7 each for 4 months We are now one hundred and fifty strong Col Crockett & Col Travis both here & Col Bowie in command of the volunteer forces. Col Neill left today for home on account of an express from his family informing him of their ill health.

There was great regret at his departure by all of the men though he promised to be with us in 20 days at furtherest. We have nominated two delegates from the Army to represent us in the Convention which I hope will be received as we were not allowed the privilege of voting here they are both staunch Independence men & damn any other than such. I have some improved demonstrations to make & send you of our Fortress whereby fewer men & less artillery will be required in case of a siege or an attack. Politics are straight here and every man in the Army your friend. I have named to Genl Houston through col Neill & others that I would like a permanent appointment in the Engineer corps. And know that my country will reward me as I may merit Your very Respectfully

G. B. Jameson[35]

Almonte Diary Entry

To the cabezeras de Sta Rita, 7 leagues, (running water); to San Maguel de Allende, 4 leagues; good roads and pasture; high hills.[36]

Advisory Committee to J. W. Robinson

COUNCIL HALL, SAN FELIPE: The advisory committee to the Executive, appointed by the General Council to act in that capacity in the absence of a quorum of the Council, are of opinion that under existing circumstance, the affairs of Government & the interests of the people could be better attended to, by an adjournment of the Genl Council to Washington together with a removal of all the offices of the Provincial Government that are required to Cooperate with the Genl Council, and such under their immediate control & supervision. Said Committee therefore advise, that the Executive, General Council, treasurer Auditor & be ready for the transaction of business at that place on Monday the 22nd Inst., and that the acting Governor advertise to that effect immediately, that the publication may appear with his proclamation now at press.[37]

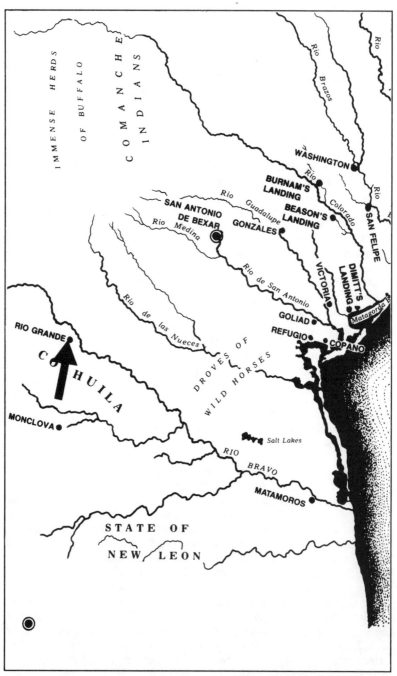

Santa Anna's army reached Presidio Rio Grande on February 12 and halted for four days while gathering provisions for the invasion of Texas.

Friday, February 12, 1836
23 DAYS TO THE FALL

Almonte Diary Entry
We arrived at Rio Grande, having left Nava 14 leagues to the left; good road and level; pasture, but no water until reaching the river.[38]

William B. Travis to His Excelly. H. Smith Governor of Texas

COMMANDANCY of BEXAR: You have no doubt already received information, by Express from La Bahia, that tremendous preparations are making on the Rio Grande & elsewhere in the Interior, for the Invasion of Texas — Sant Ana by the last accounts was at Saltillo, with a force of 2500 men & guns. Sesma was at the Rio Grande with about 2000 — He has issued his proclamation denouncing vengeance against the people of Texas — and threatens to exterminate every white man within its limits — This being the Frontier Post nearest the Rio Grande, will be the first to be attacked — We are illy prepared for their reception, as we have not more than 150 men here and they in a very discouraged state — Yet we are determined to sustain it as long as there is a man left; because we consider death preferable to disgrace, which would be the result of giving up a Post which has been so dearly won, and thus opening the door for the invaders to enter the sacred Territory of the colonies. — We hope our countrymen will open their eyes to the present danger, and wake up from their false security — I hope that all party dissentions will subside, that our fellow Citizens will unite in the Common Cause and fly to the defence of the Frontier. —

I fear that it is to waste arguments upon them — The Thunder of the Enemys Cannon and the pollution of their wives and daughters — The cries of their Famished Children, and the smoke of their burning dwellings, will only arouse them, — I regret that the Govt. has so long neglected a draft of the Militia, which is the only measure that will ever again bring the Citizens of Texas to the Frontiers. —

Money, Clothing and Provisions are greatly needed at this Post for the use of the Soldiers

I hope you Excelly, will send us a portion of the money, which has been received from the U.S. as it cannot be better applied, indeed we cannot get along any longer without Money: and with it we can do every thing. —

For God's sake and the sake of our country, send us reinforcements — I hope you will send to this Post at least two companies of Regular Troops. —

Capt. Allens Co'y. under Lt. Thornton, now at Goliad, and the company of Regulars at Copano under comand of Lt. Turner, might well be ordered to this Post, as they could reach here in four days on foot, —

In consequence of the sickness of his family, Lt. Col Neill has left this post, to visit home for a short time, and has requested me to take the Command of the Post — In consequence of which, I feel myself delicately and awkwardly situated — I therefore hope that your Excelly will give me some definite orders, and that immediately —

The troops here, to a man, recognize you as their legitimate Govr. and they expect your fatherly care & protection.

In conclusion let me assure your Excelly, that with 200 more men I believe this place can be maintained & I hope they will be sent us as soon as possible. Yet should we receive no reinforcement, I am determined to defend this place to the last, and, should Bexar fall, your friend will be buried beneath the ruins.

I have the Honor to be your Most Obt, Vet humble St.

W. Barret Travis
Lt Col. Comdt

P.S. I enclose you a Report of J. W. Smith[39] as public store Keeper, under Johnson & Grant, and reappointed by Col. Neill — Mr Smith was absent at the time my Reports were forwarded, which accounts for the delay of this.

W. B. T.[40]

William B. Travis Notebook Entry

	2.00	3.00	
For	Paper	Bread	5.00

Saturday, February 13, 1836
22 DAYS TO THE FALL

Almonte Diary Entry
At Rio Grande; weather stormy; thermometer 51 degrees; the Americans burnt the bridge over the river Nueces; the Division left the day before under the command of Sr. Sesma.[41]

William B. Travis to His Excellency Henry Smith
BEJAR: I wrote you an official letter last night as Comdt. of this Post in the absence of Col Neill & if you had taken the trouble to answer my letter from Burnam's[42] I should not now have been under the necessity of troubling you — My situation is truly awkward & delicate — Col Neill left me in the command — but wishing to give satisfaction to the volunteers here & not wishing to assume any command over them I issued an order for the election of an officer to command them with the exception of one

under me. Bowie was elected by two small company's & since his election he has been roaring drunk all the time; has assumed all command & is proceeding in a most disorderly & irregular manner — interfering with private property, releasing prisoners sentenced by court-martial & by the civil court & turning everything topsy turvey — If I did not feel my honor & that of my country compromised I would leave here instantly for some other point with the troops under my command — as I am unwilling to be responsible for the drunken irregularities of any man. I hope you will immediately order some regular troops to this place — as it is more important to occupy this Post than I imagined when I last saw you — It is the key of Texas from the Interior without a footing here the enemy can do nothing against us in the colonies now that our coast is guarded by armed vessels — I do not solicit the command of this post but as Col Neill has applied to the commander in chief to be relieved and is anxious for me to take the command, I will do it by your order for a time until an artillery officer can be sent here. The citizens here have every confidence in me, & they have shown every disposition to aid me with all they have — we much need money — can you not send us some? I read your letter to the troops & made a speech & they received it with acclamation — our spies have just returned from the Rio Grande — the enemy is there one thousand strong & is making every preparation to invade us. By the 15th of March I think Texas will be invaded & every preparation should be made to receive them. E. Smith[43] will call on you & give you all the news — so will Mr Williams the Bearer of this —

In conclusion, allow me to beg that you will give me definite orders — immediately —

W. Barret Travis

P.S. This is a private letter & is to Nibbs for fear it may fall into bad hands.[44]

William B. Travis to His Excellency Henry Smith

HEADQUARTERS of CAVALRY — BEJAR I herewith transmit to you the sentence of a Court-Martial, in the case of D. H. Barre, and other documents relative to the same, which will speak for themselves — I also enclose to you the statement of Col. D. Crockett relative to the release of S'd Barre, who refused to comply with the conditional order for his release.[45]

I make no comments upon the late transactions here, as your Excellency will be able to Judge from the enclosed impartial statements.

I have the honor to be Yr. Excy. Most ob. st.

W. Barret Travis
Lt. Col. of Cavalry[46]

J. J. Baugh to Henry Smith
GARRISON of BEXAR: Lt. Col J.C. Neill being suddenly called
home, in consequence of the illness of some of his family,
requested Col. Travis, as the Senior officer, to assume the command of the Post during his absence, — Col. Travis informed the
volunteers in the garrison, that they could, if not satisfied with
him as a commandant *Pro Tem*, elect one of their own body —
The volunteers being under a wrong impression, and ever ready
to catch at any popular excitement, objected to col Travis upon
the grounds of his being a Regular officer, and immediately
named Copl Bowie as their choice.

An election was consequently ordered by Col Travis and
Bowie was elected — without opposition none but the volunteers
voted & in fact not all of them — The consequence was a split in
the garrison Col Travis as a matter of course, would not submit
to the control of Bowie and he (Bowie) availing himself of his
popularity among the volunteers seemed anxious to arogate to
himself the entire control.

Things passed on in this way yesterday & today until at length
they have become intolerable — Bowie as Commandant of the
volunteers has gone so far as to stop carts laden with the goods
of private families removing into the country. He has ordered the
prison door to be opened for the release of a Mexican convicted
of Theft who had been tried by a Jury of 12 men, among which
was Col. Travis and Col. Bowie himself —

He has also ordered the release of D. H. Barre a private in the
Regular army attached to the Legion of Cavalry, who had been
tried by a court-martial and found Guilty of mutiny, and actually
liberated him from prison with a Corporal Guard with Loud
Huzzas —

But the most extraordinary step of all & that which sets aside
all law, civil & military, is that which follows —

James Bowie to Captains
      You are hereby required to release such Prisoners as
may be under your direction, for labor, or otherwise —
                                                    James Bowie

Under this order, the Mexican who had been convicted by the
civil authorities, and the soldiers, convicted by court-martial, &
some of whom had been placed in the Alamo, on the public
works, were released —

Antonio Fuentes who had been released as above presented
himself to the Judge under the protection of Capt. Baker of
Bowies volunteers & demanded his Clothes which were in the
Calaboose, Stating that Col. Bowie had set him at Liberty,
whereupon the Judge (Seguin) ordered him to be remanded to

prison, which was accordingly done, — As soon as this fact was reported to Bowie, he went, in a furious manner, and demanded of the Judge, a release of the Prisoner, which the Judge refused, saying that "he would give up his office & let the military appoint a Judge" — Bowie immediately sent to the Alamo for troops and they immediately paraded in the square, under Arms, in a tumultuously and disorderly manner, Bowie, himself, and many of his men, being drunk which has been the case ever since he has been in command —

Col. Travis protested against the proceedings to the Judge, and others, and as a friend to good order, and anxious to escape the stigma which must inevitably follow, has, as a last resort, drawn off his Troops to the Median, where he believes he may be as useful as in the Garrison, at all events, save himself from implication in this disgraceful business —

I have ventured to give you a hasty sketch of passing events in justice to myself and others who have had no hand in this transaction, —

J. J. Baugh
Adjt. of the Post of Bejar[47]

Amos Pollard to Henry Smith
HOSPITAL BEJAR: I am glad to learn that you are in good health and spirits. — Be assured Sir that the country will sustain you. — We are unanimous in your favor here and determined to have nothing to do with that corrupt council. — It is my duty to inform you that my department is nearly destitute of medicine and in the event of a siege I can be of very little use to the sick under such circumstances — I have a plenty of instruments with the exception of a trephining-case — some cathers and an injection syringe which would complete this station — I write you this because I suppose the Surgeon general not to be in the country and we are threatened with a large invading army

Four mexicans are to represent this jurisdiction in the convention although we might with great ease have sent the same number of americans had it not have been that a few of our people through mexican policy perfectly hood-winked head-Quarters making them believe that it was unjust to attempt to send any other then mexicans thereby exerting all that influence to the same end. — Perhaps I have said enough however I intend that those representatives shall distinctly understand previously to their leaving that if they vote *against* independence they will have to be very careful on returning here. — I wish Genl Houston was now on the frontier to help us to rush at once both our external and internal enemies — Let us show them how republicans can and will fight.[48]

J. W. Robinson to J. W. Fannin Jr.
SAN FELIPE de AUSTIN: This moment I am informed[49] that scouts sent out from San Antonio, who proceeded as far as Reo Freo [Frio], saw no troops, and the scouts returned 2 days previous to your order reaching there, and further that a Mexican arrived there from the Town of Reo Grand and says that 1600 men were there, and had halted and were baking bread &c. and was preparing to march upon San Antonio, as was reported, and that many of the men were daily deserting — *I do not think the Enemy will attack either San Antonio De Bexar or the Fortress of Goliad.* But that he will endeavor to throw reinforcements into Matamoros is more probable — Therefore you will always Keep in view the original objects of the campaign against the latter place, and dash upon it as it is prudent to do so in your opinion.[50]

J. W. Robinson to Col. J. W. Fannin Jr.
SAN FELIPE de AUSTIN: I recd yours of the 7 and 8 inst on last evening . . . and 1/3 of the militia will be ordered out to your support, and information of our situation & the pressing need of men will be be sent to the United States, without delay. . . .

You will occupy such points as you may in your opinion deem most advantageous, it is desirable to maintain the Mission of Refugio, on account of securing stores at Copano, it is proposed to occupy Gonzales and some point on the Labaca, to be occupied by the Reserve Army, & it would be well to order 2 or 3 pieces of spare cannon to each of the points above indicated. *Fortify & defend Goliad and Bexar if any opportunity fairly offers,* give the enemy battle as he advances [as] a defeat of your command would prove our ruin — all former orders given by my predecessor, Gen. Houston or myself, are so far countermanded as to render it compatible to now *obey any orders you may deem Expedient*[51]

Council to the People of Texas
COUNCIL HALL, SAN FELIPE: War with its most terrific attendants and consequences is rolling its horrors upon us! The enemy with great force is within our borders; — and Texas sleeping amidst surrounding dangers. The arch enemy of Liberty — Santa Anna, prompted by vindictive fury, leads the onset, — death, violation and extermination are determined against us. The following letters speak a language not to be misunderstood and clearly show, the alarming situation of the country and the necessity for prompt and efficient action. If we would save our country from the threatened destruction, our wives and daughters from the vilest pollution, and our families and ourselves from general massacre. Freemen of Texas — now is the

hour!! — let no consideration prevent you from coming boldly forth to the rescue! Our brethren from the United States are, by hundreds in the field, leading the van guard for our defence; and shall we look to others alone, for that protection from dangers so alarming? No Texians! shoulder your rifles, join our Patriotic Friends, and by one united and well directed effort, teach the Tyrant of Mexico and his hirelings that the sons of the Brave Patriots of '76 are invincible in the cause of Freedom and the Rights of Man.[52]

Sunday, February 14, 1836
21 DAYS TO THE FALL

Almonte Diary Entry
At the Rio Grande; the weather moderates; thermometer 46 degrees; our baggage arrived at 6 P.M. after dark.[53]

William B. Travis & James Bowie to Governor Henry Smith
COMMANDANCY of BEXAR: We had detained Mr Williams for the purpose of saying that the Garrison is in a very destitute situation we have but a small supply of provisions and are without a dollar. We therefore beg leave to call attention of your Excellency to the wants of this post, as we learn that 20,000 dollars have been sent to Copano for the use of the Troops there. We think it but just that you should send us at least 5000 dollars which we understand you have at your command.[54]

We have borrowed 500 dollars here, which has long since been Expended, and besides which, we are greatly in debt and our credit is growing worse daily. It is useless to talk of keeping up the garrison any longer without money as we believe that unless we receive some shortly, the men will all leave.

From all the information we have received there is no doubt but that the enemy will shortly advance upon this place, and that this will be the first point of attack we must therefore urge the necessity of sending reinforcements, as speedily as possible to our aid.

By an understanding of today Col. J. Bowie has the command of the volunteers of the garrison, and Col. W.B. Travis of the regulars and volunteer cavalry. All general orders and correspondence will henceforth be signed by both until Col. Neill's return.[55]

James W. Fannin, Jr. to James W. Robinson
GOLIAD: . . . I have recd. a communication from Qr, Masr, Bennet . . . they succeeded in taking 60 horses — thirty fit for service . . . I will have more and stock and some prisoners by the 18th. . . .[56]

James Fannin, Jr. to James W. Robinson and General Council
GOLIAD: Upon the documents I have sent you and Council, are
you satisfied with my course? Tell me candidly; for I will be truly
obliged to be full apprized of your and their views. I am no,
practically, an experienced commander, and may, and in all
human particularly have erred. I do not desire any command,
and particularly that of chief. I feel, I *know*, if you and the council
do not, that I am incompetent. Fortune, and brave soldiers, may
favour me and save the State, and establish for me a reputation
far beyond my deserts. I do not covet, and I do earnestly ask of
you, and any real friend, to relieve me, and make a selection of
one possessing all the requisites of a commander. If General
Houston will give up all other considerations, and devote himself
to the military, I honestly believe he will answer the present
emergency. I ask of you all, not to obtrude my name or rank
upon the approaching Convention; for I would feel truly happy
to be in the bosom of my family, and rid of the burden imposed
on me. I did not ask for my present situation, and the
Provisional Government, expiring, will give me an honourable
chance to retire. Not having discredited myself or the Texian
army, I can do so without reproach. . . . Write to me often, and
freely. Give me the news from the United States, and our
commissioners, for on them and their report, I rely mainly. *kick
for the moon, whether we hit the mark or not*; Send me all the
domestic and foreign news; and, above all things, send us men,
provisions, and ammunition. Have wagons, teams &c.
forwarded. Haste is requisite. . . .[57]

James Fannin, Jr. to James W. Robinson and General Council
GOLIAD: I should not urge our situation so strenuously upon
you, and, through you, upon the whole people of Texas, but that
I feel persuaded that a large portion of them believe the war at
an end, and that we have nothing now to do, but dictate the
terms of peace, settle down upon our form of government, and
squabble for high places and salaries. . . . Is it wise to lay at
home, and do nothing to improve the advantage already
miraculously obtained, when one week's, or one day's, work,
well and vigorously directed by a bold and skillful general, (and
Santa Anna must be acknowledged one,) would not only destroy
them all, but sacrifice the brave volunteers now in the field, and
probably jeopardize the safety of Texas! If this apathy continues,
we can never long hope for the aid of volunteers; and I am
certain we will not be worthy of the protecting Egis of the Gods;
and if we lose both, then, indeed, is our chance hopeless.

In my last, by Captain Tarleton, I informed you, that I could
find but some half dozen citizens of Texas in my ranks, and I
regret to say that it is yet the case. There is great complaint,

which, though just, I find but little difficulty in assuaging at present; there being a reasonable prospect of speedy action. This is life to a voluntary army, and though many, very many are nearly naked, and quite barefooted, and, until, my arrival here, had eaten no bread for some time, (and prospect of being out before I could get it from Demit.) I am proud to say that they manifested willingness, nay, an anxiety to meet the foe, and despoil him of his honours and illustrious deeds, won at Tampico, and more recently acted out in the unfortunate fall of Zacatecas. They look to the people of Texas, en masse, to embody and march to the rescue. Shall they be disappointed?

I hope soon to receive some intelligence from General Houston, and to see him at the head of the army. I am delicately situated, not having received any orders from him, or from your Excellency. I am well aware, that during the General's furlough, the command naturally, and of right, devolves upon me; but the fact has not been communicated to me officially, either by the General or the Governor. The steps I have taken, are those of prudence, and for defence, and would be allowable as Colonel of the volunteers, &c. May I ask for orders, and a regular communication from you, that I may be fully apprised of what is doing for us. I will obey orders, if I am sacrificed in the discharge of them; but if you are unable to afford us reasonable aid, and that in time, it would be best to destroy everything and fall back. I however, hope better things, &c. &c.[58]

D. P. Cummings to Father

BEXAR: I wrote you from Gonzales and soon after left there for this place, yet under different views from what I stated in as a sudden attack was expected on our garrison here and were called on for assistance. It is however fully ascertained that we have nothing of the kind to apprehend before a month or six weeks as the Enemy have not yet crossed the Rio Grande 180 mi. distant from this place nor are they expected to make any movement this way until the weather becomes warm or until the grass is sufficiently up to support their horses we conceive it however important to be prepared as a heavy attack is expected from Sant Ana himself in the spring as no doubt the despot will use every possible means and strain every nerve to conquer and exterminate us from the land — in this we have no fear and are confident that Texas cannot only sustain what she now holds but take Mexico itself did She think on conquest.

The Northern Indians have joined to our assistance and the volunteers from the United State are every day flocking to our ranks which from the liberal promises of the Government and desirable resources of the country seem determined to sustain themselves or sinke in the attempt. Many it is true have left the country and returned home to their friends and pleasures but of such Texas has no use for and her agents in the U. States should be careful whom they send us for assistance we want men of determined spirts, that can undergo hardships and deprivation Otherwise they are only a pest and expense to their fellow Soldiers — to the first class (tho I would be the last to advise in any case), I say come on, there is a fine field open to you all no matter how you are situated or what may be your circumstances. At least come and see the country, as a farmer, mechanic or a soldier you will do well — I believe no country offers such strong inducements to Emigration, affording all the conveniences of life that men can devise — what I write is from my own observation and from what I hear from those who have resided for years in the Country. I am to leave this to return to the Cibilo Creek in company with 10 others to take up, our lands we get as citizens which in more then 1100 acres for single men, men of family 4428 acres our volunteer pay is 20$ per month & 640 acres at close of war.

Any communication to San Felipe de Austin you may make with postage paid to the Boundary line I will get or send to Stiles Duncan Natchitoches, he could mail it to San Felipe as I would be very glad to hear from you all.

It might be that I might be of some benefit to you here provided any of you could have a mind to come out and indeed to speak sincerely this would be the Country for us all, nothing could induce me from my determination of settling here, tho my disposition may not be like most others. I should like you could once see it. — a visit by Jonathan would improve his health I have been very healthy since I have been here and am improving.

Yours affectionately
D. P. Cummings

P.S. There is one thing might be proper for me to add members have been elected to a convention of all Texas to meet on 1st March, which will make an immediate declaration of inde- pendence — upon the faith of this event great speculation is going on in Lands, tho the office for the disposal of the public lands is not yet opened but is expected will be in a Short time. The price of land has risen greatly since the commencement of the war, and a declaration of independence will bring them to vie with those of the U. States tho — they can be purchased from 50 cts to 5$ per acre by the League depending as their improve- ment. Or convenience to settlements — not Country is now settling faster — As I will most likely be engaged in surveying of public lands I might be of service to some of our friends in procuring desirable or choice locations.

D. P. Cummings[59]

J. C. Neill to Convention
GARRISON OF BEXAR: This is to certify that Jesse B. Badgett has been in the service of Texas as a volunteer from the 15th November until the present time and has discharged the duties devolving on him as such and is hereby honorably discharged from further Service giving him twenty days to return home.[60]

James Robinson to Sam Houston
SAN FELIPE: I recd. your kind note from Mr. Groce's & my papers by the boy. In a few days after Capt. Gilmine and company arrived from Tenn. and most of them left for Goliad. J. W. Fannin was recently elected Col. & Major Ward Lt. Col. of volunteers at Refugio, almost unanimously, and all is harmonious there. Report pretty well confirmed says Santa Anna is on the march for Texas in force, 1000 at Matamoros, 1600 at the town of Rio Grande, 2300 at Saltillo, where Santa Anna is himself.

I have ordered out 1/3 of the militia by volunteers if they can be had, by draft if we must.

I have sent Capt. Teal an appointment of aid de camp for that purpose, and I hope you will give any aid in advice or otherwise that he may need, and any other of the aids in the east of Texas.

I am now fully satisfied that we may soon expect an attack at all points, and we must be ready, and meet and battle with the enemy beyond the border of Texas.[61]

Monday, February 15, 1836
20 DAYS TO THE FALL

Almonte Diary Entry
At Rio Grande; weather good, thermometer 56 degrees, fine weather for traveling; despatched a part of the correspondence.[62]

W. Barret Travis to his Excellency, H. Smith Governor of Texas
BEXAR: Sir I have the pleasure to introduce to your acquaintance and friendly notice my friend and your namesake, Erastus Smith,[63] who has proven himself to be "the Bravest of the Brave" in the cause of Texas. He has been the friend of Texas in time of need: Texas ought to befriend and protect him and his helpless family — he will give you the news relative to everything here — and upon him you may rely.[64]

Asa Walker to John Grant
I take the responsibility of taking your overcoat and gun. Your gun they would have had anyhow, and I might as well have it as anyone else. If I live to return, I will satisfy you for all. If I die, I leave you my clothes to do the best you can with. You can sell

them for something. If you overtake me, you can take your rifle and I will trust to chance. The hurry of the moment and my want of means to do better are all the excuses I have to plead for fitting out at your expense. Forgive the presumption and remember your friend at heart.[65]

Erastus "Deaf" Smith, the Texas spy who was wounded at the first seige of San Antonio but recovered to play a crucial role at the Battle of San Jacinto.

Advisory Committee to J. W. Robinson

COUNCIL HALL, SAN FELIPE: The advisory committee to the Executive, appointed by the General Council to act in that capacity in the absence of a quorum of the Council, are of opinion that the advices, as to require a retrograde movement on the part of col. Fannin, or any of the troops designed for Matamoros, more especially when the forces at Bejar have considerably increased, and the Militia of Texas are now called upon to move upon the Western frontier, and where all volunteers are now directed, which together, we believe will be amply sufficient, to sustain the posts of Bejar and Goliad independent of the forces first designed for Matamoros expedition, and to meet any forces of the enemy, which may come from the upper crossing of the Rio Grande.

The committee therefore advise that Col Fannin, be required to maintain his position at Copano and if possible at San Patricio, until the movements of the Commander, which, if possible, should be directed to the accomplishment of the expedition —

The committee further advise, that a copy of this together with the corresponding orders from the acting Governor, be forwarded to col Fannin by express[66]

Advisory Committee to J. W. Robinson

COUNCIL HALL, SAN FELIPE: The advisory Committee appointed to act in the absence of a quorum of the Council, being informed that a cargo of provisions and public stores for the Government has been landed from the Schooner Caroline, at Cox's Point, on the La Vaca Bay, and that the same is in an unsafe and suffering condition, for want of a shelter and a store keeper, and furthermore they are informed that, said place before named, is without a suitable person to take charge of Government property, — Therefore the committee advise the acting Governor to constitute & appoint a public store keeper for the La Vaca Bay, to take charge of all government stores, and provisions, which may be landed there, by order of the Government, and that Mr. P. Dimmit's ware house, be designed as the place of deposit for all government stores, property or supplies landed in said Bay, to be issued and delivered by said Store Keeper to the proper accredited officers of the Government, who may require them for the use of the army, upon proper orders, and vouchers being given, also that said store Keeper be instructed to remove the public stores and property, at the store house, at Cox's point, recently landed there by the said Schooner Caroline, up to the Ware House of Mr P Dimit, and The Committee further advise that the citizen P Dimit be constituted and appointed the store keeper, before named, with the requisite instructions.[67]

Advisory Committee to J. W. Robinson

COUNCIL HALL, SAN FELIPE: The advisory committee to the Executive, appointed by the General Council to act in that capacity in the absence of a quorum. —

Are of opinion that every effort should be made, to sustain the expedition to Matamoros under command of Col Fannin and that every encouragement should be given to Citizens to co-operate in this measure, Believing that Mr Malone a member of this council would contribute to rally the citizens of the Southern Municipalities around the standard of their country. The committee advise that he be excused from attending the council until the first week in March, with a view to visit that section of Country, for that purpose and that he receive such instructions as is best calculated to facilitate this object, principally relying upon the patriotism and energy of Mr Malone for executing this important trust.

We advise that Mr Malone be allowed one of the public Horses at this place to be selected by himself —

D. C. Barrett
J. D. Clements[68]

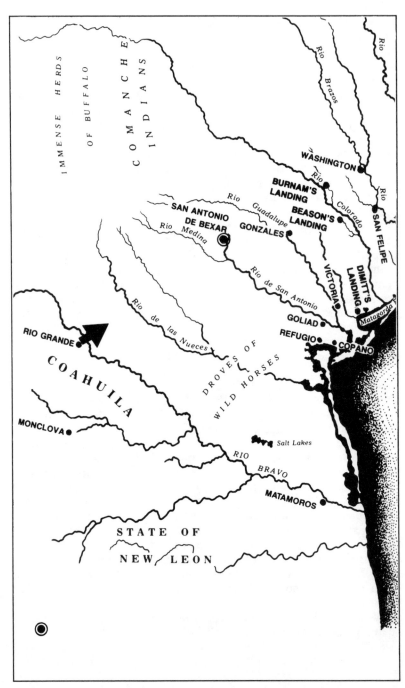

*Santa Anna's army crossed the Rio Grande into Texas and marched toward
San Antonio de Bexar.*

Tuesday, February 16, 1836
19 DAYS TO THE FALL

Almonte Diary Entry
At 4 1/2 P.M. started from Rio Grande, after writing until 3 in the afternoon; arrived at La Pena 11 o'clock at night; distance 12 leagues.[69]

William B. Travis to his Excellency Henry Smith — Governor of Texas
COMMANDANCY of BEJAR: Sir — enclosed I send you the report of the Engineer of this Post Mr. Green B. Jameson, together with a Plan or Demonstration of the Alamo & its present state of defence. I hope they will meet your approbation as Mr. G. has shown himself industrious & attentive in his department and seems willing to do everything in his power to serve the state

I must however again remind your Excellency that this Point is the key of Texas & should not be neglected by the Government. Men, money and provisions are needed — with them this post can & shall be maintained & Texas the colonies, will be saved from the fatal effects of an invasion.[70]

William B. Travis Notebook Entry[71]
      1.50   2.00
For   Firewood 17th corn 3.50

Green B. Jameson to His Excellency Henry Smith
BEXAR: I have been dilatory in communicating to you the situation as well as the plan of the Fortress whereby you might know of our exact state of defense & security in case of a siege from the enemy unless through my commander Genl. Saml. Houston — But will now send you a complete plan of the same showing its situation at the time it was surrendered to us. Also such improvement as we have made in erecting redoubts digging wells & mounting cannon. . . . all of which I send you for your information and that of your friends & the friends to our cause and country — But after seeing the improbability & perhaps the impractibility and impolicy of keeping up a strong Garrison here, I now suggest a further suggestion to you as well as the commander in Chief which you will remark to me as you both think most economical & efficient. The suggestion is, to square the Alamo and erect a large redoubt at each corner supported by Bastions & leave a ditch all around full of water. When squared in that way four cannon & fewer men would do more effective service than twenty pieces of artillery does or can do in the way they are now mounted. The Mexicans have shown imbecility and

want of skill in this Fortress as they have done in all things else — I have seen fortifications in the U.S. and find that all of the Interior ones are square and those of the Forts are generally circular.

Taking into consideration the scarcity of tools we have done well in mounting & remounting Guns and other necessary work — If I were ordered to construct a new & effective Fortress on an economical plan I would suggest a diamond with two acute & two obtuse angles — with few men & Guns with a sufficient entrenchment all around such a fortress with projecting redoubts & bastions would command all points — If you are not too much perplexed with other business I wish you to write me officially on this subject — I beg leave to tender to you my high esteem for your firm & unshaken course pursued since you have had the honor to preside over this state as chief magistrate as also that of Garrison to which I am attached and assure you that the course by you pursued has won all Philanthropists to your person & conduct, and hope that you may ever retain the same confidence you now hold and subscribe myself Yr Obt. humble Servt.[72]

J. W. Robinson to Phillip Dimmit
EXECUTIVE DEPARTMENT, SAN FELIPE: Without Knowing your views on the subject, I have sent you a Commission as public store Keeper at your own residence, by the advice of the the advisory council for the public good. I solicit you to accept, which I hope you will do, as the public stores at Coxes point, I am informed are very much exposed —

You will cause, all public property now at said point or that may hereafter arrive there, to be conveyed to your warehouse and there safely Kept, subject to the order of the competent authority.

I have given order to Cols. Neill & Fannin, & Lt. Thornton to draw on you for supplies, out of said stores, and you will report your proceedings to this department.

James W. Robinson
acting Governor[73]

J. W. Fannin to His Excellency J. W. Robinson
HEADQUARTERS ARMY OF TEXAS, GOLIAD: Since my communication of the 14th inst. inclosing several documents, recd from various sources from the interior, in relation to the movements of Santa Anna, Mr. Pantallion and young Mr. Kuykendall have arrived here, only five days from Matamoros. Both of these gentlemen are known to me, and likewise to most of the people of middle Texas; and their statements, confirming in the smallest particular my former intelligence, may be confidently relied on.

As these gentlemen will visit San Felipe, and can communicate fully with you, I will not go into a detailed account of the facts, &c., collected from them, but only draw your attention to the plan of the intended campaign against Texas.

It is designed to enter our country in Three Divisions — One to take Bejar, commanded by General Sesma, Filisola, Cos — one against Goliad under Urrea (recently Gov. of Durango) and Col Garay. The Third under Santa Anna himself, to pass either above Bejar, or between that post, & Goliad, and proceed directly into the heart of the Colony & then fortify. I understand the Genl says he will not go into the woods & swamps to find us and fight us — but proceed through open Prairie to the centre of Texas, and immediately fortify, and let us come to him, and make the best fight we can — or that he will allow us — I only say to this amen — so might it be — send 12 to 1500 men to Bejar immediately — and Provisions plenty — and anywhere from 5 to 800 here, with like stores — and then a reserve Army on Colorado, to salute the Genl with a *feu — dejoie*, and then will all be well.

Stir up the people — but do not allow them to come into camp unless organized — I never wish to see an Election in a camp, when I am responsible in any manner.

I have taken measures to forward Provisions to Bejar — and forwarded orders there to day, to place that post in a state of Defence, which if attended to, will make it safe —

If Genl Houston does not return to duty on the Expiration of his furlough, and it meets your approbation I shall make Head-quarters at Bejar — and take with me, such of the force, as can be spared.

I hope to have this place well secured by the time I can hear from You — If I do not go to Bejar. I would prefer the Reserve Army, and think, I could do some service — In this, however, do with me, whilst a public servt, as you deem best — Bejar, and Guadalupe & Colorado, I think will be the posts of danger and honor.[74]

Stephen F. Austin to Mary Austin Holley

NASHVILLE, TENNESSEE: The greatest enthusiasm pervades all ranks and sexes here in favor of Texas. The ladies of Nashville have offered to furnish the means of forming and transporting a company of Volunteers to Texas. It is now raising and will soon be ready. Such is the cause of Texas. We are contending for the right of self government. Our object is independence. March, April, and May next is the time we shall need aid, for by that time Santa Anna will be with his army.[75]

Antonio Lopez de Santa Anna to D. Vicente Filisola,
second in command
HEADQUARTERS AT GUERRERO, MEXICO: I have ordered that
fifty of the rifles and sabres that came with the general equipment of the army be turned over to the Political Chief of this
department, D. Manuel Rosas, so that by distributing them
among the villages they will serve to defend the villages from the
invasions of the Indians.[76]

Antonio Lopez de Santa Anna to D. Vicente Filisola,
second in command
HEADQUARTERS AT GUERRERO, MEXICO: I herewith forward
to your Excellency for your information the route which I have
left for the brigades so that your Excellency may order the
remaining property of the Army at the rear guard to follow the
same road. God and Liberty.[77]

Antonio Lopez de Santa Anna to D. Vicente Filisola,
second in command
GENERAL HEADQUARTERS OF VILLA GUERRERO: I approve
of the arrangements that your Excellency had made regarding the
safe forwarding of the stores of corn-meal and corn which are
being gathered there for the use of the army.

You can make use of the fortification sacks that may be
required for the transportation of the meal and grain. Your Excellency could also leave the cartridges of fifteen muskets and
carry in the wagons the cargas of meal that may fit it, leaving
instructions with the local military commandant that he is to
forward to Bejar the cartridges that remain in his care.[78]

Antonio Lopez de Santa Anna to Tornel
GENERAL HEADQUARTERS OF VILLA GUERRERO: The army
of operations under my command being already on its march to
Bexar, which I expect to occupy before fifteen days, I am going to
find myself embarrassed if the supreme government does not
send me opportunely the necessary instructions as to the policy
that I am to observe in dealing with the colonies after order has
been restored. I believe, therefore, that it is necessary for the
executive, together with the legislative body, to give its attention
to the reorganization of the government of those colonies
without delay; and that the instructions sent to me ought to be
definite, clear and ample in order that when the time comes I
may act in the most convenient manner for our national interests.[79]

Wednesday, February 17, 1836
18 DAYS TO THE FALL

Almonte Diary Entry
Exceedingly hot at mid-day on the Nueces; from La Pena to La Espantora, 5 leagues; to the river Nueces 1 1/2 and to La Fortuga [Tortuga], 3 leagues.[80]

General Jose Urrea Diary Entry
From twelve o'clock until ten o'clock at night the division was occupied in crossing the Rio Bravo for the purpose of fighting a party of about 300 colonists whom the commandant-general of those departments and I were notified were on their way to invade the city of Matamoros.[81]

General Antonio Lopez de Santa Anna to troops of the Mexican Army
Comrades in arms, our most sacred duties have brought us to these uninhabited lands and demand our engaging in combat against a rabble of wretched adventurers to whom our authorities have unwisely given benefits that even Mexicans did not enjoy, and who have taken possession of this vast and fertile area, convinced that our own unfortunate internal divisions have rendered us incapable of defending our soil. Wretches! Soon they will become aware of their folly! Soldiers, our comrades have been shamefully sacrificed at Anahuac, Goliad and Bexar, and you are those destined to punish these murderers. My friends: we will march as long as the interests of the nation that we serve demand. The claimants to the acres of Texas land will soon know to their sorrow that their reinforcements from New Orleans, Mobile, Boston, New York, and other points north, whence they should never have come, are insignificant, and that Mexicans, generous by nature, will not leave unpunished affronts resulting in injury or discredit to their country, regardless of who the aggressors may be.[82]

Alamo Receipt
Received of J. B. Badgett[83] two bottles of wine for use in the hospital & three lbs of powder for the use of the garrison, all valued at three dollars 87 1/2 which the provisional Govt. will please pay to said J. B. Badgett on order.[84]

Thursday, February 18, 1836
17 DAYS TO THE FALL

Almonte Diary Entry
To La Leona, 8 leagues; to No lo Digas, 4 leagues; no water[85]

General Jose Urrea Diary Entry
I set out to join the division. At Rancho Viejo, three good leagues from Matamoros, I was informed that the enemy was retreating precipitately to San Patricio. I spent the night at this place where two foreigners, accused of being spies detailed by the enemy to get information regarding the movements of my troops, were arrested.[86]

Unknown to Editor, Red River Herald
NACOGDOCHES: With some surprise, I have understood that a report is now in circulation, that the volunteers from the United States, lately stationed at the mission of Refugio, had refused to submit to the command of Gen Houston. The report is utterly without foundation. The troops marched under the orders of General Houston from Goliad to Refugio. And upon the arrival of Mr. Johnson, upon the second evening after their encampment, bearing the resolutions passed by the council, or a part of them. Gen. Houston returned to St. Philippe [Felipe] on the night succeeding, for the purpose of reporting to the governor, as the only office he could recognize. No doubt can be entertained, but that a great portion of the volunteers would immediately disband, had they known of the departure of their general. This General Houston wished to avoid, as he would not countenance insubordination in any form, or under any circumstance. He therefore left the post at night, and without their knowledge of the time he would leave.

An Indian treaty was also to be held, which required the immediate attention of General Houston, as one of the commissioners. In truth, this should have been a primary object with the council, and the General was preparing to accomplish it at the time orders were received from St. Philippe, to repair to the command of the army. General Houston will repair to the command, and sustain the volunteers, with whom he will put his life in the defence of Texas. Feelings of duty to his country predominate with him, and he cannot be restrained from acting as they dictate.[87]

John G. Caldwell, et al to Byers & Mercer
WASHINGTON: We subscribers do hereby bind and obligate ourselves to pay Messrs Byers & Mercer, the sum of One Hundred and Seventy Dollars, being in consideration of the rent of the house owned by them, on Main Street for the term of 3

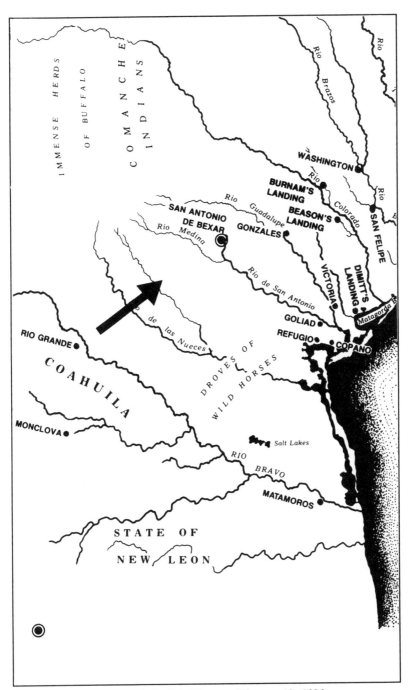

Santa Anna's army reached the Frio River on February 19, 1836.

months to commence on the 1st day of March next — Said Byers
& Mercer are to have the house in complete order & repair for
use of the members of the convention to meet in March next —
for which purpose Said building is rented by us.[88]

Signed by Hall & Lott, John G. Caldwell, John C. Neal, G. P.
Pattrick, Wood & Peebles, S. R. Roberts, Martin Clan & Co.,
William P. Smith[89]

Friday, February 19, 1836
16 DAYS TO THE FALL

Almonte Diary Entry

*At the Rio Frio, 5 leagues; found there in the morning the Division
of Sr. Rameriz; little pasture; made a new bridge; the division crossed
in the afternoon.*[90]

Wm. B. Travis to Capt. J. L. Vaughn

COMMANDANCY OF BEJAR: Sir You are hereby required to
proceed forthwith on the Recruiting service — You will take up
the line of march for the town of Rio Grande, from thence to
Peotis, thence to San Juan de Mat, thence to Aguaverde thence
to San Fernando, thence to Laredo, thence to Revilla, thence to
Alcantro, thence to Rinosa, thence to Comargo, from thence to
Florido & thence to Matamoros where you will make your headquarters until further orders. —

You will make regular reports from all the places above
named, — and make as many recruits as possible at each place
— taking care that when you shall have formed a Company to
forward the same to this post, — and proceed to recruit other
companies as fast as possible. —

Enclosed, you have the General Instructions for the Recruiting
Service, by which you will be governed in all cases. —

You have been selected for this Service on account of your
distinguished public Services, your well known patriotism,
daring valor, firmness and perseverance. — It is therefore
expected & required that this order will be executed with
Promptness & dispatch, & it is hoped & confidently believed that
my expectations will be fully realized.

I have the Honor to be
Yr. Most Ob. St.
Wm Barret Travis

P.S. The situation of the enemy must not be lost sight of, you
must report weekly in relation him. —[91]

Saturday, February 20, 1836
15 DAYS TO THE FALL

Almonte Diary Entry
Started for Arroyo Seco, 4 leagues; to Tahuacan, 2 leagues; to Rio Hondo, 2 leagues, making 8 leagues. The night was clear and pleasant, morning cloudy, 72 degrees of Fahrenheit; day cloudy, misty, no rain.[92]

Tom Find to Editor
MATAMOROS, MEXICO: Mr. Editor — the within production, which suits the present aspect of affairs in Texas was written to be published in New Orleans and Texas Gazettes. Please give the same a place in your paper.

The political horizon of affairs in this country assumes as gloomy aspect as ever, and fears are entertained some time will elapse [before] a change will take place for the better. Our military chieftain, Santa-Anna, appears to be disposed, or confident, he can exterminate the Texians from their legal residences, which he is at present attempting to hazard, by marching into the colony from 8 to 12,000 men.

About the 23d January, his first division left Saltillo for Monclova or Laredo: 2d division on the 26th and 3d on 2d February. His majesty left the 3d inst, and will arrive with part of his army at Bejar, or St. Antonio, where the brave General Cos capitulated to the *ladies*, he will make his appearance in March in due season to miss the spring buds of his prospects, "and teach the young *idea how to shoot.*" We have here an assortment of troops from the South, say from 9 to 1200; rumor reports they are destined for Labahia, and to leave on about the 10th March by land. The president does not appear to enjoy as good a reputation with the congress as he is entitled to. They are cutting off his resources by ordering all duties and liberances to be paid in the city of Mexico, which are due, or may become due in this part. That looks like a strike at his integrity.[93]

Sunday, February 21, 1836
14 DAYS TO THE FALL

James W. Fannin to James W. Robinson
and the General Council
GOLIAD: It affords me some little satisfaction to discover that you have so promptly met my expectations, and taken the first steps yet taken to force the militia to the field. But you will allow me to say I am yet a sceptic, and do not calculate to see any

Colonel James W. Fannin, from a portrait probably painted during his brief stay at West Point.

considerable force in the field, until those already there are either sacrificed, or forced to make a retrograde movement. Do not believe, for a moment, that I have any such idea at present, or ever had. . . I am fortifying here, so as to make the place tenable for a reasonable force. . .

I have caused an old priest and thirteen soldiers, including one lieutenant, (who belonged to Captain Saverago's company) and who have been making their brags, sending their couriers, &c. to be made prisoners, and forward a roll of names, tender of service, &c. I will forward them all soon, and refer you to Colonel James Powers for particulars. All I say is, secure well all prisoners, and suffer none to go on parole. This man of God is the blackest of villains, a murderer, adulterer, &c his influence is almost unbounded. I hope you will soon release me from the army, at least as an officer. But whilst I am in command, both private and public enemies shall be attended to. There is more danger from

La Bahia Mission at Goliad that was christened Fort Defiance by Colonel Fannin.

these spies, who are so intamately acquainted with the country, than from twenty times the number of armed soldiers. I again tell you, we must not rely on Mexicans. It would be a fatal decision. Give us a flag to fight under, as unlike theirs as possible. We need one, and having nothing to make it of, and hope the Convention will furnish a new one, in time to hoist it in defiance of Santa Anna. Do send some money, and clothes, and shoes, for the soldiers.

[Attached note]

In relieving guard yesterday, the corporal marched off barefooted. Many of the men are so near naked, that only certain parts of their body are covered. I will send you the padre, to officiate as your chaplain during the Convention.[94]

Almonte Diary Entry

Sunday 21st — At & 1/2 A. M. left Arroyo Hondo — weather cloudy — slight showers — not cold — wind south east. To Francisco Perez 4 leagues, (a stream of water very distant, but not on the road) To Arroyo del Chacon, good water, 3 leagues. To the River Median 2 leagues; all good road, but broken by large hills. At 1/4 before 2 o'clock the President arrived. The day completely overcast; the whole division at 5 o'clock, when it commenced raining heavily — all wet but baggage dry, at 12 o'clock at night it cleared some.[95]

Monday, February 22, 1836
13 DAYS TO THE FALL

Almonte Diary Entry

Monday 22d — Commenced cloudy, but cleared at 10 o'clock. The troops cleared their arms and dryed their clothes; no desertions whatever or sickness. We passed the day at Medina to rest the troops. Two men from the Ranchos near Bexar arrived [Menchaca] and another; killed a beef; various other persons came in, reviewed the troops. Sr. Rameriz y Sesma, marched to cut off the retreat of the enemy with — dragoons. It was believed the enemy discovered our movements.[96]

Jesse Benton to friend

NEAR NACOGDOCHES: Official information has just reached us that Santa Anna has crossed the Rio Grande and is marching against us with a large army for the purpose of exterminating us. Nearly all our troops are riflemen; no body of infantry to lodge or to form squares or rush with and crush the enemy. We will die hard, for it will be truly victory or death with us. Our volunteers have consumed our provisions and a great many have left us —

just what I expected. General Cos and his troops we are
informed have broken their parole and are returning against us
. . . If we cannot defend the country in any other way, we can
do it effectively by adopting the Russian mode of defence against
Napoleon in 1812.[97]

Governor Henry Smith to C. B. Stewart.
ON ACCOUNT OF THE PROVISIONAL GOVT OF TEXAS:

February 22, 1836

Cash paid Col. W. B. Travis as per receipt, outfit for the relief of Post of Bexar	100.00
Cash paid for an horse for Govt use	50.00
Cash paid Express from Bexar expresses	20.00
Cash paid John R. Jones for Supplies for Tennessee volunteers as per bill	89.50
	$259.50[98]

Samuel St. John to His Excellency, Henry Smith
MOBILE: On this memorable day[99] — dear to the Hearts of
every American who would venerate the memory of "the Father
of his country" — I would beg leave to offer to the People of
Texas a donation of Five Thousand Dollars to aid them in their
present struggle for Liberty — a struggle to free them from the
shackles of usurption through tyranny.

It is known to many of the early settlers in Austin's colony
that in 1832 I visited that colony — I can scarcely express the
delight I experienced in viewing this "Garden of America."
Wishing the people of Texas entire success in their threatened
overthrow by Santa Anna. . . .[100]

James W. Fannin to James W. Robinson
and the General Council
GOLIAD: You will pardon me for not giving you more of my
time, when I tell you that I have too much to do, to suffer me to
copy even my communications. I have been greatly troubled to
get my militia to work or do any kind of garrison duty: but I am
now happy to say, that I have got them quite well satisfied, and
being well-disciplined, and doing good work. The fortress will
be completely regulated by 3rd March — and in anticipation, I
have this day, christened it Fort Defiance. We had a Lottery,
placing Milam, Defiance, and Independence in the wheel: when
Defiance was drawn out. It was objected to Milam, that Bexar
should receive the honor of being called after him, as his bones
are there; and Independence it was thought, would look like
army dictation. Dame fortune settled the matter for us, and
Defiance it is.

I am critically situated. General Houston is absent on furlough, and neither myself nor army have received any orders as to who should assume command. It is my right; and, in many respects, I have done so, where I was convinced the public weal required it. I know well that many men of influence view me with an envious eye, and either desire my station, or my disgrace. The first they are welcome to — and many thanks for taking it off my hands. The second will be harder to effect. Will you allow me to say to you, and my friends of the old or new Convention, that I am not desirous of retaining the present, or receiving any other appointment in the army. I did not seek, in any manner, the one I hold, and, you well know, had resolved not to accept. . . . I am a better judge of my military abilities than others, and if I am qualified to command an Army, I have not found it out. I well know I am a better company officer than most men now in Texas, and might do well with Regulars, &c. for a Regiment. But this does not constitute a commander.[101]

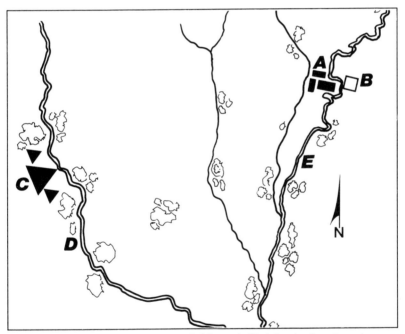

While the Texans celebrated George Washington's birthday in San Antonio, Santa Anna's army was camped near the Medina River eight miles away. Only a sudden rainstorm prevented the Mexicans from attacking while the Texans partied. A. San Antonio, B. The Alamo, C. Santa Anna's final camp on his march to the Alamo, D. The Medina River, E. The San Antonio River

Endnotes

1. *SWHQ,* 48:12. Juan Nepomuceno Almonte was Santa Anna's interpreter during the war. He was with the General at the siege of the Alamo and at San Jacinto where was taken prisoner. Almonte later accompanied the general to the United States and returned with him to Mexico in 1837. American educated, Juan Almonte continued in the diplomatic service in one station or another after the war, was active in the internal affairs in Mexico, and remained a Santa Anna follower for most of his life. He died in Paris, France in 1869. During the Texas campaign, Almonte kept a daily dairy from February 1 until the middle of April. After Almonte's capture at San Jacinto, Anson Jones, a future president of Texas, found the journal on the field of battle. He sent the ledger book to the New York Herald, a newspaper known to be most sympathetic to the cause of Texas, for publication. The Journal was printed in six parts beginning in June of 1836. It was later reprinted in Volume 48 of the *Southwestern Historical Quarterly.* The original diary has been lost so we will never know the names of the Americans who favored Mexico over Texas as referenced in the diary. The Herald publisher, James Gordon Bennett, believed the names were too well known to be published and thus omitted them.
2. Hunnicutt, 60-61.
3. William Fairfax Gray, *From Virginia to Texas* (Houston: self published 1909), 89. William Fairfax Gray came to Texas from Virginia in 1835 as a land agent and speculator. He traveled the state extensively and recorded his thoughts and observations in a carefully preserved diary. In late February, early March, Gray was an observer in the Constitutional Convention and his notes taken there have given Texans considerable insight into those wildly challenging days. After the war, Gray relocated his family to Houston, where he died in 1841. All enteries in the diary are listed by specific date.
4. Louis W. Kemp, *The Signers of the Texas Declaration of Independence* (Houston: The Anson Jones Press, 1944), 3-4.
5. Texas State Library Archives. In the actual voting, J. H. Nash kept the election from being unanimous for Maverick by casting one vote each for James Butler Bonham and John M. Hays.
6. Binkley, 2:381-383.
7. Ibid, 2:380-381.
8. Ibid, 2:383-384. George Washington Poe came to Texas from Cincinnati with his family in 1834. In 1836 he served in the infantry and fought at San Jacinto. He later held various positions, before his death in 1844, including paymaster, adjutant general, stock commissioner, and, for a short time, Secretary of war.
9. *SWHQ,* 48:12-13.
10. Foote, 2:201.
11. *SWHQ,* 48:13.
12. William Barret Travis and his group of about 30 men arrived in San Antonio de Bexar on February 3, 1836.

13. *SWHQ,* 5:316-317.
14. For a resolution to the missing shoes problem, see James C. Neill's receipt dated March 5, 1836.
15. DRT Library at the Alamo.
16. *SWHQ,* 48:13.
17. Gulick, 3:315-316.
18. *SWHQ,* 48:13.
19. Santos, 45-46. It is believed that Sesma was originally scheduled to be the commander of the invasion force that was to retake San Antonio and the Alamo but Santa Anna changed his plans and personally accompanied that force. During the final assault, however, while Santa Anna occupied a post of safety, Sesma actually led the attack and is often credited with the victory. Sesma and his force were not at San Jacinto when the decisive battle was fought and he subsequently withdrew his force below the Rio Grande and back into Mexico.
20. Barker, 4:355-356. Chief Bowles, also known as the Bowl or Colonel Bowl, brought his Cherokee tribe to Texas in about 1820. Bowl had several negotiations with the Mexicans concerning lands for his people and he had similar talks with Houston, which resulted in a treaty (see February 29). Due to the war in Texas, the treaty was never ratified and in 1837, Bowl and the Cherokees were ordered out of Texas, something they did not want. The battle of Neches resulted and Bowl, wearing a vest given him by Houston, was killed. It was the last engagement between Texans and the Cherokees.
21. *SWHQ,* 48:13.
22. Santos, 46-47.
23. Binkley, 2:398. William Bryan was a merchant in New Orleans, Louisiana that was most sympathetic to the Texas cause. He was instrumental in providing men and money for the cause. His loans of almost one hundred thousand dollars were eventually repaid by the government. He and his partner, Edward Hall, served as purchasing agents for the Republic and were instrumental in obtaining the brig *Pocket* for Texas. Hall continued to serve as agent to New Orleans until Texas was annexed into the United States.
24. Ibid, 2:399-400. Robert C. Morris was captain of the New Orleans Greys, a volunteer group that was active in the Texas struggle for Independence. After participating in the siege of Bexar and succeeding in command when Ben Milam was killed, Morris became part of the ill-fated Matamoros expedition. Morris, along with John Grant and several others, were killed by Mexican forces under General Urrea at Agua Dulce Creek on March 2, 1836.
25. *SWHQ,* 48:13.
26. Santos, 48-49.
27. Foote, 2:201-205.
28. *SWHQ,* 48:13.
29. Foote, 2:201-205.
30. *SWHQ,* 48:13.
31. Hunnicutt, 61-62.

32. *SWHQ*, 23:192-193.

33. Ibid, 48:13.

34. DRT Library at the Alamo. Historians have long known that Davy Crockett arrived at the Alamo between the 8th and 10th of February. However, those historians have been split over whether the entire contingent of Tennesseans arrived with Crockett. This receipt, signed one day after the defenders of the Alamo held a party in honor of Crockett's arrival, seems to verify that at least eight of the Tennessee boys were not with the famous frontiersman.

35. Binkley, 2:409-410.

36. *SWHQ*, 48:13.

37. Binkley, 2:410-411.

38. *SWHQ*, 48:14.

39. See February 3 for a copy of the Smith report.

40. Binkley, 416-417.

41. *SWHQ*, 48:14.

42. See William B. Travis to Henry Smith, January 28 and 29.

43. E. Smith is probably Erastus "Deaf" Smith. See Travis to Henry Smith, February 15.

44. Binkley, 2:419-420.

45. The referenced statement by Crockett could not be located.

46. Binkley, 2:421.

47. Ibid, 2:421-423. John J. Baugh, a thirty-three-year-old captain from Virginia, was the adjutant for the Alamo garrison. It is believed Baugh assumed command of the fort when William B. Travis fell early in the fighting of March 6. Baugh's command was short-lived as he perished with all the other men when the Mexicans overran the mission.

48. Binkley, 2:423-424.

49. See James Bowie letter of February 2.

50. Gulick, 3:330.

51. Ibid, 3:330-331.

52. *Telegraph, and Texas Register,* February 20, 1836.

53. *SWHQ*, 48:14.

54. Travis apparently picked up news of the council trying to get back the $5,000 in public funds held by the governor and boldly asked the governor to send it all to San Antonio.

55. Binkley, 2:425.

56. Gulick, 3:331-332.

57. Ibid, 3:332-333.

58. Foote, 2:207- 210.

59. Court of Claims Vouchers, 4271, File A-C, General Land Office, Austin, TX. David P. Cummings was a twenty-seven-year-old volunteer from Pennsylvania who died in the Alamo.

60. Kemp, 5. As the duly elected convention representative of the Alamo garrison, Badgett was discharged so he could travel to Washington.

61. A. J. Houston Papers.

62. *SWHQ*, 48:14.

63. Erastus "Deaf" Smith, the famous Texas spy, was severely wounded when the Texans took San Antonio in December of 1835. He apparently recovered, because he rejoined the army under Sam Houston and burned down Vince's bridge to prevent Santa Anna's escape from San Jacinto. Some also credit Smith with the capture of the Mexican Dictator the day following the battle.
64. State Department Records Books.
65. From phamphlet of unknown origin. Apparently Asa Walker borrowed his neighbor's gun and coat on his way to fight in the Alamo and left behind a note to show what happened to the goods. This letter was found in an unidentified, undated pamphlet. The source of the document was listed as the Washington County Courthouse at Brenham but officials of that county advise the letter is missing.
66. Binkley, 2:433.
67. Ibid, 2:433-434.
68. Ibid.
69. *SWHQ,* 48:14.
70. Binkley, 2:439-440.
71. This was the final entry in Travis' notebook concerning expenditures. The total amount spent is $143.00 which was the amount of the claim filed on behalf of the Travis estate. According to John R. Jones, executor, Travis had other expenses that were on the books of the Quarter Master, Jackson, but records concerning those expenditures are missing.
72. Binkley, 440-441.
73. Ibid, 438.
74. Foote, 2:210-211.
75. *Northwestern Gazette and Galena Advertiser* (Galena, Illinois), April 2, 1836. Mary Austin Holley, a cousin to Stephen F. Austin, was an early and frequent visitor to Texas. She was well educated (a teacher by trade), posed a keen eye for observation, and had a knack for writing. She left behind many letters that provide insight into the early colonial days of Texas. A collection of her letters was published in 1833 and she later wrote a history of the province entitled *Texas.* She remained true to the Texas cause and was active in working for independence and later annexation to the U.S. She interviewed many old settlers and the material she gathered formed the basis for a new edition of her *History of Texas.* She died of yellow fever in 1846.
76. Filisola, 68.
77. Santos, 53.
78. Filisola, 66-67.
79. Jenkins, document number 2116.
80. *SWHQ,* 48:14.
81. Castaneda, 213.
82. Enrique de la Pena, *With Santa Anna in Texas,* translated and edited by Carmen Perry (College Station: Texas A&M University, 1975), 40.

83. Since Jesse Badgett was elected to represent the Alamo garrison at the constitutional convention on March 1, 1836, he apparently intended to get reimbursed for the wine and powder.

84. Kemp, 5.

85. *SWHQ,* 48:14.

86. Castaneda, 213.

87. *Mississippi Free Trader and Natchez Gazette* (Natchez, Mississippi), March 25, 1836. *The Red River Herald* was an early and short lived Texas newspaper.

88. The Texas government was so destitute that private parties had to subscribe for the rent on a hall in which independence could be declared and a constitution written. Since the building was rented for three months, the men apparent;ly felt such documents would take some time to write. They were wrong. By march 17, the declaration and constitution had been written and the convention adjourned. The bill for the rent on the hall was never paid.

89. Kemp, 13.

90. *SWHQ,* 48:14.

91. Jenkins, document number 2135. Nothing is known of J. L. Vaughn so his activity on behalf of Texas must have been either uneventful or short lived.

92. *SWHQ,* 48:14.

93. Jenkins, document number 2137. Nothing is known of Tom Find. Judging from his name, he was an American living in Matamoros and apparently very sympathetic to the Mexican cause.

94. *SWHQ,* 48:16.

95. Foote, 2:212-213. Here Fannin is saying he is sending the padre, which is the blackest of villains, to serve as chaplain of the Texas constitutional convention — surely he was joking or he had contempt for the government. Either way he did send the padre, see Gray Diary entry for March 5.

96. Ibid, 16:280. Jesse Benton, of course, did not arrive in time to fight in the Alamo but he did join Sam Houston's army and was at Harrisburg when the battle of San Jacinto was fought.

97. *SWHQ,* 48:16.

98. Archives, Texas State Library. Charkes Bellinger Stewart, of South Carolina, was an early Texas settler and operator of a drug store type mercantile. Politically, he was secretary to the executive of the General Council and enrollment clerk for that body. He was also a delegate to the Constitutional Convention and signed the Declaration of Independence. Following the war, Stewart served as a district attorney and legislator in the Republic. He died in 1885.

99. February 22 is George Washington's birthday. Nothing is known of Samuel St. John.

100. Archives, Texas State Library. Samuel St. John was an Alabama man sympathetic enough to the cause of Texas to offer the loan of his personal funds.

101. Foote, 2:214.

The Seige

February 23 through March 6, 1836

On February 23, 1836, Santa Anna and an army of 1500 men suddenly appeared below Bexar marching smartly and closing fast. The Texans quickly looted the town for what provisions could be easily had and withdrew into the friendly confines of the huge Alamo mission compound. Santa Anna took the town of San Antonio de Bexar without firing a shot. He would not take the Alamo quite so easily.

A brief exchange between the armies produced the clear and unmistakable understanding that there could be no surrender for the Texans except unconditional. Colonel Travis answered that possibility with a cannon shot. It was the first shot in the battle and Santa Anna answered it by hoisting a blood red flag to signify that no quarter would be given to the rebels. Before nightfall on the 23rd, the men of the Alamo knew their only way out would be total victory.

On the 24th, Travis turned to his pen and authored his famous letter to the people of Texas and all Americans in the world. On the 25th, the Mexicans attempted to set up a battery of cannons within range of the Texas long rifles and a skirmish ensued that was a resounding Texas victory. Perhaps bolstered by that success, Travis sent more urgent calls for help. He looked primarily to James Walker Fannin who was 95 miles away with more than four hundred men. But Fannin, the one man in Texas who might have been able to save the Alamo, never came. Only one detachment, 32 men from Gonzales, managed to reach the Alamo after the siege began. Santa Anna, on the other hand, received another 1,000 men.

As news of the invasion spread, the universal call was *Texans to Arms!* Everywhere, patriotic broadsides were issued calling for any able-bodied man able to bring provisions and fly to the aid of his besieged countrymen in the Alamo. Intelligence came slowly; volunteers and supplies came even slower. Despite all the efforts, it appeared that little in the way of aid for the Alamo was to be forthcoming.

In San Antonio, the Mexican army proceeded to surround the Alamo and establish batteries of cannons from which they could bombard the fortress. Fortunately for the Texans, the cannon fire was largely ineffective and did not cause the loss of a single man and but one horse. Still, there was little doubt that an all-out assault was coming, and Santa Anna's blood red flag continued to wave menacingly in the soft Texas breeze. When additional Mexican reinforcements arrived on March 3, it appeared the end might be near. James Butler Bonham also returned that day with final word that Fannin was not coming. In desperation, Travis was forced to look to the colonies for aid, a prospect he must have known was hopeless since the colonies were more than 180 miles away. Still, the young colonel had to try, and thus he authored a long flowing letter explaining his position and detailing what supplies were desperately needed. When John Smith galloped out of the Alamo with that message, everyone surely knew it was their last hope.

In Washington, all talk was about the convention until the first word of the Alamo siege arrived on February 28. Suddenly, there was urgency in the affairs of the day. The convention opened as scheduled on March 1, 1836, and by March 2, independence had been declared. On March 4, Sam Houston was confirmed as commander in chief of the army, and on the sixth, the last urgent call for aid from Travis arrived. Sam Houston was ordered to the field to organize an army and march to the aid of the men in San Antonio. He left Washington on the afternoon of March 6 to try and accomplish that mission but it was too little, too late. As the old general rode across the Texas prairie toward Gonzales, the bodies of the men in the Alamo were being consumed by Santa Anna's funeral pyre. The men died fighting for an independence they never knew had been declared.

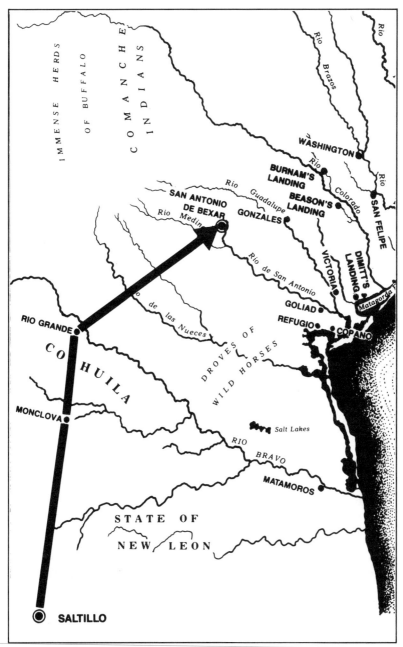

On February 23, 1836 Santa Anna's army arrived in San Antonio de Bexar. Although it is difficult to believe, the Mexican arrival was a complete surprise to the Texans, who withdrew from the town to the Alamo and prepared to meet their fate.

Tuesday, February 23, 1836
12 DAYS TO THE FALL

Almonte Diary Entry

Tuesday At 7 1/2 A.M. the army was put in march — To the Potranva 1 1/2 leagues — to the creek of Leon or Del Wedio, 3 1/2 leagues — To Bexar 3 leagues, in all 8 leagues. At half a league, from Bexar the division halted on the hills of Alazan at 12 1/2 o'clock. General Sesma arrived at 7 A.M. and did not advance to reconnoiter because he expected an advance of the enemy which was about to be made according to accounts given by a spy of the enemy who was caught. There was water, though little, in the stream of las Lomas del Alazan. At 2 the army took up their march, the President and his staff in the van. The enemy, as soon as the march of the division was seen, hoisted the tri-colored flag with the two stars, designed to represent Coahuila and Texas. The President with all his staff advanced to Campo Santo (burying ground). The enemy lowered the flag and fled and possession was taken of Bexar without firing a shot. At 3 P.M. the enemy filed off to the fort of Alamo, where there was — pieces of artillery; among them one 18 pounder; It appeared they had 130 men; during the afternoon 4 grenades were fired at them. The firing was suspended in order to receive as messenger who brought a dispatch the contents of which appears in No. 1, and the answer which was given appears in No. 2. I conversed with the bearer who was Jameson (G. B.) and he informed me of the bad state they were in at the Alamo, and manifested a wish that some honorable conditions should be proposed for a surrender. Another messenger afterwards came (Martin) late a clerk in a house in New Orleans. He stated to me what Mr. Travis said, "that if I wished to speak with him, he would receive me with much pleasure." I answered that it did not become the Mexican Government to make any propositions through me, and that I had only permission to hear such as might be made on the part of the rebels. After these contestations night came on, and there was no more firing. In the night another small battery was made up the river near the house of Veremenda. I lodged in the house of Nixon, (Major) with Urriza and Marcil Aguirre. An inventory of the effects taken was made, many curious papers were found. One Smith, carpenter and cabinet maker, they say was the owner of the effects. I did not sleep all night, having to attend to the enemy and the property, the charge of which was entrusted to me; its value was about $3,000.[1]

William B. Travis to Andrew Ponton, Judge
and Citizens of Gonzales
COMMANDANCY OF BEXAR, 3 o'clock P.M: The enemy in large force are in sight. We want men and provisions. Send them to us. We have 150 men and are determined to defend the Alamo to the last. Give us assistance.

P.S. Send an express to San Felipe with news night and day.[2]

William B. Travis and James Bowie to James W. Fannin
COMMANDANCY OF BEXAR: We have removed all the men to the Alamo where we make such resistance as is due our honor, and that of the country, until we can get assistance from you, which we expect you to forward immediately. In this extremity, we hope you will send us all the men you can spare promptly. We have one hundred and forty six men, who are determined never to retreat. We have but little provisions, but enough to serve us till you and your men arrive. We deem it unnecessary to repeat to a brave officer, who knows his duty, that we call on him for assistance.[3]

James Bowie to Commander of the Army of Texas [Mexican]
FORTRESS OF THE ALAMO: Because a shot was fired from a cannon of this fort at the time a red flag was raised over the tower, and [because] a little afterward they told me that a part of your army had sounded a parley, which, was not heard before the firing of the shot. I wish, Sir, to ascertain if it be true that a parley was called, for which reason I send my second aid, Benito Jameson, under guarantee of a white flag which I believe will be respected by you and your forces. God and Texas[4]

Jose Bartres to James Bowie
As aid-de Camp of his Excellency, the President of the Republic, I reply to you, according to the order of his Excellency, that the Mexican army cannot come to terms under any conditions with rebellious foreigners to whom there is no other recourse left, if they wish to save their lives, than to place themselves immediately at the disposal of the Supreme Government from whom alone they may expect clemency after some considerations. God and Liberty.[5]

Sam Houston Treaty with Chief Bowl
BOWLS VILLAGE: This treaty made and established between Sam Houston and John Forbes, Commissioners on the part of the Provisional Government of Texas, of the one part, and the Cherokee, and their associate Bands now residing in Texas, of the other part, to wit, Shawnee, Delaware, Kickapoos, Quapaws,

The actual message James Bowie sent to the Mexicans concerning a possible truce. The note originally included the salutation "God and the Mexican Federation," but Bowie apparently had a change of heart, because he crossed out "Mexican Federation" and inserted "Texas."

Chocktaws, Boluxies, Iowanies, Alabamas, Cochetties, Caddos of the Naches, Tahoocattakes, and Unataquous.

By the Head Chiefs, Head men, and Warriors, of the Cherokees as Elder Brother and Representative of all other Bands, agreeably to their last General Council. This treaty is made conformably to a declaration made by the last General Consultation, at San Felipe, and dated 13th November, A. D. 1835.

Article First: The parties declare, that there shall be a firm and lasting peace forever, and that a friendly intercourse shall be preserved, by the people belonging to both parties.

Article Second: It is agreed and declared that the before named Tribes, or Bands shall form one community, and that they shall have and possess the lands within the following bounds. To wit, — laying west of the San Antonio road, and beginning on the West, at the point where the said road crosses the River Angelina, and running up said river, until it reaches the mouth of the first large creek (below the great Shawnee village) emptying into the said River from the north east, thence running with said creek, at its main source, and from thence a due north line to the Sabine River, and with said river west — then starting where the San Antonio road crosses the Angelina River, and with the said road to the point where it crosses the Naches river and thence running up the east side of said river, in a northwest direction.

Article Third: All lands granted or settled in good faith previous to the settlement of the Cherokee, within the before described bounds, are not conveyed by this treaty, but excepted from its operation. All persons who have once been removed and returned shall be considered as intruders, and their settlements not to be respected.

Article Fourth: It is agreed by the Parties aforesaid that, the several bands or Tribes named in this Treaty, shall all remove within the limits or bounds as before described.

Article Fifth: It is agreed and declared by the Parties aforesaid that the Land lying and being within the aforesaid limits shall never be sold or alienated to any person or persons, power or Government of Texas. and the Commissioners on the behalf of the government of Texas bind themselves, to prevent in future all persons from intruding within the said bounds. And it is agreed upon the part of the Cherokees, for themselves and their younger brothers, that no other tribes or Bands of Indians whatsoever, shall settle within the limits aforesaid, but those already named in this Treaty, and now residing in Texas.

Article Sixth: It is declared that no individual person, member of the Tribes before named, shall have power to sell, or lease land to any person or persons, not a member, or members of this Community of Indians, nor shall any citizen of Texas be allowed to lease or buy Land from any Indian or Indians.

Article Seventh: That the Indians shall be governed by their own Regulations, and Laws, within their own territory, not contrary to the Laws of the Government of Texas. All property stolen from the citizens of Texas, or from the Indians, shall be restored to the party from whom it was stolen, and the offender or offenders shall be punished by the party to whom he or they may belong.

Article Eighth: The government of Texas shall have power to regulate Trade, and intercourse, but no Tax shall be laid on the Trade of the Indians.

Article Ninth: The Parties of this Treaty agree that one or more agencies shall be created and at least one agent shall reside, especially, within the Cherokee villages, whose duty it shall be to see that no injustice is done to them, or other members of the community of Indians.

Article Tenth: The Parties to this Treaty agree that so soon as Jack Steele, and Samuel Benge, shall abandon their improvements, without the limits of the aforesaid tract of country, and remove within the same, that they shall be valued and paid for by the government of Texas, the said Jack Steele and Samuel Benge having until the month of November next succeeding from the date of this treaty allowed them to remove within the limits before described. And that all the Lands and improvements now occupied by any of the before named Bands or Tribes, not lying within the limits before described, shall belong to the government of Texas and subject to its disposal.

Article Eleventh: The Parties to this Treaty agree and stipulate that all the bands or Tribes as before recited, except Steele Benge, shall remove within the aforesaid limits within the aforesaid Eight months from the date of this Treaty.

Article Twelfth: The Parties to this treaty agree that nothing herein contained shall effect the relations of the Saline, on the Naches nor the settlers in the neighborhood thereof until a General Council of the Several bands shall take place and the pleasure of the Convention of Texas be known.

Article Thirteenth: It is also declared, that all Titles issued to the Lands, not agreeably to the declaration of the General consultation of the People of all Texas, dated the Thirteenth day of November, 1835, within the before recited limits, are declared void — as well as all orders and surveys made in relation to the same. —

Done at Colonel Bowls village on the Twenty third day of February, 1836, and the First Year of the Provisional Government of Texas.

Signed Sam Houston, John Forbes, Colonel Bowl X (his mark), Big Mush X (his mark), Samuel Benge X (his mark), Oosoota X (his mark), Corn Tossle X (his mark), The Egg X (his mark) John Bowl X (his mark), Tunnettee X (his mark)
Witnesses: Fox Fields, Interpreter X (his mark), Henry Millard, Joesph Burst, A. Horton, George W. Case, Mathias A. Brigham, George W. Hockley, Secretary of the commission.[6]

Wednesday, February 24, 1836
11 DAYS TO THE FALL

Almonte Diary Entry
Wednesday, Very early this morning a new battery was commenced on the bank of the river, about 350 yards from the Alamo. It was finished in the afternoon, and a brisk fire was kept up from it until the 18 pounder and another piece was dismounted. The President reconnoitered on horseback, passing within musket shot of the fort. According to a spy, four of the enemy were killed. At evening the music struck up, and went to entertain the enemy with it and some grenades. In the night, according to the statement of a spy, 30 men arrived at the fort from Gonzales.[7]

William B. Travis: To The People of Texas and all Americans *in the World* —

Fellow citizens & compatriots —

I am besieged, by a thousand or more of the Mexicans under Santa Anna — I have sustained a continual Bombardment & cannonade for 24 hours & have not lost a man — The enemy has demanded a surrender at discretion, otherwise, the garrison are to be put to the sword, if the fort is taken — I have answered the demand with a cannon shot, & our flag still waves proudly from the walls — *I shall never surrender or retreat. Then,* I call on you in the name of Liberty, of patriotism & & every thing dear to the American character, to come to our aid, with all dispatch — The enemy is receiving reinforcements daily & will no doubt increase to three or four thousand in four or five days. If this call is neglected, I am determined to sustain myself as long as possible & die like a soldier who never forgets what is due to his own honor & that of his country —

VICTORY OR DEATH

William Barret Travis
Lt. Col. Comdt.

P.S. The Lord is on our side — When the enemy appeared in sight we had not three bushels of corn — We have since found in deserted houses 80 or 90 bushels & got into the walls 20 or 30 head of Beeves —

Travis[8]

with all dispatch — The enemy is receiving reinforcements daily & will no doubt increase to three or four thousands in four or five days. If this call is neglected, I am determined to sustain myself as long as possible & die like a soldier who never forgets what is due to his own honor & that of his country —

Victory or Death

William Barret Travis

Lt. Col. Comdt.

P.S. The Lord is on our side — When the enemy appeared in sight we had not three bushels of corn — We have since found in deserted houses 80 or 90 bushels & got into the walls 20 or 30 head of Beeves —

Travis

A partial reproduction of William B. Travis' famous letter "To the People of Texas and all Americans in the World." The letter is considered by many to be the most patriotic document in American history.

Albert Martin (note on back of Travis letter)
To
The People of Texas
and
All Americans

send this to San Felipe by Express night & day

Since the above was written I have heard a very heavy cannonade during the whole day think there must have been an attack made upon the Alamo We were short of Ammunition when I left Hurry on all the men you can in haste
Albert Martin

When I left there was but 150 determined to do or die tomorrow I leave for Bejar with what men I can raise [we?] will be [on the way?] at all events —

Col Almonte is there the troops are under the Command of Gen Seisma[9]

Lancelot Smithers (note on back of Travis letter)
I hope that Every one will Randeves at gonzales as soon as poseble as the Brave Soldiers are suffering do not neglect the powder is very scarce and should not be delad one moment.
L. Smither[10]

Lancelot Smithers to All the Inhabitants of Texas
In a few words there is 2000 Mexican soldiers in Bexar, and 150 Americans in the Alamo. Sesma is at the head of them, and from best accounts that can be obtained, they intend to show no quarter. If every man cannot turn out to a man every man in the Alamo will be murdered.

They have not more than 8 or 10 days provisions. They say they will defend it or die on the ground. Provisions, ammunition and Men, or suffer your men to be murder in the fort. If you do not turn out Texas is gone. I left Bexar on the 23rd. at 4 P.M.
By order of
W. V. Travis
L. Smithers[11]

Thursday, February 25, 1836
10 DAYS TO THE FALL

Almonte Diary Entry

Thursday — The firing from our batteries was commenced early. The general in Chief, with the battalion de Cazadores, crossed the river and posted themselves in the Alamo — that is to say, in the houses near the fort. A new fortification was commenced by us near the houses of McMullen. In the random firing the enemy wounded 4 of the Cazadores de Matamoros battalion, and 2 of the battalion of Jimenes, and killed one corporal and a soldier of the battalion of Matamoros. Our fire ceased in the afternoon. In the night two batteries were erected by us on the other side of the river in the Alameda of the Alamo — the battalion of Matamoros was also posted there, and the cavalry was posted on the hills to the east of the enemy, and in the road from Gonzales at the Casa Mata Antigua. At half past eleven at night we retired. The enemy, in the night, burnt the straw and wooden houses in their vicinity, but did not attempt to set fire with their guns to those in our rear. A strong north wind commenced at nine at night.[12]

William B. Travis to Major-General Sam Houston

HEADQUARTERS, FORT OF THE ALAMO: Sir; On the 23rd of Feb. the enemy in large force entered the city of Bexar, which could not be prevented, as I had not sufficient force to occupy both positions. Col. Bartes, the Adjutant-Major of the President-General Santa Anna, demanded a surrender at discretion, calling us foreign rebels. I answered them with a cannon shot, upon which the enemy commenced a bombardment with a five inch howitzer, which together with a heavy cannonade, has been kept up incessantly ever since. I instantly sent express to Col. Fannin, at Goliad, and to the people of Gonzales and San Felipe. Today at 10 o'clock A.M. some two or three hundred Mexicans crossed the river below and came up under cover of the houses until they arrived within virtual point blank shot, when we opened a heavy discharge of grape and canister on them, together with a well directed fire from small arms which forced them to halt and take shelter in the houses about 90 or 100 yards from our batteries. The action continued to rage about two hours, when the enemy retreated in confusion, dragging many of their dead and wounded.

During the action the enemy kept up a constant bombardment and discharge of balls, grape, and canister. We know from actual observation that many of the enemy were wounded — while we, on our part, have not lost a man. Two or three of our men have been slightly scratched by pieces of rock, but have not been disabled. I take great pleasure in stating that both officers and men conducted themselves with firmness and bravery. Lieutenant Simmons of cavalry acting as infantry, and Captains Carey, Dickinson and Blair of the artillery, rendered essential service, and Charles Despallier and Robert Brown gallantly sallied out and set fire to houses which afforded the enemy shelter, in the face of enemy fire. Indeed, the whole of the men who were brought into action conducted themselves with such heroism that it would be injustice to discriminate. The Hon. David Crockett was seen at all points, animating the men to do their duty. Our numbers are few and the enemy still continues to approximate his works to ours. I have every reason to apprehend an attack from his whole force very soon; but I shall hold out to the last extremity, hoping to secure reinforcements in a day or two. Do hasten on aid to me as rapidly as possible, as from the superior number of the enemy, it will be impossible for us to keep them out much longer. If they overpower us, we fall a sacrifice at the shrine of our country, and we hope prosperity and our country will do our memory justice. Give me help, oh my country! Victory or Death!

W. Barret Travis
Lt. Col. Com[13]

J. W. Fannin, Jr. to J. W. Robinson

FORT DEFIANCE GOLIAD: Herewith you have my account current with the provisional Govt. of expenditures made under my authority as Agent — You also have a list of Drafts drawn on the Prov: Govt. & a list of Receipts sundry persons which will explain themselves. The sum of two hundred & ten Dollars paid H. Foley will be charged to the Georgia Battalion of volunteers, (being for articles furnished them for private purposes, to wit seventy gallons of Brandy) and will be deducted from their pay —

You will perceive that the amount of one Hundred Dollars is to be deducted from the pay of several officers by reference to the Memorandum of Drafts — The amt of Cash advanced to Capts. Cook, & Burke & private G. F. Leonard is in the same situation and will be deducted from their pay by the proper officer — also the amt. $15. — each from Ball & Simpson as per rects. & a/c.

I have to remark in reference to the Amt. of Two thousand (2,000) Dollars received from Gay by col. F. W. Johnson, that before declining the appointment of agent by col. J. he received this amount ($2,000) in the presence of col. Wm. Pettus & Thomas F. McKinney for which he has not accounted to me or furnished a voucher or evidence of expenditure —

I send also the account of Capt. Jack Shackelford of the Red
Rovers for settlement —[14]

Very Respectfully
Your obet. Servt —
J. W. Fannin Jr

P.S. I enclose duplicates of Drafts drawn — vouchers &c with the
exceptions of a few expenditures made for the public service in
expresses &c —

J W F

I am well aware that my present movement toward Bexar is
anything but a military one — The appeal of cols Travis & Bowie
cannot however pass unnoticed — particularly by troops now on
the field — Sanguine, chivalrous Volunteers — Much must be
risked to relieve the besieger — If however I hear of the fall of
Bexar before I reach them, I shall retire on this place & complete
the fortification now in state of forwardness & prepare for a
vigorous defence, waiting anxiously in any event for the arrival
of reinforcements from the Interior —

I leave from 80 to 100 men for the present defence of this
place with the expectation of a speedy reinforcement from
Matagorda &c

J. W. Fannin Jr[15]

John Sowers Brooks to Mary Ann Brooks, my dear Sister

FORT DEFIANCE, GOLIAD: From the hurry of a preparation to
march, I have stolen a moment to write to you. An express from
San Antonio de Bexar received here a few moments since, with
intelligence that the Mexican Army under Santa Ana, were in
sight of that place and preparing to attack it. He heard the firing
of cannon after he had gained some distance towards us. He
estimated their strength at from three to five thousand men.
Bexar has a garrison of 156. They have retired to the Alamo,
determined to hold out to the last and have solicited reinforcements from us.

We have 420 men here and have been engaged in repairing the
Fort and mounting artillery. Commanding Officer, in the field,
Gen. Fannin, has made Goliad his Head Quarters, from the
conviction of its importance, as being advantageously located for
a depot of reinforcements, clothing, provisions, and military
stores. It commands the sea coast particularly, Aransas and
Matagorda Bays — and consequently the only convenient land-
ings for vessels of any tonnage. The only troops in the field at
this time are volunteers from the United States, and they
probably do not exceed 800, and perhaps but one third of them
are near the scene of action. He was therefore compelled to

remain in this place, et cetra. From the want of cavalry, we have been unable to obtain any accurate information of the enemy's movements. Thus Bexar has been left exposed and the Mexicans availing themselves of the advantages thus unavoidably offered them, have marched against it with all their force.

With a forlorn hope of 320 men, we will start tonight or tomorrow morning at the dawn of day in order to relieve the the gallant little garrison, who have so nobly resolved to sustain themselves until our arrival. Our force is small compared with that of the enemy. It is a desperate resort, but we hope the God of Battles will be with us — that victory will again perch on the bright little of banner of Texian liberty and that the civic militia, now aroused to a sense of their danger and the proximity of their implacable and mercenary form, will appear in their strength, that the young lion will arise in the majesty of his united strength and our youthful Republic make herself worthy of the high destiny at which she aims. If by forced marches we can reach Bexar, a distance of more than a hundred miles,[16] and cut our way through the enemy's lines to our friends in the Fort, our united force thus advantageously posted, may perhaps be sufficient to hold out until the militia can be collected to reinforce us. If they do not rendovous promptly, I apprehend much. But the sin be upon their own heads. We have resolved to do our duty and to perish under the walls of the Alamo, if stern necessity requires it. We are but poorly prepared to meet the formidable host of Mexicans, arrayed against us. . . .

And now my dear sister, I would ask you to look upon my situation in its proper light, and to indulge in no unnecessary fears. I am a soldier both morally and physically. Death is one of the chances of the game I play and if it falls to my lot, I shall not murmur, and you should not regret. I shall write you as soon as some thing decisive occurs. We shall probably be attacked by the Mexicans on our way to Bexar, and if I should die, my services entitle me to 1800 or more acres of land which will be valuable. It will revert to my representatives, and father should claim it. Tell him I owe Mr. Hagggerty in N.Y. and a portion of it can be applied to the discharge of that debt.

We will take with us, four pieces of artillery, two sixes and two fours. — Now is the time for the people of the U.S. to do some thing for Texas. Can nothing be done in Staunton?

Give my love to all the family, tell mother to remember me, and tell them all to write to me. They are calling me now. In the greatest haste, Ever your brother. . . .[17]

Capt. John Sowers Brooks to my dear Father
FORT DEFIANCE, GOLIAD: I wrote to Mary Ann today, and as the express does not leave before revelle tomorrow I thought that

I might profitably employ the few moments I have obtained in writing you, for it is possible I may never have another opportunity.

In my letter, I gave a hasty detail of our intended movements and the causes which produced them and I would refer you to it, if it has reached its destination.

From information received since the letter above referred to, was written, we are induced to believe that the Mexican force at and near San Antonio de Bexar does not exceed 3000. The garrison which has been withdrawn from the town to the Alamo, a Fort in the suburbs, consists in 156 effective men. They are resolute and have determined to die in the ditch rather than dishonor themselves, the cause they have espoused, or the Country they represent.

We will march at the dawn of day tomorrow with 320 men and 4 pieces of artillery, — 2 sixes and 2 fours. We have no provisions scarcely, and many of us are naked and entirely destitute of shoes. But something must be done to relieve our country. We have suffered much and may reasonably anticipate much greater suffering. But if we succeed in reaching Bexar, before the Garrison is compelled to surrender and are successful in taking the place and its gallant defenders, we shall deem ourselves amply repaid for our trials and hardships. But if we fail, I fear that our misfortunes will have an unhappy influence in prolonging the struggle in which poor Texas is engaged. We will leave a Garrison of 100 men with the hope that a portion of the Civic Militia who are embodying will be ordered here, and the remainder sent to reinforce us.

If we are successful, it will prove a check to the Mexican army from which it will not readily recover and which will ever after have a sultry influence upon our cause. But my dear father, I frankly confess that without the interposition of Providence, we can not rationally anticipate any other result to our Quixotic expedition than total defeat. If the Militia assemble, and move promptly to our aid, we may be saved. We have less than 350 men; the force of the enemy is possibly 3000 — a vast disparity. We are almost naked and without provisions and very little ammunition. We are undisciplined in a great measure; they are regulars, the elite of Santa Ana's army, well fed, well clothed, and well appointed and accompanied by a formidable battery of heavy field and battering pieces. We have a few pieces but no experienced artillerists and but a few rounds of fixed ammunition, and perhaps less of loose powder and balls. We can not therefore calculate very sanguinely upon victory. However, we will do our best, and if we perish, Texas and our friends will remember that we have done our duty.

From our information, we are induced to apprehend an attack on our march to Bexar, by a detachment of the enemy's cavalry. We hope they will not be in sufficient force to retard our march much less defeat us.

It is getting late, I slept but little last night and as we must march soon in the morning, I beg you will excuse this hasty scrawl . . . My health is good. Farewell!

P.S. I have not heard from home since I left. Direct your letters to the care of J. W. Fannin, Jr., Army of Texas, pay the postage to New Orleans. I have no money. I should like to have.

Brooks

Do not fail to write me immediately, and send me some money if possible. I am very much in want of it, I assure you. The government has obtained a loan and will soon pay us off — then I can pay you.

Brooks

Give my respects to all who remember me. Tell the youth of Staunton they may now do some thing in the cause of Liberty if they will come to Texas.[18]

R. M. Williamson to the Governor and Council of Texas
GONZALES: By express from San Antonio under date of the 23rd instant I have received information that 2000 Mexicans under the command of Siezma have arrived in Bexar and have taken possession of the public square compelling the American troops (150 in number) to confine themselves to the Alamo. The American troops are determined to defend the place to the last and have called upon their fellow citizens for aid under the 4th rule of instructions to me directed be your Excellency dated the 15th day of the present month, I have written the following communications to Capt. J. J. Tomlinson commanding the first detachment of the Ranging Corps:

Sir

Information directed from San Antonio under date of yesterday is calculated to call forth the United Effort of All Texas. Two thousand Troops under the command of Siezma have arrived in that place and are in possession of the Public square, compelling our Troops (150 in number) to retire to the Alamo where they are at present and determined to remain until death or victory, they implore aid from their fellow citizens and solicit it speedily — Provisions and men is the cry, are the fortunes of the Colorado safe? are there no hostile Indians bearing materially upon the frontier of Texas. If there be none you will forthwith fall down to Bastrop and wait further orders from me It would be well for the inhabitants of Bastrop to keep out spies in the direction of San

Antonio lest a foraging part of Mexicans surprise them, every inch of ground must be disputed by us until we can communicate and march against and crush them — If the Indians are still troublesome on the frontier I would suggest to the settlers the propriety of concentrating in the different settlements and build block houses or forts for their better defence, in the morning I will proceed to Gonzales and will advise and command what I conceive best to be done on this frontier. The information comes by Express from Col Travis and may be relied on. Do for the best and act promptly under the instructions herein contained, with sentiments of regard I am your

R. M. Williamson
Maj Comdg. &c

To Col. J. J. Tomlinson
The foregoing communication I have caused to be forwarded by express and rest assured that no exertions on my part will be wanting to give the earliest aid practical to our fellow soldiers in the Alamo. Citizens of Texas arouse, save your country and your liberties all must act and act in unison, I am in haste

Your obt servt
R. M. Williamson
Comdg. the Rangers —[19]

General Jose Urrea Diary Entry
We resumed our march at four in the afternoon. At seven o'clock that night a cold and penetrating norther began to blow. At ten I was informed by the scouting party that the enemy was occupying San Patricio. In view of this, I ordered the infantry to continue its march. Six soldiers of the battalion of Yucatan died from exposure to the cold.[20]

Friday, February 26, 1836
9 DAYS TO THE FALL

Almonte Diary Entry
Friday — The Northern wind continued very strong; the thermometer fell to 39 degrees, and during the rest of the day remained at 60 degrees. At daylight there was a slight skirmish between the enemy and a small party of the division of the east, under command of General Sesma. During the day the firing from our cannon was continued. The enemy did not reply, except now and then. At night the enemy burnt the small houses near the parapet of the battalion of San Luis, on the other side of the river. Some sentinels were advanced. In the course of the day the enemy sallied

out for wood and water, and were opposed by our marksmen. The
northern wind continues.[21]

Wm. Fairfax Gray Diary Entry

SAN FELIPE: This morning it was excessively cold for this southern
region; yesterday it was summer heat.

Last night an express was received from Lt. Col. Wm B. Travis,
at Bexar, Feb. 23, stating that 2,000 of the enemy were in sight of
that place. He had but 150 men, and was short of provisions and
ammunition, but determined to defend the place to the last, calling
for assistance. The people now begin to think the wolf has actually
come at last, and are preparing for a march. Mr. Gail Borden is
packing up the papers of the land office, in order to remove them
eastward should the enemy approach.[22]

James W. Robinson to Gen. Sam Houston

EXECUTIVE DEPARTMENT WASHINGTON: By the accompanying information from Bexar, you will see that your presence
at head quarters is absolutely necessary. 2000 Mexicans are in
San Antonio & 150 Americans in the Alamo. Come quickly and
organize our countrymen for battle. Call the militia out en masse,
send your orders East by this express for that purpose. Say it is
done by the order of the Gov. & Council & by your own order,
and by the unanimous call of Texas.

[addressed] By Express to Gen. Sam Houston Wherever he may
be. Send this by express night & day[23]

General Jose Urrea Diary Entry

The infantry arrived at dawn. It began to rain at three in the morn-
ing and it looked like snow. Taking advantage of the bad weather, I
moved foreword immediately. The night was very raw and excessively
cold. The rain continued and the dragoons, who were barely able to
dismount, were so numbed by the cold that they could hardly speak.
Nevertheless, being as brave as they were faithful, they showed no
discouragement and we continued our march.[24]

Saturday, February 27, 1836
8 DAYS TO THE FALL

Almonte Diary Entry

Saturday — The northern wind was strong at day break, and
continued all the night. Thermometer at 39 degrees. Lieutenant
Manuel Menchacho was sent with a party of men for the corn, cattle,
and hogs at the rancho of Seguin and Flores. It was determined to
cut off the water from the enemy on the side next to the old mill.

There was little firing from either side during the day. The enemy
worked hard to repair some entrenchments.

In the night a courier extraordinary was dispatched to the city of
Mexico, informing the Government of the taking of Bexar and also to
Gen'ls Urrea, Filisola, Cos & Vital Fernandez. No private letters
were sent.[25]

Wm. Fairfax Gray Diary Entry

WASHINGTON: A considerable excitement prevailing at
Washington, owing to the news from Bexar. Found that the express
to the east and north had not yet gone, owing to the want of funds
or energy on the part of those in authority[26]

Governor Henry Smith to: Fellow Citizens and Countrymen [handbill]:

SAN FELIPE: The following communication from Colonel
Travis [letter of February 24], now in command at Bexar,
needs no comment. The garrison composed of only 150
Americans, engaged in a deadly conflict against 1,000
mercenary troops of the Dictator, who are daily receiving
reinforcements, should be sufficient call upon you without
saying more. However secure, however fortunate, our
garrison may be, they have not the provisions, nor the
ammunition to stand more than a thirty days siege at the
farthest.

I call upon you as an officer, I implore you as a man, to
fly to the aid of your besieged country men, and not
permit them to be massacred by the mercenary foe. I
slight none! The call is to ALL who are able to bear arms,
to rally without a moment's delay, or in fifteen days the
heart of Texas will be the seat of war. This is not imagi-
nary. The enemy from 6,000 to 8,000 strong are on our
border and rapidly moving by forced marches for the
colonies. The Campaign has commenced. We must
promptly meet the enemy or all will be lost. Do you
possess honor? Suffer it not to be insulted or tarnished!
Do you possess patriotism? Evince it by your bold, prompt
and manly action! If you possess even humanity, you will
rally without a moment's delay to the aid of your besieged
countrymen!

Henry Smith, Governor[27]

Antonio Lopez de Santa Anna to D. Vicente Filisola, second in command.

GENERAL HEADQUARTERS OF BEJAR: . . . Your Excellency
will command the Purveyor General to gather all the food
supplies and to march immediately avoiding any delays that

might hamper the service of the Nation, as those troops are lacking in food.

Your Excellency will also order that the Treasury, with the commissary, take the lead with forced marches, and escort a convoy, as there is a very urgent need for money.

Your excellency will order that two and a half cargas of salt come with the treasury, since there is a not a single grain here, and it is needed very much.

I trust that your Excellency will act with your usual efficacy and promptness so that these dispositions be fulfilled, as all are urgent.

For God and Liberty. . . .28

Antonio Lopez de Santa Anna to D. Vicente Filisola, second in command.

GENERAL HEADQUARTERS OF BEJAR: On the 23rd of this month I occupied this city after some forced marches from the Rio Grande, with General Joaquin y Sesma's division composed of the present battalions of Matamoros and Jimenez, the active battalion of San Luis Potosi the regiment of Dolores, and eight pieces of artillery.

With the speed in which this meritorious division executed its marches in eighty leagues of road, it was believed that the rebel settlers would not have known of our proximity until we should have been within rifle shot of them; as it is they only had time to hurriedly entrench themselves in Fort Alamo, which they had well fortified, and with a sufficient food supply. My objective had been to surprise them early in the morning of the day before but a heavy rain prevented it.

Notwithstanding their artillery fire, which they began immediately from the indicated fort, the national troops took possession of this city with the utmost order which the traitors shall never again occupy; on our part we lost a corporal and a scout, dead, and eight wounded.

When I was quartering the corps of the division a bearer of the flag of truce presented himself with a paper, the original which I am enclosing for your Excellency, and becoming indignant of its content I ordered an aide, who was the nearest to me, to answer it, as it is expressed by the copy that is also enclosed.

Fifty rifles of the rebel traitors of the North, have fallen in our possession, and several other things, which I shall have delivered to the general commissary of the army as soon as it arrives, so that these forces may be equipped; and the rest will be sold and the proceeds used for the general expense of the army.

From the moment of my arrival I have been busy hostilizing the enemy in its position, so much so that they are not even allowed to raise their heads over the walls, preparing everything for the assault which will take place when at least the first brigade arrives, which is even now sixty leagues away. Up to now they still act stubborn, counting on the strong position which they hold, and hoping for much aid from their colonies and from the United States, but they shall soon find out their mistake.

After taking Fort Alamo, I shall continue my operations against Goliad and the other fortified places, so that before the rains set in, the campaign shall be absolutely terminated up to the Sabine River, which serves as the boundary line between our republic and the one of the North . . . For God and Liberty.[29]

Advisory Committee to J. W. Robinson

WASHINGTON COUNCIL HALL: The advisory Committee appointed to act in the absence of a quorum, being informed that a company of rangers, commanded by Cpt. Tomlinson, are ready for service, and also been informed, that a large force of the enemy are now at Bejar, would therefore advise your excellency that you issue your order to Cpt. Tomlinson, to immediately proceed to Bejar to aid the army there, — and that the militia class'd No 5, that are above the San Antonio road in the municipality of Mina, be ordered out to guard the frontier from Indian depredation — and signify the same to major Williamson — They would further remark that they have had the communications of Cpt Turner, and Cpt Hortcourt, under consideration, and would advise, that Cpt Turner be ordered to Bejar with all the troops he can get forthwith — And that Col. Hartcourt be informe'd that his offer, is gratefully recd and was it in our power, we would gladly comply with his proposals, but as there is no vacancy at this time we cannot, all we can do, is to place his name first on the list, and assure him that as soon as there is an opportunity, his wishes shall be comply with — and would recommend that he, and the other two gentlemen with him, should go on to the west, and join the army, as we now think their services are more needed there than any where else and in their opinion, the first fortification that will be made on the sea coast, will be on the west of the Brassos River. —[30]

San Felipe citizens to Our fellow Citizens

SAN FELIPE: At a meeting of the citizens held, in the town of San Felipe, on 27th February, Joseph Baker was unanimously called to the chair, and B. F. Cage appointed secretary. A communication from Wm. B. Travis, Lt Col Commandant of the post of Bejar, having been read, and the objects of the meeting explained. on motion of Moseley Baker Esq.

Resolved, That the chairman appoint a committee of twelve to prepare an address and draft resolutions for the adoption of the meeting.

Whereupon, the Chairman appointed Moseley Baker, J. A. Wharton, F. J. Starr, J. R. Jones, W. R. Hensley, A. Ewing, P. B. Dexter, A. Somerville, J. Fletcher, J. H. Money, James Cochrane and Thos Gay, then on motion, the meeting adjourned until 11 o'clock.

The meeting accordingly reconvened at 11 o'clock, when the following address and resolutions were reported and unanimously adopted.

TO OUR FELLOW CITIZENS

The undersigned a committee appointed by a meeting held in the town of San Felipe, on this day, present you with the accompanying letter from the commandant of Bejar. You must read and act in the same moment, or Texas is lost. You must rise from your lethargy, and march without a moments delay to the field of war, or the next western breeze that sweeps out your habitations, will bring with it the shrieks and wailings of women and children of Guadalupe and Colorado; and the last agonized shriek of liberty will follow. Citizens of the Colorado and Brazos, your country is invaded — your homes are about to be pillaged, your families destroyed, yourselves to be enslaved; and you must, one and all repair to the field of war, or prepare to abandon your country. Ere this information shall be generally circulated, the blood of many of our citizens will have crimsoned the soil; and the soul of many a devoted patriot flown to Heaven.

Inhabitants of the east, your fellow citizens of the west are in danger. Of themselves, they cannot resist the foe; we appeal to your magnanimity; we implore you for succor, and we earnestly entreat that your succor might be speedy. Unless it is, Texas, and her citizens, and her liberties, and her homes, are forever gone.

As for ourselves, we will abandon the contest only with our lives, and then earnestly appeal to all, every one to do his duty to his country, and leave the consequence to God.

The committee reports the following resolutions:

Resolved: That a committee of three persons be appointed as a standing committee, whose duty it shall be to solicit individual subscriptions for the purpose of procuring provisions, munitions &c. for the use of the army.

Resolved: That said committee forward as soon as possible provisions of every kind. . . .

Resolved: That they procure boats of all kinds on the Brazos river, for the purpose of acting as expeditively as possible.

Resolved: That said committee be appointed general guardians of our interests at home, and that they be intreated to spare no pains in raising the means for our subsistence, and that they forward on men, as fast as possible.

Resolved: That they provide expresses, to communicate with the country, so far as practicable.

Resolved: That they do all and everything necessary for the public good; and their receipts shall be sufficient vouchers to the persons from whom they may receive.

Resolved: That we recommend the establishment of depots on the road to Gonzales, for provisions, arms &c. and that the committee call on the citizens generally for subscriptions

Resolved: That two hundred copies of the proceedings of this meeting, together with colonel Travis's letter, be published as soon as possible.

In accordance with the first resolution, Wm Pettus Jr., John R. Jones, and Thos Gay were appointed for the committee.

On motion the meeting adjourned sine die.[31]

James W. Fannin to J. W. Robinson, acting Gov

GOLIAD, FORT DEFIANCE: I have to report, that yesterday, after making all the preparations *possible*, we took up our line of march, (about three hundred strong, and four pieces of Artillery,) towards Bexar, to the relief of those brave men now shut up in the Alamo, and to raise the siege, leaving Captain Westover in command of this post. Within two hundred yards of town, one of the wagons broke down, and it was necessary to **double teams** in order to draw the Artillery across the river, each piece having but one yoke of oxen — not a particle of breadstuff, with the exception of half a tierce of rice, with us — no **beef**, with the exception of a small portion which had been dried — and not a head of cattle, except those used to draw the Artillery, the ammunition, &c.: and it was impossible to obtain any until we should arrive at Seguin's Rancho, seventy miles from this place. After crossing the river, the troops camped. This morning whilst here, I received a note from the officer commanding the volunteers, requesting, in the name of the officers of his command, a Council of War, on the subject of the expedition to Bexar, which, of course, was granted. The council of War consisted of all the Commissioned officers of the command, and it was by them unanimously determined that, inasmuch as a proper supply of provisions and means of transportation could not be had; and as it was impossible, with our present means, to carry the Artillery with us; and as by leaving Fort Defiance without a proper garrison, it might fall into the hands of the enemy, with the provisions, &c., now at Matagorda, Demit's Landing, and Coxe's Point, and on the way to meet us; and, as by report of our spies (sent out by colonel Bowers, &c.) we may expect an attack on this place, it was expedient to return to this post and complete the fortifications, &c. &c. . . . I sent an express to Gonzales to apprise the committee of Safety there of our return . . . In case immediate reinforcements are not sent on to this place and Bexar, I would recommend that the Army of Reserve be concentrated near Gonzales and Victoria, for in that neighborhood must the enemy be met and driven back, if possible. We want your orders, and be assured, that they shall be obeyed to the letter.[32]

General Jose Urrea to Santa Anna

SAN PATRICIO: Sir: according to information received after my leaving Matamoros, I learnt that the insurgent forces stationed here has sent their cavalry towards Goliad, for the purpose of making incursions. I therefore made an effort; I vanquished all difficulties, and forcing a march during three days and nights, I arrived here at the dawn of day — not having with me more than 100 cavalry men, I attacked the enemy, who defended himself with firmness in the houses that served for barracks, But even there he left 16 dead; and 21 taken prisoners or wounded — among whom were some officers. There are 5 Mexicans among the prisoners. All the arms with 100 horses are in my possession.

I have the pleasure to inform you of this triumph, and however feeble it may be, it will suffice to prove to our proud and scornful enemy what the valor and courage of Mexican soldiers can effect; for in short those with me rushed into the midst of the affray like lions; and in a moment they hewed the rebels in pieces, none of whom escaped from this city.[33]

I am now in search of doctor Grant, who (according to the information that I have received) is now in the neighborhood of Meir, with 50 riflemen; and I know, not what number of Mexicans.[34]

Sunday, February 28, 1836
7 DAYS TO THE FALL

Almonte Diary Entry

Sunday, — The weather abated somewhat. Thermometer at 40 degrees at 7 A.M. News were received that a reinforcement to the enemy was coming by the road from La Bahia [Goliad], in number 200. It was not true. The cannonading was continued.[35]

Wm. Fairfax Gray Diary Entry

WASHINGTON: Cold and drizzling. Some of the citizens raised a collection, to which I contributed $1. to send the express on to the eastward.

The acting Governor, Robinson, with a fragment of the Council is here. He is treated coldly and really seems of little consequence.

Another express is received from Travis, dated the 24th, stating Santa Anna, with his army, were in Bexar, and bombarded the Alamo for twenty four hours. An unconditional surrender had been demanded, which he answered by a cannon shot. He was determined to defend the place to the last, and called earnestly for assistance. Some are going, but the vile rabble here cannot be moved.[36]

J. W. Fannin to J. W. Robinson

HEADQUARTERS, FORT DEFIANCE, GOLIAD: I have to inform you that I have just received the unpleasant intelligence that Colo Johnson's command were yesterday morning before day light was surprised by the enemy at San Patricio — I received my intelligence by express from Edward Gritten in the Mission del Refugio, who reports that Col Johnson with two men had arrived, on foot, at a Rancho near that place — I also learn that two others had arrived at the Mission — Capt Pearson was shot down & others when asking for Quarters — From those who have escaped it is impossible to learn the strength of the army or the loss sustained by our countrymen. —

Mr. Gritten writes that Col. Johnson and his Companions will as soon as fresh horses can be procured proceed to this place — They will probably arrive tomorrow morning —

This morning Col. Ferris left this post with a communication from me informing you of the return of the Troops to this place after crossing the River on the way to Bexar. The propriety of their retrograde movement will now be apparent.

It is now obvious that the enemy have entered Texas at two points, for the purpose of attacking Bexar and & this place — the first has been attacked and we may expect the enemy here momentarily — Both places are important — and this at this time particularly so — All our provisions are at Matagorda Demitts Landing Coxes point & on their way here — We have not in the garrison supplies of Bread Stuff for a single day and as yet but little beef and should our Supplies be cut off our situation will be, to say the least — disagreeable — & in case we are not reinforced and a sufficient force sent to convey the provisions (as we have no means of transportation) when famine begins to look us in the face, we shall be compelled to cut our way through the enemy leaving the artillery & munitions of war in their hands — We hope, however, for the best — we hope that before this time the people have arisen and are marching to the relief of Bexar & this post — but should the worst happen — on whose head should the burthen of censure fall — not on the heads of those brave men who have left their homes in the United States to aid us in our struggle for Liberty — but on those whose all is in Texas & who notwithstanding the repeated calls have remained at home without raising a finger to keep the Enemy from their thresholds — What must be the feelings of the volunteers now shut in Bexar — & what will be those of this command if a sufficient force of the enemy should appear to besiege us here without provisions — Will not curses be heaped on the heads of the sluggards who remained at home with a knowledge of our situation. —

Our present force in Garrison is about four Hundred & twenty, including Guena's company of Mexicans — (about five white citizens of Texas in this number —)

I omitted to mention that the force on the Nueces was divided into two parties one under Col Johnson — in the village of San Patricio & the other under Col. Grant & Major Morris on the road above — of the fate of the latter we know nothing — as yet.

[Subscription]

If this can be fowd early, so as to overtake the Express sent off this morning, it will save much time — Col. Ferris went by Dimmitts landing with it — speed — go at speed —

Forward with all dispatch and spread the alarm & cal out the whole people to arms — to arms.[37]

Capt. Phillip Dimmit to James Kerr

DIMMIT'S POINT: I have this moment, 8 p.m., arrived from Bexar. On the 23d, I was requested by Colonel Travis to take Lieutenant Nobles and reconnoiter the enemy. Some distance out I met a Mexican who informed me that the town had been invested. After a short time a messenger overtook me, saying he had been sent by a friend of my wife[38] to let me know that it would be impossible for me to return, as two large bodies of Mexican troops were already around the town. I then proceeded to the Rovia and remained till 10 p.m. on the 25th. On the 24th there was heavy cannonading, particularly at the close of evening. I left the Rovia at 10 p.m. on the 25th, and heard no more firing, from which I concluded the Alamo had been taken by storm. On the night of the 24th, I was informed that there were from four to six thousand Mexicans in and around Bexar. Urrea was at Carisota, on the Matamoros road, marching to for Goliad. If immediate steps are not taken to defend Guadalupe Victoria, the Mexican will soon be upon our families.[39]

J. W. Fannin to Jos. Mimms

GOLIAD: The advice I gave you a few days back is too true. The enemy have the town of Bejar, with a large force — and I fear will soon have our brave countrymen in the Alamo.

Another force is near me — and crossed the river yesterday morning and attacked a party by surprise, under Col. Johnson, and routed them, killing Capt. Pearson, and several others after they had surrendered. I have about 420 men here, and if I can get provisions in tomorrow or next day, can maintain myself against any force. I will never give up the ship, while there is a pea in the ditch. If I am whipped, it will be well done — and you may never expect to see me.

I hope to see all Texans in arms soon, if not, we lose our homes, and must go east of the Trinity for awhile. Look to our property — save it for my family, whatever be my fate.[40]

John A. Wharton to the Citizens of Barzoria

SAN FELIPE: I send you by express, the latest information from San Antonio, the Governor's call, and the proceedings of the meeting at San Felipe: from these you will learn the necessity for your services. I consider it unnecessary to make appeal to your patriotism, as the information from Bexar, speaks louder than words.[41]

James C. Neill Receipt

SAN FELIPE: Received San Felipe 28th Feby 1836 of Henry smith Govr of Texas Six hundred Dollars of public money, for the use of the troops at Bexar.

J. C. Neill Lt. Col
of Artillery[42]

Monday, February 29, 1836
6 DAYS TO THE FALL

Almonte Diary Entry

Monday — The weather changed — thermometer at 55 degrees in the night it commenced blowing hard from the west. In the afternoon the battalion of Allende took post at the east of the Alamo. The President reconnoitered. One of our soldiers was killed, about that time Gen Sesma left the camp with the cavalry of Dolores and the infantry of Allende to meet the enemy coming from La Bahia or Goliad to the aid of the Alamo. Gen'l Castrillon on guard.[43]

Wm. Fairfax Gray Diary Entry

WASHINGTON: A warm day, threatening rain from the south. many members [of the convention] are coming in, and it is now evident that a quorum will be formed tomorrow. Genr'l Houston's arrival has created more sensation than that of any other man. He is evidently the people's man, and seems to take pains to ingratiate himself with everybody. He is much broken in appearance, but has still a fine person and courtly manners. . . .[44]

Henry Smith to Fellow-Citizens of Texas

TEXAS
EXPECTS EVERY MAN TO DO HIS DUTY

The enemy are upon us ! A strong force surrounds the walls of San Antonio, and threaten that Garrison with the sword. Our country imperiously demands the service of every patriotic arm, and longer to continue in a state of *apathy* will be *criminal.* Citizens of Texas, descendents of Washington, awake ! arouse yourself ! ! The question is now to be decided, are we to continue as freemen, or bow beneath the rod of military despotism. The eyes of the world are upon us! Shell we disappoint their hopes and expectations? No; let us fly at once to our arms, march to the battle field, meet the foe, and give renewed evidence to the world, that the arms of freemen, uplifted in defense of their rights and liberties, are irresistible. "Now is the day and now is the hour," that Texas expects every man to do his duty. Let us show ourselves worthy to be free, *and we shall be free.* Rest assured that succors will reach us, and that the people of the United States will not permit the chains of slavery to be riveted on us.

I call upon you as your executive officer to "turn out;" it is our country that demand your help. He who longer slumbers on the volcano, must be a madman. He who refuses to aid his country in this, her hour of peril and danger is a traitor. *Our rights and liberties must be protected;* to the battlefield march and save the country. An approving world smiles upon us, the God of battles is on our side, and victory awaits us.[45]

John W. Hall to Fellow Freemen

Address to the People
The despot dictator, and his vassel myrmidonns, are
fast displaying their hostile columns on the frontier of our
heretofore happy and blessed Texas. Their war cry is,
"death and destruction to every Anglo-American, west of
the Sabine;" their watch word, actually, "beauty and
booty."

Figure to yourselves, my countrymen, the horror and
misery that will be enacted on you should the ruffians
once obtain a foothold on our soil? Your beloved wives,
your mothers, your daughters, sisters, and helpless
innocent children given up to the dire pollution, and
massacre of a band of barbarians!!

As a fellow freeman, I earnestly entreat you, at once to
prepare for the field and "let us on" to the scene of action.
Let our motto be "Victory and independence, or an
honorable grave," and our watch word "the tyrant dead or
alive, or a visit to his palace."[46]

New Orleans Notice

Texas Forever ! !
The usurper of the South has failed in his efforts to
enslave the freemen of Texas.

The wives and daughters of Texas will be saved from
the brutality of Mexican soldiers.

Now is the time to emigrate to the Garden of America.

A free passage, and all found, is offered at New
Orleans to all applicants. Every settler receives a location
of eight hundred acres of land.

On the 23rd of February, a force of 1000 Mexicans came
in sight of San Antonio, and on the 25th Gen St. Anna
arrived at that place with 2500 men, and demanded a
surrender of the fort held by 150 Texans, and on the
refusal, he attempted to storm the fort, twice, with his
whole force, but was repelled with the loss of 500 men,
and the Americans lost none. many of his troops, the
liberals of Zacatecas, are brought on to Texas in irons and
are urged forward with the promise of the women and
plunder of Texas.

The Texian forces are marching to relieve St. Antonio,
March the 2nd. The Government of Texas is supplied with
plenty of arms, ammunition, provisions, &c. &c.[47]

J. W. Hassel to his Father
TEXAS AUSTINS COLONY: I once more take my pen in hand to write you a few lines present I am not well I have had the chill and fever for a few days tho nothing of a serious kind I have injoyed better health this winter than I have had for several years past. Last summer I had the fever for seven or eight weeks tho not dangerous, I hope these lines may find you and family all well — tho I am a great way from you all dayly I think of you all. Perhaps you would like to hear something of the war in Texas and I can inform you there is plenty at present sir. We received news a few days since that the Mexicans were coming on to a large number but the people were careless about it also there was general orders for the militia to turn out in mass they were still careless. But Sir we received by express from San Antonio this evening which was written on the 24th of the present month stateing that the Mexicans had arrived at San Antonio and had attacked our garrison there which was only 150 strong and the enemy about 2000 and increasing all the time, the enemy had bin Bombarding and Cannonaiding for 24 hours but with no success they had demanded surrender of the fort but our commander replied to them with Cannon ball — they also stated that they would put all our men to the sword but our men think they can sustain themselves until we can reinforce them our commander says he will never give up the fort tomorrow evening or next morning I shall start for San Antonio with all speed the people are all to arms now and well they may be. The destroyer of liberty the Great Santa Anna of whom you have heard so much of now commands in person he swears that he will over run Texas or lose Mexico. I think the dictator will come out at the little end of the horn if he is not very careful. We have just given his right hand man a complete drubing to wit general martin perfecto de Cos who had four times our number all of which were regular troops this was at San Antonio. I served in all that campaign as a lutenant and was honorably discharged at the close of said campaign I was in every battle and skirmish except one, and was never struck with shot I was nocked down with a cannon ball one day but it only burnt my face and ear it made me feel quite foolish for a bit I also had a bullet to cut my hat I can tell you sir I have bin where balls flew as thick it seemed to me as ever I heard hail fall in that Campaign we only had five men killed and do not know what amount we killed of them as they always to conceal their dead. This might be the last time I may have the pleasure of addressing you so I remain yours till death.

J. W. Hassell[48]

Moseley Baker to Gail Borden

SAN FELIPE: In behalf of the San Felipe Company and for myself. I return to you, and through you to the ladies, our heartfelt thanks for the colors so unexpectedly presented. This banner of independence, the work and gift of worth and of beauty, is the most valuable gift, saving the independence of Texas, that could have been bestowed upon this company. Give to the ladies our solemn declaration that this Texas banner, presenting the cross, the stripes, and the star, shall wave triumphant from our ranks, so long as an arm can be raised to uphold it. Tell them that dishonored it shall never be, so long as an individual of the San Felipe Company is left to behold it. For myself, it shall never fall or retreat, until me heart ceases to beat.

Fellow citizens, and citizen soldiers, behold the banner of your country. Before you waves the gift of two fair daughters of Texas. You lot is fortunate and your distinction proud. First in your hands is placed the Texas flag; let you be the last to see it strike the invading foe; let no other feeling ever glow in your bosoms than that expressed in the motto on you banner, "our country's rights or death." He who refuses to surrender, if necessary, his life for its protection, let him be a dastard and a traitor for life, and let him have no habitation among the free. Let us all, with one accord, raise our hands to heaven and swear, The Texas flag shall wave triumphant, or we shall sleep in death.[49]

Sam Houston to Henry Smith

WASHINGTON: In accordance with a commission issued by your Excellency dated the 28th of december, 1835, the undersigned commissioners, in the absence of John Cameron, Esquire, one of the commissioners named in the above mentioned instrument, most respectfully report:

After that sufficient notice being given to the different tribes named in the commission, a treaty was held at the house of John _____ . one of the tribe of Cherokee Indians.[50]

The commissioners would also suggest to your Excellency that titles should be granted to such actual settlers as are now within the designated boundaries, and that they should receive a fair remuneration for their improvements and the expenses attended upon the exchange, in lands or other equivalent.

It will also be remembered by your Excellency that the surrender by the government of the lands to which the Indians may have had any claims is nearly equivalent to that portion now allotted to them, and most respectfully suggest that they should be especially appropriated for the use of the government.

They also respectfully call your attention to the following remarks, viz:

The state of excitement in which the Indians were first found by your commissioners rendered it impossible to commence a negotiation with them on the day set apart for it. On the day succeeding the treaty was opened, some difficulty then occurred relative to the exchange of lands, which the commissioners proposed making for those now occupied by them, which was promptly rejected. The boundaries were those established as designated in the treaty alone, and that such measures should be adopted by your Excellency for their security as may be deemed necessary.

The commissioners used every exertion to retain that portion of the territory for the use of the government, but an adherence to this would have had but one effect, viz: that of defeating the treaty altogether. Under these circumstances the arrangement was made as now reported in the accompanying treaty. They would also suggest the importance of the salt works to the government and the necessity that they should be kept for its use.

The commissioners also endeavored to enlist the chiefs of the different tribes in the cause of the people of Texas and suggested an enrollment of a force from them to act against our common enemy. In reply to which they informed us that the subject had not before been suggested to them. But a general council should be held in the course of the present month, when their determination will be made known.

The expenses attendant upon the treaty are comparatively light. A statement of which will be furnished to your Excellency. All of which is most respectfully submitted.

Sam Houston
John Forbes[51]

Tuesday, March 1, 1836
5 DAYS TO THE FALL

Almonte Diary Entry
Tuesday — The wind subsided, but the weather continued cold— thermometer at 36 degrees in the morning — day clear. Early in the morning Gen. Sesma wrote from the Mission de la Espador that there was no such enemy, and that he reconnoitered as far as the Tinja, without finding any traces of them. The cavalry returned to camp, and the infantry to this city. At 12 o'clock the President went out to reconnoiter the mill site to the north west of the Alamo. Lieut. Col. Ampudia was commissioned to construct more trenches — In the afternoon the enemy fired two 12 pound shots at the house of the president, one of which struck the house, and the other passed it. Nothing more of consequence occurred. Night cold — thermometer 34 degrees Fahrenheit, and 1 degree Reaumur.[52]

J. W. Fannin to James W. Robinson and the General Council
GOLIAD: I am pleased to inform you of the arrival of Colonel
Johnson, Messrs. Tone, Toler, and Miller, who were so fortunate
to escape from San Patricio. They can give no information as to
the remainder of their companions, except Mr. Beck, who also
escaped and is below. . . .

From all I can learn, we have to play a desperate game, on
both sides: life, liberty, and property — the honour of our
families and ancestors on the one; — a Throne and Power
Supreme on the other. Much larger preparations have been
made, and are making, (than expected) to insure the conquest
and expulsion of every man who speaks the English language,
from Mexican soil . . . General Ramirez Sezma has command of
the division approaching, or already in Texas, and probably in
Bexar. I have not sufficient information as to who comes here, or
as to number, or time of approach. . . .

Some troops are approaching from Laredo, the advance of
which we suppose to be the party who attacked and routed our
countrymen at San Patricio. I am now pretty well prepared to
make battle. I have nearly completed my fortifications, and have
beef enough for twenty days, and will have more. I hope soon to
have coffee, clothing, and some ammunition.

I learn from several sources, that as soon as Bexar is retaken,
they next march here, and thus complete their chain of
communication to the Interior and Gulf. I am resolved to await
your orders, let the consequences be what may. But I say to you,
candidly, and without fear of Mexican arms, that unless the
people of Texas, forthwith, turn out in mass, agreeably to my
plan of the 8th ult. those now in the field will be sacrificed, and
the battles that should be fought here, will be fought East of the
Brassos [sic], and probably the Trinity. I should be pleased to
have one more express from Washington, and if we are not to be
sustained in a proper manner, and in good time, receive orders
to fall back to the Provinces, and on the Colonies, and let us all
go together. I again repeat to you, that I consider myself bound
to await your orders. I cannot, in a military point of view, be
considered now as acting commander-in-chief, as I have never
received orders to that effect, nor has the army. Again, I received
furlough to the first of April. Again, I am the chosen commander
of this Regiment of Volunteers. Lastly, I have orders from you
not to make a retrograde movement, but to await orders and
reinforcements. If a large force gets here, and in possession of
the provisions and stores of Matagorda Bay, being all now in
Texas, it will be a desperate game for us all. I would, therefore,
urge the adoption of such measures as may secure them, and
without delay. I have no doubt the enemy at Bexar are already
apprized of their location; and knowing our weakness, and want

of cavalry, may, and I fear will, make a dash between us and
Provisions, and secure them . . . I am desirous to be erased from
the list of officers, or expectants of office, and leave to bring off
my brave, foreign volunteers, in the best manner I may be able.
If we should fail in the effort, and fall a sacrifice to the criminal
indifference, cold and unpardonable apathy and neglect . . .
there are people . . . who will bestow censure where it is due,
and, peradventure, drop a tear over our memory.

[Attached Note:]
Santa Anna has not, and cannot bring here exceeding five
thousand men, unless he obtain aid from the south, which is
believed he cannot do. If a general turn out be made, we can
make a clear turn, and then sow and reap our grain in quiet, and
rid the world of a tyrant.

[Second Attached Note:]
I have 420 men, and as many spare muskets, but no men to back
them.[53]

Wm. Fairfax Gray Diary Entry
*WASHINGTON: In the night the wind sprung up from the north
and blew a gale, accompanied by lightning, thunder, rain and hail,
and it became very cold. In the morning the thermometer was down
to 33 degrees and everybody shivering and exclaiming against the
cold. This is the second regular norther that I have experienced.*
*Notwithstanding the cold, the members of the Convention . . . met
today in an unfurnished house, without doors or windows. In lieu of
glass, cotton cloth was stretched across the windows, which partially
excluded the cold wind.*
*At half past 1 the convention met, and the committee reported
forty-one members present who were duly elected, and some about
which there was contest or difficulty, on which they wished the
action of the house.*
*The quarrel between the Governor and the Council was spoken of
in unmeasurable terms of reprobation. It was finally amended so as to
include the Governor, Lieutenant governor, and Council, in order, as
was avowed by members in debate, to take no cognizance of the party
quarrels or private griefs of either party, but to call on each for
whatever official information concerning the common weal they may
have to communicate.*[54]

James W. Fannin to Francis DeSauque and John Chenowith
HEADQUARTERS ARMY TEXAS: Yours of the 28th ult, was
recd. this evening & I hasten to answer it, agreeable to previous
arrangements I marched the troops [toward Bexar] & with much
difficulty got two wagons & artillery across the river one mile

above not having provisions but for one day and having only
sixty seven men & no provisions for them in the Garrison Two
wagon stalled & another could not be got over in this situation
they were encamped for the night expecting trains from below
The messenger dispatched whilst you were here not having
returned, about this time an express arrived from Matagorda
giving us intelligence of the arrival of more store clothing &c and
shortly afterwards another came in from San Patricio giving us
the unpleasant information that our countrymen under the command of Col. Johnson were attacked and inhumanely murdered
mostly after surrendering except five who have arrived here (last
night) (To wit) Col. Johnson Love Miller Fuler & Beck In this
situation not able to go forward and what was then understood
& believed to be a division or its advance to the west coming
against this post a council of war was unanimously demanded of
me by the Volunteer officers and granted of course it was
resolved to be inexpedient to attempt to go forward [to Bexar]
and that we should return and complete the Fortification and
await our doom until relieved whipped or we conquer —
    I immediately forwarded an express to Washington Demitts
Landing &c. and one after any provisions that might be on the
way to Bexar and inform them of our movements also the
committee of safety of Gonzales — I will soon bring to bear this
place — which I think can be defended some time by 200 men
and am informed by persons from Victoria that Col. Wharton
crossed the Guadalupe on Saturday with 270 men and 9 carts
with about 70 barrels flour and proceeded toward Bexar — If I
can find him or communicate with Gonzales and know how
many volunteers will form a junction & if informed speedily I
will push out 200 men and cooperate — we shall not be able to
bring teams but must be light and make force marches But will
try and bring two pieces of cannon I think Wharton will try and
go by Gonzales or if he saw my express and that was the day it
passed Victoria, may endeavor to find me near where you are
stationed — I would advise you either to return here with the
provisions or proceed to Gonzales and hold conference with the
officers in command — I am in hourly expectation of either an
attack or information of the near approach of the enemy I also
hope to hear from St. Felipe & to learn that 1000 are out — Mr.
Royall informs me that our agents in N.O. gives information of
large quantities of supplies being shipd. for here by the Mexican
Govt. and hence their desire to gain this place to keep up a chain
of communication and cover the coast. It is equally important for
us to retain it and cover our scanty stock — Under all the
circumstance I was unable to move and do trust no bad effects
will follow I would risk life and all for our brave men in the
Alamo, but circumstanced as I was and even now am I could

not, do otherwise If you can communicate this to them and adopt the following cipher in your communications double the the alphabet and uniformly an A. for Z. B. for Y. and X. for C. &c &c so vice versa inform all officers of this and should any dispatches fall into their hands they will not be the gainers by it. . . .55

David B. Macomb to James W. Robinson

NEW YORK CITY: A Mexican Minister arrived in this City two days since. A rumor prevailed that he came post haste to sell Texas to the United States. I have just learned that such is the fact, and that President Jackson declares that Texas "will belong to the United States in a week." The sources of my information are highly respectable and can be relied on. There can be no doubt of the fact. I in the absence, the protracted absence of the commissioners have drawn up an argument and protest against the right of Santa Anna to sell our sovereignty. The national law is opposed to it. I have transmitted it through a friend (Secretary Woodbury) to General Jackson, it may cause him to pause err he buy a "pig in a poke."56

Felix Huston to friend

NATCHEZ: You will be surprised probably that I am going to Texas — but such is the case. I contemplate starting about the first of May, and e x - pect to take with me about 500 emigrants.

I intend to arm and uniform the men well, and provide supplies for twelve months — and I wish not to risk my fortune, my life, and my honor, on men whom I cannot rely. Such as go with me must be willing cheerfully to undergo the hardships and privations incidental to such enterprise, and preserve discipline.

Felix Huston

I wish to get hardy, active and enterprising men, who have made up their minds, and will abide by their resolutions. I will communicate to the public the terms on which men can join me . . . but this is now certain — they will be favorable. Those who go to Texas this year will readily find employment on good terms.57

General Jose Urrea Diary Entry

*Still in San Patricio. Received news that Dr. Grant was returning from Rio Bravo with a party of forty or fifty picked riflemen and I marched that night, with eighty dragoons, to meet him. I divided my force into six groups and hid them in the woods.*58

The crude, unfinished building where convention delegates met to issue the Texas Declaration of Independence. The delegates also completed a constitution before adjourning after receiving news of the fall of the Alamo.

Wednesday, March 2, 1836
4 DAYS TO THE FALL

Almonte Diary Entry

*Wednesday — Commenced clear and pleasant — thermometer 34 degrees — no wind. An aid of Col. Duque arrived with despatches from Arroyo Hondo, dated 1st inst; in reply, he was ordered to leave the river Medina, and arrive the next day at 12 or 1 o'clock. Gen. J. Rameriz came to breakfast with the President. Information was received that there was corn at the farm of Seguin, and Lieut Menchaca was sent with a party for it. The President discovered, in the afternoon, a covered road within pistol shot of the Alamo, and posted the battalion of Jimenes there. At 5 A.M. Bringas went out to meet Gaona.*59

Wm. Fairfax Gray Diary Entry

WASHINGTON: Mr. Childress reported a Declaration of Independence which he read in his place. It was received by the house, committed to a committee of the whole, reported without amendment, and unanimously adopted, in less than one hour from its first and only reading. It underwent no discipline, and no attempt was made to amend it.

A motion was made by Mr. Scoty that the members of the Convention should arm themselves and wear their arms during the session of the Convention. It was scouted at and withdrawn.

A copy of the declaration having been made in a fair hand, an attempt was made to read it, preparatory to signing it, but it was found so full of errors that is was recommitted to the committee that reported it for correction and engrossment.

An express was this evening received from Col. Travis, stating that on the 25th a demonstration was made on the Alamo by a party of Mexicans of about 300, who, under cover of some old houses approached to within eighty yards of the fort, while a cannonade was kept up from the city. They were beaten off with some loss, and amidst the engagement some of Texan soldiers set fire to and destroyed the old houses. Col. Fannin was on the march from Goliad with 350 men for the aid of Travis. This, with the other forces known to be on the way, will by this time make the number in the fort some six or seven hundred. It is believed the Alamo is safe.[60]

Convention Delegates to the People of Texas: Independence Declared

WASHINGTON: *We, therefore, the delegates, with plenary powers, of the people of Texas, in solemn convention assembled, appealing to a candid world for the necessities of our condition, do hereby resolve and declare, that our political connection with the Mexican nation has forever ended, and that the people of Texas do now constitute a FREE, SOVEREIGN, and INDEPENDENT REPUBLIC and are fully invested with all the rights and attributes which properly belong to independent nations; and, conscious of the rectitude of our intentions, we fearlessly and confidently commit the issue to the supreme Arbiter of the destinies of nations.[61]*

Captain John Sowers Brooks to my dear Mother

FORT DEFIANCE, GOLIAD: In my letters to Father and Sister a few days since, I apprized you of some of the events transpiring on the western frontier of Texas, and of our contemplated movements. Since the date of those letters, circumstances have occurred which have materially changed our system of operations for the present. . . .

We marched at the time appointed, with 420 men, nearly the whole force at Goliad, leaving only one Company of Regulars to guard the Fort. Our baggage wagons and artillery were all drawn by oxen (no broken horses could be obtained) and there were but few yokes of them. In attempting to cross the San Antonio river, three of our wagons broke down and it was with utmost labor and personal hazard, that our four pieces of cannon were conveyed across. We remained there during the day, with our ammunition wagon on the opposite side of the River. During the night, some of the oxen strayed off and could not be found the next morning. Our situation became delicate and embarrassing in the extreme. If we proceeded we must incur the risk of starvation, and leave our luggage and artillery behind. The country between us and Bexar is entirely unsettled and there would be but little hope of obtaining provisions and we would be able to carry 12 rounds of cartridges each. Every one felt an anxiety to relieve our friends who we had been informed, had retired to the Alamo, a fortress in Bexar, resolved to hold out, until our arrival. Yet everyone saw the impropriety, if not the impossibility of our proceeding under existing circumstances and it was equally apparent to all that our evacuation of Goliad, would leave the whole frontier from Bexar to the coast open to the incursions of the enemy, who were then concentrating at Laredo and the provisions, clothing, military stores, et cetera, at Dimmitts landing and Matagorda, perhaps all that were in Texas, would eventually be lost. Intelligence also reached us that the advance of Santa Anas lower division had surprised San Patricio about 50 miles in front of our position and put the whole garrison under the command of Col. Johnson to the sword. Five of them have reached this place. Col. Johnson is one of them, and they are probably all that have escaped. Capt Pearson of the volunteers, was killed with several others, after they had surrendered. The war is to be one of extermination. Each party seems to understand that no quarters are to be given or asked. We held a council of war in the bushes on the bank of the river, and after a calm review of all the circumstances, it was concluded to return to Goliad, and place the fort in a defensible condition. We are hard at work, day and night, picketing, ditching, and mounting cannon &c. We are hourly in expectation of an attack. On the morning of the 29th ult. our pickets were driven in by a number of men supposed to be a reconnoitering party of the enemy. The Garrison was called to arms and dispositions made for defense. A party of 50 men were sent out to make discoveries and the rest remained under arms till day light. Nothing satisfactory was ascertained. There are about 450 men here. The Mexican force approaching us is variously estimated at from 1500 to 3000 men. We will endeavor to make as good a stand as possible and if we can not expect quarters and therefore do not intend to give or ask any, result as it may.

If the division of the Mexican army advancing against this place has met any obstructions, and it is probable they have been attacked by the Comanche Indians, and their advance much retarded by the loss of their horses and baggage, 200 men will be detached for the relief of Bexar. I will go with them. Our object will be to cut our way through the Mexican army into the Alamo, and carry with us such provisions as it will be possible to take on a forced march. Our united force will probably be sufficient to hold out until we are relieved by a large force from the colonies.

We have just received additional intelligence from Bexar. The Mexicans have made two successive attacks on the Alamo in both of which the gallant little garrison repulsed them with some loss. Probably Davy Crocket "grinned" them off.

We will probably march tomorrow or the next day, if we can procure fresh oxen enough to transport our baggage and two six pounders. The people in the settlements are all arming themselves. The sound of clashing steel is heard on their borders and it is time they should awake now if they wish to preserve their freedom and the fruits of so many years of toil and privation. Now is the time for volunteers from the United States. Let them come with six months clothing and one hundred rounds of ammunition, and they may be of essential service to the cause of Liberty, and no doubt will be amply rewarded by the people of Texas. Now or never. . . .

P.S. We are all nearly naked — and there are but few of us who have a pair of shoes. We have nothing but fresh beef without salt — no bread for several days.

A spy was taken last night, who will probably be shot tomorrow. One of our men is under arrest for sleeping on post. He will be tried by a Court Martial — the penalty is death.[62]

General Jose Urrea Diary Entry

Between ten and eleven in the morning Dr. Grant arrived. He was attacked and vanquished. Dr. Grant and forty of the riflemen were left dead on the field and we took six prisoners besides their arms, munitions, and horses. I countermarched to San Patricio.[63]

ARMY ORDERS.

CONVENTION HALL, WASHINGTON, MARCH 2, 1836

War is raging on the frontiers. Bejar is besieged by two thousand of the enemy, under command of general Siezma. Reinforcements are on their march, to unite with the besieging army.   By last report, our force in Bejar was only one hundred and fifty men strong.   The citizens of Texas must rally to the aid of our army, or it will perish. Let the citizens of the East march to the combat.   The enemy must be driven from our soil, or desolation will accompany their march upon us. *Independence is declared,* it must be maintained. Immediate action, united with valor, alone can achieve the great work. The services of all are forthwith required in the field.

SAM HOUSTON,
Commander-in-Chief of the Army.

P.S. It is rumored that the enemy are on their march to Gonzales, and that they have entered the colonies.   The fate of Bejar is unknown. The country must and shall be defended. The patriots of Texas are *appealed   to,   in   behalf   of   their bleeding   country.*   **S.H.**

Recreation of original broadside issued at Convention Hall, Washington on March 2, 1836. These orders were issued immediately before Houston departed for the frontier.

ARMY ORDERS

Head Quarters, Camp near Beason's
March 2, 1836

The Chairman of the Committee of Safety at San Felipe, will take such immediate measures as will arrest the deserters from the army - all persons leaving the country in a direction from the enemy will be required to return, or their arms taken from them for the use of the army. Families moving for safety will be entitled to one armed man for their protection. Victory is inevitable, if unity of action and good order is preserved. The force of the enemy before us is yet small, and if reinforcements should not arrive to him, his defeat is certain, if discipline and subordination are *firmly* established. Our spies have had a skirmish with a reconnoitering party in his advance, and evidently checked his movements.

I have sent a force of near 200 men on the west side of the river. In a few days I hope to have force sufficient to capture the enemy before he can reach the Guadaloupe.

SAM HOUSTON,
Commander-in-Chief.

Recreation of original broadside issued March 2, 1836. These orders were apparently issued after Houston left Washington and marched to Beason's Landing on the Colorado River.

FRIENDS

AND

CITIZENS OF TEXAS

Information, of a character not to be questioned, has just been received from Col. Fannin, which states that Santa Ana, at the head of four thousand men, has crossed the San Antonio river, leaving Goliad in his rear, and is moving upon our public stores, and thence to Gonzales. This force is independent of the army under Siezma before Bejar. A general turn out has commenced and is going on here and westward, and as far as known. Citizens in every part of the country, it is hoped, will be no less ready to defend their house, their wives, and children.

We advise that every armed vessel which can be had should be despatched at once, to scour the Gulf, and all points where most likely to intercept the stores and supplies of the enemy, and every precaution adopted for protecting our own stores.

John R. Jones, *Standing*
Thomas Gay, *Committee*

San Felipe, March 2, 1836

Recreation of original broadside issued by John R. Jones and Thomas Gray at San Filipe on March 2, 1836.

Thursday, March 3, 1836
3 DAYS TO THE FALL

Almonte Diary Entry

Thursday — Commenced clear, at 40 degrees, without wind. The enemy fired a few cannon and musket shots at the city. I wrote to Mexico and to my sister, directed them to send their letters to Bexar, and that before 3 months the campaign would be ended. The General-in-Chief went out to reconnoiter. A battery was erected on the north of the Alamo within musket shot. Official despatches were received from Gen Urrea, announcing that he had routed the colonists at San Patricio — killing 16 and taking 21 prisoners. The bells were rung. The battalions of Zapaderes, Aldama, and Toluca arrived. The enemy attempted a sally in the night at the Sugar Mill, but were repulsed by our advance.[64]

Wm. Fairfax Gray Diary Entry

WASHINGTON: Morning clear and cold, but became more moderate as the day advanced . . . The convention met at 9 o'clock . . . The engrossed Declaration was read and signed by all members present . . . it was forthwith dispatched by express in various directions, and the convention adjourned to give time to the committees to sit on the subjects referred to them . . . The convention has so far got on harmoniously. The only exciting subject seen ahead is the delicate subject of the schism between the governor and Council, and the doings of the latter body.[65]

Isaac Millsaps to Wife

BEXAR: My Dear, Dear Ones, We are in the fortress of the Alamo a ruined church that has most fell down. The Mexicans are here in large numbers they have kept up a constant fire since we got here. All our boys are well & Capt. Martin is in good spirits. Early this morning I watched the Mexicans drilling just out of range they were marching up and down with such order. They have bright red and blue uniforms and many canons. Some here at this place believe that the main army has not come up yet. I think they are all here even Santanna. Col. Bowie is down sick and had to be to bed I saw him yesterday & he is still ready to fight. He didn't know me from last spring but did remember Wash. He tells me that help will be here soon & it makes us feel good. We have beef and corn to eat but no coffee, bag I had fell off on the way here so it was spilt. I have not seen Travis but 2 times since here he told us all this morning that Fanning was going to be here early with many men and there would be a good fight. He stays on the wall some but mostly to his room I hope help comes soon cause we can't fight them all. Some says he is going to talk some tonight & group us better for Defence. If we fail here get to the river with the children

all Texas will be before the enemy we get so little news here we
know nothing. There is no discontent in our boys some are tired
from loss of sleep and rest. The Mexicans are shooting every few
minutes but most of the shots fall inside & no harm. I don't
know what else to say they is calling for all letters, kiss the dear
children for me be well & God protects us all.

Isaac

If any men come through there tell them to hurry with powder
for it is short I hope you get this & know — I love you all.[66]

William B. Travis to the President of the Convention

COMMANDANCY OF THE ALAMO, BEJAR: In the present
confusion of the political authorities of the country, and in the
absence of the commander-in-chief, I beg leave to communicate
to you the situation of this garrison. You have doubtless already
seen my official report of the action of the 25th ult., made on
that day to General Sam Houston, together with the various
communications heretofore sent by express. I shall, therefore,
confine myself to what has transpired since that date.

From the 25th to the present date, the enemy have kept up a
bombardment from two howitzers (one a five and a half inch,
and the other an eight inch) and a heavy cannonade from two
long nine-pounders, mounted on a battery on the opposite side
of the river, at a distance of four hundreds yards from our walls.
During this period the enemy has been busily employed in
encircling us with entrenchments on all sides, at the following
distance, to wit — in Bexar, four hundred yards west; in Lavil-
leta, three hundred yards south; at the powder-house, one
thousand yards east by south; on the ditch, eight hundred yards
north. Notwithstanding all this, a company of thirty-two men
from Gonzales, made their way into us on the morning of the
1st. inst, at three o'clock, and Col. J. B. Bonham (a courier from
Gonzales) got in this morning at eleven o'clock without molesta-
tion. I have so fortified this place, that the walls are generally
proof against cannon-balls; and I shall continue to entrench on
the inside, and strengthen the walls by throwing up dirt. At least
two hundred shells have fallen inside our works without having
injured a single man; indeed, we have been so fortunate as not
to lose a man from any cause, and we have killed many of the
enemy. The spirits of my men are still high, although they have
had much to depress them. We have contended for ten days
against an enemy whose numbers are variously estimated at
from fifteen hundred to six thousand, with Gen. Ramirez Sezma
and Col. Bartres, the aid-de-camp of Santa Anna, at their head.
A report was circulated that Santa Anna himself was with the
enemy, but I think it was false. A reinforcement of one thousand

men is now entering Bexar from the west, and I think it more than probable that Santa Anna is now in town, from the rejoicing we hear. Col. Fannin is said to be on the march to this place with reinforcements; but I fear it is is not true, as I have repeatedly sent to him for aid without receiving any. Col Bonham, my special messenger, arrived at Labahia fourteen days ago, with a request for aid; and on the arrival of the enemy in Bexar ten days ago, I sent an express to Col F. which arrived at Goliad on the next day, urging him to send us reinforcements — none have arrived. I look to the colonies alone for aid; unless it arrives soon, I shall have to fight the enemy on his own terms. I will, however, do the best I can under the circumstances, and I feel confident that the determined valour and desperate courage, heretofore evinced by my men, will not fail them in the last struggle, and although they may be sacrificed to the vengeance of a Gothic enemy, the victory will cost the enemy so dear, that it will be worse for him than a defeat. I hope your honorable body will hasten on reinforcements, ammunition, and provisions to our aid, as soon as possible. We have provisions for twenty days for the men we have; our supply of ammunition is limited. At least five hundred pounds of cannon powder, and two hundred rounds of six, nine, twelve, and eighteen pound balls — ten kegs of rifle powder, and a supply of lead, should be sent to this place without delay, under a sufficient guard.

If these things are promptly sent, and large reinforcements are hastened to this frontier, this neighborhood will be the great and decisive battle ground. The power of Santa Anna is to be met here or in the colonies; we had better meet them here, than to suffer a war of desolation to rage our settlements. A blood red banner waves from the church of Bexar, and in the camp above us, in token that the war is one of vengeance against rebels; they have declared us as such, and demanded that we should surrender at discretion or this garrison should be put to the sword. Their threats have had no influence on me or my men, but to make all fight with desperation, and that high-souled courage which characterizes the patriot, who is willing to die in defense of his country's liberty and his own honour.

The citizens of this municipality are all our enemies except those who have joined us heretofore; we have but three Mexicans now in the fort; those who have not joined us in this extremity, should be declared public enemies, and their property should aid in paying the expenses of the war.

The bearer of this will give you your honorable body, a statement more in detail, should he escape through the enemy's lines. **God and Texas ! — *Victory or Death ! !***

P.S. The enemy's troops are still arriving, and the reinforcements will probably amount to two or three thousand.[67]

William B. Travis to Jesse Grimes

Do me the favor to send the enclosed to it's proper destination instantly.[68] I am still here, in fine spirits and well to do, with 145 men. I have held this place for ten days against a force variously estimated from 1,500 to 6,000, and shall continue to hold it till I get relief from my country or I will perish in its defense. We have had a shower of bombs and cannon balls continually falling among us the whole time, yet none of us has fallen. We have been miraculously preserved. You have no doubt seen my official report of the action of the 25th ult. in which we repulsed the enemy with considerable loss; on the night of the 25th they made another attempt to charge us in the rear of the fort, but we received them gallantly by a discharge of grape shot and musquertry, and they took to their scrapers [sic] immediately. They are now encamped in entrenchments on all sides of us.

All our couriers have gotten out without being caught and a company of 32 men from Gonzales got in two nights ago, and Colonel Bonham got in today by coming between the powder house and the enemy's upper encampment. . . . Let the Convention go on and make a declaration of independence, and we will then understand, and the world will understand, what we are fighting for. If independence is not declared, I shall lay down my arms, and so will the men under my command. But under the flag of independence, we are ready to peril our lives a hundred times a day, and to drive away the monster who is fighting us under a blood-red flag, threatening to murder all prisoners and make Texas a waste desert. I shall have to fight the

An early 19th century drawing depicting Travis drawing a line in the dirt and asking any who stand with him to cross. Legend has it only one man, Moses Rose, refused to cross.

enemy on his own terms, yet I am ready to do it, and if my countrymen do not rally to my relief, I am determined to perish in the defense of this place, and my bones shall reproach my country for her neglect. With 500 men more, I will drive Sesma beyond the Rio Grande, and I will visit vengence on the enemy of Texas whether invaders or resident Mexican enemies. All the citizens of this place that have not joined us are with the enemy fighting against us. Let the government declare them public enemies, otherwise she is acting a suicidal part. I shall treat them as such, unless I have superior orders to the contrary. My respects to all friends, confusion to all enemies. God Bless you.[69]

William B. Travis to David Ayers
Take care of my little boy. If the country should be saved, I may make for him a splendid fortune; but if the country be lost and I should perish, he will have nothing but the proud recollection that he is the son of a man who died for his country.[70]

George W. Poe to Henry Smith
VELASCO: I have been ordered to this point & Galveston for the purpose of fortifying them against the enemy.

Captain Turner's company of Regular Troops & Capt Roman's of volunteers are here one (Turners) 43 strong & Romans, 35 strong — I have received letters from the citizens beseeching me not to remove the troops from here — to leave one company here to defend the place & one Company at Galveston of Batteries & mounting the Cannon — moreover there is a large supply of arms ammunitions & Clothing here which without troops cannot be protected —

Capt. Turner got an order today from James W. Robinson, self styled Commander in Chief of the Army to proceed immediately to Bexar — Capt Roman is also ordered & this place will be left defenseless — Turner's Commission comes from Robinson & Roman has received none yet —

For God sake sir consider what will become of the property & lives of the Citizens should the enemy land here — It is believed on good authority that a simultaneous attack will be made by sea & land. I am the commanding officer and the troops shall obey no other orders but yours. I don't know any other Governor — send me an express with the orders how to act discretionary or otherwise —

I will obey your orders if they are to march to the devil but the thing the other governor I will not

Did you know the anxiety here you would dispatch an express forthwith —[71]

Susan Isabella Travis, the
daughter William B. Travis
never saw.

Charles Edward Travis, who
was three years old when his
father was killed in the Alamo.

Santa Anna to General Urrea
GENERAL QUARTERS, BEJAR: [Official] In respect to the
prisoners of whom you speak . . . you must not fail to bear in
mind the circular of the supreme government, in which it is
decreed, that "foreigners invading the republic . . . shall be
judged and treated as pirates;" and as, in my view of the matter,
every Mexican guilty of the crime of joining these adventurers
loses the rights of a citizen by his unnatural conduct, the five
Mexican prisoners whom you have taken ought to be also to
suffer as traitors.

[Unofficial] In regard to foreigners who make war . . . you
will remark that what I have stated to you officially is in accordance with the former provisions of the supreme government.
An example is necessary, in order that those adventurers may be
duly warned, and the nation be delivered from the ills she is
daily doomed to suffer.[72]

Friday, March 4, 1836
2 DAYS TO THE FALL

Almonte Diary Entry
*Friday — The day commenced windy, but not cold — thermometer
42 degrees. Commenced firing very early, which the enemy did not
return. In the afternoon one or two shots were fired by them. A
meeting of Generals and colonels was held, at which Generals Cos,
Sesma, and Castrillon were present; (Generals Amador and Ventura
Mora did not attend — the former having been suspended and the
latter being in active commission,) Also present, colonels Francisco
Duque, battalion of Toluca — Orisnuela, battalion of Aldama —
Romero, battalion of Matamoros — Arnat, battalion of Zapadores,
and the Major of Battalion of San Luis — The colonels of battalion of
Jimenes and San Luis did not attend, being engaged in actual commission. I was also called. After a long conference, Cos Castrillon,
Orisniela, and Romero were of the opinion that the Alamo should be
assaulted — first opening a breach with two cannons of _____ and
the two mortars, and that they should wait the arrival of the two 12
pounders expected on Monday the 7th. The President, Gen. Rameriz,
and I were of opinion that the 12 pounders should not be waited for,
but the assault made. — Colonels Duque and Arnat, and the Major
of the San Luis battalion did not give any definite opinion about
either of the two modes of assault proposed. In this state things
remained — the General not making any definite resolution. In the
night the north parapet was advanced towards the enemy through
the water course. A lieutenant of engineers conducted the entrenchment. A messenger was dispatched to Urrea.*[73]

Wm. Fairfax Gray Diary Entry
WASHINGTON: Today several important committees have been appointed . . . No business of any importance transacted. Houston appointed Commander in Chief.[74]

Convention to Sam Houston
WASHINGTON: Be it resolved, that General San Houston be appointed Major General, to be commander in chief of the land forces of the Texian Army both Regulars, Volunteers, and Militia while in active service; and endowed with all the rights, privileges and powers due to a commander in chief in the United States of America, and that he forthwith proceed to take command, establish headquarters and organize the army accordingly.[75]

Saturday, March 5, 1836
THE EVE OF THE FALL OF THE ALAMO

Almonte Diary Entry
Saturday — The day commenced very moderate — thermometer 50 degrees — weather clear. A brisk fire was commenced from our north battery against the enemy, which was not answered, except now and then. At mid-day the thermometer rose to 68 degrees — The President determined to make the assault; it was agreed that four columns of attack were to be commanded by Generals Cos, Duque, Romero and Morales, and second in command, Generals Castrillon, Amador, and Minon. For the purpose the points of attack were examined by the commanding officers, and they came to the conclusion that they should muster at 12 o'clock tonight and at 4 o'clock tomorrow morning the attack should be made.[76]

Wm. Fairfax Gray Diary Entry
WASHINGTON: This evening two Mexican prisoners were brought here from Goliad charged with improper communications with the enemy and pointing out to them a place to build a bridge over the San Antonio. One of them is an old priest . . . the other is a young man named Eugenio Hernandez, a lieutenant in the late army of Cos, and on parole.[77]

L. Ayer's Journal Entry
GOLIAD: The Mexicans are according to the information just received closely investing the Alamo but the garrison is determined to resist to the last they however called for aid; Col Fannin 3 or 4 days before my arrival undertook to march 300 men to their aid but as I am informed all the force here insisted upon going with them and none would consent to stay except the regulars who wished to go but would obey orders under such circumstances. Col F called a council of

officers and it was concluded that the army ware in force a San Patricio and the army in such a peculiar state of mind it was best to keep them together and advisable to remain in their situation.[78]

Santa Anna To the Generals, Chiefs of Sections, and Commanding Officers

The time has come to strike a decisive blow upon the enemy occupying the Fortress of the Alamo. Consequently, His Excellency has decided that, tomorrow morning, at 4:00 a.m., the columns to attack shall be stationed at musket-shot distance from the first entrenchments, ready for the charge, which shall commence, at a signal to be given from the bugle, from the Northern Battery.

The first column will be commanded by General Don Martin Perfecto Cos, and in his absence, by myself.

The permanent Battalion of Aldama (except the company of Grenadiers) and the three right centre companies of the Active Battalion of San Luis, will comprise the first Column.

The second column will be commanded by Colonel Don Francisco Duque, and, in his absence, by General Don Manuel Fernandez Castrillon; it will be composed of the Active Battalion of Toluca (except the company of Grenadiers) and the three remaining centre companies of the Active Battalion of San Luis.

The third column will be commanded by Colonel Jose Maria Romero, and, in his absence, by Colonel Mariano Salas; it will be composed of the Permanent Battalion of Matamoros and Jimenez.

The fourth column will be commanded by Colonel Juan Morales, and, in his absence, by Colonel Jose Minon; it will be composed of the light companies of the Battalion of Matamoros and Jimenez, and of the Active Battalion of San Luis.

His Excellency the General-in-Chief will, in due time, designate the points of attack, and give his instructions to the commanding officers.

The reserve will be composed of the Battalion of Engineers and the five companies of the Battalion of Matamoros, Jimenez and Aldama, and the active Battalions of Toluca and San Luis.

The reserves will be commanded by the General-in-Chief, in person, during the attack; but Colonel Agustin Amat will assemble this party, which will report to him, this evening, at 5:00 o'clock, to be marched to the designated station.

The first column will carry ten ladders, two crowbars, and two axes; the second, ten ladders; the third, six ladders; and the fourth, two ladders.

The men carrying ladders will sling their guns on their shoulders, to be enabled to place the ladders wherever they may be required.

The companies of Grenadiers will be supplied with six packages of cartridges to every man, and the centre companies with two packages and two spare flints. The men will wear neither overcoats nor blankets, or anything that may impede the rapidity of their motions. The commanding Officers will see that the men have the chin-straps of their caps down, and that they are wearing either shoes or sandals.

The troops composing the columns of attack will turn in to sleep at dark, to be in readiness to move at 12 o'clock at night.

Recruits deficient in instructions will remain in their quarters. The arms, principally the bayonets, should be in perfect order.

As soon as the moon rises, the centre companies of the Active battalion of San Luis will abandon the points they are now occupying on the line, in order to have time to prepare.

The cavalry, under Colonel Joaquin Rameriz y Sesma, will be stationed at the Alameda, saddling up at 3 o'clock A.M. It shall be its duty to scout the country, to prevent the possibility of an escape.

The honor of the nation being interested in this engagement against the bold and lawless foreigners who are occupying us, His Excellency expects that every man will do his duty, and exert himself to give a day of glory to the country, and of gratification to the Supreme Government, who will know how to reward the distinguished deeds of the brave soldiers of the army of Operations.[79]

The topographical map, prepared by a Mexican army engineer, that Santa Anna may have used to plan his assault on the Alamo.

Telegraph,
and Texas Register

We would respectfully notify the present convention, that procured a sufficiency of hands, we are prepared to execute any order, either at night or day.

The jurisdiction of Minn, first at her post during last year, against the encroachment either of Indians or Mexicans, several days since departed a company of men to the relief of our friends in Bejar. May others, less exposed than Minn, follow this generous example.

We regret to hear of the backwardness of some of our fellow citizens, in turning out in defense of their wives and children. It is with pleasure and satisfaction, that not only the men, but even the women are nobly contributing all the service in their power in defense of our country. A few days since, when despatches were to be sent to every part of the country, an elderly lady, well known to many in this colony, on hearing of the present alarming invasion, carried, with the least possible delay, the intelligence into a settlement on the Brazos below. Many other ladies are doing every thing in their power in providing clothing, and articles of equipment for those going to the field.

We hear some complain, saying, they have already served longer, or contributed more, than some of their richer neighbors: others, that they have got no credit for what they have already done; and not unfrequently do we hear men say, they are ready to fight, but are not willing to turn out, while men possessed of lands and other property are staying at home to care of their substance, the former not having a foot of land, or little lese to fight for. We acknowledge that the burden of the present war has, thus far, fallen very unequally upon our citizens. We know men, whose names are not yet mentioned, who have generously devoted all their time, and much of their substance, in defense of our country, while others have done but very little. But it is hoped that none at the present time, when Texas is threatened to be thrown back again into a wilderness state, will count on the profit of former occupations, or will consider the cost of a few months service, when expulsion or death is at hand!

We have just learned that a treaty has been effected with the north eastern Indians; favorable, we trust to them, and beneficial to all parties.[80]

The committee of San Felipe would suggest to commandants of companies fitting out, the great utility of taking with them a quantity of bags, say two for each man. In case of an attack each man could fill his bags with sand or dirt, and in less than twenty minutes a sufficient breast work could be raised to serve for their greater security; and in a prairie county, this method of fortifying appears to the committee a good one. Common domestic for the bags would be all sufficient, and in less than twelve hours the ladies of each neighborhood could supply all the men which might turn out. The committee will furnish the San Felipe company with its quota of bags thus proposed.

John R. Jones
Thomas Gay

James C. Neill to John W. Smith, Public Store Keeper for the Garrison of Bexar

GONZALES: You will issue to the bearer five pair shoes and place them at the disposition of Mr. Fitch to be sold for the use of the garrison. Said shoes was delivered between the 16th & 24th of January 1836.[81]

J. C. Neill Lt. Col.
Comdt Bexar[82]

Sunday, March 6, 1836
THE ALAMO FALLS

Wm. Fairfax Gray Diary Entry

WASHINGTON: This morning, while at breakfast, a dispatch was received from Travis, dated Alamo, March 3. The members of the Convention and the citizens all crowded to the convention room to hear it read, after which Mr. Potter moved that the Convention organize a provisional government and adjourn and take the field. An interesting debate arose, but they adjourned without any action, the motion being lost.

A great many persons are starting and preparing to start to the seat of war. In the afternoon Houston left, accompanied by his staff, Capt. Cooke, Capt. Tarleton, etc. The town has been all day in a bustle, but is quiet now.[83]

James Collinsworth and Richard Ellis to Major General Sam Houston

CONVENTION HALL: Sir: As commander-in-chief of the Texas army, you are ordered forthwith to repair to such place on the frontier as you may deem advisable. You will proceed to establish headquarters, and organize the army. You will require of the army, of whatever grade, to report to you. And, as it is impossible, at this time, to determine any particular point of concentration, you will act according to the emergencies of the occasion and the best dictates of your own judgement, for the purpose of protecting our frontier, and advancing the best interests of our country.

You will, as often as you may deem advisable, inform this body, or such other authority as they may establish, of both your acts and the situation of the army.

John Collinsworth,
  Chairman of the Committee on Military Affairs
Richard Ellis,
  Pesident of the Convention.[84]

Convention Hall — Resolutions

WASHINGTON: *Resolved*, That one thousand copies of Colonel W. Barret Travis's letter be printed in hand bill form from the editors, Messrs. Baher & Bordens, of San Felipe.

Mr. Samuel A. Maverick, from the municipality of Bejar, appeared, produced his credentials and took his seat as a member of the Convention.

Resolved, That the safety of the country is threatened in a manner which makes it the duty of all her citizens to hasten to the field.[85]

Martin Parmer to Wife

WASHINGTON: Dear Wife: I am well and we are getting very well. We have three or four committees who are preparing a constitution, and we will soon have it ready. I shall be at home in ten or fifteen days, we have alarming news continually from the west: Frank Johnson's division is all killed, but five, it is supposed. We saw two shot begging for quarters. Dr. Grant with a company of men is supposed to be all slain.

Travis last express states San Antonio was strongly besieged; it is much feared that Travis and company are all massacred, as dispatches have been due from that place three days and none have arrived yet. The frontiers are breaking up, Gonzales must be sacked, and its inhabitants murdered and defiled unless they get immediate aid. The last accounts, the Mexicans were to a considerable number between Gonzales and San Antonio. Fanning is at La Bahia with about 500 men, and is in daily expectation of a visit from Santa Anna. Texas has been declared free and independent, but unless we have a general turn out and every man lay his helping hand too, we are lost. Santa Anna and his vassals are now on our borders, and the declaration of our freedom, unless it is sealed with blood, is of no force. I say again that nothing will save Texas but a general turnout . . . Travis closes his last expresses with these words — HELP! O my country.[86]

George W. Poe, Assist. Inspec. Gen,
Army of Texas to Editor, Mobile Register
VELASCO: Sir: I deem it my duty to my fellow citizens to inform our brethren in the United States of our perilous condition at present. Last night an express arrived with the news, that one division of the Mexican army, 4,000 strong, meeting the small force under lieut. Thornton, had driven them in, and are now in full march for the interior of Texas. Col. Travis is besieged in St. Antonio, with little provisions and a garrison of only 150 men, and we hourly expect an attack on this point of the coast, from the Mexicans by sea, under Ugarthehea, 3,500 strong. We have in the field now about 700 men to oppose this force. There is here under my command only 120 men, when we expected at least 2,000 — and it is thought the Mexican army is within a few days' march of us.

The families at a short distance from us are flying before the enemy, and have left their stock, their houses and crops to the mercy of the tyrant, who is in person at the head of his army.

We call on you by the sacred ties of country, language, habits and kindred, not to desert us in this our hour of danger. Delay for a time and we may be lost — we want immediate aid, and men and arms. Do not be deaf to our requests, but come forward as you have heretofore done, and say, "forward to the rescue."[87]

J. W. Robinson to Col. J. W. Fannin, Jr.
EXECUTIVE DEPARTMENT OF TEXAS, WASHINGTON: Yours of the 1st inst. is just recd. In answer permit us to say that unfortunately we are too much divided for the benefit of our country and promotion of the true interest to render you that effectual aid you so much need. Party spirit lays hold with her infernal fangs, upon everything that might be of any service to our country in her deadly struggle for her rights. The spirit of party rages to an unprecedented high & its bitter rancor is truly alarming & heartrending to any true friend of the country.

We however believe that under the organic law we were and are yet clothed with the power that law gives, for some days however we have not acted officially, and in fact the very letters addressed to us by you are seized by others and Read and commented upon before we are permitted to see them. Not withstanding this we feel that we are still legally in office & will continue to act until superceded by some future government. In accordance with our official duty & our oaths we have to say & instruct you to use your own discretion to remain where you are or to retreat as you may think best for the safety of the brave Volunteers Under your command, & the Regulars & Militia, and the interest of our beloved country requires unless you shall be instructed otherwise by Genl. Houston who has been by this new convention confirmed & appointed commander in chief of the Army of Texas Militia & volunteers; as well as regulars.

The bearer can give you all other information necessary as well as if it were here written.

As we are informed that this new convention intends to inform immediately an other provisional government, therefore, when you communicate again, it may be well for you to direct your communications to the Provisional Government of Texas.

This moment information has been given that about 30 men has thrown themselves into Bears[88] for its relief from Gonzales, that many more is on the way under Coll Neill Genl Burleson & to raise the siege if possible. Captain Dimmit with 200 men I am informed are marching for your relief.[89]

General Houston has been ordered to the Army by the convention forthwith . . . The God of battles shield your and our countryman from home in the field is the parting adieu of your friends.

James W. Robinson
Acting Governor[90]

James C. Neill, Col. Comdt. of the Post of Bexar to Horace Eggleston [receipt]

GONZALES: Received of Horace Eggleston a Set of medicine of amount of Ninety Dollars which sd medicines I have this day purchased from him for the use of the post of Bexar[91]

Almonte Diary Entry

Sunday — At 5 A.M. the columns were posted at their respective stations, and at half past 5 the attack or assault was made, and continued until 6 A.M. when the enemy attempted in vain to fly, but they were overtaken and put to the sword, and only five women, one Mexican soldier (prisoner) and a black slave escaped from instant death. On the part of the enemy the result was 250 killed, and 17 pieces of artillery — a flag; muskets and fire-arms taken. Our loss was 60 soldiers and 5 officers killed, and 198 soldiers and 25 officers were wounded — 2 of the latter General officers. The battalion of Toluca lost 98 men between the wounded and killed. I was robbed by our soldiers.[92]

Mexican Soldier to brothers of the heart

SAN ANTONIO de BEXAR: The attack was made in four columns, led by General Cos, General Morales, Duque de Estrada, and Romero. I marched under the immediate command of General Cos and will tell you what I saw. After a long wait we took our places at 3 o'clock A.M. on the south side, a distance of 300 feet from the fort of the enemy. Here we remained flat on our stomachs until 5:30 (Whew! it was cold) when the signal to march was given by the President from the battery between the north and east. Immediately, General Cos cried "Foreword" and placing himself at the head of the attack, we ran to the assault, carrying scaling ladders, picks and spikes. Although the distance was short the fire from the enemy's cannon was fearful; we fell back; more than forty men fell around me in a few moment. One can but admire the stubborn resistance of our enemy, and the constant bravery of all our troops. It seemed every cannon ball or pistol shot of the enemy embedded itself in the breasts of our men who without stopping cried: "Long live the Mexican Republic! Long live General Santa Anna!" I can tell you the whole scene was one of extreme terror . . . After some three quarters of an hour of the most horrible fire, there followed the most awful attack with hand arms . . . Poor things — no longer do they live — all of them died, and even now I am watching them burn — to free us from their putrification — 257 corpses without counting those who fell in the previous thirteen days, or those who vainly sought safety in flight. Their leader named Travis, died like a brave man with his rifle in his hand at the back of a cannon, but that perverse and haughty James Bowie died like a woman, in bed, almost hidden by the covers. Our loss was terrible in both officers and men.[93]

Jose Juan Sanchez Navarro Diary Entry

Long live our country, the Alamo is ours!

Today at five in the morning, the assault was made by four columns under the command of General Cos and colonels Duque, Romero, and Morales. His Excellency the President commanded the reserves. The firing lasted half an hour. Our jefes, officers, and troops, at the same time as if by magic, reached the top of the wall, jumped within, and continued fighting with side arms. By six thirty there was not an enemy left. I saw actions of heroic valor I envied. I was horrified by some cruelties, among others, the death of an old man named Cochran and of a boy about fourteen. The women and children were saved. Travis, the commandant of the Alamo died like a hero; Buy [Bowie], the braggart son-in-law of Beramendi [died] like a coward. The troops were permitted to pillage. The enemy have suffered a heavy loss; twenty-one field pieces of different caliber, many arms and munitions. Two hundred fifty seven of their men were killed; I have seen and counted their bodies. But I cannot be glad because we lost eleven officers with nineteen wounded, including the valiant Duque and Gonzales; and two hundred forty-seven of our troops were wounded and one hundred ten killed. It can be truly said that with another such victory as this we'll go to the devil.

After the capture of the Alamo, I proposed to the commandant General, Don Martin Perfecto de Cos, that the valiant officers and soldiers who died in the assault be buried in the cemetery of the chapel of the said fort, that the names of each be inscribed on a copper tablet made from one of the cannons captured to be placed on a column at the base of which these eight lines might be written:

> The bodies that lie here at rest
> Were those of men whose souls elate
> Are now in Heaven to be blest
> For deeds that time cannot abate.
>
> They put their manhood to the test,
> And fearlessly they met their fate;
> No fearful end, a patriot's fall
> Leads to the highest life of all.

My suggestion was not approved and I believe that it was not the fault of General Cos. consequently, I wished to write down the said verses here not so much for the purpose of passing myself off as a poet as to render due their tribute in the only manner within my powers to the illustrious, valiant, and untimely victims.

The dead, it appears, were not the only "untimely victims."

There are no hospitals, medicines, or doctors; and the condition of the wounded is such as to cause pity. they have no mattresses on which to lie or blankets with which to cover themselves, in spite of the fact that on entering Bexar, we took from the enemy the remnants of three or four stores and that one has been set up and called the government Store, where everything is sold at a high price and for cash.[94]

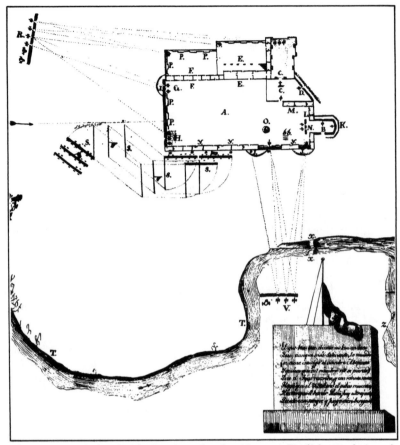

Alamo map made in 1836 by Jose Juan Sanchez Navarro. English translation of lower block reads:

> Let him who sees this crude device
> Remember every patriot must
> (If name of Mexican suffice
> To proudly bear its fame in trust)
> Return to Texas, seal the price
> Of vile rebellion low in dust,
> Until our honor, now outraged,
> In blood and fire shall be assuaged.

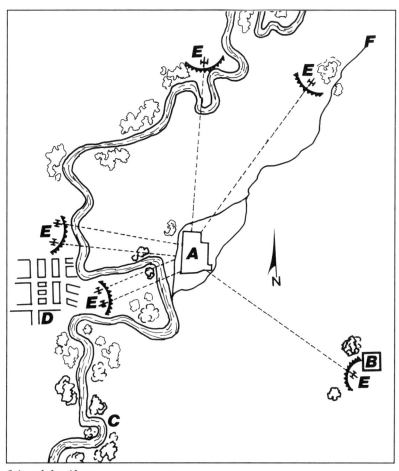

Seige of the Alamo.

A. THE ALAMO
B. POWDER HOUSE HILL
C. SAN ANTONIO RIVER
D. THE TOWN OF SAN ANTONIO
E. MEXICAN ARMY BATTERIES
F. THE ALAMO DITCH

This map depicts the placement of Mexican batteries during the siege. The placements west of the Alamo (near San Antonio) were erected when Santa Anna arrived on February 23 and proved largely ineffective. The placements north northeast and southeast were erected on March 4 and produced the most damage to the Alamo prior to the attack.

Sheet music for Duguello, the tune Santa Anna ordered played to signify that no quarter would be safe for the Texans in the Alamo.

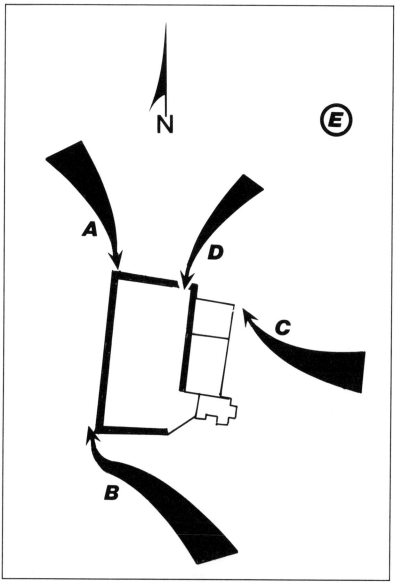

Attacking the Alamo. (A) Cos attacked from the northwest, generally considered the path of most danger and thus more honor. (B) Morales' troops attacked from the south but were forced to swing west. (C) Romero's force moved in from the east. (D) Duque's forces attacked from the northeast. (X) The northern battery where Santa Anna was stationed with the reserves and the band.

Santa Anna to Tornel

Sir: Victory belongs to the army which at this very moment, 8 o'clock a.m. achieved a complete and glorious triumph that will render its memory imperishable.

As I had stated in my report to Your Excellency of the taking of this city, on the 27th of last month, I awaited the arrival of the First Brigade of Infantry to commence active operations against the Fortress of the Alamo. However, the whole Brigade having been delayed beyond my expectation, I ordered that three of its battalions, viz: the Engineers — Aldama and Toluca — should force their march to join me. These troops, together with the Battalions of Matamoros, Jimenes, and San Luis Potosi, brought the force at my disposal, recruits excluded, up to 1400 Infantry. This force, divided into four columns of attack and a reserve, commenced the attack at 5 o'clock A.M. They met with a stubborn resistance, the combat lasting more than an hour and a half and the reserve having to be brought into action.

The scene offered by this engagement was extraordinary. The men fought individually, viewing with each other in heroism. Twenty-one pieces of artillery used by the enemy with the most perfect accuracy, the brisk fire of the musketry which illuminated the interior of the fortress and it's walls and ditches, could not check our dauntless soldiers, who are entitled to the consideration of the Supreme Government and to the gratitude of the nation.

The flag of the New Orleans Greys, the only banner proved to be flying over the Alamo during the final assault.

The fortress is now in our power, with its artillery, stores &c. More than 600 corpses of foreigners were buried in the ditches and entrenchments, and a good many, who had escaped the bayonet of the infantry, fell in the vicinity under the sabres of the cavalry. I can assure your excellency that few are those who bore to their associates the tidings of their disaster.

Among the corpses are those of Bowie and Travis who styled themselves colonels, and also that of Crockett, and several leading men, who had entered the fortress with despatches from the Convention. We lost about 70 men killed and 300 wounded, among whom are 25 officers. The cause for which they fell renders their loss less painful, as it is the duty of the Mexican soldier to die for the defence of the rights of the nation; and all of us were ready for any sacrifice to promote this fond object; nor will we, hereafter, suffer any foreigners, whatever their origin may be, to insult our country and to pollute its soils.

I shall, in due time, send to Your Excellency a circumstantial report of this glorious triumph. Now I have only time to congratulate the nation and the President, ad interim, to whom I request you to submit this report.

The bearer takes with him one of the flags of the enemy's Battalions, captured today. The inspection of it will show plainly the true intentions of the treacherous colonist, and of their abettors, who came from parts of the United States of the North.

God and Liberty![95]

Report of Francisco Ruiz, alcalde of San Antonio
On the 23rd day of February, 1836, (2 o'clock P.M.,) Gen Santa entered the city of San Antonio with a part of his army. This he effected without any resistance, the forces under the command of Travis, Bowie, and Crockett having on the same day, at 8 o'clock in the morning, learned that the Mexican army was on the banks of the Median river, they concentrated in the fortress of the Alamo.

In the evening they commenced to exchange fire with guns, and from the 23d of February to the 6th of March (in which the storming was made by Santa Anna) the roar of artillery and volleys of musketry were constantly heard.

On the 6th of March at 3 o'clock P.M.[96] General Santa Anna at the head of 4000 men advanced against the Alamo. The infantry, artillery, and cavalry had formed 1000 varas from the walls of said fortress. The Mexican army charged and were twice repulsed by the deadly fire of Travis's artillery, which resembled a constant thunder. At the third charge the Toluca battalion commenced to scale the walls and suffered severely. Out of 830 men only 130 of the battalion were left alive.

When the Mexican army entered the walls, I with the political chief (Gefe politico) Don Ramon Musquiz and other members of the corporation, accompanied by the Curate, Don Refugio de la Garza, who by Santa Anna's orders, had assembled during the night at a temporary fortification on Protero Street, with the object of attending the wounded, etc. As soon as the storming commenced we crossed the bridge on Commerce street with this object in view, and about 100 yards from the same a party of Mexican dragoons fired upon us and compelled us to fall

Jose Francisco Ruiz

back on the river and place we occupied before. Half an hour elapses when Santa Anna sent one of his aide-de-camps with an order for us to come before him. He directed me to call on some of the neighbors to come with carts to carry the [Mexican] dead to the cemetery and to accompany him as he desired to have Colonels Travis, Bowie and Crockett shown to him.

On the north battery of the fortress lay the lifeless body of Col. Travis on the gun carriage, shot only through the forehead. Toward the west and in a small fort opposite the city, we found the body of Colonel Crockett. Col Bowie was found dead in his bed in one of the rooms on the south side.

Santa Anna, after all the Mexicans were taken out ordered wood to be brought to burn the bodies of the Texans. He sent a company of dragoons with me to bring wood and dry branches from the neighboring forest. About three o'clock in the afternoon they commenced laying the wood and dry branches upon which a pile of dead bodies was placed; more wood was piled on them, and another pile brought, and in this manner they were arranged in layers. Kindling wood was distributed through the pile, and about 5 o'clock in the evening it was lighted.

The dead Mexicans of Santa Anna were taken to the graveyard, but not having sufficient room for them, I ordered them to be thrown into the river, which was done that same day.

Santa Anna's loss was estimated at 1600 men.[97] These were the flower of his army.

The gallantry of the few Texans who defended the Alamo was really wondered at by the Mexican army. Even the generals were astonished at their vigorous resistance, and how dearly victory was brought.

The Generals who, under Santa Anna, participated in the storming of the Alamo, were Juan Amador, Castrillon, Ramirez, Sesma, and Andrade.

The men burnt numbered one hundred and eighty two.[98] I was an eyewitness. . . .[99]

Fall of the Alamo, *painting by Jean Louis Theodore Gentilz, ca. 1885.*

Beginning here and continuing on the following pages is a series of paintings, drawings, and photographs depicting the attack on the Alamo and conditions of the mission following the Mexican   victory. The first painting (above), completed in about 1885 by Jean Louis Theodore Gentilz, shows the initial attack by Santa Anna's army on the morning of March 6, 1836. The original painting was destroyed when fire ravaged the offices of C. H. Mueller, a San Antonio paint manufacturer, in the early 1900s.

This version of the assault on the Alamo was done for W. W. Dexter's Texas: Imperial State of America *that was distributed at the 1904 World's Fair in St. Louis.*

This 1953 painting by Ruth Conerly Zachrisson illustrates the traditional version of Travis' death. It is generally believed that Travis died early in the fighting while he was commanding a cannon on the north wall.

The Fall of the Alamo, *painting by Robert J. Onderdonk, 1903.*

Dawn at the Alamo, *painting by Henry Arthur McAudle.*

Death of Dickinson, *painting by Jean Louis Theodore Gentilz, ca. 1844.*

The Funeral Pyre, *painting by Jose Arpa.*

Artist's conception of the Alamo chapel ruins.

Drawing depicting the Alamo chapel ruins.

Interior view of the Church of the Alamo, *watercolor by Edward Everett,*
1847.

Ruins of the Alamo Mission.

RUINS OF THE CHURCH OF EL ALAMO.

This 1854 Alamo illustration first appeared in Gleason's Pictorial Drawing-Room Companion.

Alamo Church + Plaza

The earliest known actual photograph of the Alamo which was taken 14 years after the fall. By the time this photo was taken, the U. S. Army had reconstructed the facade of the chapel and added two windows.

Endnotes

1. *SWHQ,* 48:16-17.
2. Ibid, 37:13-14. Andrew Ponton, the last Alcalde of Gonzales, participated in the battle of Gonzales where the first shots of the Texas revolution were fired. In response to Travis' appeal for help, thirty-two men from Gonzales, not including Ponton, rode to the Alamo and became the only group to respond to the urgent pleas from Travis.
3. Foote, 2:224.
4. *SWHQ,* 37:16.
5. Ibid.
6. Texas State Library Archives, Austin. Sam Houston, who did not expect the Mexican campaign to begin until the grasses were up in the spring, was away making a treaty with the Indians when Santa Anna arrived in Bexar. Due to the hostilities with the Mexicans, action on this treaty was delayed and it was ultimately rejected by the Republic of Texas Senate. In 1839, then President Mirabeau B. Lamar ordered the Cherokees removed from Texas. Chief Bowles, wearing a vest given him by Sam Houston, was killed in the battle of the Neches on July 16, 1839.
7. *SWHQ,* 48:17.
8. Ibid, 37:14. This letter is considered by many to be the most patriotic letter in the history of America.
9. Ibid, 37:307 The bracketed portions of this letter are estimates of the actual words since the original is no longer readable.
10. Ibid, 37:306. Many historian believe Smithers, about twenty years old, rode out of the Alamo as a messenger for Travis. However, others believe Smithers was not actually in the fort but rather simply saw a copy of Travis' dispatch and then rode on to spread the word.
11. Ibid, 37:305. This letter is considered by many as proof that Smithers was not actually in the Alamo and sent out by Travis. This letter was certainly written by Smithers and it is believed, if Travis had sent him out, there would have been a formal message written by the commander.
12. Ibid, 48:17-18.
13. Ibid, 37:28.
14. This letter seems to be evidence that the financial position in Goliad was much better than in the Alamo, especially since there was enough to purchase (and presumedly consume) seventy GALLONS of brandy.
15. Gulick, 3:338-339.
16. San Antonio is actually about 95 miles from Goliad.
17. *SWHQ,* 9:178-180. John S. Brooks was a twenty-two-year-old volunteer in Fannin's command at Goliad. He left behind several lengthy letters that have helped researchers gain insight into the situation that existed in Texas in early 1836. Because of his

inspired, patriotic style of writing, anyone reading his letters cannot help but develop a sense of sympathy for the young man and a sense of loss and regret that he was lost to Texas in the Fannin massacre.

18. Ibid, 9:180-182.
19. Binkley, 2:453-454. Robert McAlpin Williamson, of Georgia, was one of the most prominent lawyers in early Texas. He was widely known as "Three Legged Willie" because his right leg was drawn up at the knee and he wore a wooden leg to compensate. He participated at the battle of San Jacinto and later became a judge and member of the Texas Supreme Court. He also served in the House and Senate of Texas before his death in 1859.
20. Castaneda, 214. The soldiers of the Yucatan battalion were primarily Mayan Indians accustomed to tropical climate, so they suffered considerably in the winter conditions of Texas in early 1836.
21. *SWHQ,* 48:18.
22. Gray, 119.
23. A. J. Houston Papers.
24. Castaneda, 215.
25. *SWHQ,* 48:19.
26. Gray, 120.
27. Brown, 303-304.
28. Filisola, 74-75.
29. Ibid, 70-73.
30. Binkley, 2:461.
31. Gulick 3:339.
32. Foote, 2:225 (Misdated as February 29th). Despite being less than 100 miles away with more than 400 men, Fannin never again attempted to go to the aid of the Alamo.
33. The General either lied to inspire the favor of Santa Anna or did not know that F.W. Johnson and four other men did, in fact, escape the fight.
34. Jenkins, document number 2192.
35. *SWHQ,* 48:19.
36. Gray, 120.
37. Lamar Papers, 1:341-42.
38. Mrs. Dimitt was a Mexican citizen.
39. Archives, Texas State Library. This is one of the most curious letters of the entire Texas Revolution. For a complete discussion, see *Exploring the Alamo Legends* by Wallace O. Chariton.

James Kerr, of Kentucky, was a close friend of Stephen F. Austin and he came to Texas in 1825. He was active in the political and Indian affairs of the time and was ultimately elected to the Constitutional Convention although he did not attend. He did serve in the congress of the province and authored bills to outlaw dueling in Texas and to relocate the capital from Houston to Austin.
40. Archives, Texas State Library.

41. *The Texas Republican* (Brazoria, Texas), March 2, 1836. John A. Wharton, of Tennessee, served as "Texas Agent" to New Orleans, adjutant general to Sam Houston at San Jacinto, and later as a representative to the congress of the Republic.
42. Daughters of the Republic of Texas Library, the Alamo. This recently uncovered receipt apparently solves the mystery of why James C. Neill left the Alamo on February 11, 1836. His stated excuse for leaving was due to illness in his family but historians have long believed he actually left to try and get much needed funds for the men in the Alamo. For a complete discussion of what happened to James C. Neill after he left the Alamo, see *Exploring the Alamo Legends* by Wallace O. Chariton
43. *SWHQ*, 48:19.
44. Gray, 121.
45. Gulick, 3:343-344. This document is actually dated only February but is included here because it fits the natural sequence.
46. *Telegraph, and Texas Register*, March 5, 1836. This document is also dated only February but it fits here.
47. From original broadside in private collection. This circular is dated only February but it is included here because, based on the information in the notice, it must have been issued near the end of the month.
48. Hassell Family Papers, University of Texas Library. Apparently, J. W. Hassel never reached San Antonio, despite his stated intentions, because there is no record of his having been in the Alamo.
49. Archives, Texas State Library.
50. For a copy of the complete treaty, see *The Writings of Sam Houston*, pages 358-360.
51. Barker, 3:356-358. While the men of the Alamo desperately needed their commander in chief, he was in the field treating with the Indians. Due to the hostilities of war, the treaty was not ratified until after Sam Houston had served his first term as President of the Republic of Texas and the treaty was broken within a year.
52. *SWHQ*, 48:19.
53. Foote, 2:216-218.
54. Gray, 121.
55. Binkley, 474-476. John Chenowith was a veteran of the siege of Bexar, served with Fannin for a while, was at the battle of San Jacinto, and resigned from the army to serve in the first Congress of the Republic.
56. Archives, Texas State Library.
57. *SWHQ*, 21:43. Felix Huston, of Kentucky, was very much pro-Texas and spent a considerable amount of his own money training men and provisions for the cause. He did not start for Texas himself until after the victory at San Jacinto. He served as a general in the army and was actually commander in chief for a short time. After the war, Huston attempted to arouse interest in a campaign against Mexico but failed in the effort. He left Texas in 1840 but continued to support the cause of annexation with frequent speeches on behalf of Texas.

58. Castaneda, 216.
59. *SWHQ*, 48:19-20.
60. Gray, 123-124.
61. Wallace, 99.
62. *SWHQ*, 9:182-185
63. Castaneda, 216.
64. *SWHQ*, 48:20.
65. Gray, 124.
66. DRT Library at the Alamo. Forty-one-year-old Isaac Millsaps, of Mississippi, went to the Alamo with the thirty-two men from Gonzales on March 1, 1836. He died with the Alamo defenders on March 6 and was survived by a blind wife and six children. This particular letter is thought by many to be a forgery. Some of the phrasing used was not in common use in 1836 and the signature does not appear to match an existing Millsaps signature. However, until expensive scientific tests are conducted, the validity of this letter will remain uncertain.
67. Foote, 2:219-222.
68. Whatever "the enclosed" was has been lost to history. Many believe it was a private good-by letter to Travis' sweetheart Rebecca Cummins. If that's true and the letter could be found, it would be one of the most valuable pieces of Texanna.
69. *SWHQ*, 37:24-25. Jesse Grimes, of North Carolina, came to Texas in 1827. He was a representative to the Constitutional Convention and signed the Declaration of Independence. After the convention, he enlisted for a three-month tour of duty in the army. Following the war he served in the congress of the Republic.
70. *The Texas Monument*, March 31, 1852. David Ayers, of New Jersey, came to Texas in 1832 and brought his family to the province two years later. He was in the mercantile and land business until he volunteered for the army. Because of deafness, his activity was limited to helping Texas citizens escape the advance of the Mexicans in the Runaway Scrape. He also cared for Charles E. Travis while his father, William B. Travis, was in the Alamo.
71. Jenkins, document number 2229.
72. *United States Magazine and Democratic Review*, October 1838, 143.
73. *SWHQ*, 48:20.
74. Gray, 124.
75. Yoakum, 2:510.
76. *SWHQ*, 48:22-23.
77. Gray Diary, 124-125. The prisoners were the ones captured by James Walker Fannin and subsequently sent to the convention.
78. Gulick, 1:336. L. Ayers joined Fannin's command in early March. He apparently left the command as a messenger before the men were forced to surrender since his name does not appear on any list of casualties of the Goliad massacre.
79. Potter, 56-57.
80. The completion of this treaty was what took Sam Houston away from the field of battle for the entire month of February.

81. This receipt was issued to clear up the discrepancy in the shoe inventory of the Alamo. See February 3 report by John W. Smith.
82. Daughters of the Republic of Texas Library, the Alamo.
83. *SWHQ,* 48:23.
84. Gray, 125.
85. Gammel, 1:847.
86. Texas Almanac, 1870:39-40.
87. Hunnicut, 62-64.
88. *SWHQ,* 37:35-36. This eyewitness account was printed in *El Mosquito Mexicana.*
89. Bexar.
90. This was apparently just a rumor since Dimitt did not march to Fannin's relief.
91. Binkley, 2:481-482.
92. Yoakum, 2:511. James Collinsworth came to Texas from Tennessee in early 1835. He served in the Constitutional Convention where he nominated Sam Houston for commander in chief of the army. Following the convention, Collinsworth served in the army, was instrumental in helping with the Runaway Scrape and distinguished himself at the battle of San Jacinto. After the war he served as commissioner to the U.S., declined an appointment as attorney general of the Republic, and became Chief Justice of the Supreme Court. In 1838, while a candidate for the Texas presidency, Collinsworth took his own life by jumping off a bridge on Galveston Bay. Despite the misspelling, Collingsworth County was named in his honor.
    Richard Ellis, of Virginia, came to Texas briefly in 1826 and returned permanently in 1834. He was elected president of the Constitutional Convention and later served in the congress of the Republic. He died in 1846.
93. Jenkins, document number 2255. Martin Parmer, of Virginia, originally came to Texas in the mid-1820s but was expelled by the Mexicans in 1831. He returned in 1835, was elected a delegate to the Constitutional Convention, and signed the Declaration of Independence. Known as the "Ring-tailed Panther," Parmer was married either four or five times, depending on some questionable circumstances. After the war he served as a judge before his death in 1850. Parmer county is named in his honor.
94. Mobile *Register,* March 28, 1836.
95. Archives, Texas State Library. Little is known of Horrace Eggleston but he apparently was in some sort of mercantile business since he was supplying medical supplies.
96. This should be A.M. since the movement of the army commenced early in the morning of the 6th, not in the afternoon.
97. The number of Mexican losses has been widely disputed. Most dedicated Alamo scholars now believe the total loss of killed and wounded was around 600.
98. The number of Texas casualties will be forever argued about. This Ruiz account is almost certainly responsible for the widespread use of the 182 figure. However, Ruiz apparently did not count the

body of Gregorio Esparza, which was removed and buried. There may have also been other Texans who were not burned or the count may have been wrong. See *Exploring the Alamo Legends* by Wallace O. Chariton for more information.

99. Texas Almanac, 1860:56-57. This account was not written on the 6th (probably shortly thereafter) but is included to show the disposition of the bodies of the Alamo victims. While Ruiz was contending with the Mexican army, his father, Don (Jose) Francisco Ruiz, was attending the Constitutional Convention as an elected representative of San Antonio. He signed the Declaration of Independence on March 2, 1836.

CHAPTER SIX

After the Fall

March 7, 1836 to March 17, 1836

It took five days for word of the fall of the Alamo to reach Sam Houston and the rest of the Texas army. General Houston arrived in Gonzales, 70 miles from San Antonio, on March 11, 1836. Shortly after his arrival at about 4:00 P.M., two Mexican gentlemen showed up carrying the first news that the Alamo had fallen. The commander-in-chief believed the men were spies and had them detained. But he also feared the story they told was largely true. He accordingly issued orders for Fannin to fall back from Goliad to Victoria and blow up Fort Defiance before leaving.

On March 13, Houston received official confirmation of the fall of the Alamo when Erastus "Deaf" Smith piloted the few survivors of the disaster, including Susanna Dickinson and Travis' slave Joe, into the army camp at Gonzales. The worst fears of all Texans were realized. Santa Anna had crushed the outpost in San Antonio and was intent on marching through Texas to exterminate all non-Spanish speaking people west of the Sabine river. It appeared Fannin's army was open to attack at any moment.

The Alamo was back in Mexican hands and it appeared all of Texas might soon follow suit. News of the disaster spread like a prairie fire across the whole of Texas. Everywhere, families quickly packed up what few possessions they could easily carry and retreated to the east to try and put themselves out of harm's way. Urgent and patriotic calls went up from all sections imploring any man able to carry a rifle to rise up and meet the enemy. Sam Houston ordered Gonzales burned and began a retreat destined to allow him sufficient time to rebuild an army. By March 17, sentiment was already building that the men of the Alamo must be avenged.

Monday, March 7, 1836
FALL PLUS 1 DAY

Almonte Diary Entry
Monday — Commenced with a north wind. A special despatch was received from gen Urrea, dated 3d March, from San Patricio, in which he communicated that the preceding day, at a place called Los Cohates, he attacked Dr. Grant and his party, and killed Dr. Grant and 41 of his men, and afterwards 2 out of 5 who fled. There was no loss on our side. By the 14th General Urrea would be in Goliad. The greater part of the 1st brigade arrived under command of general Gaona. The mail arrived from Matamoras and Mexico dates to the 2d and 3d of February.[1]

Wm. Fairfax Gray Diary Entry
WASHINGTON: The Convention proceeded to work on the constitution. It is reported in part only . . . It is awkwardly framed, arrangement and phraseology both bad; general features much like that of United States.[2]

Nicolas Rodrigues to D. Jose M. Guerra
SAN PATRICIO: Yesterday at 3 p.m. we commenced the attack on the rebel columns, below the habitation of Agua Dulce. The surprise occasioned them by our ambuscade was such that they did not perceive us till they were in our power. They fired pistol shots; but so badly directed that they only wounded one horse. We charged them in the plain for the distance of two leagues and a half; and pursued them as if they were savage horses (mes-tanos). They forgot they carried muskets and pistols, with which they had learned to direct their fires. Thirty-two dead were found on the field of battle; and we took 4 prisoners. Among the slain were Col. Grant. The fact is that our troops pursued them with poised lance which was sufficient to achieve all.[3]

The General-in-Chief of the Army of Operations of the Mexican Republic to the Inhabitants of Texas
HEADQUARTERS, BEXAR: **Citizens!** The causes which have conducted to this frontier a part of the Mexican army are not unknown to you: a parcel of audacious adventurers, maliciously protected by some inhabitants of a neighboring republic, dared to invade our territory, with an intention of dividing amongst themselves the fertile lands that are contained in the spacious department of Texas, and even had the boldness to entertain the idea of reaching the capitol of the Republic. It became necessary to check and chastise such enormous daring; and in conse-quence, some exemplary punishment have already taken place in Saint Patrick, Lipantitlan and this city. I am pained to find

General Antonio Lopez de Santa Anna

amongst these adventurers the names of some, to whom had been granted repeated benefits, and who had no just motive of complaint against the government of their adopted country — These ungrateful men must also necessarily suffer the just punishment that the laws and the public vengeance demand. But if we are bound to punish the criminal, we are not the less compelled to protect the innocent. It is thus that the inhabitants of this country, let their origin be whatever it may, who should not appear to have been implicated in such iniquitous rebellion, shall be respected in their persons and property, provided they come forward and report themselves to the commander of the troops within eight days after they should have arrived in their respective settlements, in order to justify their conduct and to receive a document guaranteeing to them the right of enjoying that which lawfully belongs to them.

Bexarians! Return to your homes and dedicate yourselves to your domestic duties. Your city and the fortress of the Alamo are already in possession of the Mexican army, composed of your fellow citizens; and rest assured that no mass of foreigners will ever interrupt your repose, and much less, attack your lives and plunder your property. The supreme government has taken you under its protection, and will seek for your good.

Inhabitants of Texas! I have related to you the orders that the army of operations I have the honor to command comes to execute; and therefore the good will have nothing to fear. Fulfill always your duties as Mexican citizens, and you may expect the protection and benefit of the laws; and rest assured that you will never have reason to report yourselves of having observed such conduct, for I pledge you in the name of the Supreme authorities of the nation, and as your fellow citizen and friend, that what has been promised you will be faithfully performed.

Antonio Lopez de Santa Anna[4]

Tuesday, March 8, 1836
FALL PLUS 2 DAYS

Almonte Diary Entry
Tuesday — Fine clear day, but cold. Letters were written to Mexico under date of 6th inst. Commenced blowing hard. Official reports were forwarded to-day.[5]

Wm. Fairfax Gray Diary Entry
WASHINGTON: Fine weather. The Convention are diligent in their meetings, but get on slowly with business. Too much talk.[6]

Moseley Baker to Jones, Gray, & Pettus
GONZALES: On day before yesterday I arrived here, accompanied by the companies of Captain McNutt and Robb. I found about one hundred sixty men here, which, with our force, made about two hundred and seventy, fifty of which started on yesterday for the Alamo. Our force now at this place is about two hundred and twenty men, with an army seventy-five miles in our front, five thousand strong. Our own situation is critical — too weak to advance, and insufficient to protect the place — and daily expecting two thousand cavalry to attack us. To retreat, however, would be the ruin of Texas: and we have all resolved to abide an attack, and to conquer or die. We are now busily engaged fortifying ourselves, with the hope that the people of Texas, en masse, are on the march to our assistance. Unless they are, the Alamo and our post must fall, and all, every man be destroyed. Not one of us will return to tell the dreadful tale or to reproach those that remain for their supineness, or their cowardice. We have come to repel the enemy, and my company will die beneath their standard sooner than the enemy shall advance, or they retreat. Will the people of Texas longer remain at home? Will any man, under these circumstance, longer refuse to turn out, because his interest requires his attention? Will any one dare to have the effrontery to say, that his interest must be attended to, when Texas is in danger of being overrun, and all the women and children in cold blood massacred, when a portion of his fellow citizens are closely besieged, and another portion daily expecting to be attacked by ten time their number. The truth is not to be disguised, unless Texas turns out to a man — unless in two weeks from this day, three thousand men are concentrated here, Texas is gone, and one universal destruction and conflagration will be the result. In the name of God, send us assistance — send out the men; and let all who remain without satisfactory reasons, be henceforth branded as a coward and a traitor, and an enemy to Texas, and let him so be treated. Their doctrine appears to be, that we must fight the battles of Texas,

endure all privation, and all toil, and spill our blood and our lives, that they may enjoy the privilege of staying at home. Such a man is a traitor, and as a traitor treat him. Send as fast as possible, arms and ammunition. Some of my company, are without guns, and no possible means of procuring them here. Not a pound of lead except what I brought . . . send these things, and speedily; and be assured, that unless Texas is victorious, I shall never return.[7]

F. W. Johnson to the Genl. Convention of Texas

LACY'S COLORADO [river]:[8] I hasten to inform you of the disaster of my party at San Patricio and also that of Col. Grant on the 2nd Inst. — which I have by Don Placido who was in company with Col. Grant when attacked — Grants party of 26 men were attacked some 15 miles from San Patricio by a party in ambush — At the onset the party were thrown into disorder and soon became an easy prey to the enemy owing to their superiority of numbers — but two of Grants party escaped — Grant himself a prisoner — of my party which consisted of only 25 men four escaped. — I have from Placido that the Enemies strength is from 1000 to 1200 men about 200 of whom had advanced as far as Refugio on the 1st — I left Goliad on the 3d. and arrived in Victoria on the 4th where I found but fifteen Volunteers — the people are much alarmed and unless some efficient measures are taken the whole settlements west fo Colorado will be broken up — all — all have left Labaca & Navidad — But a part of the provisions at Coxes point & Dimitts have been taken off — that part remaining is in great danger of being cut off by the enemy — Their first object will be to secure Copano, keep a few troops at Refugio and with the main body attack Goliad or advance into the Country — from the best information I get it is Ureah that has advanced by the lower route and Seisma on Bejar — Santa Anna in in Monclova with from 3 to 4000 men with a heavy train of battering & field artillery. —

The success of the enemy at San Patricio and easy entrance into Bexar will stimulate them to turn out and march freely into the Country — Heretofore they have refused —

The keeping of Garrisons at a time like this is to deprive the country of the services of those in Garrison — the Enemy can pass Bexar and Goliad with impunity as soon as they may think proper —

Action, the united action of the whole people is necessary to the salvation of the country. —[9]

General Jose Urrea Diary Entry

I was informed that the enemy was taking steps to attack me in San Patricio. I marched during the night to meet them, taking 300 men and the four-pounder in our division. Ten leagues from Goliad I ambushed my troops on the road to await the enemy.[10]

Thomas B. Rees to Gerald Birch

FORT DEFIANCE, TEXAS: Dear Sir, I avail myself of the opportunity to address you a few lines to let you know that I am with _____ I am at this time stationed at Laberdio [LaBahia or Goliad] on the St. Antonio river. The enemy is at hand & we expect to be attacked every hour they have arrived at St Antonio six thousand troops & have been fighting the American troops for the last fifteen days. We received an express this evening that the Americans have not had a man killed & only three slightly wounded.[11] There is about two hundred that has possession of the fort & will keep possession of it if their ammunition holds out till they can be reinforced. The citizens of Texas is turning out to a man. The Mexicans has got possession of San Patricio & are concentrating their troops & fortifying that place. Col Johnson with about twenty men was attacked at that place in the knight and only four or five made there escape and John Love was one of the men that lived. Doct Brodnart [sic] was seen to fall in the street & has not been heard of since. Rubin Brown & Col Grant with about thirty men was attacked in a open prairie & both of them fell and all of there men that was not killed was taken prisoner. I have not time to write you the perticulars I wish you to attend to my business & not let my family want for any thing till I return. State to my wife that I am well & was going to write to knight & send the letter with this but since I have been writing this letter they have been an express received that two thousand Mexicans has landed at a creek in nine miles of us and there is no doubt but what we shall be attacked before day. They have four cannon with them I have no time to write more you shall here from me every opportunity. This letter is sent with apprehension.

Thos B. Rees

A. B. the express received to night from the source it came by all probability is not true but we are preparing for them — Texas has declared Independence.[12]

Wednesday, March 9, 1836
FALL PLUS 3 DAYS

Almonte Diary Entry
Wednesday — Commenced with a violent north wind, weather not very cold. Generals Filisola, Araga &c. &c. arrived. Orders to march were given to Gen'l Sesma and colonel Gonzales. Two persons arrived from the interior to see the President. The wind continued all night.[13]

Wm. Fairfax Gray Diary Entry
WASHINGTON: The business of the Convention drags. There are some questions that they seem afraid to approach. They are sure to induce excitement, come up when they may. The land question is one, and the loan they are unwilling or afraid to ratify. Such miserable narrow-mindedness is astonishing. There is a great want of political philosophy and practical political knowledge in the body.[14]

B. H. Duval to Father
GOLIAD: By last express, yesterday, from San Antonio we learned that our little band of 200 still maintained their situation in the Alamo. Santa Anna is there himself and has there and in the vicinity at least 6000 troops — Contrary to the expectation of every one he has invaded the Country when least expected. Not a Texan was in the field, not has even one yet made his appearance at this post.

San Antonio I fear has fallen before this; from its situation and construction, I cannot believe it possible so small a band could maintain it against such fearful odds . . . D. Crockett is one of the number of the fort . . . we are expecting an attack hourly.

We have just learned from Washington that they have declared independence. If such be the fact of which I have no doubt, we must whip the Mexicans. For young men who wish to acquire distinction and fortune now is the time.[15]

George W. Hockley [memorandum]
BURNAM'S, COLORADO [river]: This day a letter was forwarded by return express from this place to Colonel C. Neill, commanding at Gonzales, ordering the original to be forwarded to Colonel Fannin, Commanding at Goliad, and a copy to be kept as follows: 'Colonel Fannin to march immediately with all his effective force (except one hundred and twenty men, to be left for the protection of his post), to co-operate with the command of Colonel Neill, at some point to be designated by him, to the relief to Colonel Travis, now in the Alamo. Colonel N. to recommend a route to Colonel F. from Goliad to the point of co-operation. Colonel F. to bring two light pieces of artillery, and no more; fifty muskets, with thirty to forty rounds ball cartridges

for each. Both to use immediate despatch — Colonel F. — with ten days provision.'

A letter to General Burleson, requesting him to unite with Colonel Neill in recommending the route — forming the battalion, or regiment, according to the number of troops at Gonzales.[16]

John S. Brooks to James Hagerty

FORT DEFIANCE: I have written to you several times since my arrival in Texas; but, as I have received no answer from you, I presume my letters have miscarried. An opportunity now occurs of forwarding to Matagorda, whence it will more probably be shipped to New Orleans, than the usual route, now infested by the enemy.

A brief retrospect of our heretofore bloodless campaign, will perhaps, be interesting to you. I write in great haste, and may possibly, omit events necessary to elucidate our conduct. Indeed, it is impossible within the compass of a single letter, to give you any idea of the manner in which our little army has been influenced by the policies of the Country; though most of them are strangers to it, and consequently unable to realize the motives, which actuate the different parties. — For Texas is not, as you would probably suppose, united, in the great struggle before her. Party spirit has taken a form even more malignant than she has assumed in the U. States; and to such an extent has domestic cavilling been carried, that the Council have deposed, impeached, and arrested the Governor, while he, by an official fiat, has dissolved the Council; and thus we see the striking anomaly of two Governors, created by different authorities, ruling the same country.

But, to return — On the 24th day of January 1836, the Georgia Battalion of Volunteers, in which I held a responsible office, sailed from the Brazos, under the command of J W Fannin, Jr. The object of this expedition was to take the City of Matamoros, to revolutionize the State of Tamaulipas, to form a nucleus, or point of rendezvous for volunteers from the U. States, to harass the enemy at sea, to relieve ourselves from the burden of the war by carrying it out of the Country, and to give employment to the volunteers who had lately arrived. On the 4th day we arrived Copano, at the head of the Aransass Bay, where we debarked, and landed our stores, munitions, and artillery. After a days march, we pitched our tents at the Mission of Refugio, in Mr. Power's grant, and remained for a few days, in order to make cartridges and prepare our artillery, which was defective, for service. In the mean time, the scout who had been sent ahead, returned with information, that Santa Ana had already commenced the concentration of his army on our frontiers. They were rendezvousing at Matamoros, Monclova, Saltillo, Montery, and Laredo, to the number of from 6 to 10000 men, and designed attacking Bexar and Goliad simultaneously, with two divisions of his army and marching the third between those points to San Felipe, where he intended fortifying. We immediately apprised Government of these facts, and fell back to Goliad with our small force of 450 men, and commenced repairing the Fort. Bexar was garrisoned by 150 or 200 men; and with this handful of 6 or 700 Volunteers, we are left by the generous Texians, to roll back the tide of invasion from their soil.

On the 23rd ult. the Mexican advance, reached Bexar, and attacked the subsequent morning with 1800 men. The gallant little garrison retired to the Alamo, a fortress in the suburbs, resolved to hold out to the last. The Mexicans made several assaults, and were repulsed with loss at every instance. On the receipt of the intelligence at Goliad, we promptly marched with 320 men and four pieces of artillery. While consulting on what course to pursue, we received news of the successive defeats of the parties of Cols. Johnson and Grant, in Tamaulipas, and of the approach of the lower division Of Santa Ana's army on our position in Goliad. A council of War was held in the bushes, and it was determined to return to the post we had vacated in the morning, as its abandonment would leave the road open to the settlements, and completely uncover our depot of provisions, the only one now in Texas, and consequently the main stay of the Army.

The Mexicans, to the number of 700, are now in San Patricio, about 60 miles in front of our position; and another party of 200 have been discovered within 18 miles of us, between us and Gonzales. Every thing indicates that an attack will be speedily made upon us. Their scouts, well mounted, frequently push up to our walls, and, from the want of horses, we are unable to punish them.

We have again heard from Bexar, Santa Ana has arrived there himself, with 3000 men, making his whole force 4800. He has erected a battery within 400 yards of the Alamo, and every shot goes through it, as the walls are weak. It is feared that Bexar will be taken and that the devoted courage of the brave defenders will be of no avail.

We have had no bread, for several days. I am nearly naked, without shoes, and without money. We suffer much, and as soon as Bexar falls, we will be surrounded by 6000 infernal Mexicans. But we are resolved to die under the walls rather than surrender.

You shall hear from me again as soon as possible.

I am acting Aid-de-camp to the Commander-in-Chief, with the rank of Lieutenant. The Express is anxious to start, and I am compelled to close this letter, unfinished.

Independence has probably been declared. We are in a critical situation. I will die like a soldier.

Farewell,
John S. Brooks[17]

John Cross to My Dear Brother and Sister
FORT DEFIANCE: From the name of the place and being in a manner surrounded by a treacheous and bloody foe you may think I have little time to devote to private feelings or friends. However, I will steal a few minutes to write to those I love. You may perhaps wonder what could induce me to engage in this war at this advanced age, but I will explain my motives and sanction or condemn as your feelings may prompt you.

To begin then, I had business to transact in Nashville, Tenn . . . two days after my arrival on the 27th of December a committee was appointed to wait on me as one of the oldest members of the lodge with a request that I attend and assist at the installation of new officers which I did . . . and was informed that on Tuesday there was to be a meeting to assist the cause of Texas . . . of course, I attended. When money was liberally given the Proclamation was read and an appeal to all true patriots to join them and some appropriate speeches were made tending to touch the feelings, when Lo, my heart responded to the call and I found as Burns says "My mother's Highland blood rising in my veins and rushing like a torrent through my heart." . . . I immediately enrolled my name as a volunteer and many followed my example I knew if I was killed they could not rob me of my years and if it pleased God that I should survive I should have a sufficient quantity of the richest land in the world situated in a healthy, lovely climate for all my nephews who would settle it. On land that will raise from 1 1/2 to 2 bales of cotton to the acre, as I shall get one league of land which I shall lay on a river. A league consists of 4444 acres and then I will get 800 in another grant and when the struggle is over there will be thousands of rich planters from all parts flock in with their negroes and cash which will enhance the value of land to an enormous price. We are about 100 miles below the town of San Antonio, where there is a fort of about 20 pieces of artillery and we have at present about 200 men surrounded by 6000 Mexicans supposed to be commanded by Santa Anna himself, and I am sorry to say the citizens are very backward in turning out as they ought to do, but trust in the volunteers entirely. Santa Anna made several tremendous attacks on the little spartan band but they always kill as many with their cannon and rifles as takes their enemies the next day to bury them. We have about 500 men and a large force is close to us. Their advance guard is at St. Patricia, or in english, St. Patrick, but let me come, we are determined only to surrender our liberty with our lives as they murdered their prisoners in cold blood. This may be the last you will hear of me although it may please God to conduct me safely through. Then I will see you all again in this life.

There is a super abundance of cattle and horses in this country

and some tame and some wild. For instance, I can if I wish to
breed my own horses, I can buy for $100, a stud of horses
consisting of 20 mares and one stallion, but through this country
is an abundance of game. I would have paid the postage of this
but I am under a compliment to get it carried by a Capt. to New
Orleans. I have joined the artillery as I found but very few who
understood it. If you should think enough of me to answer this
by directing to me in Capt. Westover's company of Artillery in
the army of Texas and pay 25 cts. but to conclude accept my love
and give my love to all sisters and brothers and all my relatives
and friends. An express has just arrived that the enemy is
advancing in haste.[18]

Your affectionate brother,
John Cross[19]

Thursday, March 10, 1836
FALL PLUS 4 DAYS

Almonte Diary Entry
*Thursday — Day broke mild, but soon the cold north wind com-
menced blowing, through with clear weather. The cavalry under
command of General Andrade came in. They were quartered in the
Alamo. The Commissary and the Treasury of the Army arrived.*[20]

Wm. Fairfax Gray Diary Entry
*WASHINGTON; The business of the Convention moves slowly. The
Constitution is on tapis every day. It is a good one, on the whole, but
clumsily put together, indifferent in arrangement, and worse in
grammar.*
*No news yet from the Alamo, and much anxiety is felt for the fate
of the brave men their. It is obvious they must be surrounded and all
communications with them cut off.*[21]

James C. Neill to General Sam Houston
GONZALES: I have received with great satisfaction your
communication of the 9th inst . . . I shall forward your communications to Colonel Fannin by express, agreeably to your
instructions, giving him due time to concentrate his forces with
mine at the time and place I shall designate.[22]

E. Thomas to Father
GOLIAD: . . . we are 500 strong in the fort and 200 strong in the
town. Santa Ana has 5,000 troops at San Antone, 100 miles from
here and we expect him daily . . . Davy Crockett and James
Bowie are fighting like Tigers 200 Americans are in the fort
against 5,000 troops and Santa Ana at the head the fort is the

strongest in the world they have thrown 2,000 bums and not kild
a single American but 3 wounded 1,800 mexicans are Laying on
the field Dead it is a Real landed fact Santa Ana comes to a
parley Every half our and sends a flag of truse to Carry his Dead
it takes 12 mexicans to whip 1 American they are old convicts
Presd to fight they have to whip them to fight I like Texas better
Every Day wild horses plenty mustangs

Land here is so rich you can raise cotton sugar tobacco anything at all They turn the cattle out for 2 or 3 months an they
come home fat

Independence has been declared. Land Speculators falls

Optimistic about Bexar; Santa Anna hourly calls for truce

E. Thomas
Death or Victory[23]

General Jose Urrea Diary Entry

*I received news that the enemy had changed its plan and was making
ready to march with 400 men, to the aid of those who were besieged
by our army in the fortress of the Alamo. I countermarched to San
Patricio and ordered the cavalry to make ready to fight the enemy on
the march.*[24]

John S. Brooks to My Dear Father

FORT DEFIANCE: I wrote to Mother and to Mary Ann a few
days since; but, as the route over which the Government's
courier, who carried the letters, must have passed has been
infested by advanced parties of the enemy, it is possible they
have been intercepted; and, as an officer will be sent to
Matagorda to morrow, I have concluded to write again.

In the letters referred to, and some others I have previously
written, I gave a brief detail of the events of our campaign up to
this period. As some of these epistles, must have reached their
destination, I will not again trouble you with a narration of
incidents, which I presume, are familiar to you.

A party of 70 men, under the joint command of Col's. Grant
and Johnson, has been in Temaulipas, for the purpose of
acquiring information, as to the designs of the enemy, ever since
the fall of Bexar in December last. They had taken from 2 to 300
horses, for the use of the army; and were gradually retiring on
this post, when half the party, with Col. Johnson at its head, was
attacked by about 200 of the enemy, and totally defeated. Six,
among whom was their leader, escaped. Capt. Pearson, and two
others were inhumanly butchered, after they had surrendered.
They, of course, lost all their horses and arms. The party under
col. Grant, were attacked between 8 and 9 o'clock in the morning. They were bringing on a large herd of horses, and in their
attempt to save them, and, at the same time, fight the enemy,

who amounted to 150, they were cut to pieces. Five only escaped. col. Grant was either killed on the ground, or now is a prisoner. Scarcely had the intelligence of these disasters to our advance in Tampaulipas reached us, when we were informed by express, that the Mexicans had entered Bexar with an effective force of 1800 men. The garrison there consisted of 156 Americans, who retreated, on the approach of the enemy to the Alamo, a spanish fortress in the neighborhood, which was immediately invested, and has been vigorously besieged up to the date of our latest intelligence.

Immediately on receipt of the news we promptly took up the line of march, in order to relieve them. After proceeding three miles,[25] several baggage wagons broke down; and it was found impossible, to get the ammunition carts or artillery over the river San Antonio. We accordingly halted. During the night our oxen strayed off. In the morning a council of War was convened. While it was in session, a courier apprised us, that 650 of the enemy, the same, probably, who had defeated Grant and Johnson, had reached San Patricio on the Neuces and would attack our depot of provisions on the La Baca, and at Matagorda. With these facts before us, it was concluded to return to Goliad, and maintain that place, which was done.

Thirty two men have cut their way into the Alamo, with some provisions. The enemy have erected a battery of nine pounders within 400 yards of the fort, and every shot goes through the walls. A large party of the enemy are between this and Bexar, with a design of cutting off reinforcements. another division of 3000 Mexicans have arrived at Bexar, making their whole force now more than 4800 men. The little garrison still holds out against this formidable force. It is said that Santa Ana is himself with the army before the Alamo.

It is said that Santa Anna designs driving all the Americans beyond Sabine. We have just been advised that he intends detaching 1000 men from Bexar, to form a junction with the 650 at San Patricio, and then reduce this place. We have 450 men here, and twelve pieces of small artillery. We have strengthened the fort very much; and he will find it difficult with his 1650 men to drive us from our post.

We are hourly anticipating an attack, and preparing for it. We are short of provisions, and that is now our deadliest foe. Unless we are soon supplied, we can not hold out much longer. We have had no bread for some time. We suffer much from the want of shoes and clothing.

Excuse this hasty letter. I have just returned from a weary and unsuccessful march in pursuit of a party of Mexicans, who appeared a few miles from this place.

I have not heard from home since I have been in Texas, and I am at a loss to account for your silence.

The Convention, which met the first of this month, it is rumored, have declared Texas independent. No official or authentic information, however has come to hand.

You shall hear from me again as soon as possible.

Your affectionate son,
John S. Brooks

P.S. I have neither clothes nor money to buy them. The government furnishes us with nothing, — not even ammunition. I have written nearly twenty letters home, all of them unanswered.

Brooks[26]

Jos. B Tatom to Sister
GOLIAD: In haste I write you a few lines to inform you that I am in fine health and brother's is increasing. We (have been increased) with eight more volenteer Companies, the whole amounting to five Hundred men and forted at Goliad and expect an attack daily. San Antone was attacked Sixteen days ago. The mexican forces are between five & Six thousand strong, ours were one hindred & fifty I believe they have been reinforced by about fifty malitia making two hundred men they are in the Alamo which is a strong Garrison they were attacked on the 20 February early in the morning and the firing has not yet ceased for one moment They have thrown 2 thousand bomb shells into the Allomo and cannonaded it continual though they have not yet even wounded an american The conveniences of writing are So bad that I must stop. . . .

Your Brother,
Jos. B. Tatom

The slaughter among the mexican have been great Some hundreds.[27]

Friday, March 11, 1836
FALL PLUS 5 DAYS

Almonte Diary Entry
Friday — Day pleasant, but somewhat windy. Gen'l Tolsa came in with the 3rd brigade, but the divisions of Sesma and Gonzales had already marched with four six pounders and one howitzer. Marches detailed being 9 days to Goliad, 5 to Gonzales and 14 to San Felipe.[28]

Wm. Fairfax Gray Diary Entry
WASHINGTON: Nothing of interest to-day, in Convention. Intrigues for the high office of State are said to be going on, much log rolling on the land issue.

Among the persons attracted by the convention is David G. Burnett, one of the Empressarios of this country, who is spoken of as the President. He is said to be an honest, good man, but I doubt his ability for such a station.[29]

L. Ayer's Journal Entry
GOLIAD: A council of officers were held this morning in consequence of an express arriving from Gonzales with another call for assistance to be rendered to the brave defenders of the Alamo I understand three hundred men will march there tomorrow. I should have stated 4 day since that it has been decided to march with 300 men to San Patricio which expedition had failed for the same reason as the first for Bexar all the volunteers insisted on going in the expedition.[30]

Sam Houston to J. W. Fannin, Commanding in Goliad
HEADQUARTERS, GONZALES Sir: On my arrival here this afternoon, the following intelligence was received through a Mexican, supposed to be friendly though his account has been contradicted in some parts by another, who arrived with him. It is therefore only given to you as a rumor, though I fear a melancholy portion of it will be found true.

Anselmo Bergara states that he left the Alamo on Sunday, the 6th inst; and is three days from Arroche's rancho; that the Alamo was attacked on Sunday morning at the dawn of day, by about two thousand three hundred men, and carried a short time before sunrise, with a loss of five hundred and twenty-one Mexican killed and as many wounded. Colonel Travis had only one hundred and fifty effective men out of his entire force of one hundred eighty seven. After the fort was carried, seven men surrendered, and called for Santa Anna and quarter. They were murdered by his order. Colonel Bowie was sick in bed, and also murdered. The enemy expect a reinforcement of fifteen hundred men under General Condelle, and a reserve of fifteen hundred to follow them. He also informs us that Ugartechea had arrived with two millions of specie for the payment of the troops. The bodies of the Americans were burnt after the massacre. Alternate layers of wood and bodies were laid together and set on fire. Lieutenant Dickenson, who had a wife and child in the fort, after having fought with desperate courage, tied his child to his back and leaped from the top of a two story building. Both were killed by the fall.

I have little doubt the Alamo has fallen whether above particulars are all true may be questionable. You are therefore referred to the enclosed order.

P.S. In corroboration of the truth of the fall of the Alamo, I have ascertained that colonel Travis intended firing signal guns at three different periods of each day until succor should arrive. No signal guns have been heard since Sunday, though a scouting party have just returned who approached within twelve miles of it, and remained there forty eight hours.[31]

Sam Houston to Colonel J. W. Fannin, Commanding in Goliad
HEADQUARTERS, GONZALES: Sir: You will, as soon as practical after receipt of this order, fall back upon Guadalupe Victoria, with your command, and such artillery as can be brought with expedition. The remainder will be sunk in the river. You takes the necessary measures for the defense of Victoria, and forward one third the number of your effective men to this point, and remain in command until further orders.[32]

Every facility is to be afforded to women and children who may be desirous of leaving that place. Previous to abandoning Goliad, you will take the necessary measures to blow up that fortress; and do so before leaving its vicinity. The immediate advance of the enemy may be confidently expected, as well as a rise of water. Prompt movement are therefore highly important.

Sam Houston Commander-in-Chief of the Army[33]

Barsena et al Deposition
GONZALES: Examination of Andrew Barsena and Ansolma Bergara.

Andrea Barsena, says that last Saturday night Anselmo Bergara arrived at the rancho of Don Jose Flores, where he who declares was and that Bergara informed him that his mother had solicited him Bergara to take her son if he could find him to the Colorado River to avoid the military who was gathering up all they could and making soldiers of them.

Antonio Peres left the rancho of Don Jose Ma. Arocha on Sunday morning last and returned in the evening with the notice that the soldiers of Santa Anna had that morning entered the Alamo and killed all the men that was inside and that he saw about 500 of the Mexicans soldiers that had been killed and so many wounded.

Bergara landed at the rancho Saturday evening and gave no notice of the fall of the Alamo, but that Antonio Peres brought the news to the rancho that Musquiz had advised him to leave as it was not prudent for him to remain.

Antonio Peres was called to Bejar by Don Louisiana Navarro for the purpose of sending him to Gonzales with a letter calling all Mexicans to come forward and present themselves to the President to receive there pardon and enter on their own proper pursuits. Antonio refused to come unless Santa Anna would give a passport which could not then be obtained but was promised in three or four days and that on tomorrow if he (Antonio) comes he will leave the rancho for this place. Genl'l Cos entered Bejar with 700 men (so says Bergara)[34]

James W. Fannin to General Mexia

HEADQUARTERS ARMY OF TEXAS, FT. DEFIANCE: Dr. Genl. I avail myself of the politeness of Capt. Guerra (a soldier of 1824) who feels himself bound to retire from our services for reasons which will be apparent to you.

I am pleased to say of him and his men, that since they have been under my command, each and every one has done his duty — and owing to his and their particular situation, and political aspect of this newborn nation, so widely different from what it was when they entered its service; I have this day given them an Honorable discharge, with permission and passport to proceed to N. Orleans &c.

We are in the midst of a revolution the ending whereof, no one can foresee. Sa. Anna with 5000 men are in Bejar, and have been since 23rd. ult., but has not been able to take the Alamo defended by only 146 men. If he does not get it in four days, he never will, as the people en masse are on their march to the relief of their friends — and in all this month, we will not have less than from 4 to 5000 Texicans under arms.

If 216 could & did take Bejar, how many of Sa. Annas men will be left him, should this force encounter him ?? I know not as yet what has been the action of the Convention — but do not entertain a doubt but a declaration of Independence will follow shortly. This my dear sir will not interfere with your favourite project. You can go ahead with more safely, and may calculate upon aid from Texas — and her Volunteers.

I know not how long I may remain in the service — circumstances unexpected and over which I had no control, have placed me, where I cannot retreat, but in disgrace. This I am not disposed to suffer — rather preferring to encounter death in any shape. If I had men, over whom I could exercise reasonable authority, I should glory in the present opportunity as I should most certainly do myself some credit, and the country great service, and teach Genl. Sa. Anna a lesson, which he might remember, and the states of Mexico profit by.

I hope I may be in it, as it is — and that I may hear from you to the west, waging battle for your injuried and oppressed countrymen.

J. W. Fannin, Jr.[35]

T. Green to Burnley

WASHINGTON D.C.: It is true The Mexican minister has come to sell Texas to the U. States and I have no doubt the sale will be made. Santa Anna is willing to take even less than we are willing to give . . . The Settlers rights — each to 4428 acres — and all secure — so will be the larger grants when the terms are complied with . . . *communicate this to our friends. It is certain Texas will be ceded and perhaps in a few days or weeks*[36]

Gray to - [unknown]

GONZALES: At 4 - O'clock, this afternoon, Anselmo Bergara and Andrew Bargarra, came to this town with the disagreeable intelligence of the taking of the Alamo by General Santa Anna. The event is related in the following manner: — On Saturday night, the 5th of the present month, he marched his infantry under the walls, and surrounded them with cavalry, to prevent escape in case they should attempt to fly. At daybreak on Sunday morning he planted his ladders, which were carried by the infantry, against the sides of the four walls, and carried the place by assault, with great loss of infantry. All within the Fort perished. Seven of them were killed by order of Santa Anna when in the act of giving up their arms. Travis killed himself. And Bowie was killed while lying sick in bed.

All of the above is derived from what was told to Bergara by D[illegible] on Sunday night when he, Bergara, went in from the country. It must be understood that Bergara remained at large in Bejar thirteen days after the entrance of Santa Anna, and walked about undisturbed by him all that time.

Barcena says that Bergara came to the rancho of my father-in-law, on Saturday night, before the entrance of the troops into the walls, and that he knows nothing about it — only what was told by Antonio [Peres?] had been called by D. L. on Sunday in the night, who said that he had been in the battle, — that 521 of the infantry were killed and as many more badly wounded.

The contradiction of these two men makes me suspect that they are spys sent by Santa Anna; — because, why should Bergarra fly from Bejar after remaining so many days there undisturbed and enjoying himself?

E. N. Gray[37]

Saturday, March 12, 1836
FALL PLUS 6 DAYS

Almonte Diary Entry

Saturday — Day broke mild — became windy — but clear and temperate. We consumed many fish. Sesma wrote from El Salaldo, giving the details — Romero likewise. The troops were reviewed in the afternoon in the square.[38]

Wm. Fairfax Gray Diary Entry

WASHINGTON: Weather warm and pleasant. No intelligence yet from the Alamo, nor from Houston. . . .[39]

Sam Houston to Captain Phillip Dimmit

HEADQUARTERS: You are ordered with your command to this place — bring all your disposable force — and, should there be any companies, or troops, at Victoria, whose services are not indispensable to the present emergencies of that section of the frontier, you will notify that it is my order that they forthwith repair to this point. Colonel Fannin is ordered to fall back on Victoria, after blowing up La Bahia. You will send expresses to headquarters as often as practicable.

Unofficial,
I am induced to believe from all the facts communicated to us that the Alamo has fallen, and all our men are *murdered*. We must not depend on Forts; the roads, and ravines suit us best.[40]

Telegraph, and Texas Register

SAN FELIPE: Capt. Bird, with a company of sixty volunteers from the different settlements with a good baggage wagon, marched from this place on Monday last to the westward; half of the company being mounted.

The citizens of the jurisdiction of Washington, are, we are told, turning out almost to a man for the relief of Col. Travis and his brave associates in Bejar.

It is reported that Col. Johnson's party, who went to the west, were surprised, and all, with the exception of himself and two or three others, killed by the Mexicans. Col Grant is not heard of.

We learn that Gen'l Houston left Washington on Saturday last, for the purpose of repairing forthwith to the seat of war. No general has ever had more to do. At this time, like the turn out last fall, our citizens are rushing to the field, without any other officer than a captain. We believe, however, that an organization will be speedily effected

---

under the direction of Gen'l Houston, whose experience renders him eminently qualified in the discharge of so arduous a duty; and it is hoped, that every officer and private will contribute every aid in promoting that organization so indispensable to our very existence. And we trust that our citizens at home will not presume to give orders to our army in the field, or lay out plans for the commander-in-chief. Let us suppose that he on the spot, knows better the plan of attack than those in the chimney corner.

Intelligence has just reached this place, that there is a French company at the mouth of the Brazos, consisting of 100 men, and about 150 others, making say 250 men, who have come to our assistance in the present struggle; and report says there are 2 or 300 more at the mouth of the Mississippi and in New Orleans, who are on their way.

We understand that Major Hampt Norton, who has recently returned to this country from the United States, and who, in the city of New York, was presented with a splendid sword, to be given by him to a volunteer in the cause of Texas, who should wield it in defense of her rights and independence, has presented the same to Captain U. Bullock, of the Georgia volunteers. Captain Bullock, on receiving it, pledged himself to sacrifice his last heart's blood before he would yield it to the enemy.

Sunday, March 13, 1836
FALL PLUS 7 DAYS

Almonte Diary Entry
*Sunday — Day clear but windy. Heard Mass in the square. Very warm in the afternoon. Thermometer 85 degrees. Nothing particular.*41

Wm. Fairfax Gray Diary Entry
WASHINGTON: No intelligence yet from the Alamo. The anxiety begins to be intense. Mr. Badgett and Dr. Goodrich, members of the Convention, have brothers there, and Mr. Grimes, another member, has a son there.

*Zavala expresses the belief that in twelve months he will be in Mexico. He thinks that Santa Anna's race is nearly run; that a revolution will take place in Mexico, and the liberal party will be in the ascendency; that he is the most popular man of that party, and he thinks he will be called to head it. The seeds of ambition are not yet extinct in him, and vanity is his weak side.*42

Sam Houston to James Collinsworth,
Chairman of the Military Committee
HEADQUARTERS, GONZALES I have the honor to report to
you my arrival at this place on the 11th inst, at about four o'clock
P.M. I found upward of three hundred men in camp, without
organization, and who had rallied on the first impulse. Since
then the force has increased to more than four hundred. I have
ordered their organization at ten o'clock this morning; and hope
to complete it, and prepare to meet the enemy.

The enclosed statement[43] which came here a few moments
after my arrival, has induced me to adopt a course very different
from that which I intended before the information was received.
The enclosed order to Colonel Fannin will indicate to you my
convictions, that, with our small, unorganized force, we can not
maintain sieges in fortresses, in the country of the enemy. Troops
pent up in forts are rendered useless; nor is it possible that we
can ever maintain our cause by such a policy. The want of
supplies and men, will insure the success of our enemies.

The conduct of our brave men in the Alamo was only equalled
by Sparton valor.

I am informed Colonel Fannin had about seven hundred men
under his command; and, at one time, had taken up the line of
march for the Alamo, but the breaking down of a wagon induced
him to fall back, and abandon the idea of marching to the relief
of our last hope in Bexar. Since then he has written letters here,
indicating a design to march upon San Patricio, and also the
occupation of Copano, So I am at a loss to know where my
express will find him. From the colorado I forwarded, by this
place, an express to him to meet me, with all his disposable
force, on the west side of the Cibolo, with a view to relieve
Bexar. The news of the fall of Bexar, corroborated by so many
circumstances, compelled me to change my plan, as the enclosed
order will indicate. On seeing the various communications of
Colonel Fannin at this point, I could not rely on any co-operation from him. The force under my command here was such as
to preclude the idea of my meeting the enemy — supposing their
force not to exceed the lowest estimate which has ever been
made of it. My reason for delaying my despatch until the
present, was, the assurance of Captain Seguin, that two men had
been sent by him to his rancho, and would return on last night.
They have not returned; and the belief is, that they have been
taken by the enemy, or deserted. I am using all my endeavors to
get a company to send in view of the Alamo; and if possible,
arrive at the certainty of what all believe — its fall. The scarcity
of horses, and the repulse of a party of twenty-eight men, the
other day, within eighteen miles of Bexar, will, I apprehend,
prevent the expedition.

This moment Deaf Smith and Henry Karnes have assured me,that they will proceed in sight of Bexar; and return within three days. The persons, whose statement is enclosed for your information, are in custody; I will detain them, for the present as spies.

I beg leave to suggest the great importance of fortification on Live-Oak point and Copano, and the defence of Matagorda and Lavaca bays.

You must rest assured that I shall adopt and pursue such course of conduct as the present emergencies of the country require, and as the means placed at my disposal may enable me to do, for the defence of the country and the protection of its inhabitants.

The projected expedition to Matamoros, under the agency of the council has already cost us over two hundred and thirty seven lives; and where the effects are to end, none can foresee. Doctor Grant's party, as well as Colonel Johnson's, have been murdered. Major Morris, as reported. was struck down with a lance, while gallantly fighting. Doctor Grant surrendered, and was tied by the enemy. Be pleased to send all possible aids to the army; and keep an eye to the coast.

Intelligence from the seat of government, if favorable, has a most happy effect upon the spirits of the men. Frequent expresses sent to me, may be highly beneficial to the army. I fear La Bahia (Goliad) is in siege.

Sam Houston[44]

Sam Houston to Henry Raguet

GONZALES: On the 11th Inst I reached this place assured that I would find 700 men — only the rise of 300 unorganized were on the Ground — since then my force has increased to near 500.

A few moments after my arrival the awful news of the fall of the Alamo reached us. A statement will be forwarded from Washington with the last of the facts. Our dear Bowie, as is now understood, unable to get out of bed, shot himself as the soldiers approached. Despalier, Parker, and others, when all hope was lossed followed his example. Travis, 'tis said, rather than fall into the hand of the enemy, stabbed himself.

Our spies have been driven back from within 12 miles of Bexar. They heard none of the previously concerted signals, which were to be given by our friends: all was silent, as they report. I will send two spies in a few minutes to view Bexar, and they will report in 3 days.

Colonel Fannin should have relieved our brave men in the Alamo. He had 430 men with artillery under his command, and had taken the line of march with a full knowledge of the situation of those in the Alamo, and owing to the breaking down of a wagon abandoned the march, returned to Goliad and left our Spartans to their fate.

We are now compelled to take post on the east side of the Guadalupe, and make battle if the enemy should press upon us. I am informed that Fannin has upward of 700 men now under his commands. I have ordered Goliad to be blown up and if possible, prevent all future murders where our men have no alternative but to starve in forts, or remain inactive, and useless to the defence of the country. With our force we cannot fight the enemy ten to one, in their own country where they have every advantage. It is reported and I do believe that (Labard) or Ybarbo, who has lately been at San Antonio de Bexar, has gone on to incite the Indians in the neighborhood of Nacogdoches. Keep an eye to this, but be prudent. Arouse our friends in the States.

I would have sent the express as soon as I heard the news from the Alamo, but was assured that two spies are now out, but hourly expected in, on whose statement I might place unbounded reliance as to the fate of the Alamo. The conduct of the general Council and that of their "Agent," has already cost us the lives of more then 230 men. Had it not been for that we should have kept all the advantages which we had gained. We must repair our losses by prudence and valour. I have no doubt as to the issue of the contest. I am in good spirits! tho not ardent ! ! !

Susanna Dickinson, one of the few Alamo survivors.

Johnson & Grant parties are cut off. The enemy at the Alamo are said to have lossed 521 killed and an equal number wounded. Murdered americans, 187. . . . Three Negroes and Ms Dickinson were all in the fort who escaped massacre as reported! Several Mexicans in the fort were also murdered. and all killed in the fort were burned: The Mexicans killed in the assault were buried — This is the report of the matter in substance!

Tell the Red landers to awaken and aid in the struggle!

Salute affectionately your family with Dr. Porter's and all friends. Write to me.

Sam Houston

P.S. Our force tomorrow, I hope, will be 600 men. I am in great haste — will Major Allen join me? Let the People beware of [name obscured] and [name deleted] ! ! ! They are enemies to Texas and Liberty. Be vigilant! Major Hockley salutes yourself and family. I send a paper to your care.

Houston[45]

General Jose Urrea Diary Entry
I marched towards Goliad and was informed enroute that the enemy had dispatched a strong detachment to occupy the port of Copano and that they would halt at Refugio Mission[46]

Monday, March 14, 1836
FALL PLUS 8 DAYS

Almonte Diary Entry
Monday — Cloudy and windy, and warm — Weather cleared and the wind abated a little. The correspondence from Mexico, Monterey and Matamoras was received, and a despatch from Gen'l Urrea stating that he would be at Goliad the 14th, that is to-day. — Orders to march were issued to the battalion of Tres Villas.[47]

Wm. Fairfax Gray Diary Entry
WASHINGTON: No intelligence yet from the Alamo. The weather is gloomy and warm, indicating rain.

Conrad to-day introduced a series of resolutions, giving large bounties to the volunteers. It is necessary to conciliate the military, and scarcely anything that they can ask will be refused.[48]

General Jose Urrea Diary Entry
I arrived at the said mission [Refugio] at daybreak where I found the enemy in the church where they had taken refuge. The enemy opened a brisk fire upon our men.

According to the information I secured, the number of the enemy that had shut themselves in the church was 200 and they lacked water and supplies. This would make it imperative, unless they succeeded in escaping during the night, for them wither to come out and fight us the following day or surrender.[49]

Tuesday, March 15, 1836
FALL PLUS 9 DAYS

Almonte Diary Entry

Tuesday — Windy and warm. The battalion of Queretaro was ordered to march to Goliad, with one 12 pounder and corresponding munition. To-marrow the two battalions of Queretaro and Tres Villas will march. In the afternoon the courier was despatched to Gen'l Urrea. Accounts came from Gonzales by a Mexican that the Americans, in number 500 fled as soon as they heard of the taking of the Alamo and the approach of our troops, leaving their stores and many goods, and throwing two cannon in the water, &c.&c. This was Sunday in the afternoon. The same man said that the Convention had met at Washington and declared the independence of Texas. . . .[50]

Wm. Fairfax Gray Diary Entry

WASHINGTON: In the afternoon, while the convention was sitting, a Mr. Ainsworth, from Columbia, arrived and brought news that an attack had been made on the Alamo, which was repulsed with great loss to the enemy. The rumor was doubted, on account of the circuitous route by which it came. All hoped it true, but many feared the worst. In half an hour after an express was received from General Houston, bringing the sad intelligence of the fall of the Alamo, on the morning of the 6th. His letters were dated on the 11th and 13th, and a letter from Juan Seguin, at Gonzales, to Ruis and Navarro, brought the same account. Still some did, or affected to, disbelieve it.[51]

Sam Houston to James Collinsworth,
Chairman of Military Committee

Since I had the honor to address you from Gonzales, the lady of Lieutenant Dickenson, who fell at the Alamo, has arrived and confirms the fall of that place, and the circumstances, pretty much as my express detailed them. She returned in company with two negroes — one the servant of Colonel Travis, the other a servant of Colonel Almonte. They both corroborate the statement first made and forwarded to you. Other important intelligence arrived at Gonzales — that the army of Santa Anna had encamped at the Cibolo on the night of the 11th inst., after a march of twenty-four miles that day. The army was to encamp on the 12th at Sandy, and proceed direct to Gonzales. The number of the enemy could not be ascertained, but was represented as exceeding two thousand infantry. Upon this statement of facts, I deemed it proper to fall back and take post on the Colorado, near Burnhams's which is fifteen miles distant from this point. My morning report, on my arrival in camp, showed three hundred and seventy-four effective men, without two days' provisions, many without arms, and others without any ammunition. We could have met the enemy, and avenged some of the wrongs; but, detached as we were, without supplies for the men in camp, of either provisions, ammunition, or artillery, and remote from succor, it would have been madness to hazard a contest. I had been in camp two days only, and had succeeded in organizing the troops. But they had not been taught the first principles of the drill. If starved out, and the camp once broken up, there was no hope for the future. By falling back, Texas can rally, and defeat any force that can come against her.

I received the intelligence of the enemy's advance between eight and nine o'clock at night; and, before twelve, we were on the march in good order, leaving behind a number of spies, who remained and were reinforced next morning by a number of volunteers and brave spirits from Pecan creek. H. Karnes, R. E. Handy, and Captain Chenowith, have been very active. Only about twenty persons deserted the camp (from the first sensation produced by the intelligence) up to this time. I intend desertion shall not be frequent; and I regret to say that I am compelled to regard as deserters all who have left camp without leave; to demand their apprehension and that, whenever arrested, they be sent to me at headquarters for trial. They have disseminated throughout the frontier such exaggerated reports, that they have produced dismay and consternation among the people to a most distressing extent.

I do not apprehend the immediate approach of the enemy upon the present settlements; I mean those on the Colorado, for the country west of it is an uninhabited waste. This season the grass refuses to grow on the prairies.

When the approach of the enemy was known, there was but two public wagons and two yoke of oxen in camp, and the few horses we had were very poor. I hope to reach the Colorado on to-morrow, and collect an army in a short time. I sent my aide-de-camp, Major William T. Austin, to Columbia this morning, for munitions and supplies, to be sent me immediately; and to order the troops now at Velasco to join me, provided they had not been previously ordered by you to fortify Copano and Dimit's Landing. I am fearful Goliad is besieged by the enemy. My order to colonel Fannin, directing the place to be blown up, the cannon to be sunk in the river, and to fall back on Victoria, would reach him before the enemy could advance. That they have advanced upon the place in strong force, I have no doubt; and when I heard of the fall of the Alamo, and the number of the enemy, I knew it must be the case.

Our forces must not be shut up in forts, where they can neither be supplied with men nor provisions. Long aware of this fact, I directed, on the 16th of January last, that the artillery should be removed and the Alamo blown up; but it was prevented by the expedition upon Matamoras, the author of all our misfortunes.

I hope that our crusiers on the gulf will be active, and that Hawkins and _____ may meet the notice of the government. Let the men of Texas rally to the Colorado!

Enclosed you will receive the address of General Santa Anna sent by a negro to the citizens. It is in Almonte's handwriting. Santa Anna was in Bexar when the Alamo was taken. His force in all, in Texas is, I think, only five or six thousand men — though some say thirty thousand! This can not be true. Encourage volunteers from the United States — but I am satisfied we can save the country. Had it not been for the council, we would have had no reserves. We must have the friendship of the Comanches and other Indians.

Gonzales is reduced to ashes!

Sam Houston, Commanding General[52]

John Sturat to General Sam Houston

FORT COFFEE: Dear General, I have your rifle and will send it to you by the first safe opportunity. Capt. Dodge brought it to me about a week ago, he has mended the old stock, not being able to make a new one — your dog is at fort Gibson. . . .

A report has reached this country, that yourself and Col. Bowie, have both, from some whim of the authority of Texas been removed from office, but the report is not believed.[53]

Benj. Briggs Goodrich to Edmund Goodrich

WASHINGTON, TEXAS: Texas is in mourning, and it becomes my painful duty to inform my relations in Tennessee of the massacre of my poor brother John. He was murdered in the Texas fortress of San Antonio de Bexar (known as the Alamo) on the night[54] of the 6th of this month, together with one hundred and eighty of our brave countrymen, gallantly defending that place against an invading army of Mexicans, eight thousand strong; not one escaped to tell the dreadful tale. The Alamo had been surrounded for many days by a besieging party at from 3 to 8 thousand men, commanded by Genl. Lopez de Santa Anna in person; the fortress, as before stated, was besieged, and it fell and every man was put to the sword. They effected their purpose by a general charge aided by scaling ladders. Upward of five hundred of the enemy were killed and as many more mortally or dangerously wounded. Col. Travis, the commander of the fortress, sooner than fall into the hands of the enemy, stabbed himself to the heart and instantly died.

Seven of our brave men, being all that were left alive, called for quarter and to see Santa Anna, but were instantly shot by the order of the fiendish tyrant. Col. Bowie was murdered, sick in bed. Among the number of your acquaintances, murdered in the Alamo, were Col. David Crockett, Micajah Autry, formerly of Haysborough, John Hays, son of Andrew Hays of Nashville, and my unfortunate brother John C. Goodrich: but they died like men, and posterity will do them justice. Santa Anna is now in Texas with an invading army of eight or ten thousand men strong — determined to carry on a war of extermination. We will meet him and teach the unprincipled scoundrel that freeman can never be conquered by the hireling soldiery of a military despot.

The struggle is great and our difficulties many — but the army of the patriot is doubly nerved, when his friends and his liberties are invaded — We rush to combat, and our motto is Revenge, Liberty or Death. Approach our poor old mother cautiously with the awful news, for I fear her much worn out constitution will not survive the shock. — Publish this information if you think proper — We ask for help and in the name of everything that is sacred to Liberty and Independence.

So soon as the convention (of which I am a member) adjourns, I shall proceed forthwith to the army — The blood of a Goodrich has already crimsoned the soil of Texas and another victim shall be added to the list or I see Texas free and independent. —

Benj. Briggs Goodrich

P.S. News has just reached that the enemy are on their march to this place and we know not at what moment we shall be compelled to move our women and children beyond their reach. Their mode of warfare is strictly savage; they fight under a Red banner, and we ask nor expect no quarter in the future, — I will advise you from time to time (if alive) and would highly appreciate hearing from you. —

Goodrich[55]

General Jose Urrea Diary Entry

This day at dawn, as I approached the church [Refugio] I noticed the absence of the enemy and ordered the place to be occupied. Having reinforced the detachments that I had on the road to Goliad and El Copano, I ordered all the available cavalry to pursue the enemy. We killed sixteen and took thirty-one prisoners.[56]

Wednesday, March 16, 1836
FALL   PLUS   10   DAYS

Almonte Diary Entry

Accounts were received from Gen'l Rameriz — it was determined that Gen'l Tolsa should march with two battalions to Goliad, and he started at 3 o'clock P.M. It was also determined that I should join Sesma. Montoga left with two battalions for Goliad, to reach there in seven days. Wind continues.[57]

Council Hall, Washington

On Motion of Mr. Waller, an address to the people of the United States of America, was ordered to be prepared to accompany the letter of Sam Houston, Commander-In-Chief of the Army, &c. announcing the fall of the Alamo.

Mr. Carson asked that the rules be suspended, with leave to introduce the following resolution. Resolved: That Spies be immediately despatched under direction of this house, for the protection of this Convention and also; for the procuration of arms.[58]

TO THE

PEOPLE OF TEXAS

Fellow Citizens,

I have just received information by Col. William T. Austin of the fall of the Alimo, and massacre of our countrymen in that garrison. Goliad is attacked ere this and possibly has shared the fate of the Alimo. The enemy had advanced as far as Gonzales on the evening of the 14th, with a detachment of about 2000 Cavalry. Gen Houston is on the retreat to Brennam's on the Colorado with about 500 Infantry. Gen Santa Ana is at the head of the army which is at this time from 6 to 7000 strong, so says Mrs. Dickinson who was in the Alimo when it was stormed. John Seguin gives the same information. Gen Santa Anna is already advanced into he interior of our country. Our force in the field at this time does not exceed 1000.

The united action and exertion of all are now necessary to the salvation of Texas and the cause in which we are engaged. It is confidently expected that all will turn out and join the main body at Burnham's, or such other point as they occupy. All - all, must be satisfied of the necessity as well as importance of making a desperate defence in support of their lives, fortunes, and sacred liberty. It is confidently hoped that none, in this hour of trial and danger, will prove recreant, but, like men and freemen, maintain all at the point of the bayonet.

Committee room, San Felipe de Austin, March 16, 1836.

Attest,   Thomas Gay,
F. W. Johnson,   Committee
Edward Bailey,

Recreation of original broadside issued March 16, 1836.

Wm. Fairfax Gray Diary Entry

WASHINGTON: A Dr. Southerland [Sutherland] arrived this morning from Gonzales, who puts the intelligence of the fall of the Alamo beyond a doubt.

Some members are going home. Col. Parmer was authorized by resolution to press wagons, horses, etc. and to take possession of the public arms at Nacogdoches. Expresses and dispatches were sent off in different directions and authority given to move and provide for some defenseless families from the Colorado.

Great confusion and irregularity prevailed in the convention to-day. The President has lost all dignity and all authority. The house adjourned until to-morrow morning.

Frequent alarms were brought in during the night. Spies and patrols were ordered out; much excitement prevailed.[59]

General Jose Urrea Diary Entry

I marched with 200 men, infantry and cavalry, to Goliad. A messenger of Fannin was intercepted and we learned beyond all doubt that the enemy intended to abandon the fort at Goliad and concentrate its force to Refugio to execute this operation[60]

A. Briscoe to Editor, Red River Herald

Sir — Bexar has fallen! Its garrison was only 187 strong, commanded by lieut Col. W. Travis. After standing repeated attacks for two weeks and an almost constant cannonade and bombarding during that time, the last attack was made on the morning of the 6th inst. by upwards of 2000 men, under the command of Santa Anna in person; they carried the place about sunrise, with the loss of 520 men killed and about the same number wounded. After about an hour's fighting the whole garrison was put to death, (save the sick and wounded and seven men who asked for quarter) — all fought desperately, until entirely cut down; the rest were cooly murdered. The brave and gallant Travis, to prevent his falling into the hands of the enemy shot himself. Not an individual escaped, and the news is only known to us by a gentleman of Bexar, who came to our army at Gonzales — but from the cessation of Travis siege guns, there is no doubt of its truth. The declaration of independence you have no doubt received, and you will, in a few days, receive the constitution proposed by the republic.

Cols. James Bowie and David Crockett are among the slain — the first was murdered in his bed, to which he had been confined by illness — the later fell, fighting like a tiger. The Mexican army is estimated at 8000 men; it may be more or less.

A. Briscoe[61]

Thursday, March 17, 1836
FALL PLUS 11 DAYS

Almonte Diary Entry

A courier Extraordinary was despatched to Tolsa and Sesma, and to Matamoras; one for Mexico will start tomorrow; by it go my letters for Mexico and the United States; I could not start to-day, because the mules did not arrive in time.[62]

General Jose Urrea Diary Entry

I broke camp early in order to march to join the division that was coming from Bexar. I passed near Goliad and reconnoitered it from as close as possible. In the afternoon my advance guards notified me that the enemy was approaching and shortly after, a body of cavalry was seen advancing along the edge of a woods. I ordered Col Morales to go out and meet them. This operation was sufficient to make the enemy retreat.[63]

Council Hall, Washington

The Committee to whom was referred the Resolution to take into consideration the condition of the families compelled to retreat from beyond the San Antonio and Guadalupe to seek protection from their fellow countrymen to the East, beg leave to report as follows:

That there are a number of families who have been compelled to retreat into the Colonies to the East, and many of them unable to provide for themselves.

Resolved, therefore; that any contracting or other agent of the Government who may have provisions, Clothing, or any other necessaries that they may require, shall supply them with the same, at the expense of the Government.

On Motion of Mr. Childress, the convention adjourned Sine die.[64]

Wm. Fairfax Gray Diary Entry

WASHINGTON: The Alamo has now fallen, and the fate of the country is becoming every day more and more gloomy. In fact, they begin now to feel that they are hourly exposed to attack and capture, and, as on the approach of death, they begin to lat aside their selfish schemes, and to think of futurity. An invaded, unarmed, unprovisioned country, without an army to oppose the invaders, and without money to raise one, now presents itself to their hitherto besotted and blinded minds, and the awful cry has been heard from the midst of their assembly, ''What shall we do to be saved?''

The members are now dispersing in all directions with haste and in confusion. A general panic seems to have seized them. Their families are exposed and defenseless, and thousands are moving off to the east. A constant stream of women and children, and some men, with wagons, carts and pack mules, are rushing across the Brazos night and day. The families of this place, and storekeepers, are packing up and moving.[65]

General Sam Houston

Sam Houston to James Walker Fannin, Jr.

HEADQUARTERS, COLORADRO RIVER: Colonel J. W. Fannin, Jr. will take a position on the bay of Lavaca, or any other point best calculated for the protection of the provisions, ammunition, &c., at Coxe's point and Dimit's landing. The army now near Burnham's, on the the Colorado, will remain for a time, and, according to circumstances, fall down the river. Colonel Fannin will therefore hold himself in constant readiness to join the commander-in-chief. The Redlanders are already in motion, and will join the army as soon as possible. Regulars and volunteers are also on their march to headquarters.

If Colonel Fannin can not maintain his position, he will fall back on the main army — the object of the movement now ordered being only for the protection of the arms, ammunition, &c. The present force on the Colorado numbers four hundred and twenty effective men.

Should a permanent fortification be necessary on the bay of Lavaca, or other point, for the protection of the stores, &c., Colonel Fannin will judge of the expediency (with the command under him) of erecting them. The commanding general, not having a detailed report of his force, can only order that such measures shall be taken as will be best for the good of the services and the protection of the country.

Stock of all descriptions will be driven to the east side of the Colorado.

Sam Houston[66]

Sam Houston to James Collinsworth,
Chairman of Military Committee
BURNAM'S COLORADO: Sir: To-day, at half past four in the afternoon, I reached this point with about six hundred men, including my rear-guard, which is a few miles behind with the families, which were not known to be on the route as the army marched, and for which the guard were sent back.

It pains my heart that such consternation should have been spread by the deserters from camp. We are here; and, if only three hundred men remain on this side of the Brazos, I will die with them, or conquer our enemies. I would most respectfully suggest the assemblage of the troops at this point. It serves more of the country than any other known to me. when they are assembled, I will detach suitable numbers to each point as I may deem best. The Mexican army will not leave us in the rear. If they do, and find San Felipe in ashes, it will astound them. I am assured that the mules and horses of their army are miserably poor; and that there are several hundred women and children with the army, with a view to colonize Texas. If La Bahia was blown up, previous to their march upon it, I should be satisfied.

As to the state of the coast — keep the navy busy. To do it we must look for essential aid. Would it not be well to send a special active agent to the United States — one who will act efficiently and promptly? Appeal to them in the holy names of liberty and humanity!

Our own people, if they would act, are enough to expel every Mexican from Texas. Do let it be known that, on close examination, and upon reflection, the force of Santa Anna has been greatly overrated. He must have lost one thousand, or perhaps more, at the Alamo. It is said the officers have to whip and slash the soldiers on the march. And, if they should advance to the Colorado, it will be some time, as there is such scanty subsistence for animals. I have had the impression that the advance upon the Cibolo was to prevent our co-operation with Fannin, and hold us in check.

If you can by any means soothe the people, and get them to remain, they shall have notice, if I deem it necessary. Let them entertain no fears for the present. We can raise three thousand men in Texas, and fifteen hundred can defeat all that Santa Anna can send to the Colorado. We would then fight on our own ground, and the enemy would loose all confidence from our annoyance. Let the men from east of the Trinity rush to us! Let all the disposable force of Texas fly to arms! If the United States intend to aid us, let them do it now !

I shall raise a company of spies to-morrow, to range the country from this to Gonzales. Send all the good horses you can get for the army. If possible, let it be done speedily; and send ammunition for fifteen hundred men: but first send eight hundred men. I will do everything in my power for Texas.

Sam Houston

The Alamo after partial reconstruction by U.S. Army troops in 1845.

P.S. I entertain a belief that Santa Anna has returned to Mexico, but it will not be known to the troops. In the attack upon the Alamo, the ramparts were swept twice, and the enemy as often repulsed; but Santa Anna was by, and urged the troops. He was not in danger. There was not a man in the Alamo but what, in his death, honored the proud name of an American. *Let the men of Texas avenge their deaths.*[67]

Endnotes

1. *SWHQ,* 48:23.
2. Gray, 126.
3. Jenkins, document number 2264.
4. *Telegraph, and Texas Register,* October 11, 1836.
5. *SWHQ,* 48:23.
6. Gray, 126-127.
7. *Telegraph, and Texas Register,* March 12, 1836. This letter was addressed to John R. Jones, who may have been the John R. Jones who served in the military until being elected postmaster general on December 11, 1835. See also earlier note concerning John Rice Jones III, who could have been the object of this letter. The Gray was Thomas, who may have been the Thomas Gray that was part of Austin's colony and helped organize the town of Washington-on-the-Brazos, Texas. Pettus was William, who has previously been identified.
8. Lacy's was a trading post on the Colorado River.
9. Jenkins, document number 2273.
10. Castaneda, 217.
11. Rees indicates a messenger from the Alamo arrived on March 8, which means he would have left after John Smith on the third, disrupting the popular theory that Smith was the last messenger out of the Alamo. This other messenger is also mentioned in the letters of B. H. Duval and John S. Brooks, both on March 9.
12. Daughters of the Republic of Texas Library, the Alamo. There is no Thomas Rees listed among the victims or survivors of the Goliad Massacre. There is, however, a Thomas Ross and a Thomas Reives, either of which might have been mistaken spellings for Rees.
13. *SWHQ,* 48:23.
14. Gray, 127-128.
15. *SWHQ,* 21:49-50. Burr H. Duval came to Texas from Kentucky in late 1835 and volunteered to fight with the force at Goliad. He was killed in the massacre of March 27.
16. A. J. Houston Papers. George Washington Hockley, of Philadelphia, followed Sam Houston to Texas in 1835. When Houston was named commander in chief, Hockley became chief of staff. He was in command of the artillery at San Jacinto and later accompanied Santa Anna when the dictator was sent to Washington D. C. Hockley later served as secretary of war and negotiated an armistice with Mexico in 1843. He died in 1845.

    We have only this memorandum to identify that letters were sent to Neill and Fannin. The actual documents are missing. We do know Neill received his since he replied on March 10. There is no record as to whether or not Fannin received his copy.
17. *SWHQ,* 9:190-192. James Haggerty was apparently a friend of the Brooks family but no other information is available.

18. The parts of this letter that were omitted deal with John Cross' personal business in Nashville that had no bearing on the affairs of Texas. Also, written on this letter was the following note: "By public accounts on the 23rd March, 1836, the garrison of Fort Definace Goliad endeavored to break through the Mexicans who besieged them but were intercepted and entirely cut to pieces, so that it is feared the writer of the above perished with them. Hugh Somers"
19. Daughters of the Republic of Texas Library, the Alamo. John Cross was a volunteer in Fannin's army and he died in the massacre.
20. *SWHQ,* 48:23.
21. Gray, 128.
22. Yoakum, 2:104.
23. Jenkins, document number 2291. E. Thomas was probably Evans M. Thomas who died in the Fannin massacre. Despite the poor grammar and spelling, Thomas was a true patriot. There is, however, no proof that Santa Anna had to fly a flag of truce every half hour to remove his dead and wounded soldiers.
24. Castaneda, 217.
25. The distance of Fannin's aborted march seems to have grown with the passage of time. In the initial reports of the incident it was reported the march lasted but 200 yards.
26. *SWHQ,* 9:192-195.
27. Jenkins, document number 2290.
28. *SWHQ,* 48:23-24.
29. Gray, 129.
30. Gulick, 1:336. There is no record of Fannin actually attempting a second march to the Alamo.
31. Barker, 3:364-365.
32. Despite these orders, Fannin delayed his retreat, failed to destroy the mission, and did not sink the cannons in the river. He and his men were subsequently captured and massacred.
33. Barker, 3:365-366.
34. Chabot, 146-47.
35. James W. Fannin Papers, University of Texas Library, Austin.
36. Jenkins, document number 2296. Burnley may have been Albert T. Burnley of Virginia who was sympathetic to the Texas cause and was commissioned by Sam Houston, in 1837, to arrange for huge loans for the Republic.
37. Ibid, document number 2295.
38. *SWHQ,* 48:24.
39. Gray, 129-130.
40. Barker, 3:366.
41. *SWHQ,* 48:24.
42. Gray, 130.
43. Barsena deposition.
44. Barker, 3:367-368.

45. Barker, 4:17-19. Henry Raguet, of Pennsylvania, met Sam Houston in New Orleans and accompanied him to Texas on a visit. He subsequently relocated to the area and settled in Nacogdoches where he was active in the Committee of Vigilance and Safety.

46. Castaneda, 218.

47. *SWHQ*, 48:24.

48. Gray, 130.

49. Castaneda, 220.

50. *SWHQ*, 48:24.

51. Gray Diary, 130-131.

52. Yoakum, 2:475.

53. A. J. Houston Papers.

54. It was actually early in the morning of the sixth.

55. *SWHQ*, 37:262-263. Goodrich, a native of Virginia, came to Texas after completing medical school in Baltimore. He represented Washington at the Constitution Convention and signed the Declaration of Independence. He also was careful to record the age, birthplace, and location from which each delegate emigrated to the province of Texas. While Benjamin worked on a Declaration of Independence in Washington, his brother John was in the Alamo and perished there when the mission was overrun.

56. Castaneda, 220.

57. *SWHQ*, 48:24.

58. Gammel, 1:900-901.

59. Gray, 131-132.

60. Castaneda, 221.

61. DRT Library at the Alamo.

62. *SWHQ*, 48: 25.

63. Castaneda, 222.

64. Gammel, 1:900-901.

65. Gray Diary, 133. The mass exodus to the east following the fall of the Alamo came to be known as the "Runaway Scrape."

66. Yoakum, 2:479.

67. Ibid, 2:477-478.

Photo Credits

Abbreviations:
Archives = The archives of the Texas State Library in Austin.
Author = the author's collection.
Alamo = The Alamo museum in San Antonio.
Barker = Barker Texas History Center at the University of Texas in Austin.
DHS = The Dallas Historical Society.
DRT = The Daughters of the Republic of Texas Library at the Alamo in San
    Antonio.
Scrap Book = *A Texas Scrap-Book* by D. W. C. Baker.
Streeter = Thomas Streeter collection at Yale University.

17. Barker
23. top-Scrap Book,
    bottom-Archives
34. Archives
35. Archives
45. DRT
49. DRT
50. DRT
56. Archives
108. DRT
113. Streeter
116. DRT
119. DRT
133. DRT
139. Streeter
156. DRT
157. DRT
164. DRT
199. Author
202. Archives
209. Author
306. DRT
212. Scrap Book
218. Author
224. Author
236. Archives
238. Author
245. Author
248. top-DHS,
    bottom-DRT
251. Author
261. Author

264. DRT
268. Archives
295. Archives
296. Barker
300. Streeter
301. Streeter
302. Streeter
308. DRT
312. Barker
321. Author
322. DRT
323. Author
324. DRT
326. DRT
327. Archives
328. top - Archives,
    bottom - DRT
329. top - DRT,
    bottom - DRT
330. top - Archives,
    bottom - Alamo
331. top - DRT,
    bottom - DRT
332. top - DRT,
    bottom - DRT
333. top - DRT,
    bottom - DRT
346. Scrap Book
366. DRT
372. Streeter
375. Barker
377. DRT

Sources

Austin, Stephen F. *The Austin Papers*. Complied and edited by
Eugene C. Barker. Volume 1 and 2, Washington: Government
Printing Office. 1924 and 1928. Volume 3, Austin: University of
Texas Press, 1927.
Baker, D. W. C. *A Texas Scrap-Book*. New York: A. S. Barnes &
Company, 1875.
Barker, E. C. and Williams, A. W., editors. *The Writings of Sam
Houston*. Austin: University of Texas Press, 1938.
Binkley, William C., editor. *Official Correspondence of the Texas
Revolution, 1835-1836*, 2 vols. New York: D. Appleton-Century
Company, 1938.
Castaneda, Carlos E. *The Mexican Side of the Revolution*. Dallas: P.
L. Turner, 1928.
Cloud, Daniel William. Various letters in the Daughters of the
Republic of Texas Library at the Alamo.
De Zavala, Adina. *History and Legends of the Alamo and Other
Missions In and Around San Antonio*. San Antonio: by the
author, 1917.
Foote, Henry S. *Texas and the Texans*, 2 volumes. Philadelphia:
Thomas, Cowperthwait & Co., 1841.
Gammel, H. P. M., compiler and arranger. *The Laws of Texas,
1822-1897*, 10 volumes. Austin: The Gammel Book Company,
1898.
Gray, William Fairfax. *From Virginia to Texas*. Houston: 1909.
Gulick, Charles A., Jr., editor. *The Papers of Mirabeau Buonaparte
Lamar* 3 volumes Austin: Texas State Library.
Hunnicutt, Helen, editor. "A Mexican View of the Texas War:
Memoirs of a Veteran of the Two Battles of the Alamo." *The
Library Chronicle*, Volume 4. Austin: University of Texas,
Summer 1951.
Jenkins, John H., General Editor. *The Papers of the Texas
Revolution, 1835-1836*, 10 volumes. Austin: Presidial Press,
1973.
Kemp, Louis W. *The Signers of the Texas Declaration of Independence*.
Houston: The Anson Jones Press, 1944.
Mixon, Ruby. *William Barret Travis, His Life and his Letters* Masters
Thesis, University of Texas, 1930.
Muster Rolls of the Texas Revolution. Austin: Daughters of the
Republic of Texas, Inc., 1986.
Niles *Weekly Register*, December 26, 1835.
Pena, Enrique de la. *With Santa Anna in Texas*. Translated and
edited by Carmen Perry. College Station: Texas A&M
University, 1975.
Santos, Richard G. *Santa Anna's Campaign Against Texas*. Waco:
Texian Press, 1968.

Shackford, James A. and Stanley Folmsbee. *A Narrative on the Life of David Crockett*. Knoxville: University of Tennessee Press, 1973.

Streeter, Thomas W. *A Bibliography of Texas*. Portland Maine: Anthoesen Press, 1955.

Telegraph, and Texas Register, various issues from the Texas State Library Archives in Austin.

Wallace, Ernest, editor. *Documents of Texas History*. Austin: The Steck Company, 1960.

Williams, Amelia W. *A Critical Study of the Siege of the Alamo and of the Personnel of Its Defenders*. Ph.D Thesis, University of Texas, 1931.

Yoakum, Henderson. *History of Texas From Its First Settlement in 1685 to Its Annexation to the United States in 1846,* 2 volumes. New York: Redfield, 1856.

Index